2ND NATIONAL EDITION

Your Rights in the Workplace

BY ATTORNEY BARBARA KATE REPA

EDITED BY MARCIA STEWART

NOLO PRESS  BERKELEY

YOUR RESPONSIBILITY WHEN USING A SELF-HELP LAW BOOK

We've done our best to give you useful and accurate information in this book. But this book does not take the place of a lawyer licensed to practice law in your state. If you want legal advice, see a lawyer. If you use any information contained in this book, it's your personal responsibility to make sure that the facts and general information contained in it are applicable to your situation.

KEEPING UP-TO-DATE

To keep its books up-to-date, Nolo Press issues new printings and new editions periodically. New printings reflect minor legal changes and technical corrections. New editions contain major legal changes, major text additions or major reorganizations. To find out if a later printing or edition of any Nolo book is available, call Nolo Press at (510) 549-1976 or check the catalog in the *Nolo News,* our quarterly newspaper.

To stay current, follow the "Update" service in the *Nolo News.* You can get the paper free by sending us the registration card in the back of the book. In another effort to help you use Nolo's latest materials, we offer a 25% discount off the purchase of any new Nolo book if you turn in any earlier printing or edition. (See the "Recycle Offer" in the back of the book.) This book was last printed in **June 1994**.

SECOND EDITION	June 1994
EDITOR	Marcia Stewart
BOOK DESIGN	Jackie Mancuso
COVER DESIGN	Toni Ihara
PRODUCTION	Dave McFarland
PROOFREADER	Ely Newman
INDEX	Susan Cornell
PRINTING	Consolidated Printers, Inc.

Copyright © 1994 Nolo Press

ISBN 0-87337-200-X

Nolo books are available at special discounts for bulk purchases for sales promotions, premiums and fund-raising. For details contact: Special Sales Director, Nolo Press, 950 Parker Street, Berkeley, CA 94710.

ACKNOWLEDGMENTS

Many people gave their time, expertise and wise counsel to help make this tome possible.

Some of them merit special thanks, including:

Marcia Stewart, editor extraordinaire, whose special brand of encouragement worked its way onto every page.

Jackie Mancuso, express designer, who made the innards look grand.

Katherine Jaramillo, who researched and reresearched the quick-changing laws that fill these pages.

Susan Cornell, who took the index to new heights with her nitpicking mind.

Stanley Jacobsen, who worked tirelessly—and pleasantly—to keep the facts current.

Ely Newman, whose sharp proofreading eyes caught the gremlins.

And finally, a special thanks to my beacons—Joel and Thomas.

Dan Lacey, one of the primary authors of the first edition of *Your Rights in the Workplace*, died in 1992. Some of his words live on here.

Contents

C H A P T E R   4

HEALTH INSURANCE

C H A P T E R   5

FAMILY AND MEDICAL LEAVE

PRIVACY RIGHTS

HEALTH AND SAFETY

ILLEGAL DISCRIMINATION

SEXUAL HARASSMENT

LOSING OR LEAVING A JOB

CHALLENGING A JOB LOSS

CHAPTER 17

IMMIGRATION ISSUES

CHAPTER 18

LAWYERS AND LEGAL RESEARCH

APPENDIX

Maybe you're just curious. Or maybe you're the cautious type of soul who likes to think ahead and prevent a wrong before it happens. But the best bet is that you're reading this book because you already have a work-related problem:

- You were not hired for a job and you have good reason to suspect it was because of your race. Or your disability.
- Your employer promoted a less qualified person to fill a position you were promised.
- You want to know your legal rights if you consistently work overtime. Or if you want to take a leave to care for a sick parent. Or if you are called to serve on a jury.
- You have just been laid off and you're wondering if you have any right to get your job back. Or to get unemployment payments in the meantime. Or whether your employer owes you severance pay.
- You want to help evaluate a new job you've been offered. Or you want to find out your legal rights as a jobseeker.

This book will help you understand the legal rights that apply to your situation. It explains federal workplace laws—such as the right to be paid fairly and on time and to work free from discrimination. And it also explains the twists state law may place on your workplace rights—regulating, for example, both your right to smoke and to work in a smokefree place, or whether or not you are entitled to time off work to vote or to care for a sick child.

When pondering how to tackle a potential workplace problem, heed that noble adage: Simplify, simplify. Better still: Simplify. Woe unto the reader whose concerns span every chapter. First skim Chapter 2 on determining your legal employment status. Then proceed to the chapters that discuss the substance of your problem.

Also, be aware that there are many public and private agencies, groups and organizations that specialize in workplace issues, and many of them provide free—or low cost—counseling, support or referrals. You will find lists of such organizations peppered throughout the book, and a comprehensive listing in the Appendix.

A. Analyzing Your Options

If something is amiss in your workplace and you have tuned into water-cooler wisdom, commuter train skinny or locker room recounts, you may have come away with the same urging: Sue.

For most people, that is bad advice. The courtroom is usually the worst place to resolve workplace disputes. Most of them can be handled more efficiently and much more effectively in the workplace itself—through mediation, arbitration or, most often, by honest conversation.

If you have suffered an insult, an injury or a wrong at work, you are probably feeling angry or hurt. If you have lost your job, you may be hurting financially, too. All of this is likely to cloud your ability to make well-reasoned decisions. So go slowly. Decide what you want to gain. If an apology from your employer would suffice, save yourself the time and expense of filing a legal action.

B. Talking It Over With Your Employer

Do not overlook the obvious: First try talking over your workplace problem with your employer. An intelligent discussion can resolve most wrongs—or at least get your differences out on the table. Most companies want to stay within the law and avoid legal tangles. So the odds are that your problem is the result of an oversight, a misunderstanding or a lack of legal knowledge. Here are a few tips on how to present your concerns to your employer or former employer.

Know your rights. The more you know about your legal rights in the workplace—to be paid fairly and on time, to do your job free from discrimination and retaliation, to labor in a safe and healthy place—the more confident you will be in presenting your problem. This book offers a wealth of information about the basic laws of the workplace—and tells you where to turn if you need more specifics in clarifying your rights.

Stick to the facts. Keeping your legal rights firmly in mind, write a brief summary of what has gone wrong and your recommendation for resolving the problem. It often helps to have someone who is more objective, such as a friend or family member, review the facts of your workplace problem with you and discuss possible approaches to resolving it.

Then doublecheck the facts. The human memory is not nearly as accurate as we would like to think it is—particularly when it comes to remembering numbers and dates. Before you approach your employer with a complaint about your pay, check to be sure your math is correct. If your beef is about a discriminatory remark, be sure you can quote it verbatim. Review any of your written records to make sure you have not overlooked a past event or pivotal memo.

Do not be overly emotional. Dealing with a workplace problem can be stressful. After all, if you are like most workers, you spend about half of your waking hours on the job. But you also know friends, relatives and acquaintances who are out of work—and who are having hard times finding new jobs.

Do not tolerate abuse. But if your job is on shaky ground, try not to jeopardize it further by losing your temper and getting fired as a result. A calm presentation of a complaint is always better than an emotional confrontation. Remember the common wisdom that it is easier to find a new job while you still have your old one. At the very least, it's easier to blaze a new career trail if you have no muddy tracks behind you.

Be discreet. Discussions of workplace problems are often very personal, and should take place privately—not in front of co-workers. Employment problems can be divisive for an entire workplace. You don't want to be justly accused of poisoning the workplace atmosphere or of filling it with disgruntled workers forming pro and con camps. Ask for an appointment to discuss your complaint privately with your supervisor or another appropriate manager. Give them a chance to resolve your problem rationally and privately—and they will be more apt to see things your way.

C. Documenting Your Problem

Most employers now heed the workplace mantra reinforced by thousands of court cases: Document, document, document. If your once good working situation has gone bad—or you have recently been fired—you, too, must heed the call: Document all that happened. You are nowhere, legally, without evidence of where and when things went wrong.

A little bit of workplace paranoia may later prove to be a healthy thing. Even if everything seems fine now, take the extra seconds to make a paper trail. Collect in one place all documents you receive on the job: initial work agreements, employee handbooks, management memos, performance reviews. To be safe, keep your file at home, away from the office.

If you have what seems to be a valid complaint, it is crucial to gather evidence to bolster your claim. From the start, beware of deadlines for filing specific types of legal claims. The deadlines may range from a few weeks to a few years, but will likely signal that you will have to act quickly.

There are several kinds of evidence you should collect as soon as possible.

Company policy. Statements of company policy, either written or verbal, which indicate arbitrary or wrongful treatment—including job descriptions, work rules, personnel pamphlets, company notices or anything else that either indicates or implies that company policy treats workers unfairly.

Written statements by management. Statements by supervisors, personnel directors or other managers about you are also important. Save any written statements and note when and from whom you received them. If you have not received any written reasons for a job decision you feel is discriminatory or otherwise wrongful, make a written request for a statement of the company's reasons.

Verbal comments. In many cases, employers and their managers do not write down their reasons for making an employment decision. In such cases, you may still be able to document your claim with verbal statements by supervisors or others concerning unwritten company policy or undocumented reasons for a particular action involving your job.

Make accurate notes of what was said as soon as you can after the statement is made. Also note the time and place the statement was made, who else was present and the conversation surrounding it. If others heard the statement, try to get them to write down their recollections and have them sign that statement. Or have them sign your written version of the statement, indicating that it accurately reflects what they heard.

WE'RE ALL IN THIS TOGETHER

Co-workers may be reluctant to help you with your workplace complaint, whether by giving statements of their own experiences or by backing up your story of what has occurred. You may run into the same common reaction: "I don't want to get involved."

People may be afraid they will lose their own jobs or suffer in some other way because of having created bad blood with the company. You may be able to persuade them to help you by reassuring them that the law which prohibits the initial wrongful treatment also specifically prohibits retaliatory actions by the company or union against anyone who helps in an investigation of your claim.

D. Considering Legal Action

Wipe the dollar signs from your eyes. While it's true that some workers have won multi-million dollar judgments against their employers, it's also true that such judgments are very few and very far between. There are several things to think about before you decide to launch a no-holds-barred legal challenge to your firing or wrongful workplace treatment.

Be honest. Answer one question honestly: What do you expect to gain by a lawsuit? Are you angry, seeking some revenge? Do you expect to teach your former employer a lesson? Do you just want to make your former employer squirm? All of these are not usually strong bases on which to construct a lawsuit that is likely to succeed. If an apology, a letter of recommendation or a clearing of your work record would make you feel whole again, negotiate first for those things.

Keep good documentation. As this book stresses again and again, the success of your claim or lawsuit is likely to depend upon how well you documented the circumstances surrounding your workplace problem. If your employer claims you were fired because of incompetence, for example, make sure you can show otherwise by producing favorable written performance reviews or evidence that your employer circumvented the company's disciplinary procedures before firing you.

Before you discuss your case with a lawyer, look closely at your documentation and try to separate the aspects of your problem that you can prove from those you merely suspect. If you cannot produce any independent verification of your workplace problem, you will be in the untenable position of convincing a judge or jury that your word alone should be believed.

It will require time and effort. You can save yourself some time and possibly some grief by using this book to objectively analyze your job loss or problem. If possible, do it before you begin talking with a lawyer about handling your case. Once again, the keys to most successful wrongful discharge lawsuits are good documentation and organized preparation—both of which must come from you.

It's likely to be expensive. Because many challenges to workplace problems are legal longshots, lawyers who specialize in this type of case often refuse to handle them. In fact, these days, many originally well-meaning employment lawyers have switched to where the money is: They represent employers.

So your initial search is likely to be frustrating. And if you do find a lawyer willing to take your case, you will probably have to pay dearly. If you hire a lawyer with expertise in wrongful discharge lawsuits and your case is less than a sure win, you can expect to deposit several thousands of dollars to pay for the lawyer's time if your lawsuit fails, plus thousands more to cover other costs. ■

CHAPTER

2

YOUR
LEGAL
EMPLOYMENT
STATUS

As a worker, you may be labeled a variety of things—an independent contractor, a temporary, parttime, fulltime or permanent employee. The semantics can be befuddling. But the meaning behind the words is important. Most workplace laws protect only those workers who are legally defined to be employees. You must first determine which legal category fits your work situation and responsibilities before you will know whether laws covering employees apply to you.

Beware, too, that within many workplace laws there are specific exceptions. For example, some laws exempt government employees from their protections, while some laws only cover public employees. Some laws exempt domestic workers. There is even a workplace law that specifically does not apply to those who work harvesting almonds. Some of these exceptions and exemptions seem spurious, some hard-hearted. But these intricacies point up the need to make sure that you are protected by a specific law before you assert some legal right or decide to take legal action against an employer.

A. The Definition of Employee

The Internal Revenue Service—because it routinely requires that money be withheld from the paychecks of employees—is the agency responsible for determining who is and is not an employee, legally. If you have had dealings with the monolithic IRS, or even if you have used its allegedly simple forms for filing taxes, this news may not inspire much confidence in you.

Luckily, the IRS has demonstrated uncharacteristic restraint over the years by classifying workers into only a few categories: common law employees, independent contractors and statutory employees.

1. Common Law Employees

Most working people are common law employees. The IRS will most heavily weigh one fact in deciding whether to classify a worker as a common law employee: whether an employer retains the right to control both the type and method of work being done. (See Section B for a complete list of considerations the IRS uses in classifying workers.) The title that you or a supervisor assign to your work situation simply does not matter for legal purposes.

One strong indication that you are legally an employee is if the company you work for gives you a W-2 Form at the end of each calendar year. If your employer does not consider you to be a common law employee, it will either give you an IRS Form 1099-Miscellaneous to report your work income, or it will not report your income to the IRS at all.

Employers have specific legal obligations to their employees. For example, employers must:

- withhold state and federal income taxes and Social Security from paychecks
- pay unemployment insurance taxes, and
- pay for workers' compensation insurance.

In addition, many workplace laws—including those controlling wages and hours—protect employees, not other categories of workers. For example, most employees must be paid overtime at a rate of one-and-a-half times the regular rate for all hours worked beyond a 40-hour workweek.

2. Independent Contractors

As in the employee category, the employer's control over the work is a key fact in determining whether a worker is legally an independent contractor. The person or company paying for the work controls the outcome of the independent contractor's work. The independent contractor, however, retains control over how the work gets done.

Example: *Moira, a freelance writer, agrees to write a technical guide for new software being produced by the Dikus Company. The completed draft must be 40 double-spaced, typewritten pages and is due on February 1. Moira can use a word* *processor to complete the draft. If she's hearty—or possibly foolhardy—she can write the entire thing the evening of January 31. Because Moira controls the process and means by which she prepares the technical guide, she is legally considered an independent contractor.*

Another major earmark of independent contractors is that they offer services to the public at large, not just to one employer.

Example: *Jeffrey does machine repairs and gets most of his income from one company that operates several factories containing hundreds of machines. When a machine breaks down, a factory manager calls Jeffrey, who makes on-site repair calls. Sometimes, Jeffrey takes the machines to his shop to be worked on there. Other times, he repairs the machines at the factory. Jeffrey also advertises his services in the local telephone directory, from which he gets a few repair calls from other companies.*

Because he determines how to do the repairs and also offers his work to more than one company, Jeffrey is legally considered an independent contractor with every company for which he works—even the one that provides most of his income.

Most workplace rights guaranteed by law to employees are not guaranteed to people who work as independent contractors. In general, the relationship between independent contractors and the company or person paying for their work is covered not by the law of the workplace, but by state business codes and contract laws. From a legal standpoint, an independent contractor is just a one-person business and must live by the laws that govern all businesses, large or small. For example, an independent contractor who agrees to perform a task for a specific amount of money must fulfill that contract and cannot demand to be paid time-and-one-half rates for spending more than 40 hours in one week to complete that task.

However, being an independent contractor holds great appeal for some workers. It offers flexibility in workhours and the chance to pick and choose assignments. Independent contractors are allowed to deduct, for tax purposes, 100% of their expenses that are related to self-employment— such as supplies and travel; most employees may deduct only business expenses exceeding 2% of their gross incomes.

In addition, many workers just like the sound of being an independent contractor. The term seems to imply that you are your own boss—and not under anyone else's thumb.

INDEPENDENTS: ON THE UPSWING?

According to the IRS, the number of workers claiming to be independent contractors is burgeoning, but a growing number are claiming the status when they don't deserve it. The Taxman tracks independent contractors by monitoring the number of those who file federal income tax Schedule C, the form reserved for sole proprietors. The IRS recently reported that:

- In 1985, 12 million taxpayers filed returns as sole proprietors; by 1990, that number had reached 15 million.
- From 1988 to 1992, the IRS reclassified more than 400,000 workers from independent contractors to employees and collected $52.5 million in back taxes.
- In 1992 alone, the IRS audited 1,700 businesses on suspicion of misclassification, reclassified 90,000 workers and collected $19 million in tax assessments.

Industries most likely to be audited: computer, medical, entertainment, construction, and travel and resort.

Most likely locales for audited businesses: California, Georgia, Illinois, Michigan, New York and Texas.

Source: *Nation's Business*; August, 1993

3. Statutory Employees

This category includes groups of workers—such as delivery people and some home workers—who might not seem to qualify as employees, but who have been designated by specific laws as being subject to tax withholding requirements imposed upon employees. Other specific legal obligations of employers are generally also spelled out in the statute. An employer's control is irrelevant here. What matters most is the specific type of work being done.

Most of the laws defining statutory employees were passed in response to special interest political lobbying. For example, labor unions usually view independent contractors and people who work at home as threats to the work standards of unionized factories, so they exerted political pressure to keep as many home workers as possible under the wage and hour laws that govern employees.

Because of such piecemeal lobbying, there is no central logic to the statutory employee category. If the law labels you as one, you are one. There is little to be gained by trying to figure out why.

The most common types of workers who are statutory employees are discussed here.

- *Delivery drivers.* Drivers who deliver meat, vegetables, fruits, bakery products, or beverages other than milk, or who pick up and deliver laundry or dry cleaning, but who are legally agents of a company—authorized by the company to act on its behalf. These workers are most often paid on commission.

    Example: *A bread truck driver who sells on commission to a customer route on behalf of only one bakery would typically be an agent of that bakery—and therefore, a statutory employee of the bakery. But a restaurant supply distributor who buys bread at wholesale prices and resells it at a profit would typically be considered neither an agent nor a statutory employee of the bakery that produced the bread.*

- *Life insurance agents.* Insurance sales agents whose main job is selling life insurance or annuity contracts, or both, primarily for one life insurance company.

- *Home workers.* People who work at home according to a company's explicit instructions on materials or goods that are supplied by the company and which must be returned to that company or to someone designated by that company.

- *Business-to-business salespeople.* People whose main job is to sell on behalf of a company and take orders from wholesalers, retailers, contractors, hotels, restaurants or other business establishments. The goods sold must be merchandise for resale or supplies for use in the buyer's business operation, as opposed to goods purchased for personal consumption at home.

    This category applies only to those whose main job is selling business-to-business. Because the IRS sets no firm statistical standards for this type of work, the definition of "main job" is not interpreted consistently. In general, this category is directed at traveling salespeople who might otherwise be considered independent contractors because their employers exercise so little control over their daily work activities.

Example: *Mary is an on-the-road salesperson for a roofing manufacturer that supplies building contractors. Because she works primarily out of her car and an office in her home, and visits the company's headquarters only twice a month, the company has very little control over how and when she does her work. Nevertheless, the IRS considers her to be a statutory employee.*

STATUTORY NONEMPLOYEES: A RARE BREED

The IRS has designated one additional category of rare worker: the statutory nonemployee. Like statutory employee, the category of statutory nonemployee lacks a central logic. It also has been specifically created through efforts by special interest lobby groups, and the rights and responsibilities that attach to the status are also made clear in the laws defining them. However, statutory nonemployees are excluded from the protections of most workplace laws—and are treated as self-employed for federal income and employment tax purposes.

There are only two categories of statutory nonemployees recognized by the IRS: licensed real estate agents and direct sellers. A direct seller is someone who sells goods to a consumer who intends to use them personally—for example, a person who sells household vacuum cleaners through in-home demonstrations.

People working in these occupations are considered statutory nonemployees if:

- most payments for their services are directly related to sales, rather than to the number of hours worked, and
- their services are performed under a written contract providing that they will not be treated as employees for federal tax purposes.

Direct sellers must satisfy one additional requirement to qualify as statutory nonemployees: They must do their selling someplace other than in an established retail store or salesroom.

B. Guidance in Determining Your Legal Status

Some unscrupulous employers have tried to classify workers as independent contractors when they should be deemed employees. It simply is workier and costs more in benefits and taxes to have employees on staff than it does to use independent contractors.

Being misclassified by your employer may mean that you miss out on paid benefits to which you are legally entitled. Employers who misclassify employees as independent contractors can be held liable for back unemployment, Social Security, Medicare and income taxes owed, interest, legal fees and penalties—and may also lose tax advantages previously claimed.

The IRS has been cracking down on the practice of misclassifying employees. (See Section A2.) According to a 1993 government investigation, small employers—those with less than $3 million in assets—are the most likely to offend. But the reality is that few employers get caught in the process of misclassifying their workforces. All the more reason to spend some time and effort wading through the legal definitions to be sure you are accurately classified.

If your work situation presents a close call as to whether you are an employee or independent contractor, take a closer look at the following facts—the most important of the ones that the IRS considers in determining your official status.

Instructions. An employee must comply with instructions about when, where and how to work. Even if no instructions are given, it may be enough demonstration of employer control if the employer has the right to give instructions. Independent contractors must only deliver a finished product; how they produce it is up to them.

Training. An employee is trained to perform services in a particular manner. Independent contractors use their own methods and receive no training from those who pay for their services.

Integration. An employee's services are integrated into the business operations because the services are important to the success or continuation of the business. Independent contractors are typically consulted only for short-term or occasional projects.

Hiring assistants. An employee works for an employer who hires, supervises and pays assistants. An independent contractor hires, supervises and pays assistants under a contract that requires him or her to provide materials and labor—and is responsible only for the result.

Continuing relationship. An employee has a continuing relationship with an employer. However, a continuing relationship may exist where work is performed frequently, although at irregular intervals. An employee who is called in to work for only a few days each month is still an employee. Independent contractors may work for several different employers—often completing only a brief stint with each.

Set hours of work. An employee has set hours of work established by an employer. An independent contractor establishes his or her own work schedule.

Fulltime work. An employee normally works fulltime, exclusively for one employer. An independent contractor can work when and for whom he or she chooses. Note that this factor does not exclude parttime workers from being employees. (See Section B3.)

Work done on premises. An employee works on the premises of an employer, or works on a route or at a location designated by an employer. An independent contractor is usually free to complete the work assignment wherever it is convenient and feasible.

Set work duties. An employee must perform services in the order or sequence set by an employer. An independent contractor is free to complete the job as he or she deems best.

Pay. An employee is paid by the hour, week or month. An independent contractor is paid by the job or on a straight commission.

Expenses. An employee's business and travel expenses are paid by the employer. Unless their agreements specify otherwise, independent contractors are usually responsible for paying for their own expenses.

Tools and materials. An employee is furnished with tools, materials and other equipment by an employer. An independent contractor must usually supply his or her own.

Working for more than one person or firm. An employee usually works for only one employer. An independent contractor may work for two or more unrelated people or firms at the same time and offer services to the general public.

Right to fire. An employee can be fired by an employer. An independent contractor cannot be fired as long as he or she produces a result that meets the specifications of the contract.

Right to quit. An employee can quit his or her job at any time without incurring liability. An independent contractor usually agrees to complete a specific job and is responsible for completing it satisfactorily—or is legally obliged to make good for failure to complete it.

WHERE TO GO FOR MORE HELP

The IRS publishes a free pamphlet, "Employment Taxes and Information Returns, IRS Publication 937." While its aim is to spell out tax responsibilities for employers, it provides valuable information for employees who want to doublecheck their employer's tax treatment of them. To obtain a copy, call the IRS toll-free number for forms and publications: 800/829-3676.

C. Additional Categories of Workers

The following definitions cover what might be called conversational categories of work. These are tags that people and companies often give to various work relationships, but that are not really legal categories of work according to IRS rules. No matter what you, your employer or your associates call your job, it falls under one of the official categories of employment set out by the IRS. (See Section A.)

The following explanations offer some guidance on which legal category generally best fits a hard-to-place work situation.

1. Consultants and Subcontractors

In some areas of the United States, and within some industries, the terms consultant and subcontractor are frequently used to describe work relationships. However, the IRS does not recognize either one as a legal category of work. The business arrangements under which people who are really consultants and subcontractors work typically make them independent contractors.

2. Personal Service Contractees

Because some feel it has a flattering ring to it, people who work as independent contractors will say that they have a personal service contract with a company. But a personal service contract is more correctly defined as a written agreement between a company and an employee that spells out the terms of the employee's work and compensation over and above what is required by law.

For example, engineers with rare technical skills sometimes agree to leave one company for another only after their new employer promises, in a personal service contract, to employ them for several years—or to pay them the equivalent of the salary they would have received for those years if they are fired before their contract expires.

Many workplace specialists now recommend that you negotiate a personal service contract before taking a new job. It is a nice thought, but the truth is that very few working people have sufficient power on their side of the employment transaction to negotiate a personal service contract. And for many positions, such contracts are simply impractical or unnecessary.

Consequently, personal service contracts are rare except at the highest levels of corporate management, in professional sports and other forms of commercial entertainment, and where an employee has unique skills or is required to move to a distant country—in essence, to give up a lifestyle completely for a time—to perform a job for a limited number of years before returning home.

If you are someone's employee but also have an individual contract that specifies such things as how much you will be paid, what hours you will be expected to work, what bonuses you will receive and how many years you will be employed, you are among the lucky. Such a contract does not, however, negate the fact that you are an employee. It merely gives you some extra rights—enforceable under contract law.

If you are working under an individual employment contract but are not legally an employee or statutory employee (as described in Section A), then you are either an independent contractor or statutory nonemployee, depending on the nature of the work.

3. Parttime Workers

There is no single, overriding definition of a parttime worker in workplace law. Some state workplace laws—and a number of individual employers—specify their own definitions of fulltime and parttime workers. But for the most part, it is merely contemporary American culture that defines fulltime work as 40 hours of work spread over a five-day period within a given week.

Therefore, describing a job as parttime does not change a worker's legal status. A worker who puts in fewer than 40 hours weekly who fits the description of an independent contractor is an independent contractor. And a person who works substantially fewer than 40 hours per week and whose work situation fits the description of an employee is an employee.

While some workplace benefits—such as vacation time and retirement fund contributions—may be reduced proportionately to the amount of time worked, parttime workers generally have the full arsenal of employee rights at their disposal.

4. Job Shares

In some workplaces, two or more people share a job that requires 40 or more hours of work per week. For example, two workers might agree to work 20 hours each weekly, taking a prorated share of fringe benefits. The flexibility of the arrangement is good for the workers—allowing them time off work to pursue other interests or attend other obligations, while assuring them the security of enduring employment. The arrangement is also good for employers that want to promote employee satisfaction and save time and money in training a new employee to take over job duties.

But job sharing is not a legal category of work. Workers involved in job sharing are legally employees when all other aspects of their work situation fit the definition of an employee, and legally independent contractors when all other aspects of their work situation fit the definition of an independent contractor.

5. Temporaries

On a typical day, more than one million jobs in America are filled by workers from services that specialize in temporary staffing.

Most people working through temporary services are legally employees of the services, not the companies to which they are assigned. The temporary services pay workers' wages, withhold taxes from their paychecks and contribute to programs such as Social Security and workers' compensation, just as any other employer would. Many of the temporary services also offer benefit programs such as health insurance to those they employ.

6. Leased Employees

Employee leasing allows companies to cut costs and simplify management of workforces by paying another specialized company to hire and fire workers, for example, and to manage benefit programs. As the American workplace has grown more legally complex, employee leasing has become increasingly popular.

Like temporary workers, most leased workers are legally employees of the service firm supplying workers to the client company in which they work. The basic difference between leased workers and temporaries is that the leased employees are expected to be assigned to one job for a substantial amount of time—usually a year or more.

WORKING FOR AN EMPLOYEE-OWNED CORPORATION

Since the late 1970s, there has been a trend within corporate America toward a great variety of financing schemes that have been lumped under the title of employee ownership. In some cases, corporations have sold—or given—entire divisions to the employees of those divisions.

But in many cases, employee ownership programs have amounted to little more than transferring a small percentage of corporate stock to employees. Employees' retirement funds are sometimes blended with money provided by investors to create an entity described as employee-owned, but to which the nonemployee investors have first claim.

Consequently, hundreds of thousands of American workers are now regularly reminded by their bosses that they are part of an employee-owned company—implying that they are something other than employees. But workers whose day-to-day relationship with an employee-owned corporation fits all the IRS criteria for the category of employee are still employees of that corporation. The percentage of the corporation's stock owned or controlled by its employees does not affect their employee status.

D. The Definition of Employer

There are far fewer legal permutations in the legal definition of employer than there are of employee. In most cases, there is little room for confusion over who hires, fires or signs the paychecks.

1. Who Is Responsible

Confusion over who is the legally responsible individual sometimes arises during workplace disputes. As a general rule, employer, as used in most workplace laws, includes all individuals that a company holds out to have authority to act and to make decisions—the owner of the business, the chief executive officer or president. It may also include supervisors, managers and sometimes even other employees.

2. Employer Identification Numbers

The IRS and other government agencies need a way to track employees and employers by numbers, rather than by names. There are many thousands of Smiths in America, for example, but when keyed in by their individual, nine-digit Social Security numbers, computers can easily distinguish them.

You, too, can refer to a government-assigned number if you want to be sure of your employer's identity. This may seem unnecessary. But many working people today who appear to be employed by one company are, in fact, employed by another. Look at the name badges of some service station attendants, for example. Although they are wearing uniforms done up in the colors of the oil company, their badges point out in small print that they are really working for an employee-leasing subsidiary of the oil company.

Some small, unincorporated employers use their personal Social Security numbers to identify their companies to the IRS. Larger employers, and all those that are incorporated, are assigned an Employer Identification Number (EIN) by the IRS. Each corporation is allowed to have only one EIN, so one number often is used by several divisions of a corporation that conducts business under different names.

Employment-related IRS forms such as the W-2 and the 1099-Miscellaneous include spaces in which the person or company paying you must note their identification numbers. That number is then used to track the records of the company and its employees within the IRS system.

Consequently, your employer's identification number is an important component of your employment status and history. Your true employer is the one that owns the employee identification number that appears on your records.

There are a number of reasons why a less-than-honest employer might use an identification number other than its own. One typical example would be at a hazardous waste clean-up site, where workers think they are working for a well-heeled company but are technically being paid by a financially unsound subcontractor which is likely to go out of business about the time that it gets sued because of worker injuries.

Because of privacy laws, there is no official way to verify the validity of the employer identification number that your employer is using. Nevertheless, the IRS encourages people who suspect that an employer is using false or incorrect employer identification numbers—a tip from a disgruntled payroll office worker would be a typical reason—to report it to the criminal investigation department of their local IRS district office. ■

CHAPTER 3

WAGES AND HOURS

The French writer Voltaire once pointed out that work spares us from three great evils: boredom, vice and need. Most of us can tolerate a little boredom, and some may even enjoy a small helping of vice. But need is something we would all rather avoid. Although most people like their jobs to be fun and fulfilling, what they likely want most is to be paid—fairly and on time—so that they can enjoy the other aspects of their lives.

A. The Fair Labor Standards Act

The most important and most far-reaching law guaranteeing a worker's right to be paid fairly is the federal Fair Labor Standards Act or FLSA (29 U.S.C. §§201 and following). The FLSA:

* defines the 40-hour workweek
* covers the federal minimum wage
* sets requirements for overtime, and
* places restrictions on child labor.

Basically, the FLSA establishes minimums for fair pay and hours—and it is the single law most often violated by employers. An employer must also comply with other local, state or federal workplace laws that set higher standards. So in addition to determining whether you are being paid properly under the FLSA, you may need to check the other laws discussed in this chapter that apply to your situation.

The FLSA was passed in 1938 after the Depression, when many employers took advantage of the tight labor market to subject workers to horrible conditions and impossible hours. One of the most complex laws of the workplace, the FLSA has been amended many times. It is full of exceptions and exemptions—some of which seem to contradict one another. Most of the revisions and interpretations have expanded the law's coverage, for example:

* requiring that male and female workers receive equal pay for work that requires equal skill, effort and responsibility

- including in its protections state and local hospitals and educational institutions
- covering most federal employees and employees of states, political subdivisions and interstate agencies, and
- setting out strict standards for determining, paying and accruing compensatory or comp time—time given off work instead of cash payments.

UNLIKELY CHAMPIONS OF WOMEN'S RIGHTS

Probably unwittingly, the U.S. Supreme Court tipped its sexist hand in deciding a 1937 case, *West Coast Hotel Co. v. Parrish* (300 U.S. 379). That case was the first to challenge the constitutionality of a state minimum wage law.

In it, a hotel chambermaid sued because she was paid less than Washington's minimum wage—then set at $14.50 per week for a 48-hour workweek.

Interestingly, the state set no minimum wage for men.

The U.S. Supreme Court upheld the state law, because, the Court opined, "the health of women is peculiarly related to the vigor of the race." It also cited the need to protect women, creatures of "weak bargaining power," from "unscrupulous and overreaching employers."

The dissent in the case, simultaneously forward-thinking and socially naive, was equally indignant. Wrote dissenting Justice Sutherland: "Women today stand upon a legal and political equality with men. There is no longer any reason why they should be put in different classes in respect of their legal right to make contracts; nor should they be denied, in effect, the right to compete with men for work which men may be willing to accept."

---

1. Who Is Covered

The FLSA applies only to employers whose annual sales total $500,000 or more, or who are engaged in interstate commerce. You might think that this would restrict the FLSA to covering only employees in large companies, but in reality the law covers nearly all workplaces.

This is because the courts have interpreted the term interstate commerce very broadly. For example, courts have ruled that companies that regularly use the U.S. mail to send or receive letters to and from other states are engaged in interstate commerce. Even the fact that employees use company telephones to place or accept interstate business calls has placed an employer under the FLSA.

2. Who Is Exempt

A few employers, including small farms—those that use relatively little outside paid labor—are explicitly exempt from the FLSA.

In addition, some employees are exempt from the FLSA even though their employers are covered. A few common categories of employees are exempt from FLSA requirements, such as pay for overtime.

- *Executive, administrative and professional workers.* To qualify as an exempt executive, the employee must:
  —use discretion in performing job duties
  —regularly direct the work of two or more people
  —have the authority to hire and fire other employees, or to order such hiring and firing
  —be primarily responsible for managing others, and
  —devote no more than 20% of worktime to other tasks that are not managerial. For certain retail and service companies, 40% of nonmanagerial time is allowed.
  The definitions of administrative and professional employees are similar, but contain minor differences. For example, employees categorized as professionals must perform work that is primarily intellectual. The definitions also change with the employee's salary level. For example, if the weekly salary of the executive, administrative or professional employee exceeds a certain minimum, fewer factors are required to qualify for the exemption.

HOLD THE PICKLE, HOLD THE LAW

The FLSA definition of executive is tied into the amount of salary earned. But that definition has not kept up with the times, allowing many employers to bend federal wage and hour laws.

Current U.S. Labor Department guidelines permit employers to pay executives weekly salaries of $155—less than the minimum wage of $170 for a 40-hour workweek. And because these poorly paid execs are exempt from the FLSA, they are also free to work an unlimited number of overtime hours. No extra charge.

This egregious practice came to light well over a decade ago when several Burger King assistant managers sued the fast food chain. The employees took issue with the corporate policy of requiring FLSA-exempt assistant managers to spend much of their 54-hour workweeks doing the same work as the people they supervised. The appeals court ruled, however, that if assistant managers were allowed to shun burger production duties, more hourly employees would be needed, breaking the restaurant's hourly labor budget (*Donovan v. Burger King Corp.*, 675 F. 2d 516 (2d Cir. 1982)).

The abuses continue. According to the most recent survey by the National Restaurant Association, one-quarter of fast food assistant managers earn less than $15,000 annually. But they have impressive titles.

Other employees who are exempt from the FLSA include:

- *Amusement park and camp workers,* including those employed by religious or nonprofit educational centers.
- *Fishing specialists,* who catch, harvest or farm fish and shellfish.
- *Farm workers,* most of whom, however, are covered by other federal and state laws.
- *Newspeople,* who work to produce a local newspaper with a circulation of less than 4,000.
- *Switchboard operators,* who work for small, independently owned companies.
- *Employees who work out of the country,* except for workers in Puerto Rico,

the U.S. Virgin Islands, American Samoa, Guam, Wake Island, Eniwetok Atoll, Kwajalein Atoll, Johnston Island and the Outer Continental Shelf lands, who are specifically covered by the FLSA.

- *Special situations.* People with severe physical handicaps employed in special workshops, volunteers in nonprofit organizations, mental patients or patient-workers at rehabilitation facilities and prison laborers are also exempt from the FLSA. The employer should have documentation of the Department of Labor's permission to employ people under special FLSA exemptions.

- *Personal companions and casual babysitters.* Officially, domestic workers—housekeepers, childcare workers, chauffeurs, gardeners—are covered by the FLSA if they are paid at least $50 per calendar quarter, or if they work eight hours or more in a week for one or several employers. For example, if you are a teenager who babysits only an evening or two each month for the neighbors, you probably cannot claim coverage under the FLSA; a fulltime au pair would be covered.

INDEPENDENT CONTRACTORS ARE EXEMPT

The FLSA covers only employees, not independent contractors (discussed in Chapter 2, Section A). However, whether a person is an employee for purposes of the FLSA generally turns on whether that worker is employed by a single employer, not on the Internal Revenue Service definition of an independent contractor.

If nearly all of your income comes from one company, a court would probably rule that you are an employee of that company for purposes of the FLSA, regardless of whether other details of your worklife would appear to make you an independent contractor.

The FLSA was passed to clamp down on employers who cheated workers of their fair wages. As a result, employee status is broadly interpreted so that as many workers as possible come within the protections of the law.

In recent cases determining close questions of employment status, a growing number of courts are finding workers to be employees rather than independent contractors. Key realities cited by the courts: the relationship appeared to be permanent, the workers lacked bargaining power with regard to the terms of their employment (*Martin v. Albrecht*, 802 F. Supp. 1311 (1992)) and the individual workers were economically dependent upon the business to which they gave service (*Martin v. Selker Bros., Inc.*, 949 F. 2d 1286 (1991)).

B. Rights Under the FLSA

The FLSA guarantees a number of rights, primarily aimed at ensuring that workers get paid fairly for time worked. (See Sections G and H for an explanation of how to take action for FLSA violations.)

1. Minimum Wage

Employers must pay all covered employees not less than the minimum wage—$4.25 per hour. Keep in mind that some states have established a minimum wage that is higher than the federal one—and you are entitled to the higher rate if your state allows for one. Employers not covered by the FLSA, such as small farm owners, are required to pay all workers the state minimum wage rate. (See the chart, State Minimum Wage Laws, in Section E.)

The FLSA does not require any specific system of paying the minimum wage, so employers may pay based on time at work, piece rates or according to some other measurement. In all cases, however, an employee's pay divided by the hours worked during the pay period must equal or exceed the minimum wage.

GUIDANCE IN CHECKING YOUR WAGES

Many employers either become confused by the nuances and exceptions in the wage and hour law—or they bend the rules to suit their own pocketbooks. Whatever the cause, you would do well to doublecheck your employer's math. A few simple rules distilled from the law may help.

- *Hourly*. Hourly employees must be paid minimum wage for all hours worked. Your employer cannot take an average—or pay you less than minimum wage for some hours worked and more for others.
- *Fixed rate or salary*. Employees paid at a fixed rate can check their wages by dividing the amount they are paid in a pay period by the number of hours worked. The resulting average must be at least minimum wage.
- *Commissions and piece rates*. Your total pay divided by the number of hours you worked must average at least the minimum hourly wage rate.

a. Form of pay

Under the FLSA, the pay you receive must be in the form of cash or something that can be readily converted into cash or other legal forms of compensation, such as food and lodging. Your employer cannot, for example, pay you with a coupon or token that can only be spent at a store run by the employer. Employee discounts granted by employers cannot be counted toward the minimum wage requirement.

b. Pay for time off

Neither the minimum wage section nor any other part of the FLSA requires employers to pay employees for time off, such as vacation, holidays or sick days. Although most employers provide fulltime workers some paid time off each year, the FLSA covers payment only for time on the job.

However, some state laws mandate that employees get paid time off for jury duty (see Section E2), for voting (see Section E3) and for family and medical leave (see Chapter 5, Section B). And most state laws provide that if employers offer paid days off, employees are entitled to be paid for the portion they earn when they quit or are fired.

c. Tips

When employees routinely receive at least $30 per month in tips as part of their jobs, their employers are allowed to credit half of those tips against the minimum wage requirement—that is, they can credit up to $2.12 an hour of the tips received toward their wage obligation and actually pay you only $2.13 an hour. However, the employer's offset may not exceed the tips the employee actually receives. (See Section B3b for more on tips as wages.) Also, the employee must be allowed to keep all of the tips he or she receives.

Example: *Alfonse is employed as a waiter and earns more than $10 per hour in tips. The restaurant's owner, Denis, may use those tips to make up one-half of the minimum wage requirement of $4.25 an hour. Denis is still required, how-*

ever, to pay Alfonse at least $2.13 per hour on top of his tips for the first 40 hours worked in each week.

The two weeks or so following a negative review by a local newspaper columnist, the restaurant business slows to a crawl, and Alphonse's tips dip to $1 an hour. Denis may credit half the tip amount—or 50 cents—toward Alphonse's hourly minimum wage; he must pay an additional $3.75 to make up the full amount of minimum wage Alphonse is owed: $4.25 an hour.

d. Commissions

When people are paid commissions for sales, those commissions may take the place of wages. However, if the commissions do not equal the minimum wage, the FLSA requires that the employer make up the difference.

Example: *Julia, a salesperson in an electronics store, is paid a percentage of the dollar volume of the sales she completes. During one slow week, she averaged only $2 in commissions per hour. Under the FLSA, her employer must pay her an additional $2.25 for each hour she worked through the first 40 hours of that week, and more for any overtime hours.*

FINDING OUT MORE ABOUT THE FLSA

FLSA exemptions for employers change often. Doublecheck any exemption your employer claims by calling the local U.S. Labor Department, Wage and Hour Division office, listed in the federal government section of your telephone directory. Keep in mind, however, that the FLSA is so broadly written and so full of amendments and cross-references that it applies to most employers.

Most of the exemptions to FLSA coverage are listed in federal statute, 29 U.S.C. §213. The most direct way to become familiar with these exemptions is to read about them in an annotated edition of the code, which is what your local law library is most likely to have. (See Chapter 18, Section E, for more information about how to do your own legal research.)

2. Equal Pay for Equal Work

Men and women who do the same job, or jobs that require equal skill and responsibility, must be compensated with equal wages and benefits under a 1963 amendment to the FLSA called the Equal Pay Act (29 U.S.C. §206). Beware, however, that some payment schemes that may look discriminatory at first glance do not actually violate the Equal Pay Act. The Act allows disparate payments to men and women if they are based on:

- seniority systems
- merit systems
- systems measuring earnings by quantity or quality of production, such as a piece goods arrangement, or
- any factor other than sex—for example, salary differentials that stem from unequal starting salaries because of differences in experience levels.

Although the Equal Pay Act basically covers the same employers and employees as the rest of the FLSA, there is one important difference. The Equal Pay Act also protects against discriminatory pay arrangements for executive, administrative and professional employees—including administrators and teachers in elementary and secondary schools.

Because the Equal Pay Act is enforced along with other anti-discrimination laws by the Equal Employment Opportunity Commission, illegal wage discrimination based on gender is discussed in detail in Chapter 8, Section C.

3. Pay for Overtime

The FLSA does not limit the number of hours an employee may work in a week—except through some of the child labor rules (discussed in Section B5). But it does require that any covered worker who works more than 40 hours in one week must be paid at least one-and-one-half times his or her regular rate of pay for every hour worked in excess of 40.

Example: *Raymond works for a software shipping company at the wage of $8 per hour. When he works 50 hours in one week filling back orders in preparation for a national exhibition, Raymond must be paid $12 per hour for the last ten hours he worked that week.*

Jody, who is vice president of the software shipping company and Raymond's boss, also worked 50 hours the same week. Since Jody qualifies as an executive and so is exempt from the FLSA (see Section A2), she is not entitled to overtime pay, but receives her regular weekly salary.

There is no legal requirement that workers must receive overtime pay simply because they worked more than eight hours in one day. Nor is there anything that requires a worker to be paid on the spot for overtime. Under the FLSA, an employer is allowed to calculate and pay overtime by the week—which can be any 168-hour period made up of seven consecutive 24-hour periods. There are some special exceptions that allow employers that require odd work schedules—for example, some healthcare institutions and nursing homes—to pay employees according to multiple-week standards.

It is custom, not law, that determines that a workweek begins on Monday. However, the FLSA requires consistency. An employer cannot manipulate the start of the workweek to avoid paying overtime.

Also, there are a few additional exceptions to the overtime pay rules that are dictated by common sense. Some types of jobs are exempt from the portions of the FLSA that set out overtime pay requirements. The most common of these jobs are live-in domestic workers, taxi drivers, truck drivers, delivery people and outside salespeople who spend most of their worktime away from their employers' offices.

a. Piece rates and commissions

People who work on piece rates and commissions instead of by the clock have a more complicated task in calculating their rates of pay.

For piece rate workers, the regular wage rate may be calculated by averaging hourly piece rate earnings for the week. Calculating overtime is a bit trickier.

Example: *Max is an assembler in a photocopier factory who is paid a piece rate of 50 cents for each copier cover he installs. One week, he worked 40 hours and installed 400 covers, so his regular rate of pay for that week was $5 per hour (400 x .50, divided by 40).*

One of two alternatives may be used to determine Max's overtime pay:

- *Increase the piece rate by 50% during the overtime hours. For example, Max's employer could raise his piece rate to 75 cents per copier cover (150% of .50) for overtime hours.*
- *Estimate an average hourly wage and then use that estimated average to compute overtime.*

Keep in mind that if the U.S. Labor Department investigates the legality of your pay rate, it may require proof that any estimates used to calculate your pay are in line with the piece rate pay you actually earned over a substantial time—usually several months.

The methods for calculating and paying commissions vary tremendously. If you have questions about whether your employer is complying with the wage laws on piece rates and commissions, call or visit the nearest office of the Labor Department's Wage and Hour Division, listed in the government section of the telephone book.

b. Jobs involving tips

If you regularly work for tips, all of the tips you usually receive are not counted as part of your regular rate of pay when calculating overtime pay. Only the wage that your employer has agreed to pay you counts, and in most cases where people work for tips, that is the federal minimum wage. Of course, tip money that you receive beyond the minimum wage amount is still taxable to you as income.

Example: *Lisa works as a waitress for wages plus tips. Because she receives a substantial amount in tips, her employer is allowed to take a 50% set-off against the minimum wage requirement, paying her a wage of just $2.13 per hour. Nevertheless, her regular rate of pay for calculating overtime pay under the FLSA standards is still the minimum wage of $4.25 per hour.*

One week, Lisa worked 41 hours—one hour of overtime. For that overtime hour, she must be paid $4.25, regardless of the tips she received during that hour: the $2.12 per hour that she would normally receive after the tip credit, plus one-half her regular rate of pay, which equals another $2.13.

c. Split payscales

If your job involves different types of work for which different payscales have been established, you must calculate your regular rate of pay for each category of work, then apply the appropriate rate to any overtime hours. The payscale that applies to the type of work you did during overtime hours is the one on which you calculate the time and one-half rule.

Example: *Matt works for a company that manages a large apartment complex. For landscaping work, he is paid $8 per hour. When he works as a guard with the company's private security force for the complex, Matt gets $5 per hour. For payroll purposes, his workweek begins on Monday.*

During one week in the spring, he worked eight hours a day, Monday through Friday, for a total of 40 hours with the landscaping crew. But the landscaping crew does not work on weekends, and Matt needed some extra money, so he worked eight hours on Saturday with the security patrol. He took Sunday off.

Because the FLSA's overtime pay rules take effect only after an employee works 40 hours in one week, the eight overtime hours Matt worked with the security force were at security patrol rate of $5 per hour. His overtime pay for that week is $60 ($5 x 8 x 1½).

EXEMPTION FOR SKILLS TRAINING

Up to ten hours per week of otherwise payable time is exempt from the overtime rules in wage and hour law for some types of skills training. To qualify, the extra hours must be used to provide employees who never graduated from high school or otherwise demonstrated that they have attained at least an eighth grade education with general training in reading and other basic skills. To qualify for this exemption, the training cannot be specific to the worker's current job, but must cover skills that could be used in virtually any job (29 U.S.C. §207(q)).

d. Multiple employers

No matter how many jobs you hold, the overtime pay rules apply to each of your employers individually. If in one week you work 30 hours for one employer and 30 additional hours for another, for example, neither one owes you overtime pay.

4. Compensatory Time

Most workers are familiar with compensatory or comp time—the practice of employers offering employees time off from work in place of cash payments for overtime. What comes as a shock to many is that the practice is illegal in most situations. Under the FLSA, only state or government agencies may legally allow their employees time off in place of wages (29 U.S.C. §207(o)). Even then, comp time may be awarded only:

- according to the terms of a collective bargaining unit (see Chapter 16), or
- if the employer and employee agree to the arrangement before work begins.

When compensatory time is allowed, it must be awarded at the rate of one-and-one-half times the overtime hours worked—and comp time must be taken during the same pay period that the overtime hours were worked.

Example: *John, a state employee, is paid a fixed salary every two weeks. His standard workweek is made up of five shifts, each eight hours long. During the first week of a pay period, John works 44 hours, earning four hours of overtime pay. During the second week of that pay period, he can take six hours off as comp time (4 hours x 1½). In the second week of the pay period, he works only 34 hours, but is paid his full salary as though he had worked 40 hours.*

Some states do allow private employers to give employees comp time instead of cash. But there are complex, often conflicting laws controlling how and when it may be given. A common control, for example, is that employees must voluntarily request in writing that comp time be given instead of overtime pay—before the extra hours are worked. Check with your state's labor department for special laws on comp time in your area. (See the Appendix for contact information.)

WHAT'S SO NORMAL ABOUT YOUR WORKWEEK?

Most Americans consider a normal workweek to be 40 hours, spread over a five-day period that begins each Monday, with each day's work starting in the morning and ending as evening approaches. But, in fact, that kind of schedule is a leftover from the decades when factories dominated the American economy.

Production line manufacturing techniques made it necessary for all workers to gather around a factory's machines at the same time. The lack of strong artificial light in the early factories made the daylight hours the best time to run the production line. Biblical warnings against working on Sundays inspired the factory tradition of closing for one day at each week's end.

In the 1930s, the Fair Labor Standards Act restricted the normal factory workweek to 40 hours so that fewer people would be worked to physical exhaustion. This restriction forced industry to spread work among more employees, rescuing some unemployed people from the financial humiliation of the Depression. Consequently, the typical factory employee's weekend break from work grew to include Saturdays.

Today, the factory-style work schedule has faded in popularity. Companies are slowly beginning to acknowledge that most people's work no longer requires them to gather in the same place, at the same time, around the same set of machines.

In 1991, for example, The Bechtel Group engineering company in San Francisco began scheduling its employees for nine days of work in every two-week period. Each of the workdays that falls on Monday through Thursday is nine hours long. On Friday, only one-half of the staff works, and the shift is only eight hours long. The Bechtel employees still work the equivalent of 40 hours per week. But their schedules give them each the enviable total of 26 three-day weekends per year.

Many employers and employees routinely violate the rules governing the use of compensatory time in place of cash overtime wages. However, such violations are risky. Employees can find themselves unable to collect money due them if a company goes out of business or they are fired. And employers can end up owing large amounts of overtime pay to employees as the result of a labor department investigation and prosecution of compensatory time violations.

5. Restrictions on Child Labor

Minors under 18 years old may not work in any job that is considered to be hazardous—including those involving mining, wrecking and demolition, logging and roofing. The Secretary of Labor defines what jobs are deemed hazardous, and so out of bounds for young workers. To find out which jobs are currently considered hazardous for the purposes of the FLSA, call the local office of the U.S. Labor Department's Wage and Hour Division, located in the government section of your telephone book.

There are additional restrictions on when and how long workers between ages 14 and 16 may be employed in nonhazardous jobs.

- They may work no more than three hours on a school day and no more than 18 hours in a school week.
- They may work no more than eight hours on a nonschool day and no more than 40 hours in a nonschool week.
- During the period that starts with the day after Labor Day and ends at midnight May 31, their workday may not begin earlier than 7 a.m. or end later than 7 p.m.
- From June 1 through Labor Day, their workday may not begin earlier than 7 a.m., but it can end as late as 9 p.m.

Some industries have obtained special exemptions from the legal restrictions on child labor. Youths of any age may deliver newspapers, for example, or perform in television, movie or theatrical productions.

The farming industry has been fighting the child labor restrictions as well as the rest of the FLSA ever since the law was first proposed in the 1930s, so less strict rules apply to child farm workers. For example, children as young as 12 may work on their parents' farms.

C. Calculating Your Pay

To resolve most questions or disputes involving the FLSA, you must first know the regular rate of pay to which you are legally entitled.

Whether you work for hourly wages, salary, commissions or a piece rate, the courts have ruled that your regular rate of pay typically includes your base pay plus any shift premiums, hazardous duty premiums, cost of living allowances, bonuses used to make otherwise undesirable worksites attractive, and the fair value of such things as food and lodging that your employer routinely provides as part of your pay.

Obviously, there is much room here for individual interpretation and arbitrary decisions. But the overriding concept is that everything that you logically consider to be a routine part of your hourly pay for a routine day is a part of your regular rate of pay.

The courts have often ruled that the regular rate of pay does not include contributions that an employer makes to benefit plans, paid vacations and holiday benefits, premiums paid for working on holidays or weekends, and discretionary bonuses. And some employee manuals clarify what is included in your regular rate of pay by specifying that some benefit programs are regarded by the company to be extra compensation that is not part of an employee's regular pay.

The regular rate of pay for people who work for hourly wages is their hourly rate including the factors just mentioned. For salaried workers, the hourly rate is their weekly pay divided by the number of hours in their standard workweek.

D. Calculating Workhours

When a work pay period begins and ends is determined by a law called the Portal-to-Portal Pay Act (29 U.S.C. §251). This amendment to the FLSA and several other workplace laws requires that an employee must be paid for any time spent that is controlled by and that benefits the employer.

This aspect of wage and hour law has generated a tremendous number of clashes—and cases in which the courts have attempted to sharpen the definition of payable time.

Worktime for which you must be paid includes all the time you must be on duty or at the workplace. However, the courts have ruled that on-the-job time does not include the time employees spend washing themselves or changing clothes before or after work, nor does it include time spent in a regular commute to the workplace.

Employers are not allowed to circumvent the Portal-to-Portal Pay Act by simply "allowing" you to work on what is depicted as your own time. You must be paid for all the time you work—voluntary or not. This issue has come up frequently in recent years because some career counselors have been advising people that volunteering to work free for a company for a month or so is a good way to find a new job. Although working for free may be legal in situations where the job being sought is exempt from the FLSA—for example, a professional fundraising position with a nonprofit organization—it is not legal when the job involved is governed by the Act. (See Section A2 for details on FLSA exemptions.)

For ease of accounting, employers are allowed to round off records of worktime to the nearest five-minute mark on the clock or the nearest quarter hour. But rounding off becomes illegal if it results in employees being paid for less time than they actually worked. In practice, this means that your employer will usually round your worktime off to add a few minutes each day to the time for which you are paid.

In calculating on-the-job time, most concerns focus on how to deal with specific questionable situations, such as travel time, meal and coffee breaks, on-call periods and sleeping on the job.

1. Travel Time

The time you spend commuting between your home and the place you normally work is not considered to be on-the-job time for which you must be paid. But it may be payable time if the commute is actually part of the job.

If you are a lumberjack, for example, and you have to check in at your employer's office, pick up a chainsaw, then drive ten miles on company lands to reach the cutting site for a particular day, your workday legally begins when you check in at the office.

And if your employer requests that you attend an out-of-town conference or meeting, the time it takes you to go back and forth from the conference or meeting site is legally considered worktime—and you must be paid for it.

Otherwise, you can only claim that you should be paid for your time in commuting to and from work when you are required to go back and forth from your normal worksite at odd hours in emergency situations.

Example: *Ernest normally works 9 to 5 as a computer operator and is paid hourly. One day, about two hours after he arrived home from work, he got a call from his office notifying him that the computer was malfunctioning and that he was needed there immediately to help correct the problem. It took him one-half hour to drive back to the office, two hours to get the computer back on track and one-half hour to drive home again.*

The company must pay Ernest for three extra hours, two of them workhours and the third for the extra hour of commuting time required by the company's emergency.

2. Meal and Break Periods

Contrary to common sense, federal law does not require that you be allotted or paid for breaks to eat meals.

However, many states have laws specifically requiring that employees be allowed a half-hour or so in meal and rest breaks during each workday. (See the chart below.) Meal breaks of 30 minutes or more usually need not be counted as part of your payable work hours—as long as you are completely relieved of work duties during that time. Technically, however, if your employer either requires that you work while eating—or allows you to do so—you must be paid for time spent during meals. Also, you must be paid for break periods that are less than 20 minutes.

STATE MEAL AND REST BREAK LAWS

Alabama	No statute
Alaska	No statute
Arizona	No statute
Arkansas	No statute
California	Meal—30 minutes within 5 hours of starting work if workday is 6 hours or more. If less, waivable.
	Rest—10 minutes per 4-hour period. Compensated.
	Industrial Welfare Commission Order No. 1-89. (Does not apply to motion picture, agricultural and household occupations.)
Colorado	Meal—30 minutes within 5 hours of starting work. Optional if workday is not over 6 hours.
	Rest—10 minutes per 4 hours.
	Wage Order No. 19
Connecticut	Meal—30 minutes per 7-1/2 hour workday. Given after 2nd hour and before last 2 hours.
	Conn. Gen. Stat. §31-51ii
Delaware	Meal—30 minutes for 7-1/2 hour workday. Given after 2nd hour and before last 2 hours.
	Del. Code Ann. tit. 19, §707
District of Columbia	No statute
Florida	No statute
Georgia	No statute
Hawaii	Meal—45 minutes for government employees only.
	Haw. Rev. Stat. §80-1
Idaho	No statute
Illinois	Meal—20 minutes for a 7-1/2 hour workday beginning no later than 5 hours into the work period.
	820 Ill. Compiled Stat. §140/3
Indiana	No statute
Iowa	No statute
Kansas	No statute
Kentucky	Meal—"Reasonable" break between 3 and 5 hours into the work period.
	Rest—10 minutes per 4 hours.
	Ky. Rev. Stat. Ann. §§337.355 and 337.365
Louisiana	No statute

Maine	Meal—30 minutes per 6 hours of work for meals or rest. Me. Rev. Stat. Ann. tit. 26, §§601 and 602
Maryland	No statute
Massachusetts	Meal—30 minutes per 6-hour work period. Mass. Gen. Laws Ann. ch. 149, §100
Michigan	No statute
Minnesota	Meal—Employer must allow "sufficient time" to eat a meal during an 8-hour work period. Minn. Stat. Ann. §177.254 Rest—Employer must allow a "reasonable" amount of time in a 4-hour period to use the restroom. Minn. Stat. Ann. §177.253
Mississippi	No statute
Missouri	No statute
Montana	No statute
Nebraska	All employees in assembly plants, workshops, or mechanical establishments are required to have at least 30-minute lunch breaks between noon and 1 p.m. without having to remain on the premises unless it operates 24 hours per day. Neb. Rev. Stat. §48-212
Nevada	Meal—30 minutes per 8 hours of work. Rest—10 minutes per 4 hours of work. Nev. Rev. Stat. Ann. §608.155
New Hampshire	Meal—30 minutes per 5 hours of work. N.H. Rev. Stat. Ann. §275:30-a
New Jersey	No statute
New Mexico	Meal—30 minutes. N.M. Stat. Ann. §50-5-4
New York	Meal—Mercantile or similar establishments: 45 minutes; Factory: 60 minutes; If shift begins before noon and extends past 7 p.m., an additional 20 minutes is given between 5 p.m. and 7 p.m.; If shift is more than 6 hours long and begins between 1 a.m. and 6 a.m., then mercantile employees are to receive 45 minutes and factory employees 60 minutes. N.Y. Labor Law §162
North Carolina	No statute
North Dakota	Meal—30 minutes if shift is over 5 hours. By wage order. Commissioner of Labor sets the standards. N.D. Century Code §34-06-03
Ohio	No statute

Oklahoma	No statute
Oregon	Meal—30 minutes for each work period of between 6 and 8 hours within the 2nd and 5th hour worked. Or, if work period is more than 7 hours, break to be given between the 3rd and 6th hour worked.
	Rest—10 minutes for every 4 hours worked.
	Or. Administrative Rules §839-020-050
Pennsylvania	No statute
Rhode Island	Meal—20 minutes per 6 hours of work.
	R.I. Gen. Laws §28-3-14
South Carolina	No statute
South Dakota	No statute
Tennessee	Meal—30 minutes for 6-hour work period.
	Tenn. Code Ann. §50-2-103
Texas	No statute
Utah	No statute
Vermont	No statute
Virginia	No statute
Washington	No statute
West Virginia	Meal—20 minutes.
	W.V. Administrative Regulations §42-5-2.6
Wisconsin	Meal—30 minutes close to usual meal time or near middle of shift. Shifts of more than 6 hours without a meal break should be avoided.
	Break mandatory for minors.
	Wisc. Admin. Code, Ind. 74.02
Wyoming	Two rest periods of not less than 15 minutes, one before the lunch hour and one after lunch, for employees who are required to be on their feet continuously.
	Wyo. Stat. Ann. §27-6-101

3. On-Call Periods

Time periods when employees are not actually working, but are required to stay on the employer's premises or at some other designated spot while waiting for a work assignment, are covered as part of payable time. For example, a driver for a private ambulance service who is required to sit in the ambulance garage waiting for calls must be paid for the waiting time.

But if your employer requires you to be on call but does not require you to stay on the company's premises, then the following two rules generally apply.

- On-call time that you are allowed to control and use for your own enjoyment or benefit is not counted as payable time.
- On-call time over which you have little or no control and which you cannot use for your own enjoyment or benefit is payable time.

Example: *Jack works in an office, 9 to 5, Monday through Friday, as a client services representative for a funeral director. His employer also requires him to be on call at all times in case a business question arises—and it furnishes him with a message beeper. Jack can spend his free time any way he wants. All his employer requires him to do is to call the office as soon as is convenient after his beeper registers a message, so Jack's on-call time is not payable time.*

Example: *Elizabeth is a rape crisis counselor with a social service agency. The agency that employs her must constantly have someone with her expertise available. During weekends when Elizabeth is the on-call counselor, she is allowed to stay at home but must remain near her telephone at all times. She cannot leave her apartment except in response to a rape report, and she cannot drink any alcohol. Practically speaking, she cannot even throw a little dinner party because, if a call were to come in, she would have to leave her guests immediately. Elizabeth's on-call time is not hers to control and enjoy, so it is payable time.*

4. Sleep as Payable Time

If you are required to be on duty at your place of employment for less than 24 hours at a time, the U.S. Labor Department allows you to count as payable any time that you are allowed to sleep during your shift of duty. If you are required to be at work for more than 24 hours at a time—for example, if you work as a live-in housekeeper—you and your employer may agree to exclude up to eight hours per day from your payable time as sleep and meal periods.

However, if the conditions are such that you cannot get at least five hours of sleep during your eight-hour sleep-and-eat period, or if you end up working during that period, then those eight hours revert to being payable time.

Example: *Bill works on an offshore oil rig for two days at a time. At the start of each shift, the boat takes him out to the platform and does not come back for him until two days later. Bill and his employer have an agreement that requires that Bill gets an unpaid eight-hour sleep period each day, so his payable time for each 48-hour period he spends on the platform totals 32 hours. During one of Bill's shifts, a storm blew up and caused so much trouble that he had to keep working through the night. That reduced one of his sleep periods to only two hours. Bill must be paid for the sleep period that was cut short, so his payable time at the end of that shift would be 40 hours, or 32 + 8 hours payable sleep time..*

DIFFERENT PAY RATES ARE ALLOWED

Unless there's an employment contract that states otherwise, employers are generally allowed to pay a different hourly rate for on-call time than they do for regular worktime, and many do. The employer need only make sure that the employees are paid at least the minimum amount required under wage and hour regulations.

Example: A hospital emergency room has a policy of paying medical technicians a high hourly rate when they are actually working on a patient, and just the minimum wage when they are merely racking up on-call time on the hospital's premises. If such a technician were to record 20 hours active time and 20 hours on-call time in one week, the FLSA requires only that he or she receive the minimum wage for the 20 on-call hours.

The courts have generally approved such split-rate pay plans for the purposes of both the minimum wage and overtime requirements if there are marked differences in the types of work performed and the employer has clearly informed employees that different wages are paid for different types of work. (See Section B3 on split payscales.)

E. State and Local Laws

Although the niggling matters of wage and hour requirements are not among the most scintillating workplace topics, disputes over either tend to hit employees hard and fast. In addition to broad controls over wages and hours that are set out in federal law, a number of state and local regulations are thrown into the fray. If your dispute involves a wage and hour issue, check all these sources of legal controls to get a clear picture of your possible rights and remedies. (See Section F for a discussion and state listing of wage garnishment laws.)

In particular, check the discussions of state laws and charts below on:

- minimum wages (Section 1)
- time off for jury duty (Section 2)
- time off for voting (Section 3)
- military leave (Section 4), and
- protections for filing wage and hour complaints (Section 5).

PAY INTERVAL LAWS: HOW OFTEN IS OFTEN ENOUGH?

The question of how often you must be paid is most often addressed by state wage and hour laws. The FLSA states only that the pay period must be no longer than once a month, but state laws controlling pay intervals often require that most employees be paid at least every two weeks or twice a month.

Like state wage and hour laws, state laws governing how often you must be paid are complex, usually covering only certain types of companies and employees. If you have a question about how often you must be paid under your state's laws, contact the local office of your state's labor department. (See the Appendix for contact details.)

1. Minimum Wage Laws

All but a few states have laws specifying wage and hour standards. Some of these laws are virtually meaningless because they set standards less stringent than those set by federal law. On the other hand, some state wage rates are significantly higher than those set by federal law. (See the chart below.)

Alaska is a good example. Its minimum wage is $4.75 per hour—and must remain 50 cents higher than the federal minimum should the federal law change. In addition, Alaska is one of the few states that does not allow tips to be used as a credit against its minimum wage.

Each state has its own rules for who is covered by its minimum wage law, and they are usually complex. The best way to determine whether your job is covered by a state wage and hour law that has a standard higher than the FLSA is to call the local office of your state's labor department. (See the Appendix for contact details.)

In the last few years, some counties, cities and towns have also passed their own wage laws. Such local wage laws are still rare and controversial, but you may want to check with the law department of the county or municipality in which you work if you have reason to think that it has passed a wage and hour law covering your job.

Whenever the FLSA sets a standard higher than one at the state or local level, the FLSA rules. When a state or local law sets standards higher than the FLSA, the state or local law is the one that applies.

STATE MINIMUM WAGE LAWS	
Alabama	No statute
Alaska	$4.75. 50 cents above federal minimum wage. Alaska Stat. §23.10.065
Arizona	No statute
Arkansas	$4.15 as of 8/1/93; $4.25 as of 7/1/94. Ark. Code Ann. §11-4-210
California	$4.25. At least the federal minimum wage. Cal. Labor Code §1182
Colorado	$3.00. By minimum wage order #19. For wage setting procedure, see Colo. Rev. Stat. §§8-6-109; 8-6-110; 8-6-111

Connecticut	$4.27. Or at least 1/2% above the federal minimum wage. Conn. Gen. Stat. §31-58j
Delaware	$4.25. Or at least the federal minimum wage. Del. Code Ann. tit. 19, §902a
District of Columbia	$5.25. Federal minimum wage plus $1.00. D.C. Code Ann. §§36-220.1 and 36-220.2
Florida	No statute
Georgia	$3.25. Ga. Code Ann. §34-4-3a
Hawaii	$5.25. Haw. Rev. Stat. §387-2
Idaho	$4.25. Idaho Code §44-1502
Illinois	$4.25. Ill. Compiled Stat. ch. 820, ¶105/4a
Indiana	$3.35. Ind. Code Ann. §22-2-2-4
Iowa	$4.65. Iowa Code Ann. §91D.1
Kansas	$2.65. Kan. Stat. Ann. §44-1203
Kentucky	$4.25. Ky. Rev. Stat. Ann §337.275
Louisiana	No statute
Maine	$4.25. Same as federal minimum wage up to $5.00. Me. Rev. Stat. Ann. tit. 26, §664
Maryland	$4.25. At least the federal minimum wage. Md. Code Ann., Labor and Employment, §3-413
Massachusetts	$4.25. Mass. Gen. Laws Ann. ch. 151, §1
Michigan	$3.35. Mich. Stat. Ann. §17.2554
Minnesota	$4.25 for large employers—those grossing more than $362,500 per year. For others, $4.00. Minn. Stat. Ann. §177.24
Mississippi	No statute
Missouri	$4.25. Mo. Ann. Stat. §290.502
Montana	$4.25 for businesses with gross annual sales of $110,000 or more. For others, $4.00. Mont. Code Ann. §§39-3-404; 39-3-409; Dept. of Labor & Industry Rules §24.16.15104
Nebraska	No statute
Nevada	$4.25. Notice of the Labor Commissioner. 4/1/91
New Hampshire	$4.25. Federal minimum wage or $3.95, whichever is higher. N.H. Rev. Stat. Ann. §279:21
New Jersey	$5.05. N.J. Stat. Ann. §34:11-56a4
New Mexico	$4.25. N.M. Stat. Ann. §50-4-22
New York	$4.25. N.Y. Labor Law §652
North Carolina	$4.25. N.C. Gen. Stat. §95-25.3
North Dakota	$4.25. By wage order. Commissioner of Labor sets the standards of minimum wages, hours of employment and conditions of employment. N.D. Century Code §34-06-03

Ohio	$4.25. Ohio Rev. Code Ann. §4111.02
Oklahoma	$4.25. Not less than current federal minimum wage. Okla. Stat. Ann. tit. 40, §197.2
Oregon	$4.75. Or. Rev. Stat. §653.025
Pennsylvania	$4.25. 43 Pa. Cons. Stat. Ann §333.104
Rhode Island	$4.45. R.I. Gen. Laws §28-12-3
South Carolina	No statute
South Dakota	$4.25. S.D. Codified Laws Ann. §60-11-3
Tennessee	No statute
Texas	$3.35. Tex. Labor Code Ann. §62.051
Utah	$4.25. Utah Code Ann. §4487-1-3A
Vermont	$4.25. Not less than current federal minimum wage. Vt. Stat. Ann. tit. 21, §384a
Virginia	$4.25. Equal to federal minimum wage. Va. Code Ann. §40.1-28.10
Washington	$4.90. Wash. Rev. Code Ann. §49.46.020
West Virginia	$4.25. W.Va. Code §21-5C-2a
Wisconsin	$4.25. Set by wage order. Dept. of Industry, Labor and Human Relations Regulations, Ind. 72.031. Wis. Stat. Ann. §104.02
Wyoming	$1.60. Wyo. Stat. §27-4-202

2. Time Off for Jury Duty

Most states have some specific requirements that apply to employees who are called to serve on juries. Most of these laws fall under the broad rubric of wage and hour controls. Some laws require that employees must be paid for time away from work spent on jury duty; some states require only that unpaid time off be allowed. And many state laws contain an anti-discrimination twist—baldly stating that employees called to serve on juries may not be fired for doing so. And a few laws broadly restrict employers from attempting to intimidate employees not to serve on juries.

STATE LAWS ON JURY DUTY

Alabama	Employees may not be fired for taking time off to serve on a jury. A fulltime employee is entitled to usual pay less any compensation received from the court for service. Ala. Code §12-16-8
Alaska	Public employees may not be fired or penalized for taking time off to serve on a jury and are entitled to paid leave for their absence from employment. Alaska Stat. §39.20.270
Arizona	Employees may not be fired for serving on a jury. Employers are not required to pay employees when absent from employment for jury service. Ariz. Rev. Stat. Ann. §21-236
Arkansas	City, county, school employees may not be fired for taking time off to serve on a jury. Ark. Stat. Ann. §21-12-304
	State employees may not be fired for taking time off to serve on a jury. Ark. Stat. Ann. §16-31-106
California	Employees may not be fired for taking time off to serve on a jury. Cal. Labor Code §230
Colorado	Employees may not be fired for taking time off to serve on a jury. Regular employees, including parttime, temporary and casual workers, are entitled to regular wages up to $50 per day for the first three days of jury service. Colo. Rev. Stat. §13-71-126
Connecticut	Employees may not be fired for taking time off to serve on a jury. Conn. Gen. Stat. Ann. §54-247a
	Fulltime employees are entitled to be paid their regular wages by their employer for the first five days of jury service. Conn. Gen. Stat. Ann. §51-247
Delaware	No statute
District of Columbia	No statute
Florida	Employees may not be fired for taking time off to serve on a jury. Fla. Stat. §40.271
	Regular employees, including parttime, temporary and casual workers, who continue to receive their regular wages are not entitled to be compensated by the court for the first three days of jury duty. Employers are not required to pay jurors during absence. Fla. Stat. §40.24
Georgia	No statute
Hawaii	Employee may not be fired for taking time off to serve on a jury. Hawaii Rev. Stat. §612-25.
	Public employees may not be fired for taking time off to serve on a jury and are entitled to paid leave during their absence from employment. Hawaii Rev. Stat. §70-14

Idaho	Employees may not be fired for taking time off to serve on a jury. Idaho Code §2.2181
Illinois	Employees may not be fired for taking time off to serve on a jury. Ill. Compiled Stat. ch. 705, ¶310/10.1
Indiana	No statute
Iowa	Employees may not be fired for taking time off to serve on a jury. Iowa Code §607A.45
Kansas	No statute
Kentucky	Employees may not be fired for taking time off to serve on a jury. Ky. Rev. Stat. §29A.160
	Public employees may not be fired for taking time off to serve on a jury and are entitled to paid leave during their absence. Ky. Rev. Stat. §161.153
Louisiana	Employees may not be fired for taking time off to serve on a jury. La. Rev. Stat. Ann. §23:965
Maine	Employees may not be fired for taking time off to serve on a jury. Me. Rev. Stat. Ann. title 14, §1218
Maryland	Employees may not be fired for taking time off to serve on a jury. Md. Cts. and Jud. Proc. Code Ann. §8-105
Massachusetts	Employees may not be fired for taking time off to serve on a jury. Regular employees, including parttime, temporary and casual workers, are entitled to regular wages for the first three days of jury service. Mass. Gen. Laws Ann. ch. 234A, §§48 and 49
Michigan	Employees may not be fired for taking time off for jury service. Mich. Comp. Laws §600.1348
Minnesota	Employees may not be fired for taking time off to serve on a jury. Minn. Stat. Ann. §593.50
Mississippi	Employers may not intimidate employees to keep from jury service. Miss. Code Ann. §13-5-23
Missouri	No statute
Montana	No statute
Nebraska	Employees may not be fired for taking time off to serve on a jury and are entitled to regular pay during absence from employment less any compensation received from court. Neb. Rev. Stat. §25-1640
Nevada	Employees may not be fired for taking time off to serve on a jury. Nev. Rev. Stat. §6.190
New Hampshire	No statute
New Jersey	State, county, local and mass transit employees may not be fired for taking time off to serve on a jury. N.J. Stat. Ann. §2A:69-5

New Mexico	Employees may not be fired for taking time off to serve on a jury. N.M. Stat. Ann. §§38-5-18 and 38-5-19
New York	No statute
North Carolina	No statute
North Dakota	Employees may not be fired for taking time off to serve on a jury. N.D. Cent. Code §27-09.1-17
Ohio	Employees may not be fired for taking time off to serve on a jury. Ohio Rev. Code Ann. §2313.18
Oklahoma	Employees may not be fired for taking time off to serve on a jury. Okla. Stat. Ann. title 38, §§4 and 35
Oregon	Employees may not be fired for taking time off to serve on a jury. Or. Rev. Stat. §§10.090
Pennsylvania	Employees may not be fired for taking time off to serve on a jury. Pa. Cons. Stat. Ann. title 17, §§920 to 922.
Rhode Island	Employees may not be fired for taking time off to serve on a jury. R.I. Gen. Laws §9-9-28
South Carolina	Employees may not be fired for taking time off to serve on a jury. S.C. Code Ann. §41-1-70
South Dakota	Employees may not be fired for taking time off to serve on a jury. S.D. Codified Laws Ann. §§16-13-41.1 and 16-13-41.2
Tennessee	Employees may not be fired for taking time off to serve on a jury. Tenn. Code Ann. §22-4-108
Texas	Employees may not be fired for taking time off to serve on a jury. Tex. Rev. Civil Stat. Ann. art. 5207b
Utah	Employees may not be fired for taking time off to serve on a jury. Utah Code Ann. §78-46-21
Vermont	Employees may not be fired for taking time off to serve on a jury. Vt. Stat. Ann. tit. 21, §499
Virginia	Employees may not be fired for taking time off to serve on a jury. Va. Code §18.2-465.1
Washington	Employees may not be fired for taking time off to serve on a jury. Wash. Rev. Code Ann. §2.36.165
West Virginia	Employees may not be fired for taking time off to serve on a jury and are entitled to regular wages for time absent. W. Va. Code §§52-3-1
Wisconsin	Employees may not be fired for taking time off to serve on a jury. Wis. Stat. Ann. §756.25
Wyoming	Employees may not be fired for taking time off to serve on a jury. Wyo. Stat. §1-11-401

3. Time Off for Voting

Another set of state laws that fall under the broad category of wage and hour controls regulates the time off employers must allow for employees to vote. Some state laws set out a specific amount of time that employees must be allowed off from work to cast their ballots. In some states, the time off must be paid, not in others. And a number of state laws prohibit employers from disciplining or firing employees who take time off work to vote.

STATE LAWS ON VOTING	
Alabama	No statute
Alaska	Employees may not be fired for taking two hours off without loss of pay unless the employee has two nonwork hours to vote. Alaska Stat. §15.56.100
Arizona	Employees may not be fired for taking three hours off without loss of pay unless the employee has three nonwork hours to vote. Ariz. Rev. Stat. Ann. §16-402
Arkansas	Employers must change work schedules to allow employees to vote. No specific amount of time off is required. Ark. Stat. Ann. §7-1-102
California	Employees may not be fired for taking time off to vote. No specific amount of time off is required. Up to two hours may be taken without loss of pay if the employee does not have time before or after work. Cal. Elec. Code §14350
Colorado	Employees cannot be fired for taking two hours off without loss of pay unless the employee has three nonwork hours to vote. Colo. Rev. Stat. §1-7-102
Connecticut	No statute
Delaware	No statute
District of Columbia	No statute
Florida	No statute
Georgia	Employees cannot be fired or disciplined for taking two hours off of unpaid time unless the employee has two nonwork hours to vote. Ga. Code Ann. § 21-2-404
Hawaii	Employees cannot be fired for taking two hours off without loss of pay unless they have two nonwork hours to vote. Hawaii Rev. Stat. §11-95

Idaho	No statute
Illinois	Employees cannot be fired for taking two unpaid hours off to vote. 10 Ill. Compiled Stat. 5/17-15
Indiana	No statute
Iowa	Employees may not be fired for taking three hours off without loss of pay to vote. Iowa Code §49.109
Kansas	Employees cannot be fired for taking two hours off without loss of pay to vote. Kan. Stat. Ann. §25-418
Kentucky	Employees cannot be fired for taking off four unpaid hours to vote. Ky. Rev. Stat. §118.035
Louisiana	No statute
Maine	No statute
Maryland	Employees cannot be fired for taking two hours off without loss of pay unless they have two nonwork hours in which to vote. Md. Ann. Code Const. art. 33, §24-26
Massachusetts	Employees must be given time off to vote and manufacturing, mercantile and mechanical employees must be given the first two hours the polls are open without loss of pay. Mass. Gen. Laws Ann. ch. 149, §178
Michigan	No statute
Minnesota	Employees cannot be fired for taking time off to vote and must be given an unspecified amount of morning time without loss of pay for this purpose. Minn. Stat. Ann. §204C.04
Mississippi	No statute
Missouri	Employees cannot be fired for taking three hours off to vote without loss of pay. Mo. Ann. Stat. §115.639
Montana	No statute
Nebraska	Employees cannot be fired for taking two hours off to vote without loss of pay. Neb. Rev. Stat. §32-1046
Nevada	Employees cannot be fired for taking up to three hours off, depending upon where they live in relation to the polling place without loss of pay unless they have enough time during nonwork hours to vote. Nev. Rev. Stat. §293.463
New Hampshire	No statute
New Jersey	No statute
New Mexico	Employees cannot be fired for taking two hours off without loss of pay unless they have two hours before or three hours after work to vote. N.M. Stat. Ann. §1-12-42
New York	Employees cannot be fired for taking up to two hours off without loss of pay unless they have four hours of nonwork time to vote. N.Y. Elect. Law §3-110

North Carolina	No statute
North Dakota	Employers are encouraged to grant employees time off to vote. No specific requirements are mandated. N.D. Cent. Code §16.1-01-02.1
Ohio	Employees cannot be fired for taking a reasonable amount of time off to vote without loss of pay. Ohio Rev. Code Ann. §3599.06
Oklahoma	Employees cannot be fired for taking two hours off to vote without loss of pay. Okla. Stat. Ann. title 26, §7-101
Oregon	No statute
Pennsylvania	No statute
Rhode Island	No statute
South Carolina	No statute
South Dakota	Employees may not be fired for taking two hours off without loss of pay unless they have two nonwork hours to vote. S.D. Codified Laws Ann. §12-3-5
Tennessee	Employees cannot be fired for taking three hours off to vote without loss of pay. Tenn. Code Ann. §22-4-108
Texas	Employees cannot be fired for taking a reasonable amount of time off without loss of pay unless they have two nonwork hours to vote. Tex. Elect. Code §276.004
Utah	Employees cannot be fired for taking two hours off to vote without loss of pay. Utah Code Ann. §20-13-18
Vermont	No statute
Virginia	No statute
Washington	Employees cannot be fired for taking two hours off, other than meal or rest breaks, to vote without loss of pay. Wash. Rev. Code Ann. §49.28.120
West Virginia	Employees cannot be fired for taking three hours off without loss of pay unless they have three nonwork hours to vote. W. Va. Code §3-1-42
Wisconsin	Employee cannot be fired for taking three hours off to vote without loss of pay. Wis. Stat. Ann. §6.76
Wyoming	Employees cannot be fired for taking one hour, other than meal time, without loss of pay to vote. Wyo. Stat. §22-2-111

4. Time Off for Military or National Guard Duty

Most states have laws requiring employers to give time off for National Guard or state militia members or reservists to serve. A number of laws set a minimum amount of paid or unpaid time off that must be given. Some apply only to public employees, some to both public and private. And most laws include a provision preventing discrimination against employees who take military leave. When leave is required, the employer must usually reemploy service member employees without loss of benefits, status or reduction in pay.

STATE LAWS ON MILITARY LEAVE	
Alabama	Active members of the Alabama National Guard or any reserve of the armed forces are entitled to up to 21 days paid leave of absence. Ala. Code §31-2-13(a). But see *White v. Associated Industries of Alabama, Inc.*, 373 So. 2d 616 (Ala. 1979), which held this statute unconstitutional as applied to private employers.
Alaska	Public employees are entitled to 16½ days of paid leave if they are members of the reserves and called to training duty or a search and rescue mission. Alaska Stat. §39.20.340
	Private employers must grant unpaid leaves of absence to state militia members called to active service. Alaska Stat. §26.05.070
Arizona	Employers may not discriminate against employees because of membership in the National Guard or for absence from work for military duty. Employers must allow National Guard members an unpaid leave of absence for active duty or training. Ariz. Rev. Stat. Ann. §§26-167 and 26-168
Arkansas	Public employees may not be fired or discriminated against for membership in the military reserves. Ark. Stat. Ann. §21-3-306
	Public employees who are National Guard members or reservists must receive two weeks paid leave for training per year. If called to active duty in an emergency situation, they must receive 30 days of paid leave. Ark. Stat. Ann. §21-4-212
	Private employees or applicants who are members of the state militia or National Guard must not be fired, penalized or discriminated against for being called to active duty. Ark Stat. Ann. §12-62-413

California	Employees who are members of the National Guard or reserves are entitled to 17 days leave for active military duty for training. National Guard members who are called into active service are to be regarded as being on a leave of absence. Cal. Mil. & Vet. Code §§394 through 395.9
Colorado	Employees who are members of the National Guard or reserves are entitled to 15 days of unpaid leave per year for military training. Colo. Rev. Stat. §28-3-506
Connecticut	Employees who are members of the military reserves or National Guard are entitled to paid leave for up to 30 days for training or active duty. Conn. Gen. Stat. Ann. §27-33
Delaware	Military reservists and National Guard members must be given leaves of absence for training. Del. Code Ann. tit. 20, §905
District of Columbia	No statute
Florida	Employees cannot be fired or penalized for active service in the National Guard. Fla. Stat. §250.482
	Public employees get 17 days paid leave per year for reserve and National Guard training and unpaid leave when called to duty. Fla. Stat. §115.07
Georgia	Employees are entitled to unpaid leave for state militia or National Guard duty. Ga. Code Ann. §38-2-280
	Public employees are entitled to 18 days paid leave per year for military training. If called to active duty, 30 days. Ga. Code Ann. §38-2-279
Hawaii	Private employees are entitled to unpaid leaves of absence for National Guard duty. Hawaii Rev. Stat. §121-43
	Public employees are entitled to 15 days of paid leave per year for National Guard or reserves duty. Hawaii Rev. Stat. §79-20
Idaho	Employees are entitled to 15 days unpaid leave per year for serving in National Guard or military reserves. Idaho Code §46-224
	Public employees entitled to reinstatement after military duty. Idaho Code § 65-511
Illinois	Employees cannot be fired for serving in the National Guard or naval militia. Ill. Ann. Stat. ch. 129, ¶220.100 and 20.307
Indiana	No statute
Iowa	Employees may not be fired, discriminated against or penalized for membership in the National Guard or military reserves. Employer must give leaves of absence for training or service. Iowa Code §29A.43

Kansas	Employees may not be fired or punished for absence for National Guard service. Kan. Stat. Ann. §48-222
Kentucky	Employees cannot be fired or discriminated against for service in National Guard or active militia. Ky. Rev. Stat. §38.460
Louisiana	Employees cannot be fired or discriminated against for duty in state militia or National Guard and are entitled to unpaid leaves of absence for such service. La. Rev. Stat. Ann. §29:38
	Public employees are entitled to 15 days paid leave per year for fulfilling military reserves or National Guard duty. La. Rev. Stat. Ann. §42:394
Maine	Employees cannot be fired or penalized for membership in National Guard or military reserves. Public employees are entitled to paid leave while on annual training duty. Me. Rev. Stat. Ann. title 37-B, §342
Maryland	Employees cannot be fired or penalized for taking time off for duty in the state militia. Md. Ann. Code art 65, §32A
Massachusetts	Employees may not be fired for membership in National Guard or the reserves. Mass. Gen. Laws Ann. ch. 33, §13
	Employees must be given 17 days per year of unpaid leave of absence for military training. Mass. Gen. Laws Ann. ch. 149, §52A
Michigan	Employees cannot be fired, hindered or dissuaded from performing duty as a member of National Guard or state naval militia. Mich. Stat. Ann. §4.1487(2)
Minnesota	Employee cannot be fired for being members of military. Minn. Stat. Ann. §192.34
	Public employees are entitled to 15 days per year of paid leave for National Guard or reserves active duty or training and are entitled to leave without pay if called to extended duty. Minn. Stat. Ann. §§192.260 and 192.261
Mississippi	No statute
Missouri	Employees cannot be fired or threatened for membership in state militia or hindered or prevented from performing their militia service. Mo. Ann. Stat. §41.730
Montana	Members of the state militia may not be deprived of employment or an employment benefit due to their membership in the militia. Mont. Code §10-1-603
	Public employees get 15 days paid leave of absence for military or state militia duty. Mont. Code Ann. §10-1-604

Nebraska	Pubic employees who are members of the National Guard or reserves are entitled to an unpaid leave of absence for up to four years during active duty and a paid leave of absence for up to 15 days per year for training or duty. Neb. Rev. Stat. §55-161
Nevada	Employers cannot fire or discriminate against employees because of National Guard duty or membership. Nev. Rev. Stat. §§412.1393 and 412.606
New Hampshire	Employers cannot fire employees because of membership in or performance of duty in the National Guard. N.H. Rev. Stat. Ann. §110-B:65
New Jersey	Employers cannot fire or discriminate against employees because of National Guard or armed forces membership. N.J. Stat. Ann. §10:5-12
New Mexico	Employers cannot fire employees because of membership in the National Guard. N.M. Stat. Ann. §§20-9-6 and 20-9-7
	Employers must give members of reserves or National Guard unpaid leaves of absence during active duty. N.M. Stat. Ann. §§28-15-1 to 28-15-3
New York	Employers should not fire employees because they are subject to National Guard or military duty. N.Y. Mil. Law §318
	Employees are entitled to unpaid leave of absence when called for active duty. N.Y. Mil. Law §317
North Carolina	Employers cannot fire employees because of National Guard duty. N.C. Gen. Stat. §127A-202
	Employers cannot fire employees because of state militia or reserves duty. N.C. Gen. Stat. §127B-14
North Dakota	Public employees cannot be fired for performance of National Guard, military reserves or federal service duty. Such employees must be granted 30 days of paid leaves of absence when ordered to active duty and 20 days of paid leave per year for training. N.D. Cent. Code §37-01-25
Ohio	Employees must be granted leaves of absence for up to four-and-a-half years during military service. Ohio Rev. Code Ann. §§5903.02 and 5903.08
	Employees cannot be discriminated against for membership in the National Guard, reserves or state militia. Ohio Rev. Code §5903.08
	Employees are entitled to unpaid leaves of absence for up to 15 days for military service or training. Ohio Rev. Code §5903.061
Oklahoma	Employers cannot hinder or prevent employees who are members of the National Guard from performing their military duty. Okla. Stat. Ann. title 44, §208

	Public employers must give leave of absence when service members are called to active duty and 20 days of paid leave per year for training. Okla. Stat. Ann. title 44, §209
Oregon	Public employers must give employees unpaid leaves of absence to perform active military duty. Or. Rev. Stat. §408.210
	Public employees are entitled to 15 days of paid leave for training per year. Or. Rev. Stat. §408.290
	Private employees who are state militia members are entitled to unpaid leaves of absence when called into active service. Or. Rev. Stat. §399.230
Pennsylvania	Employers cannot fire or discriminate against employees because of performance of military duty in the National Guard or reserves. Pa. Cons. Stat. Ann. title 51, §7309
	Employees are to be granted unpaid leaves of absence for the duration of their service. Pa. Cons. Stat. Ann. title 51, §7302
Rhode Island	Employers cannot fire or discriminate against employees for duty in the National Guard or reserves. R.I. Gen. Laws §§30-11-2 and 30-11-6
	Employees who are National Guard members are entitled to unpaid leave for training periods and active military service. R.I. Gen. Laws §30-11-3
South Carolina	Private employers cannot fire employees for membership or performance of duty in National Guard. S.C. Code Ann. §25-1-2310
	Public employees who are members of the National Guard are entitled to leaves of absence for training. S.C. Code Ann. §25-1-2250
South Dakota	Employees who are members of the National Guard or reserves are entitled to 15 days per year of unpaid leave of absence for training or when called to active duty. S.D. Codified Laws Ann. §33-17-15
Tennessee	Employers cannot fire or refuse employment because of membership in the National Guard or because of employee's absence for training. Tenn. Code Ann. §58-1-604
Texas	Private employers cannot fire an employee who is called to active service in the state militia. Tex. Gov't Code Ann. §431.006
	Public employees are entitled to 15 days of paid leave of absence per year for training or duty in the state militia or armed forces reserves. Tex. Govt. Code Ann. §431.005
Utah	Employers cannot fire employees who are National Guard members and must grant them leaves of absence for service. Utah Code Ann. §§39-1-36 and 39-3-1

Vermont	Employers cannot fire employees for engaging in military training and must grant them 15 days of unpaid leave per year. Vt. Stat. Ann. tit. 21, §491
Virginia	Employers cannot fire or refuse to hire members of the National Guard. Va. Code §44-98
	Public employees who are members of the reserves, National Guard or state naval militia are entitled to 15 days per year of paid leave for the performance of military duties. Va. Code §44-93
Washington	Employers cannot fire employees for military service and must grant an unpaid leave of absence when employees are called to active duty in the National Guard, armed forces reserves or U.S. public health service. Wash. Rev. Code Ann. §73.16.033
West Virginia	Employees in the National Guard are entitled to an unpaid leave of absence when called to active duty. W. Va. Code §15-1F-8
	Public employees are entitled to 30 days paid leave per year for training or active duty. W.Va. Code §15-1F-1
Wisconsin	Employers cannot fire employees for performance of National Guard or reserves duty and must grant unpaid leave of absence for not more than four years. Wis. Stat. Ann. §§45.50 and 45.51
Wyoming	Employers cannot fire, hinder or penalize employees for performing National Guard duty. Wyo. Stat. §19-2-105
	Public employees are entitled to 15 days of unpaid leave per year for military training or duty. Wyo. Stat. §19-2-504

5. Penalties for Retaliation

Nearly half the states have laws that specifically protect employees who file complaints or testify in investigations controlled by the wage and hour statutes from retaliation. Most simply provide that employees cannot be fired for filing wage and hour complaints. And a number of the laws protect those who testify at a wage and hour dispute on their own behalf or on behalf of another employee.

STATE LAWS PROHIBITING RETALIATION	
Alabama	No statute
Alaska	No statute
Arizona	Employees cannot be fired or discriminated against for serving on or testifying before a wage board. Ariz. Rev. Stat. Ann. §23-329
Arkansas	No statute
California	Employees cannot be fired for asserting rights under the jurisdiction of the Labor Commissioner. Cal. Lab. Code §98.6
	Employees cannot be fired for refusing to work hours in excess of those permitted by the Industrial Welfare Commission. Cal. Lab. Code §1198.3
Colorado	Employers cannot fire or otherwise discriminate against employees for participating in any wage and hour proceeding. Colo. Rev. Stat. §8-6-115
Connecticut	Employees may not be disciplined in any manner for reporting violations of minimum wage laws. Conn. Gen. Stat. Ann. §31-69
Delaware	Employees may not be fired for participating in proceeding under wage payment and collection law. Del. Code Ann. tit. 19, §1112
District of Columbia	Employees may not be fired for participating in proceeding to enforce the minimum wage law. D.C. Code Ann. §36-213
Florida	No statute
Georgia	No statute
Hawaii	Employees may sue employers if fired for reporting to public agency a violation of law. Hawaii Rev. Stat. §§378-63 and 378-65

Idaho	Employees cannot be fired or discriminated against for participating in proceedings under minimum wage law. Idaho Code §44-1509
Illinois	Employees cannot be fired for bringing claim under state wage and hour law. Ill. Ann. Stat. ch. 48, §39m-14
Indiana	Employees may not be fired for participating in action to recover wages under state wage and hour law. Ind. Code Ann. §22-2-2-11
Iowa	Employees cannot be fired for participation in wage and hour proceeding. Iowa Code §91A.10(5)
Kansas	No statute
Kentucky	Employees cannot be fired for exercising rights under wage and hour law. Ky. Rev. Stat. §337.423
Louisiana	Employees may not be fired for testifying regarding labor violations. La. Rev. Stat. Ann. §23:964
Maine	No statute
Maryland	No statute
Massachusetts	No statute
Michigan	Employees may not be fired for protesting violations or participating in proceedings regarding state minimum wage law. Mich. Comp. Laws §408.395
Minnesota	Employees cannot be fired for giving testimony with regard to minimum wage violations. Minn. Stat. Ann. §177.32 The same protections apply to testimony with regard to the Minnesota Labor Relations Act. Minn. Stat. Ann. §179.120
Mississippi	No statute
Missouri	No statute
Montana	No statute
Nebraska	No statute
Nevada	No statute
New Hampshire	No statute
New Jersey	No statute
New Mexico	No statute
New York	Employers cannot fire employees because of labor complaints to the employer or Labor Commissioner. N.Y. Lab. Law §215 Employers cannot fire employees because of wage complaints. N.Y. Lab. Law §662
North Carolina	Employers cannot fire employees for filing a wage claim. N.C. Gen. Stat. §95-25.20

North Dakota	No statute
Ohio	No statute
Oklahoma	No statute
Oregon	Employers cannot fire employees because of filing a wage claim. Or. Rev. Stat. §652.355
Pennsylvania	No statute
Rhode Island	No statute
South Carolina	No statute
South Dakota	Employers may not fire employees for wage complaints. S.D. Codified Laws Ann. §12-26-13
Tennessee	No statute
Texas	No statute
Utah	Employers cannot fire employees for wage complaints. Utah Code Ann. §34-22-12
Vermont	Employers cannot fire employees for labor relations law complaints. Vt. Stat. Ann. tit. 21, §1621
Virginia	No statute
Washington	No statute
West Virginia	Employers cannot fire employees for wage complaints. W. Va. Code §21-5C-7
Wisconsin	Employers cannot fire employees for wage complaint proceedings. Wis. Stat. Ann. §104.12
Wyoming	No statute

F. Payroll Withholding and Deductions

Since the end of the Depression of the 1930s, the right and responsibility of employers to withhold a portion of your pay has become a virtually undisputed part of American culture. The laws that created the income tax and Social Security programs for which funds are withheld typically authorize payroll withholding to finance those programs.

But a growing number of additional deductions are now also authorized.

1. What Can Be Deducted or Withheld

In addition to Social Security and local, state and federal taxes, an employer may also make several other deductions from minimum wages: costs of meals, housing and transportation, loans, debts owed the employer, child support and alimony, payroll savings plans and insurance premiums. As in most other workplace laws, there are exceptions to these rules. There are often limitations on how much may be withheld or deducted from a paycheck.

a. Meals, housing and transportation

Employers may legally deduct from an employee's paycheck the "reasonable cost or fair value" of meals, housing, fuel and transportation to and from work.

But to deduct any of these amounts, an employer must show that it customarily paid these expenses and that:

- they were for the employee's benefit
- the employee was told in advance about the deductions from a paycheck
- the employee voluntarily accepted the meals and other accommodations against minimum wage.

Example: *Bob accepted a job as a guide at a remote wilderness ski resort after the employer told him that the job paid $10 per hour plus room and board. But when he got his first paycheck, Bob saw that charges for housing and meals had been deducted from his pay. And the charges were so high that he really was earning only $3 per hour, far less than the minimum wage.*

Asking around among other employees at the resort, Bob learned that the exorbitant meal charges were billed to his payroll account by a catering service owned by the resort owner's brother-in-law. Bob's employer had violated several of the FLSA's rules governing noncash compensation, so he filed a complaint with the U.S. Labor Department's Wage and Hour Division.

Some state laws offer some guidance as to what is deemed reasonable by setting out specific meal and lodging credits. In California, for example, when credit for lodging is used to meet part of the employer's wage obligation, no more than $20 per week may be credited for a room occupied by one person.

> ## ADDITIONAL GUIDANCE ON PAYROLL WITHHOLDING
>
> The Internal Revenue Service rules for payroll withholding and reporting vary greatly among the legal categories of work: employee, statutory employee, statutory nonemployee and independent contractor. (See Chapter 2, Section A.)
>
> You can obtain a detailed explanation of those rules free by calling the IRS forms distribution center at 800/829-3676 and requesting Publication 937, entitled "Business Reporting." This booklet is also available at your local IRS office.
>
> State and local payroll withholding taxes usually parallel the IRS rules, but the taxing authorities in your state and city should be able to provide you with publications outlining their payroll withholding rules.

b. Loans

An employer that has loaned you money can withhold money from your pay to satisfy that loan. However, it is illegal to make any such deduction if it would reduce your pay to below the minimum wage.

Example: *Bruce works 40 hours a week at $5 per hour making deliveries for an auto parts store. He is paid each Saturday. One Monday morning, the battery in his car went dead. His employer authorized him to replace his car's battery with a new one out of the store's stock—if he agreed that the price of the new battery, $60, would be deducted from Bruce's pay.*

However, it took two weeks for the store to be fully paid for the battery. Under the FLSA, Bruce's employer could legally deduct no more than $30 per week (40 hours x .75) from his gross pay to cover the battery. To deduct more would drop Bruce's pay rate to below the required minimum of $4.25 per hour.

c. Debts and Wage Garnishments

If you owe someone money and do not pay, that person might sue you and obtain a court judgment against you. If you do not pay the judgment, the creditor may try to collect by taking a portion of your paycheck until the judgment is paid in full. This is called a wage attachment or wage garnishment. Except in a few situations—student loans, child support, alimony and taxes—a creditor must sue you and obtain a court judgment before he or she can garnish your wages.

A wage garnishment works simply. Once the creditor has a judgment, he or she delivers a copy of it to a sheriff or marshal, who in turn sends a copy to your employer. Your employer must immediately:

* notify you of the garnishment
* begin withholding a portion of your wages, and
* give you information on how you can protest the garnishment.

Protesting is straightforward. You file a paper with the court and obtain a hearing date. At the hearing, you can present evidence showing that your expenses are very high and that you need all of your paycheck to live on. The judge has the discretion to terminate the wage garnishment or let it remain.

A federal law, the Consumer Credit Protection Act (15 U.S.C. §1673), prohibits judgment creditors from taking more than 25% of your net earnings through a wage garnishment to satisfy a debt. A few states offer greater protection, however. In Delaware, for example, judgment creditors cannot take more than 15% of your wages.

The Consumer Credit Protection Act also prohibits your employer from firing you because your wages are garnished to satisfy a single debt. If two judgment creditors garnish your wages or one judgment creditor garnishes your wages to pay two different judgments, however, you can be fired. Again, some state laws offer employees stronger protection. In Washington, for example, an employer cannot fire you unless your wages are garnished by three different creditors or to satisfy three different judgments within a year. In Connecticut, you cannot be fired unless your employer has to deal with more than seven creditors or judgments in a single year.[1]

There are basically four types of statutes that prohibit employers from retaliating against an employee for being subject to a wage garnishment. (See the chart below.) They differ in how many garnishments an employee is allowed per year and still have his or her job protected.

---

[1]For more information on debts, getting sued and wage garnishments, see *Money Troubles: Legal Strategies to Cope With Your Debts,* by Robin Leonard (Nolo Press).

The majority of the states just have a general prohibition of employer retribution against employees who have their wages garnished. Some states prohibit retaliation if the employee has one garnishment per year; some laws apply to more than one garnishment. Another type of anti-retribution for wage garnishment statute is when income is withheld to satisfy child support obligations. (See also Section F1e.) Employers may not fire employees merely because they are subject to this type of order regardless of the quantity. Of course, none of these statutes prohibit firing for cause. They just prohibit firing an employee solely because of the wage garnishment.

STATE LAWS ON WAGE GARNISHMENTS

Alabama	Employees may not be fired for having wages garnished for child support obligations. Ala. Code §30-3-70
Alaska	Employees may not be fired for having wages assigned for child support obligations. Alaska Stat. §47.23.062
Arizona	Employees may not be fired or disciplined because of wage assignment to provide child support obligations. Ariz. Rev. Stat. §12-2454
Arkansas	Employees may not be fired or disciplined for having a wage assignment for child support obligations. Ark. Stat. Ann. §9-14-1226
California	Employees may not be fired for having one wage garnishment in a year. Cal. Lab. Code §2929b
Colorado	Employees may not be fired for having wages garnished. Colo. Rev. Stat. §13-54.5-110
Connecticut	Employees may not be fired for having wages garnished unless they have more than seven in one year. Conn. Gen. Stat. Ann. §52-361aj
Delaware	Employees may not be fired for having wages garnished. Del. Code Ann. tit. 10, § 3509
District of Columbia	Employees may not be fired for having wages garnished. D.C. Code Ann. §16-584
Florida	No statute
Georgia	Employees may not be fired for having one wage garnishment in a year. Ga. Code Ann. §18-4-7

Hawaii	Employees may not be fired for having a wage assignment for child support obligations. Hawaii Rev. Stat. §378-2
	Employees may not be fired for having wages garnished. Hawaii Rev. Stat. §378-32
Idaho	No statute
Illinois	Employees may not be fired for having one wage garnishment in a year. Ill. Ann. Stat. ch. 48, §39.11 and ch. 110, §12-818
Indiana	Employees may not be fired for having one or more wage garnishments in one year. Ind. Code Ann. §24-4.5-5-106
Iowa	Employees may not be fired or penalized for having wages garnished for child support obligations. Iowa Code §598.22
	Employees may not be fired for having wages garnished. Iowa Code §42.21
Kansas	Employees may not be fired for having wages garnished. Kan. Stat. Ann. §60-2311
Kentucky	Employees may not be fired for having one wage garnishment in a year. Ky. Rev. Stat. §427.140
Louisiana	Employees may not be fired for having one wage garnishment in a year. La. Rev. Stat. Ann. §23:731
Maine	Employees may not be fired for having wages garnished. Me. Rev. Stat. Ann. tit. 14, §3127-B
Maryland	Employees may not be fired for having one wage garnishment in a year. Md. Com. Law Code Ann. §15-606
Massachusetts	No statute
Michigan	Employees may not be fired for having one or more garnishments in a year. Mich. Comp. Laws §600.4015
Minnesota	Employees may not be fired for having wages garnished. Minn. Stat. Ann. §571.927
Mississippi	Employees may not be fired for having wages garnished for child or spousal support obligations. Miss. Code Ann. §93-11-111
Missouri	Employees may not be fired or discriminated against for having one wage garnishment in a year. Mo. Ann. Stat. §525.030
	Employees may not be fired for having wages assigned for child support obligations. Mo. Ann. Stat. §452.350
Montana	Employees may not be fired or discriminated against for having wages assigned for child support obligations. Mont. Code Ann. §40-5-422
Nebraska	Employees may not be fired for having one wage garnishment in a year. Neb. Rev. Stat. §25-2558
	Employees may not be fired for having wages assigned for child support obligations. Neb. Rev. Stat. §43-1725

Nevada	Employees may not be fired for having wages garnished for consumer transaction or child support obligations. Nev. Rev. Stat. §31.298
New Hampshire	Employees may not be fired for having wages garnished for child support obligations. N.H. Rev. Stat. Ann. §458-B:6
New Jersey	Employees may not be fired for having one or more wage garnishments in a year. N.J. Stat. Ann. §2A:170-90.4
	Employees may not be fired for having wages garnished for child support. N.J. Stat. Ann. §§2A:17-56.8 and 2A:4-30.34
New Mexico	Employees may not be fired for having wages garnished for child support obligations. N.M. Stat. Ann. §40-4A-11
New York	Employees may not be fired for having wages garnished. N.Y. Civ. Prac. L. & R., §5253
North Carolina	Employees may not be fired for having wages garnished for child support obligations. N.C. Gen. Stat. §110.136.8
	Employees may not be fired for having wages garnished to pay debts for services rendered at a public hospital. N.C. Gen. Stat. §131E-50
North Dakota	Employees may not be fired for having wages garnished. N.D. Cent. Code §32-09.1-18
	Employees may not be fired for having wages assigned for child support obligations. N.D. Cent. Code §§14-09-09.1 and 14-09-09.6
Ohio	No statute
Oklahoma	Employees may not be fired for having wage assignment for child support obligations. Okla. Stat. Ann. title 12, §1171.37
	Employees may not be fired for having wages garnished, unless more than two in a year. Okla. Stat. Ann. title 14A, §5-106
Oregon	Employees may not be fired for having wages garnished. Or. Rev. Stat. §23.1855
	Employees may not be fired for having wages garnished for child support obligations. Or. Rev. Stat. §25.0508
Pennsylvania	Employees may not be fired for having wages garnished for child support obligations. Pa. Cons. Stat. Ann. tit. 23, §4348
Rhode Island	Employees may not be fired for having wages garnished for child support obligations. R.I. Gen. Laws §15-5-26
South Carolina	Employees may not be fired for having wages garnished for consumer debt. S.C. Code Ann. §37-5-106
	Employees may not be fired for having wages garnished for child support S.C. Code Ann. §20-7-1315H1

South Dakota	Employees may not be fired for having wages garnished for child support obligation. S.D. Codified Laws Ann. §27-7A-46
Tennessee	Employees may not be fired for having wages garnished for child support obligations. Tenn. Code Ann. §50-2-105
Texas	Employees may not be fired for having wages garnished for child support obligations. Tex. Fam. Code Ann. §14.43m
Utah	Employees may not be fired for having one wage garnishment in a year. Utah Code Ann. §70C-7-104
	Employees may not be fired for having wages garnished for child support. Utah Code Ann. §78-45d-510
Vermont	Employees may not be fired for having wages garnished. This is known in Vermont as the "trustee process." Vt. Stat. Ann. tit. 12, §3172
	Employees may not be fired for having wages assigned for child support. Vt. Stat. Ann. tit. 15,§790
Virginia	Employees may not be fired for having one wage garnishment in a year. Va. Code §34-29f
	Employees may not be fired for having wages garnished to pay child support. Va. Code §20-79.1
Washington	Employees may not be fired for having wages garnished, unless employee has 3 or more within a year. Wash. Rev. Code Ann. §7.33.160
	Employee may not be fired for having wages withheld for child support. Wash. Rev. Code Ann. §26.18.110
West Virginia	Employees may not be fired for having wages garnished for a regular consumer transaction. W. Va. Code §46A-2-131
	Employees may not be fired for having wages garnished for child support obligation. W. Va. Code §48A-5-3
Wisconsin	Employees may not be fired for having one wage garnishment in a year. Wis. Stat. Ann. §812.235
	Employees may not be fired for having wages garnished for child support. Wis. Stat. Ann. §767.265
Wyoming	Employees may not be fired for having wages garnished. Wyo. Stat. §1-15-509
	Employees may not be fired for having wages garnished for child support obligations Wyo. Stat. §20-6-218

d. Student loans

The federal Emergency Unemployment Compensation Act of 1991 extended unemployment insurance for Americans who are out of work (20 U.S.C. §1095a). A rider to that bill authorizes the U.S. Department of Education or any agency trying to collect a student loan on behalf of the Department of Education to garnish up to 10% of a former student's net pay if he or she is in default on a student loan.

The Department of Education does not have to sue you before garnishing your wages. But at least 30 days before the garnishment is set to begin, you must be notified in writing of:

- the amount the Department believes you owe
- how you can obtain a copy of records relating to the loan
- how to enter into a voluntary repayment schedule, and
- how to request a hearing on the proposed garnishment.

The law includes only one specific ground upon which you can object to the garnishment—that you returned to work within the past 12 months after having been fired or laid off.

e. Child support and alimony

The federal Family Support Act of 1988 (102 U.S. Stat. §2343) requires that all new or modified child support orders include an automatic wage withholding order. If child support is combined with alimony and paid as family support, the wage withholding applies to the payment. It is not required for orders of alimony only.

In an automatic wage withholding order, a court orders you to pay child support; then the court or your child's other parent sends a copy of the order to your employer. At each pay period, your employer withholds a portion of your pay and sends it on to the parent who has custody.

States have implemented the mandatory wage withholding orders with some variation. In Texas and Vermont, for example, all current orders include automatic wage withholding, regardless of your payment history. The rationale is that by not distinguishing between parents with poor payment histories and parents who have paid regularly, no parent is stigmatized. In California and New York, wage withholding orders are automatic as well. But parents who show a reliable history of paying or who agree not to implement the wage withholding order may be exempt.

In most states, employers must withhold wages if you are one month delinquent in paying support. But an employer cannot discipline, fire or refuse to hire you because your pay is subject to a child support wage withholding order. If an employer does discriminate against you, the employer can be fined by the state. (See Section F1c for specific state law provisions.)

f. Back taxes

If you owe the IRS and do not pay, the agency can grab most—but not all—of your wages. The amount that you get to keep is determined by the number of your dependents and the standard tax deduction to which you are entitled. For example, a married couple with two children get to keep about $300 per week, while a single taxpayer with no dependents gets only about $116.

If the IRS wants your wages, it sends a wage levy notice to your employer, who must immediately give you a copy. On the back of the notice is an exemption claim form. You should fill out, sign and return this simple form to the IRS office that issued it within three days after you receive it. Your employer should not pay anything to the IRS until you have your chance to file your exemption claim.

If you do not file the claim form, your employer must pay you only $116 per week and give the rest to the IRS. An employer who ignores the IRS wage levy notice and pays you anyway is liable to the IRS for whatever amounts were wrongly paid. Once the wage levy takes effect, it continues until either the taxes are paid in full or the collection period expires—ten years from when the taxes are assessed.

Most state and some municipal taxing authorities also have the power to seize a portion of your wages—and some act even more quickly than the IRS does when you owe back taxes. State laws vary, however, as to the maximum amount of wages that the state can take. In California, for example, the state taxing authority cannot take more than 25% of your net pay.

2. What Cannot Be Deducted or Withheld

Only a few things are sacrosanct and may not usually be deducted from an employee's paycheck:
- the value of time taken for meal periods (see Section D2)
- the cost of broken merchandise
- tools and materials used on the job
- required uniforms, and
- cash register shortages and losses due to theft.

THE HISTORY OF PAYROLL WITHHOLDING

The Social Security Act of 1935, a part of President Franklin D. Roosevelt's New Deal, was the first law to sink its teeth firmly into the typical paycheck. Intended only to save industrial and commercial hourly workers of the Depression era from poverty in old age, the original Social Security program required employers to withhold a mere 1% of workers' pay.

Since then, the Social Security Act has been amended many times. The age of eligibility has been lowered from 65 to 62, and coverage has been extended to people unable to work because of physical disabilities, government employees, self-employed people and a number of other groups not covered by the original Act. Consequently, the amount withheld from most wages to pay for Social Security programs now is more than 7%.

The federal income tax, the other major cause of paycheck shrinkage, was created when the 16th Amendment to the U.S. Constitution was passed in 1913. The original federal income tax rates ranged from 1% to 7% of annual income above $3,000—a lot of money back then.

To pay for World War II, however, the government raised the income tax rates so dramatically that the tax on the top income level bracket hit a record of 94% in 1944 and 1945. The minimum income subject to taxation was lowered so that most working people were for the first time subject to some income tax.

Politicians, hoping to assuage the public angst over paying a large yearly lump sum, decided to lessen the trauma by making employers withhold the income tax, little by little, from workers' pay each week.

By the 1970s, employees had become so accustomed to having large sums of money withheld from their pay that most states and cities—as well as nongovernment groups such as health insurance companies and pension fund managers—instituted additional withholding programs.

Today, it is common for employees to have more than a third of their pay withheld by their employers on behalf of government, with still more withheld to finance private benefit plans.

G. Enforcing Your Right to Be Paid Fairly

Your first step in enforcing your right to be paid fairly should be to decide whether your complaint involves a violation of a law, or is simply a matter of disagreement or misunderstanding between you and your employer.

If, for example, your employer refused to pay you time-and-one-half for five hours of overtime that you worked, then the issue would be covered by the FLSA. But if you had been working under the impression that you would get a raise every year—a matter not covered by the FLSA—and your employer will not give you one, then the issue is not covered by federal wage and hour law.

Once you have refined your complaint, try discussing it with your employer or former employer before filing any official action. Some companies have dispute resolution programs—usually outlined in their employee manuals—that can help you resolve a pay dispute without resorting to legal action. (See Chapter 18, Section A.)

H. Filing a Complaint or Lawsuit

If your complaint involves what you believe is a violation of the FLSA—for example, you have not been paid fairly or on time—contact your local office of Wage and Hour Division of the U.S. Department of Labor, listed in the federal government section of the telephone directory.

If you call, visit or write to your local Wage and Hour Division office, workers there will take down the information you provide and transcribe it onto a complaint form. You can request one of these forms and fill it out yourself. But since the staff members are familiar with which details are legally pertinent, they usually prefer to fill it out for you. They will probably ask you to provide photocopies of documents relevant to your dispute, such as pay stubs.

Be sure to review the completed complaint form and attached documents to be sure they are correct and as complete as possible. If you are assigned to a staff person who seems particularly unsympathetic or unhelpful, calmly and politely ask to speak with someone else. Also, keep in mind that a huge dollop of patience is required. The process—from filing a complaint through investigation and the final outcome—typically takes from one to three years.

Once your complaint has been put together, U.S. Labor Department investigators will take over the job of gathering additional data which should either prove or disprove your complaint.

If the thought of reporting your employer to the authorities frightens you, take some comfort in knowing that Labor Department investigators must keep the identities of those who file such complaints confidential. Also, it is illegal for an employer to fire or otherwise discriminate against an employee for filing a complaint under the FLSA, or for participating in a legal proceeding related to its enforcement. Many state laws also provide protection for employees who file state wage and hour complaints. (See Section E5.)

Where the federal investigators find violations of the FLSA, the action that they then take will depend upon the severity of the violations and whether or not the employer appears to have been violating the law willfully.

When the violations are severe and apparently willful, the Labor Department may ask the Justice Department to bring criminal charges against the employer. Government lawyers will handle the matter for you. If convicted, a first-time violator of the FLSA may be fined by the courts; subsequent convictions can result in both fines and imprisonment.

If the violations are not too severe, or if the Labor Department investigators feel the infractions were not willful, one of the following steps may be taken:

- The Labor Department may set up and supervise a plan for your employer to pay back wages to you and anyone else injured by the violations.
- The Secretary of Labor may file a lawsuit asking the court to order your employer to pay you the wages due, plus an equal amount as damages. The court may also issue an injunction or order preventing your employer from continuing the illegal behavior.
- You may file your own lawsuit under the FLSA to recover the wages you're owed, plus other damages, attorney fees and court costs. You will probably need to hire a lawyer to help with this type of lawsuit. (See Chapter 18, Section D.)

WHEN YOU CANNOT SUE UNDER THE FLSA

You cannot file an FLSA lawsuit if your employer has already paid back wages to you under the supervision of the Labor Department. This amounts to an incentive system for employers: An employer who cooperates in correcting any violations discovered by the Wage and Hour Division investigators must pay only the back wages that are due. An employer who refuses to cooperate by paying back wages stands the chance of having to pay double the wages, plus your attorney's fees and costs, plus the cost of its own defense.

You cannot bring a lawsuit under the FLSA if the Secretary of Labor has already done so on your behalf. And if you file a lawsuit and then the Secretary of Labor files a lawsuit over the same violations, your right to sue ends and the Labor Department takes over.

I. Violations of State and Local Laws

The laws of each state and municipality specify which branch of government is responsible for enforcing state and local wage and hour laws, and what remedies—criminal, civil or both—are available. In most states, the Labor Department is authorized to take action on your behalf to recover unpaid wages. (See the Appendix for contact information.)

If you are dissatisfied with the action taken by the government agency responsible for enforcing state or local wage and hour laws, consider resolving your problem in small claims court. Because of the relatively small amounts of money typically involved, disputes over wages, commissions or other forms of compensation can often be pursued quickly and inexpensively in small claims courts without requiring help from a lawyer.[2] ■

---

[2]For details on how to pursue your claim through small claims court, see *Everybody's Guide to Small Claims Court,* by Attorney Ralph Warner (Nolo Press).

CHAPTER

4

HEALTH INSURANCE

Despite sweeping reforms proposed by the Clinton Administration, health insurance remains an expensive necessity. Long term treatment of a medical condition or even a short hospital stay is likely to quickly bankrupt most Americans. To help foot the bills, most employers offer their employees some type of group insurance plan.

The specifics of insurance coverage are dictated by the terms of individual policies. This chapter discusses the broader state and federal legal controls on health insurance and will help you evaluate whether any insurance you have meets the minimum legal standards.

A. A Benefit, Not a Right

While many workers feel insurance coverage is an entitlement, in reality, offering health insurance to employees is purely voluntary—a matter of tradition, not law. This truth flies in the face of many firmly-held beliefs about what people are entitled to at work. But in fact, there is no federal law that requires employers to provide or pay for health insurance coverage for all current employees, or even fulltime employees. In fact, over eight million employed workers have no health insurance. And millions more are underinsured.

No federal legal scheme requires every employer to offer insurance coverage. However, an employer who promises to provide health insurance—in an employee manual, for example—must follow through on the promise. And benefits must be provided without discriminating against any employee or group of employees. That includes employees who are statistically more likely to incur high medical costs. For example, federal laws specifically provide that women workers and older workers (see Chapter 8, Sections C and E) must be provided with the same coverage as other workers.

BUT WAIT—THERE'S MORE

Insurance—and all its crafty permutations—has insinuated itself into many aspects of workplace law. You will find discussions of other insurance-related issues peppered throughout the book, including:

- privacy issues, such as employers' access to medical records (see Chapter 6, Section A)
- coverage for unemployed workers provided by state unemployment insurance programs (see Chapter 12)
- coverage for sick or disabled workers provided by state workers' compensation programs (see Chapter 13), by the Social Security disability system (see Chapter 14) and by private and state disability programs (see Chapter 10, Section K)
- coverage or time off provided for family and medical leave (see Chapter 5), and
- continuing coverage after retirement (see Chapter 15).

In recent years, some companies have discontinued or cut back on insurance coverage they offer employees, simply because of the expense. Again, the legal rule emerging is that of evenhandedness: Employers cannot offer insurance coverage to some employees and deny it to others.

But because health insurance is a job benefit that is not regulated by law, employers are otherwise free to fashion a plan of any stripe. They may:

- require employees to contribute to the cost of premiums
- offer reduced reimbursement or pro rata coverage to parttime employees
- limit options to one insurance plan or offer a variety of choices, or
- give employees a sum of money earmarked for insurance coverage that may be applied to any chosen plan.

As anyone who has read the fine print on a health insurance policy can attest, insurers, too, place conditions on the coverage they provide. The most nettling of these limitations is on pre-existing conditions. Under these provisions, if you have had a recent illness or have a chronic medical condition, you may be denied coverage, made to wait a specific time period until your condition will be covered—or forced to pay high premiums for specialized coverage. The greatest headway on doing away with the pre-existing condition denial of coverage has been made in the federal law requiring continuing coverage for former employees. (See Section C3.)

There are two main categories of employee health insurance: coverage for current employees and coverage for former employees.

B. Coverage for Current Employees

There is no federal law mandating insurance coverage. But a few states, counties and cities now require some employers to provide health insurance coverage for some employees who work there. For example, Hawaii requires employers to provide coverage to employees earning a set amount per month or more (Hawaii Rev. Stat. §393-11).

In addition, some state laws require that employers who offer insurance to employees must provide certain minimum coverage. The state requirements vary considerably, but typical minimums include: medical and surgical benefits, treatment of mental illness, alcoholism and drug abuse, and coverage for preventative testing such as mammograms and PAP smears. Check with your state's health commissioner to find out whether there is any minimum mandated coverage in your area.

Some states impose additional restrictions on workplace health insurance. In Illinois, for example, it is illegal for employers to fire employees because they file a legitimate claim against their company's health insurance (Illinois Pub. Act 85-930).

WHY MANY EMPLOYERS NO LONGER PAY

For many people, the greatest shock involved in finding their first job or securing a new one comes from learning that few employers pay all the costs of health insurance anymore—and that a growing number of employers do not pay anything at all.

The sad truth is that America's healthcare costs are so out of control that most companies are no longer willing or able to pay for them. In recent years, U.S. healthcare costs have been rising at nearly three times the rate of inflation.

Employers who pay for health insurance as an employee benefit now spend more than $3,500 per year for healthcare coverage for each employee, on average. If healthcare costs continue to rise, the cost of providing coverage at the start of the 21st century will be $22,000 per employee per year, according to estimates by the consulting firm of Foster Higgins in New York City. That is about $10.50 for every hour that a typical employee works.

C. Coverage for Former Employees

A federal workplace law, the Consolidated Omnibus Budget Reconciliation Act, or COBRA (29 U.S.C. §1162), requires your employer to offer you—and your spouse and dependents—continuing insurance coverage if:

- you lose insurance coverage because your number of workhours is reduced, or
- you lose your job for any reason other than gross misconduct. Because the law is still relatively new, the courts are still grappling with the question of how egregious the workplace behavior must be to qualify as gross misconduct. So far, courts have ruled that inefficiency, poor performance, negligence or errors in judgment on the job are not enough. There must be some deliberate, wrongful violations of workplace standards to qualify as gross misconduct.

COBRA was intended to extend access to group health insurance coverage to people who would otherwise be totally unprotected—and unlikely to be able to secure coverage on their own. The law applies to all employers with 20 or more employees. Under the law, employers need only make the insurance available; they need not pay for it. Employers may charge up to 102% of the base premium for continued coverage—the extra 2% thrown in to cover administrative costs.

Those covered under COBRA include:

- all individuals who are or were provided insurance coverage under an employer's group plan, and
- those individuals' beneficiaries—who typically include a spouse and dependent children.

1. Continuing Coverage

Qualified employees and former employees may elect to continue coverage up to 18 months following their termination from employment or the reduction in hours that makes them ineligible for coverage. Those who become disabled, however, can get COBRA coverage for 29 months—until Medicare payments typically kick in.

No one can choose to enroll in an insurance plan upon becoming ineligible for workplace coverage. COBRA extends only to those already enrolled when their health insurance coverage ceases.

In addition, COBRA provides that covered individuals must be given the right to convert to an individual policy at the end of the continuation period—although that coverage is usually significantly more expensive.

2. Coverage for Dependents

Beneficiaries or dependents may also elect to continue coverage for 18 months.

However, they may opt to have coverage continued for up to 36 months if any of the following occur:

- the covered employee dies
- they are divorced or legally separated from the covered employee
- a minor dependent child turns 18 or otherwise ceases to be considered a

dependent under the plan, or

- they become disabled and eligible for Social Security disability insurance benefits. (See Chapter 14.)

COORDINATION IS KEY FOR SOME PLANS

Many group insurance plans contain coordination of benefits (COB) provisions where two policies provide overlapping coverage—a common situation for families with two working spouses. A COB provision establishes a hierarchy for determining which policy provides primary coverage and which provides secondary coverage.

Most COBs provide that if the primary insurer's obligation is less than the amount of the total bill, the insured can then submit a claim to the secondary insurer, asking for coverage for the amount not paid. If only one policy has a COB provision, the policy that does not have a COB clause is the primary payor; if the same person is covered as an employee and a dependent, the employee policy coverage is primary.

In addition, as for coverage of children of two working parents covered by insurance, most states now follow the Birthday Rule. That rule provides that the parent who has a birthday earlier in the year is the one whose insurance will cover the children.

---

3. Pre-Existing Conditions

COBRA addresses the most common health insurance bugaboo: denial of coverage for pre-existing conditions.

Under COBRA, coverage must be offered regardless of any pre-existing medical conditions. And importantly, if an employee obtains new employment with coverage that contains exclusions or limitations for any such conditions, the former employer may not terminate coverage before the end of the COBRA coverage period. However, the employer may end coverage if a beneficiary such as a spouse is covered by another group health plan—as long as there is no significant gap in benefits provided.

4. Enforcing COBRA

COBRA provides for a number of fines for employers and health insurance plan administrators who violate its requirements. However, the Act has so many complexities that no one can agree on exactly what circumstances release an employer from its requirements. And, frustratingly, there is no one place you can call to get help if you think your rights under COBRA have been violated. Parts of the law are administered by the U.S. Labor Department and other parts fall under the Internal Revenue Service—and the two agencies frequently refer COBRA complaints back and forth to each other.

If you have a COBRA-related question or complaint, you can try calling your local office of either of those agencies, but neither has a track record of actively enforcing COBRA requirements. Your employer is required to provide you with an explanation of your COBRA rights when you are enrolled in a group healthcare plan covering 20 or more employees. However, these materials are seldom well written or easy to understand.

In general, COBRA can be enforced only through an expensive lawsuit. That means that it typically can be used only by large groups of former employees who have been denied their rights to continue group health insurance coverage—and who can share the expense of hiring a lawyer and filing a lawsuit to enforce that right. (See Chapter 10, Section H.)

5. Where to Get More Information

If you need detailed information on when and how COBRA governs your right to continue health insurance coverage, a good source is a report entitled "COBRA Continuation Coverage" available for $10 per copy from the International Foundation of Employee Benefit Plans; 18700 West Bluemound Road; P.O. Box 69; Brookfield, WI 53008-0069; 414/786-6700.

If you need advice or run into problems claiming COBRA benefits, contact the Older Women's League; 730 Eleventh Street, NW; Suite 300; Washington, DC 20001; 202/783-6686. The organization also assists younger women and men.

D. State Laws on Insurance Continuation

Because COBRA generally cannot be enforced by any means other than a complex and expensive lawsuit, state laws that give former employees the right to continue group health insurance coverage after leaving a job are often a better alternative. (See the chart below.) In nearly all instances, any continuation of coverage will be at your expense—just as it would be under COBRA.

However, the specific requirements of these laws and how they are enforced vary tremendously. For more specific information, contact your state's insurance department, or read the controlling laws at a local law library. (See Chapter 18, Section E.) In addition, the plant closing laws of a few states also may give you the right to continue group health insurance coverage. (See Chapter 10, Section H.)

STATE HEALTH INSURANCE CONTINUATION LAWS	
Arkansas	Former employees and their dependents have the right to continue group insurance coverage for 120 days after the coverage would have ended because of a change in employment status. Ark. Stat. Ann. §23-86-114
California	Former employees and their dependents, including widows and widowers and divorced spouses, have the right to continue group insurance coverage for 90 days after termination. Cal. Health & Safety Code §§1373.62 and 1373.6
Colorado	Former employees who were terminated and had been covered for at least three months by group health insurance and their dependents have the right to continue that coverage 90 days or until re-employed, whichever comes first. Colo. Rev. Stat. §10-8-116
Connecticut	Former employees and their eligible dependents have the right to continue group health insurance for 78 weeks after the coverage would have ended, or until they are covered by another group plan, whichever comes first. Conn. Gen. Stat. §38-262d

Florida	Former employees who were terminated and had been covered by group health insurance for at least three months and their eligible dependents have the right to covert the coverage to an individual policy. Fla. Stat. §627.6675
Georgia	Former employees and their eligible dependents who have been covered by group health insurance have the right to continue coverage for three months after the end of employment. Ga. Code Ann. §33-24-21.1
Illinois	Former employees who were terminated and had been covered by group health insurance for at least three months have the right to continue group coverage unless they are covered by another group plan. Ill. Stat. Ann. ch. 73 §979e
Iowa	Former employees who were terminated have the right to continue group health insurance for nine months, but some types of coverage such as prescription drug benefits are excluded. Iowa Code Ann. §509B.3
Kansas	Former employees have the right to continue group health insurance for six months after the end of employment. Kan. Stat. Ann. §40-2209
Kentucky	Former employees who had been covered by group health insurance for at least three months have the right to continue that coverage for nine months. Ky. Rev. Stat. Ann. §304.18-110
Louisiana	A former employee's surviving spouse who is 50 years old or older can continue group health coverage. La. Civ. Code Ann. art. 22, §215.7
Maine	Former employees who have been covered by group health insurance for six months and has been terminated because of layoff or work-related injury or occupational disease can continue group coverage. Me. Rev. Stat. Ann. tit. 24-A, §2809-A
Maryland	Former employees who were involuntarily terminated and had been covered by group health insurance for at least three months have the right to continue that coverage. Md. Ann. Code Art. 48A, §§354FF, 477GG, 477K and 490G
Massachusetts	Former employees and their dependents may continue group health insurance for 31 days. If employment was terminated by plant closing, then insurance may be continued for 90 days. If employment ended by layoff or death, then insurance may be continued for 39 weeks. Mass. Gen. Laws Ann. ch. 175 §110G; ch. 176A, §8D; ch. 176B, §6A; ch. 176G, §4A
Minnesota	Former employees who quit or were terminated for reasons other than gross misconduct have the right to continue group health coverage for themselves and their families for 12 months

	after it would otherwise end or until they become covered by another group plan, whichever comes first. Minn. Stat. Ann. §62A.17
Missouri	Former employees who have been covered by a group health plan for at least three months have the right to continue that insurance for up to nine months after it would otherwise end. Mo. Ann. Stat. §376.428
Nebraska	Former employees are entitled to continue group health insurance for six months after employment ends unless termination was due to employee misconduct. Neb. Rev. Stat. §44-1633.
Nevada	Former employees who have been covered by a group health plan for at least three months are entitled to continue coverage for 18 months unless terminated for misconduct. Eligible dependents are entitled to continue coverage for 36 months. No coverage if employee voluntarily quits. Nev. Rev. Stat. Ann. §§689B.245 and 689B.246
New Hampshire	Former employees and eligible dependents are entitled to group health plan continuation if employee is terminated or dies, unless the termination is for misconduct or is for less than six months. Coverage continues for 29 months if termination is due to disability, 36 months for spouse upon separation or divorce or if employee dies, and 18 months in all other situations. N.H. Rev. Stat. Ann. §415.18
New Jersey	Former employees are entitled to continuation of group health coverage if termination is due to total disability and they have been covered for three months. N.J. Stat. Ann. §17B:27-51-12
New York	Former employees have the right to continue group health coverage for up to six months after date of termination. N.Y. Ins. Law §3221
New Mexico	Former employees have the right to continue group health insurance coverage for up to six months after it would otherwise end. Covered family members may convert to individual policies upon the former employee's death or divorce. N.M. Stat. Ann. §59-18-16(A)
North Carolina	Former employees and their eligible dependents are entitled to continue group health plan coverage for three months if they have been covered by the plan for at least three months. N. C. Gen. Stat. §58-53-35
North Dakota	Former employees who had been covered by group health insurance for at least three months have the right to continue that coverage. N.D. Cent. Code §26.1-36-23

Ohio	Former employees who were terminated involuntarily have the right to continue group health insurance coverage for six months after termination. Ohio Rev. Code. Ann. §1737.30
Oklahoma	Former employees are entitled to continue group health coverage for 30 days after termination. If the employee has been covered by the plan for at least six months and is suffering from a continuing medical condition, then basic medical coverage continues for three months and major medical coverage continues for six months. Okla. Stat. Ann. tit. 40, §§172 and 173
Oregon	Former employees and eligible dependents who have been covered by a group health insurance plan for least three months are entitled to continuation of coverage for six months after the end of employment. Or. Rev. Stat. §742.850
Rhode Island	Former employees who were terminated due to an involuntary layoff or death have the right to continue group health insurance coverage for themselves and their dependents for up to 18 months after it would otherwise end. R.I. Gen. Laws §27-19.1-1
South Carolina	Former employees who have been covered by group health plan for at least three months are entitled to continue coverage after employment ends for one month. S.C. Code Ann. §38-45-946
South Dakota	Former employees and their dependents who have been covered by a group health insurance plan for at least six months have the right to continue that coverage for up to 18 months after it would otherwise end. S.D. Codified Laws Ann. §58-18-7.5
Tennessee	Former employees who had been covered by group health insurance for at least three months have the right to continue that coverage for up to three months after it would otherwise end. The employee is required to pay the premium in advance. Tenn. Code Ann. §56-7-1501
Texas	Former employees who have been covered by a group health insurance plan for at least three months and who are not terminated for cause are entitled to continue coverage for six months. Tex. Rev. Civ. Stat. Ann. art. 3.51-6
Utah	Former employees who have been covered by a group health insurance plan for at least six months are entitled to continue coverage for two months after end of employment. Utah Code Ann. § 31A-22-703
Vermont	Former employees who have been covered by a group health insurance plan for at least three months are entitled to continue such coverage unless terminated for misconduct. Vt. Stat. Ann. tit. 3, §§4090a through 4090g

Virginia	Former employees who have been covered by a group health insurance plan for at least three months may either continue coverage for 90 days after employment ends or convert to an individual policy at the employer's option. Va. Code Ann. §38.2-1541
Washington	Former employees are entitled to continue group health insurance benefits for a period of time and at a rate that employer and employee have agreed upon. Wash. Rev. Code Ann. §§48.21.250 through 48.21.270
West Virginia	Former employees who have been involuntarily laid off are entitled to continue group health benefits for 18 months. W.Va. Code §33-16-3
Wisconsin	Former employees who had been covered by group health insurance for at least three months have the right to continue coverage or convert it to an individual policy, unless they were fired for misconduct. If the former employee chooses group coverage, it will continue indefinitely and cannot be terminated unless the former employee moves out of state or becomes eligible for similar coverage. Wis. Stat. §632.897

E. Individual Health Insurance

Even if your state does not have a law that gives you the right to continue group healthcare coverage after employment ends, it may have a law that requires health insurance companies to offer you the option of converting your group policy to individual coverage.

Individual coverage typically is much more expensive than group coverage—and the coverage limits are usually much lower than those offered under group coverage. For example, a group health insurance policy often will not have any limit on total benefits paid during your lifetime, while individual coverage often limits total lifetime benefits to $500,000. However, laws that give you the right to convert to individual health coverage usually do not require you to lose your job to be eligible.

If your employer cancels your group healthcare coverage but continues to employ you—an increasingly common situation—these laws can give you the right to convert to individual coverage until you can find a better insurance deal, or a job with better health insurance benefits. You can usually find the laws guaranteeing you the right to convert group health insurance coverage to individual coverage among the statutes governing your state's insurance industry. Some states have a consumer complaint section in their insurance departments that can help you with this.

WHY HEALTH INSURANCE FOR RETIREES IS FADING

During the booming manufacturing decades following World War II, many big corporations promised to pay for their employees' health insurance—not only while they were on the company payroll, but also after they retired.

The problem was that many of those corporations never put away enough money to pay for their promises. When healthcare costs got out of control in the 1980s, many corporations were hit by enormous medical bills for former employees who had since retired.

It did not take long for those corporations' investors to begin complaining about the big healthcare bills and the way they were cutting into stockholders' profits. The investors argued that it was dishonest for a corporation not to put aside money to cover long-term commitments such as retiree healthcare costs.

The result was a rule from the Financial Accounting Standards Board—the group that governs the art of accounting in the United States—requiring that companies that promise retirement health insurance coverage to employees must put aside money to cover the cost of those promises on a pay-as-you-go basis.

The formula for estimating how much companies have to set aside to pay for retiree healthcare is remarkably complex. It is sufficient to know that for a company with 10,000 employees, the amount that would typically have had to be put aside in 1990 alone to pay for future retiree healthcare coverage was $21.5 million, according to the consulting firm of Towers Perrin in New York City.

Faced with such huge bills, most corporations now admit that they really cannot afford to pay for retiree healthcare coverage. So they are doing everything they can to cut back on promises of retiree healthcare coverage that they have already made—and to avoid making any more such promises.

F. Utilization Review

If your health insurance coverage provider has joined the swelling ranks of those who use a process called utilization review, you may get caught in the crossfire of one of the greatest workplace legal feuds on record if you become ill.

The idea behind utilization review is simple: By having an objective eye, usually an independent agency, take a look at your medical problem and approve or disapprove the things your doctor recommends, insurance companies can cut down on treatments that are unnecessary and expensive. The savings can then be passed along to the employers and employees who are finding it ever more difficult to pay for health insurance coverage.

Most physicians hate utilization review—and the reason for their attitude is simple: Any process that prevents doctors from prescribing unnecessary treatment significantly reduces the charges that they can bill to your insurance company. But employers like utilization review. So lawyers have found a lucrative place for themselves in the middle of that opinion clash—routinely filing lawsuits on behalf of doctors, employers and their insurance companies.

UTILIZATION REVIEW AND INSURANCE COVERAGE

Unless the legal feud over utilization review is settled, employees must be particularly careful in making sure they understand what role it would play in their healthcare coverage if they became ill and needed to file a claim.

Here are some questions to ask to help you evaluate coverage.

- Does my health insurance coverage include a provision for utilization review?
- If so, who will perform the review? Will it be someone on the company's staff? Someone on the insurance company's staff? An outside agency?
- What kind of professional credentials are required of the people who would review my doctor's recommendations for treating me?
- What methods does my health insurance coverage use to enforce its utilization review decisions? For example, some health insurance plans merely compile lists of doctors whose charges are habitually high, and then try to talk them into exercising restraint. Others use more aggressive tactics, such as reducing by 25% the fees paid to doctors who fail to obtain permission from the insurance company before performing a treatment on a patient.
- Do I have the option of electing to participate in a health insurance plan that doesn't include utilization review? If so, will it cost me more to be covered by that plan?
- If my doctor or I disagree with a decision made by a reviewer, would I have the option of rejecting the utilization reviewer's decision?

Having this information is not likely to keep you completely out of the utilization review feud, but at least you will understand what is happening to you and what options you have if you get caught in it. ■

CHAPTER

5

FAMILY AND MEDICAL LEAVE

The typical American household has changed dramatically in the decades since the 1950s, when most American families were rigidly organized around a wage-earning father and a housekeeping, stay-at-home mother.

The workforce, too, has changed dramatically as women, single parents and two-paycheck couples have entered in droves. And it is projected that by the year 2000, 75% of all women with children will work in jobs outside the home. Economics has made working a necessity for most people.

And due to the astronomical costs of medical care, more workers find they are yoked with the responsibility for providing at least some of the care for sick or injured family members and aging parents.

There have been some additions to workplace legal rights that recognize these grand changes. But by and large, legislation has limped far behind societal shifts.

A. The Family and Medical Leave Act

The most sweeping federal law to help workers with the precarious balance between job and family is the Family and Medical Leave Act, or FMLA (29 U.S.C. §§2601 and following), signed by President Clinton in February 1993 after prolonged congressional gridlock. Under the FMLA, an employee is eligible for up to 12 weeks of unpaid leave during a year's time for the birth or adoption of a child, family health needs or the employee's own health needs.

The employer must not only allow an employee to take the leave, but must allow the employee to return to the same or a similar position to the one he or she held before. And during the leave, the employer must continue to make the same benefit contributions, such as paying insurance policy premiums, as the employee was receiving before going on leave. However, the FMLA does not require that employers pay any benefits that are not generally provided to employees—and seniority and pension benefits need not accrue during an employee's leave.

Employers who violate the Act, including its provisions against retaliating against those who take advantage of its protections (see Section 4), may be required to pay backpay, damages, attorneys' and expert witnesses' fees—and importantly, for the cost of up to 12 weeks of caring for a child, spouse or parent.

1. Who Is Covered

The FMLA applies to all private and public employers with 50 or more employees—an estimated one-half of the workforce.

In addition, to be covered under the law, an employee must have:

* been employed at the same workplace for a year or more, and
* worked at least 1,250 hours—or about 24 hours a week—during the year preceding the leave.

2. Restrictions on Coverage

Anticipating that some of the leave provisions in the FMLA might cause a hardship on smaller and some specialized employers, Congress included a number of exceptions to its coverage. Some of the exceptions sound rather harsh, and would likely result in fractionating some workplaces—providing some employees with benefits that others are blanketly denied. So to maintain morale and encourage company loyalty, many employers are opting to adopt uniform standards for all employees rather than adhere slavishly to the exceptions allowed.

a. 50 employees within 75 miles

Companies with fewer than 50 employees within a 75-mile radius are exempt from the FMLA. This means that small regional offices of even the largest companies may be exempt from the law's requirements. However, the magic number of 50, for purposes of the FMLA, is computed by adding up the employees on the payroll, so that those already on leave and those who work erratic schedules are tallied into the final count.

b. The highest paid 10%

The law allows companies to exempt the highest paid 10% of employees. This exception recognizes that in many companies, the highest paid employees are the executives, the leaders and the manager—the most essential to have in attendance to keep work running smoothly. Employers may choose to provide these employees with unpaid leave, however, and many do—recognizing that the standard is broader than the reality of most workplaces. For example, in a smallish workplace of 100 employees, it is highly unlikely that ten workers will be deemed top-level executives.

c. Teachers and instructors

Those who work as schoolteachers or instructors are partially exempt from the FMLA—that is, they may not be allowed to take their unpaid leave until the end of a teaching period, commonly a quarter or semester, to avoid disrupting the continuity of the classroom. Teaching assistants and school staff, however, are fully covered under the FMLA.

d. Two spouses, one employer

Unless their need for leave is due to a personal medical problem, spouses who work for the same employer must aggregate their 12 weeks of leave time—that is, together, they are entitled to a total of 12 weeks off.

Congress defends that it wrote this exception into the FMLA to ease an employer's unwillingness to hire a married couple. In reality, it forces a couple to choose who should be the caregiver in the family. Note, however, that because of the loophole allowing time off for medical problems, if a woman qualifies for a pregnancy leave, her husband may be entitled to family leave to care for her.

SCHEDULING TIME OFF

Theoretically, an employee and employer are required to agree in advance on scheduling leave time to be taken under the FMLA. The law requires the employee to give at least 30 days notice for "foreseeable medical treatment."

But the reality is that the FMLA provides time off from work for events that are often unpredictable and impossible to schedule—birth, adoption, sudden illness. In cases of medical emergencies, premature births or surprise adoption placements, employee leave is allowed—even without the employer's advance approval.

3. Reasons for Time Off

The FMLA establishes what has been long-awaited in the workplace: a federal standard guaranteeing many workers the right to leave for the birth or adoption of a child and to care for their own or a family member's serious health condition.

a. Time off for childcare

The law is targeted so that workers can provide adequate care for ill or injured children under 18, and those 18 and older who cannot take care of themselves because of a physical or mental disability. Leave is available to care for an employee's son or daughter—which is broadly defined to include biological, adopted or foster children, stepchildren and legal wards. Also covered are children for whom employees stand in the place of parents—such as where a grandparent, aunt or uncle has complete caretaking responsibilities.

The FMLA states that all covered employees must be given 12 weeks of unpaid leave for the birth, adoption or foster placement of a child, as long as that leave is taken within a year of the child's arrival. Also, if the leave is for a new child, it must be taken in a 12-week chunk; whereas leave for medical problems may be scheduled more flexibly.

WHEN IS A BENEFIT NOT A BENEFIT?

Your employer can count your accrued paid benefits—vacation, sick leave and personal leave days—toward the 12 weeks of leave you are allowed under the FMLA. If you use three weeks of vacation, for example, and another week of sick leave, you are left with only eight weeks of protected job leave under the FMLA.

To ease the strain, however, many employers let employees decide whether to include paid leave time as part of their family leave allotment.

---

b. Time off for healthcare

The FMLA also provides for time off for health problems—physical and psychological—that affect either the employee or his or her spouse or parents. The required care need only limit the employee's ability to work, or limit the employee's family member's ability to carry on with daily activities.

In the FMLA, the definition of spouse is limited to "a husband or wife, as the case may be"—overtly banning unmarried partners from the Act's coverage. In-laws are not included in the definition of parents.

The FMLA's definition of a medical condition entitling an employee to take a leave is quite liberal. It includes, for example, time off to care for a parent or spouse who has Alzheimer's disease or clinical depression, has suffered a stroke, is recovering from major surgery or is in the final stages of a terminal disease. It also covers employees who need time off to recover from the side effects of a medical treatment—including chemotherapy or radiation treatments.

However, the employee's or family member's health condition or medical treatment must require either an overnight stay in the hospital or a three-day absence from work. For example, a one-time health problem that is expected to require a short recovery period, such as an appendectomy or orthodontic treatments, are not covered under the FMLA. In fashioning the law, Congress presumed, rightly or wrongly, that most workplace sick days or personal leave policies would be sufficient to cover these situations.

IF YOUR EMPLOYER DOUBTS YOUR WORD

The cautious Congress that fashioned the FMLA took special care to guard against employees' potential abuse of the leave time policy.

And so the law includes a means of routing out cheaters.

If your employer doubts that you or yours has a serious health condition that requires you to take a leave, your employer may request that the condition be certified—that is, that a physician, psychologist, mental health counselor or other healthcare worker vouch for the condition in writing.

An employer who doubts even that confirmation can request, but is required to pay for, a second—and a third—medical opinion of the condition.

---

4. Penalties for Retaliation

By passing the FMLA, Congress intended to signal that employers must foster employees' needs to preserve both family and job. As in other workplace laws prohibiting unfair practices, the FMLA prohibits employers from demoting or firing an employee solely because he or she took a legally sanctioned leave.

The law also provides that an employer may not use either a carrot or a stick in handling leave requests. That is, an employee may not be promised a raise or promotion as an inducement not to take a leave; nor may an employee be denied a raise or promotion because of taking a leave.

5. Returning to Work

When you return to work after taking a family leave, the FMLA requires that you be returned to your old position or to an equivalent one.

This is a strict requirement. Congress has intimated that it is not enough that the position to which you are returned be "comparable" or "similar." It has stated that the "terms, conditions and privileges"—including the security of the position within the company—must be the same as the previous position.

Example: *A credit manager, responsible for supervising several employees, took a leave from her position due to pregnancy. When she returned to work, she was given a job with the same pay, the same benefits and the same office as her previous position, but she no longer had a job title, she supervised fewer employees—and a fourth of her worktime was to be spent in clerical work. Focusing on the diminished responsibility and authority, a court held that the new position was not equivalent under the terms of the FMLA (Kelley Co., Inc. v. Marquardt, 493 N.W. 2d 68 (1992)).*

6. If You Do Not Return to Work

An interesting twist in the law provides that if an employee does not return to work after an FMLA-sanctioned leave, the employer may seek return of the benefits paid while he or she was away.

Although it has not yet been questioned in court, this recapture provision seems to be an oversight in the law, as it enables employers to set off benefit amounts from an employee's final paycheck or from a severance award. However, the set off most often involves health insurance premiums, which the employer usually pays directly to the insurer.

7. Enforcing Your Rights

You must file a claim under the FMLA within two years after an employer violates the Act—or within three years if the violation is willful. Since the law is fairly new, it is still unclear what conduct will be required to be considered willful, but retaliation is likely to be found such an offense.

As mentioned, employers found to violate the FMLA may be liable for a number of costs and benefits, including:

- wages, salary, employment benefits or other compensation an employee has lost
- the cost of providing up to 12 weeks of care for a baby or ill family member
- reasonable attorneys' and expert witness fees, and
- interest on the amounts described above.

The employee may also win the right to be promoted or reinstated to a particular job.

The FMLA is now enforced by the U.S. Department of Labor, much the same as the Fair Labor Standards Act, which controls work hours and wages. (See Chapter 3, Section H.) Because the law is fairly new and fairly radical, there is still much concerning its practicality and effect that will be decided in the years to come. If you have specific questions about the

FMLA, contact the local office of the Labor Department, listed under U.S. Government, Department of Labor, in the telephone book.

B. State Laws on Family Leave

The majority of states now have leave laws, but their provisions differ wildly—leaving a patchwork of protections, benefits and loopholes that are often confusing to both employers and employees.

1. Choosing Federal or State Protections

If your state also has a family leave law in some incarnation, you are free to seek benefits under the federal FMLA or your state law—whichever law offers you the greatest benefit. If you have a baby one year, you may use the leave allotted you by the state; if you become ill the next year, you may be entitled to benefits guaranteed by the FMLA. However, several states have recently amended their laws to provide that state and federal coverage cannot be piggybacked; their coverage runs concurrently.

LEAVES WITH PAY

In general, state family leave laws only require employers to grant an employee a leave without pay. Paid leaves are uncommon, but some companies—typically very large ones or very small ones that regard their employees as family members—do provide at least partial paid leave.

Check with your supervisor well before you anticipate needing a leave to determine your workplace's policy on paid leaves. Make sure that you fulfill all the requirements for receiving your regular pay during the time that you're away from work—such as giving your employer adequate notice of your need to take such a leave.

2. State Laws

State laws governing family leaves differ greatly as to:

- the size of workplace covered—varying from 4 to 100
- the reasons allowed for time off—some states provide leaves for birth and adoption only; others also provide it for family members' illnesses
- who is covered—a number of states specify that an employee must have worked for one employer for a minimum time before being entitled to leave
- the length of leave allowed
- the length of notice that an employee must give before taking a leave
- whether or not benefits must be continued and at whose expense
- whether or not an employee is entitled to the same or an equivalent position after returning to work—in some states, this is required only if proper advance notice has been given
- how rights to parental leaves are divided when both parents are employed by the same company, and
- how the laws can be enforced.

A few states—including California, Minnesota and Nevada—also provide that parents must be given a certain amount of unpaid leave to attend a child's school conferences.

On their faces, many state laws are more liberal than the federal law. But many state laws are rife with large loopholes, too. For example, the family leave laws in many states provide that an employer is free to deny an employee's request for leave if the time off would be an undue hardship in the workplace.

FAMILY AND MEDICAL LEAVE LAWS

Nearly half the states have laws that specifically guarantee people employed in private industry the right to take work leaves because of pregnancy, childbirth or the adoption of a child. A few also have laws that give employees the right to take time off from work to care for a family member who is ill. In addition, several states that are not listed here provide leaves for state employees only. Here is a synopsis of the basic rights granted to employees in private industry by state laws.

Alaska	Employers with 21 or more employees must grant any employee who has worked fulltime for six months or halftime for one year 18 weeks of unpaid leave per 12-month period for pregnancy, childbirth or adoption, or 24 months for care of a family member during a serious illness. Employees who take such leave must be restored to their same or comparable position. Alaska Stat. §23.10.500
California	Employers with 50 or more employees must grant any employee who has worked for more than one year up to four months of unpaid leave per 24-month period for pregnancy, childbirth, adoption, foster care, or care of a child, spouse or parent during serious illness. Employees who take such leave must be restored to their same or comparable position. Cal. Gov't. Code §§12945, 12945.2 and 19702.3
Colorado	Employer policies applying to leaves for biological parents must also be extended to adoptive parents. Colo. Rev. Stat. §19-5-211
Connecticut	Employers with at least 75 employees are required to give 16 weeks of unpaid leave within any two-year period. Leave may be for birth or adoption of child or for care of a child, spouse, or parent during serious illness. Employees who take such leave must be allowed to return to either their original or equivalent jobs. Conn. Gen. Stat. §§31-51cc, 31-51dd, 31-51ff
District of Columbia	An employee who has worked with a company of at least 20 employees for at least one year, and who has worked at least 1,000 hours during the previous 12-month period, must be granted up to 16 weeks of unpaid leave during any 24-month period in connection with the birth or adoption of a child or serious illness of a family member. (D.C. Code Ann. §36-1302). Family member includes a child who lives with the employee and for whom the employee resumes parental responsibility. It also includes a person with whom the employee shares a residence and maintains a residence. Employees who take such leaves must be restored to either their original or equivalent jobs.

Hawaii	Employers with at least 100 employees must grant employees an unpaid leave of up to four weeks per calendar year for the birth or adoption of a child or for care of a child, spouse or parent during a serious illness. Employees who take such leave must be restored to their same or comparable position. Haw. Rev. Stat. §398-1
Iowa	Employers with at least four employees must grant employees who are disabled by pregnancy, childbirth or related medical conditions an unpaid leave for the duration of their disabilities, up to a maximum of eight weeks. Iowa Code Ann. §601.A.6
Kentucky	An employer of any size must grant up to six weeks unpaid leave to an employee who has adopted a child under seven years old. Ky. Rev. Stat. Ann. §337.015
Louisiana	Employers that have at least five employees must grant employees up to four months of unpaid leave for the birth of a child and any related medical conditions. La. Rev. Stat. Ann. §23:1008
Maine	An employee who has worked at least 12 consecutive months with a company employing at least 25 people must be granted up to ten consecutive weeks of unpaid leave in any two-year period for the birth or adoption of a child 16 years old or younger or to care for a family member during illness. Employees who take such leaves must be restored to either their original or equivalent jobs. Me. Rev. Stat. Ann. tit. 26, §844
Massachusetts	Employers of at least six employees must grant employees who have completed their probationary periods or three months of employment and have worked full-time for at least three months must be given up to eight weeks of unpaid leave for the birth or adoption of a child. Mass. Gen. Laws Ann. ch. 149, §105D
Minnesota	A company employing 21 or more people must grant employees up to six weeks of unpaid leave for the birth or adoption of a child. However, only employees who have worked for the company an average of at least 20 hours per week for at least 12 months before the request for leave is made are covered. During the leave, the employer must offer the employee the option of continuing group healthcare insurance coverage. Employees who take such leave must be returned to either their original or equivalent jobs, unless the employee would have been laid off. Minn. Stat. Ann. §181.941
	An employee may use paid sick leave to care for a sick child. Minn. Stat. Ann. §181.943
Montana	An employer of any size may not dismiss an employee who becomes pregnant, or refuse to allow a reasonable unpaid leave for pregnancy, or refuse to allow accrued disability or other leave benefits for a pregnancy leave. Employees also cannot be required to take pregnancy leave for an unreasonable period of time. Employees who take

pregnancy-related leaves must be returned to their original jobs or equivalents. Mont. Code Ann §49-2-310 and §49-2-311

Nevada

The same leave policies that apply to other medical conditions must be extended to female employees before and after childbirth, or after a miscarriage. Nev. Rev. Stat. §608.159

New Jersey

Employers of at least 50 employees must grant to those who have worked for at least 12 months, and who have worked at least 1,000 hours in the preceding 12 months, up to 12 weeks of unpaid leave in any 24-month period for the birth, adoption or care during the serious illness of a child under 18 years old, or one older than 18 who is incapable of self-care or a parent or a spouse. Employees who take such leaves must be restored to either their original or equivalent jobs. N.J. Stat. Ann. §§34:11B-1 and 34:11B-4

New York

If an employer permits leave for the birth of a child, then leave must be granted for adoption. N.Y. Labor Law §201-c

Oregon

Employees who have worked with a company with at least 25 employees for at least 90 days must be granted up to 12 weeks of unpaid leave for childbirth or the adoption of a child less than six years old. The employer may require employees to give 30 days notice of intent to take such a leave, and employees returning from such a leave must be returned to either their original or equivalent jobs. Pregnant employees must also be given the right to transfer to a less strenuous job. Or. Rev. Stat. §659.360

Employers with 50 or more employees must grant to employees who have worked an average of at least 25 hours per week for 180 days or more a leave of absence to care for a seriously ill family member of up to 12 weeks in a two-year period. Or. Rev. Stat. §659.570

Rhode Island

Employers with 50 or more employees must grant those who have worked for them for at least 12 consecutive months up to 13 weeks of unpaid leave for the birth or adoption of a child (R.I. Gen. Laws §28-48-3) or for the care of a family member during illness (R.I. Gen. Laws §28-48-2). Employees who take such leaves must be restored to either their original or equivalent jobs.

Tennessee

Companies with 100 or more employees must grant up to four months of unpaid leave to any female employee for pregnancy or childbirth. If the employee gives the employer at least three months advance notice of her intent to take such a leave, or, if a medical emergency makes the leave necessary, she must be restored to her original job or its equivalent upon returning to work. The employer must allow an employee who takes such a leave to continue benefits such as healthcare insurance, but the employer is not required to pay for the benefits during the leave period. Tenn. Code Ann. §4-21-408

Vermont	Companies with 15 or more employees must allow employees who have worked with them an average of at least 30 hours per week, for at least one year, to take up to 12 weeks of unpaid leave for pregnancy or childbirth, or the serious illness of a family member. The employee must provide the employer with written notice of her intent to take such a leave and of its anticipated duration. The employee must be allowed to use accrued vacation or sickness leave for up to six weeks of leave. The employee must also be given the option of continuing benefit programs at his or her own expense. After returning from such a leave, the employee must be restored to her original job or its equivalent. An employee who does not return to the job after taking such a leave must refund to the employer any compensation paid during the leave, except payments for accrued vacation or sickness leave. Vt. Stat. Ann. tit. 21 §472
Washington	Employers with 100 or more employees must grant up to 12 weeks of unpaid leave during any two-year period in connection with the birth or adoption of a child. The employee must provide the employer with at least 30 days advance notice in most situations. Employees who take such leaves must be restored to their original jobs or equivalent jobs. If circumstances have changed to the point that no equivalent job is available, the employee must be given any vacant job for which he or she is qualified. An employee may use accrued sick leave to care for an ill child under age 18. An employee also may take up to 12 weeks of unpaid leave within any 24-month period to care for a child under 18 years old who is terminally ill. Wash. Rev. Code §49.12.270
Wisconsin	Employers with 50 or more employees must grant employees who have been with the company one year and worked 1,000 hours up to six weeks of unpaid leave for the birth or adoption of a child and up to two weeks for the care of a parent, child or spouse with a serious health condition. This leave, when combined with any other family-related leave, may not exceed a total of eight weeks within a 12-month period. Wis. Stat. Ann. §103.10

CHANGING YOUR MIND

A common sore point with employers is that some employees officially state they are taking a parental leave of only a few months, but then decide to become fulltime parents and quit their jobs outright.

This strategy is particularly popular among employees who are having their first baby because, at the very least, it seems to allow the option of going back to a job after experimenting with a few months of stay-at-home parenting.

But this strategy is far from new—and most employers have seen it before. Many companies now require employees who take paid parental leaves and then decide to leave their jobs permanently to pay back all compensation received during the leave. The FMLA specifically guards against this practice. (See Section A6.)

To enforce this type of policy, employers usually need you to sign an agreement in which you agree to make such a repayment, so be careful to read and understand anything you sign in connection with any paid leave that is granted to you.

3. Anti-Discrimination Provisions

Some state laws also forbid workplace discrimination on the basis of gender. In states that have no specific family leave laws, anti-discrimination laws often can be used to establish a right for parents to take time off from work for pregnancy and childbirth.

The anti-discrimination laws of most states include marital status among the factors that may not be used as the basis for work-related discrimination. Some states, such as Alaska, for example, go a step further, protecting even unmarried couples by specifically listing parenthood as an illegal basis for discrimination. (See the Chart in Chapter 8, Section B, for a listing of state anti-discrimination laws.)

4. Enforcing Your Rights

Anti-discrimination laws often can be applied to such leaves only through slow-moving complaints to the Equal Employment Opportunity Commission, or through complex and expensive lawsuits. But, in general, state laws that grant family leaves offer a clear basis for enforcing the right to take such a leave.

For example, in Oregon, you can file a complaint with the state Labor Department against an employer that refuses to allow you to take a leave for childbirth (Or. Rev. Stat. ¶659.365). And in New Jersey, you can ask the state Attorney General's office to file a lawsuit against an employer who violates your right to take a parental leave (N.J. Stat. Ann. §34:11B-10).

The most direct and constructive way to exercise your right to take a family leave is to know your rights and to make sure your employer is aware of them as long before you need to take a leave as possible. Nearly all state family leave laws have been enacted recently and your employer may be sincerely unaware of them.

If you have made your employer aware of your right to take such a leave and the employer refuses to comply, the options available to you will vary with the situation.

- If your problem seems to be merely a matter of disagreement over interpretation of the law, you can suggest to your employer that a mediator or arbitrator help settle the dispute. (See Chapter 18, Section A.)

- If your state is listed in this chapter as having a specific leave law, you may be able to have a state agency intervene in your case. To find the appropriate state agency, start with the one responsible for overseeing your state's anti-discrimination law. (See Chapter 8, Section B.)

- If your case involves a violation of Title VII of the Civil Rights Act, you can file a complaint with the Equal Employment Opportunity Commission (EEOC). If the EEOC decides not to take action in your case, you may be able to file a federal lawsuit on your own. (See Chapter 8, Section A.)

- If your state has no agency to enforce its law, you may be able to file a lawsuit on your own behalf. (See Chapter 8, Section A.) In some states, those who sue under family leave laws are allowed to collect punitive damages, court fees and the cost of hiring a lawyer to help.

WHEN PARENTS' RIGHTS ARE PARENTS' WRONGS

According to many experts, the next wave of legal reform in the workplace is likely to be championed by an unexpected source: workers who have no chiildren.

The backlash, ironically, may first be felt most strongly in companies that attempted to provide the most accommodations for workers. Corning, Inc., a large optical fiber and ceramics company based in New York, is one good example. The company recently began providing a number of innovative benefits for workers—childcare programs, childcare counseling, flexible work schedules for parents. "After the first couple of years, people who didn't have young children started quietly saying, 'What about us? Does my personal life count?'" recalls Sonia Werner, a workplace consultant at Corning. Corning recently righted its shortsightedness by offering flexible work schedules to workers who have no children, changing the name of its Family Support Program to Work Life and offering employee seminars in assertiveness training and other general concerns.

The murmurs of resentment are becoming louder in many other work-places, too. Many workers who feel the sting—and nearly two-thirds of U.S. workers do not have children under age 18—say this form of discrimination takes more subtle forms, so it is often more difficult to document, speak up about and correct. But an increasing number of childless workers are beginning to voice their grievances, including that they are customarily:

- expected to work more hours than their co-workers who have children
- made targets for frequent transfers and out-of-country assignments
- forced to absorb extra work to cover for parents who arrive late or leave early to drop off and pick up their children
- deprived of paid benefits such as childcare and counseling offered only to traditional families, and
- exclusively called upon to cover weekend and after-hour assignments.

Some companies are beginning to get the message. For example, Quaker Oats, a food company based in Chicago, began in 1993 to offer workers a more equitable benefits program, as masterminded by a team of workers in various ages and stages holding various positions throughout the company. Quaker's new Flexplan gives an additional $300 to employees who claim no dependents on company-reimbursed insurance coverage. Their employees can opt to take the $300 in cash, as an investment to their 401k plans—or they can use it to buy other employee benefits, such as vacation time.

C. The Pregnancy Discrimination Act

Additional workplace rights for new parents come from the Pregnancy Discrimination Act, or PDA (92 Stat. §2076), passed in 1978 as an amendment to Title VII of the Civil Rights Act of 1964. It clearly outlaws discrimination based on pregnancy, childbirth or any related medical condition.

CAUSE FOR PREGNANT PAUSES

In 1992, the federal Equal Employment Opportunity Commission reported that nearly 3,500 pregnancy-related discrimination claims were filed—an 11% increase over the previous year.

And 9to5, a working women's advocacy organization (see the Appendix for contact details) recently noted that at least one-third of the 5,000 job problem calls it receives each month have to do with pregnancy discrimination in the workplace.

1. Who Is Covered

Like other provisions of Title VII, the federal law that widely prohibits many types of discrimination, the PDA applies to all workplaces that:
- engage in some type of interstate commerce—today, broadly construed to include all employers that use the mails or telephones, and
- have 15 or more employees for any 20 weeks of a calendar year. (See Chapter 8, Section A, for more on Title VII protections.)

2. Available Protections

The PDA specifies that pregnant employees—and those recovering from an abortion—who need time off from work, must be treated the same as other temporarily disabled employees. For example, a company that allows employees to return to work with full seniority and benefit rights after taking time off for a surgical operation and recovery must similarly reinstate women who take time off because of a pregnancy.

On the flip side, this law may also help sanction the denial of a benefit to a pregnant worker if that benefit has been denied any other temporarily disabled worker. If it is company policy, for example, to suspend seniority rights and benefits for employees who require extended medical leave, those work benefits must also be denied to pregnant workers on leave.

Also, while the PDA bars discrimination based on pregnancy, unlike the Family and Medical Leave Act (see Section A), it does not require an employer to provide a pregnant employee with leave—and does not guarantee job security while a worker is out on leave.

a. Forced leaves

The PDA bars mandatory maternity leaves—and those that are prescribed for a set time and duration. The focus instead is on whether an individual pregnant worker remains able to perform her job. And a pregnant woman cannot be required to take a leave from work during her pregnancy as long as she remains able to do her job.

Example: *Judy's pregnancy is proceeding without problems, and she has no difficulty performing her job as an office manager. Even though she is a week past her delivery due date according to her doctor's calculations, her employer cannot force her to take off work in anticipation of labor.*

b. Hiring and promotion discrimination

In addition, an employer cannot refuse to hire or promote a woman solely because she is pregnant—or because of stereotyped notions of what work is proper for a pregnant woman to do or not to do.

Example: *Marsha is the most qualified applicant for a job, but is six months pregnant during her job interview. The company cannot choose another applicant simply because it does not want to find a replacement for Marsha when she takes a leave to give birth.*

c. Insurance discrimination

The PDA also states that an employer cannot refuse to provide healthcare insurance benefits that cover pregnancy if it provides such benefits to cover other medical conditions.

Example: *The Dumont Company provides complete hospitalization insurance to spouses of female employees, but has a $500 cap on childbirth coverage for spouses of male employees. This policy is illegal under the PDA.*

The sole exception here is that an employer need not pay for health insurance benefits for an abortion—except where the life of the pregnant woman would be endangered if the fetus is carried to term or where there are medical complications following the abortion.

3. Men's Rights to Leaves

Under Title VII, an employer must grant men the same options for taking leave from their jobs to care for a child as it grants to women. To do otherwise would constitute illegal discrimination based on gender.

Example: *Steven works for a company that provides a 12-week unpaid leave for women who give birth to or adopt a child. If his employer refuses to allow Steven to take such a leave to adopt a child, he can file a complaint against his employer under Title VII, alleging gender discrimination.*

However, a study released by the U.S. Small Business Association in 1991 showed that this is one area where the law is routinely violated: Most companies offer some type of leave for childbirth to female workers, the study found, but less than 8% offer the same option to their male employees.

For details about who is covered by Title VII and how to file a complaint under it, see Chapter 8, Section A. But first read Section B of this chapter to see if your state offers a more direct approach. Also, see the Appendix for organizations that provide information on work and family issues.

D. Balancing Work and Family: Other Ways to Cope

Some companies help employees juggle work and family responsibilities in various ways, including:

- allowing employees to work parttime or to share a job (see Chapter 2, Section B)
- allowing employees to put in some of their work hours at home
- allowing flexible onsite work hours, and
- providing additional assistance to employees, such as counseling and seminars on work and family issues.

If you feel that one of these options is feasible in your workplace and would make your life more manageable, talk with your employer. Better still, come to the talk armed with success stories of similar set-ups in local companies.

1. Work at Home Agreements

These days, many jobs use computers as essential tools. And computers can easily be transported, or hooked up to communicate with the main worksite from various locales. And many other kinds of work are portable and may lend themselves well to work at home arrangements for employees.

These arrangements often involve an agreement between the worker and the company—best if it is in writing—that spells out who is responsible for any legal liabilities that arise from the work at home arrangement and how worktime will be measured.

For example, a work at home agreement may specify that you are responsible for any damage that occurs to a company-owned laptop computer while it is being used in your home. Most homeowners' and renters' insurance policies do not automatically cover business equipment, so you may have to purchase additional coverage.

Also, check the agreement against the wage and hour laws (discussed in Chapter 3) to make sure that neither you nor your employer would be breaking the Fair Labor Standards Act through your work at home plan. In general, if you are not an exempt employee, the wages and hours provisions of the Act still apply even when you are working at home.

2. Flexible Workhours

In many urban workplaces, where rush hour commuting makes for immense amounts of downtime, 9 to 5 workdays are all but extinct. In fact, a growing number of employers everywhere are putting less credence in the rigid Monday to Friday, 9 to 5 workweek and allowing employees to adopt more flexible work schedules.

When this idea was newer, it was referred to by the high-tech appellation of flextime. Flextime is not a reduction in hours, but simply a shift in the times employees are required to clock in and out of work. An increasingly popular flextime option, for example, is the ten-hour/four-day workweek, as it gives employees at least the illusion of a three-day weekend. Since flextime employees usually maintain 40-hour workweeks, they lose no benefits—such as healthcare coverage or vacation time—in the bargain.

A CLOSER LOOK AT EMPLOYEE BENEFITS:
ALL THAT GLITTERS MAY NOT BE GOLD

U.S. West is a regional telephone company headquartered in Colorado that has won accolades recently for its "family friendly" employee benefit programs. The smorgasbord of benefits offered by U.S. West include:

Information services: counseling for family problems; a toll-free referral service on how to care for children, the elderly and disabled adults; workshops on topics including children's self-esteem and estate planning for the elderly; free videos on parenting and eldercare.

Flexible work schedules: eight paid and one unpaid personal days; three paid days off for deaths of family members, including grandparents; six weeks paid sick leave for mothers; six months unpaid leave for childcare, with paid insurance benefits—with a possible additional six months off without benefits; 12 months unpaid leave to care for other family members; ten-hour day/four-day workweeks, job sharing and excused time off.

Financial assistance: discounts for childcare with several approved centers; pretax dependent-care stipend; reimbursements for childcare expenses during travel.

The list looks impressive—and many U.S. West workers say their company provides a refreshing and progressive list of benefits.

But a number of U.S. West workers now complain that the programs are not universally enforced; they are only as effective—and only as much a reality—as the managers in each branch office make them. In fact, some such well-documented complaints emanating from the Seattle area offices caused U.S. West not to enter its name in *Working Mother* magazine's annual contest for The Best Places for Mothers to Work. (It had emerged as an easy winner in 1989, 1990 and 1992.) Also, many workers say threats of layoffs mean that the best-laid plans of workplace flexibility are taking a backseat to their need to hang onto their jobs tooth and nail.

3. Counseling and Other Benefits

Many employers now make employee counseling an integral part of their discipline procedures. That is, fewer employees are surprised by being fired from a company, since more have had the option of getting some form of counseling first—to improve their work performances, to help them conquer drug or alcohol abuse problems, to help raise awareness about potential sexual harassment.

And more enlightened employers now also offer employees a number of seminars and workshops more indirectly related to the workplace— workshops on building self-esteem, dealing with long-term healthcare for aging parents, First Aid and CPR certification. These educational workshops not only train employees in more valuable skills, they also have the more nebulous value of improving morale.

At some workplaces, employees have taken the initiative in setting up their own workshops during lunchtimes or after work hours. Volunteers from local special interest groups—the Red Cross, stress management groups, battered women's shelters, self-defense trainers—are often available to present the training free or at a very low cost. ■

CHAPTER
6

PRIVACY RIGHTS

Technology has made it easier to pry into peoples' lives and psyches—through computerized recordkeeping, drug and alcohol testing, videotaping and audiotaping. And that has caused more workers to want to protect something of themselves, to jealously guard their rights to privacy, to be left alone at work.

Theoretically, at least, employers sit on the other side of the fence. They are understandably concerned about stomping down on wrongdoing in the workplace, such as drug and alcohol abuse, theft, incompetence and low productivity. And usually, their concerns center on finding the best qualified employee for a particular position. Employers want to know as much as possible about what goes on and who spends time in a workplace.

While there are some legal controls on what an employer or prospective employer can find out about you and on how they can use that information, there are still many ways an employer can invade your privacy—for example, by requiring you to take a drug test under some circumstances. But there are some subtle limits on the extent to which your privacy can be invaded. In general, employers are entitled to intrude on your personal life no more than necessary for legitimate business interests.

Most abuses of privacy rights occur when people are not aware of the legal constraints and how to enforce them. This chapter covers these legal constraints and outlines some of the most profound current workplace privacy issues: access to personnel records, medical and psychological testing and high tech surveillance.

> **WE DO BELIEVE**
>
> Results of a recent survey indicate that while most American workers think it's fine for employers to probe into whether employees may be convicted felons or drug users, they draw the line at prying into health and lifestyle matters.
>
> Percent of Americans who believe employers should be allowed to test job applicants for drugs: 83
>
> Percent who believe employers should be able to check whether an employee has a criminal record: 80
>
> Percent who believe in random drug testing of employees: 66
>
> Percent who think written honesty tests are appropriate: 55
>
> Percent who approve of AIDS testing for job applicants: 46
>
> Percent who feel it is appropriate for employers to check into a job applicant's lifestyle or political association: 12
>
> *Source: 1990 national opinion survey conducted by Louis Harris & Associates*

A. Your Personnel Records

Your employer is required by law to keep some tabs on you—including information on your wages and hours, workplace injuries and illnesses, tax withholding, as well as records of accrued vacation and other benefits. That information is usually gathered together in one place: your personnel file. Your file will usually contain little information you did not know or provide to your employer in the first place.

But personnel files can also become the catch-alls for other kinds of information—references from previous employers, comments from customers or clients, employee reprimands, job performance evaluations, memos of management's observations about an employee's behavior or productivity. When employment disputes develop, or an employee is demoted, transferred or fired, the innards of his or her personnel file often provide essential information—often unknown to the employee—about the whys and wherefores.

A federal law, the Privacy Act (5 U.S.C. §552a), limits the type of information that federal agencies, the military and other government employers may keep on their workers.

However, private employers have a nearly unfettered hand when it comes to the kind of information they can collect. The laws in a few states restrict the information in personnel files. Michigan, for example, bars employers from keeping records describing an employee's political associations (Mich. Stat. Ann. §17.62 (8)). And in Maryland, an employer may not ask a job applicant about psychiatric or psychological illness or treatment unless it is directly related to his or her fitness to perform a job (Md. Labor & Emp. Code §3-701).

While many states now have some type of law regulating personnel files for private employers (see the chart below), most of these laws control not the content of the files, but:

- whether and how employees and former employees can get access to their personnel files
- whether employees are entitled to copies of information in them, and
- how employees can correct erroneous information in the file.

FORCING AN EMPLOYER TO KEEP YOUR SECRETS

Employers are supposed to collect only information about you that is job-related. And only those others with a proven need to know are supposed to have access to your personnel file. For example, your employer cannot tell your co-workers the results of a drug screening test you were required to take. But the truth is that employers frequently give out information about their employees to other people—other employers, unions, police investigators, creditors, insurance agents.

Job applicants or employees who wish some personal information about themselves to remain confidential—their address and phone number, for example, if they fear physical violence at the hands of a former spouse—should request in writing that the information be kept confidential. That request may end up being worth little more than the paper it is written on. But it may also be the strongest evidence of an employer's negligence should problems develop later.

1. Getting Access to Your File

The best way to find out what a company knows about you, or what it is saying about you to outside people who inquire, is to obtain a copy of the contents of your personnel file from your current or former employer.

In some cases, the only way you would get to see those files is while collecting evidence after filing a lawsuit against the employer or former employer. And even then you might be in for a legal battle over what portions of the files are relevant to the case. But in many states, you have the right to see the contents of your personnel file without filing a lawsuit. For example, Oregon law gives employees the right to a copy of any documents an employer uses in making a workplace decision—including promotions, raises or firings. (See the chart below.)

State laws on employee access to personnel records generally cover technical matters, such as when your request must be made and how long the employer has to respond. Before you request your file, read the law on procedures for your state. In general, you must make your request to see your personnel files in writing to your employer or former employer as soon as you decide that you want to see them. If you send your request by certified mail, you will be able to prove when the request was submitted, should you need that evidence later.

If you live in a state that does not have a specific law ensuring you access to your personnel records, all is not lost. If you wish to see and copy your personnel files, you should still make that request. If you meet with resistance, make a more formal request in writing. If that request is denied, and you genuinely believe your records may contain information that is critical to your position, you may need to consult with an expert such as a private investigator or experienced attorney.

STATE LAWS ON EMPLOYEE ACCESS TO PERSONNEL RECORDS

Alabama	No statute
Alaska	Employees have the right to see their personnel files and make a copy of them. Alaska Stat. §23.10.430
Arizona	No statute
Arkansas	Employees may demand to see their own personnel and workplace evaluation records. Ark. Stat. Ann. §7-1-102
California	Employees have the right to see their personnel files and to demand a copy of any document relating to employment that they have signed. Employers must maintain a copy of the employee's personnel file where the employee reports to work, or must make the file available at that location within a reasonable time after the employee asks to see it. Cal. Lab. Code §§432 and 1198.5
Colorado	No statute
Connecticut	Employees have the right to see their personnel files and to insert rebuttals of information with which they disagree. Conn. Gen. Stat. Ann. §31-128b
Delaware	Employees have the right to see their personnel files and to insert rebuttals of information with which they disagree. Del. Code Ann. tit. 19, §§730 through 735
District of Columbia	No statute
Florida	No statute

Georgia	No statute
Hawaii	No statute
Idaho	No statute
Illinois	Employers with five or more employees must allow them to see their personnel files and to insert rebuttals of any information with which they disagree. Ill. Rev. Stat. ch. 48, §2010(c)
Indiana	No statute
Iowa	Employees have the right to see and copy personnel files, including performance evaluations and disciplinary records, but not references. Iowa Code §91B.1
Kansas	No statute
Kentucky	No statute
Louisiana	No statute
Maine	Employees have the right to see and make copies of their personnel files, including workplace evaluations. Me. Rev. Stat. Ann. title 26, §631
Maryland	No statute
Massachusetts	Employees have the right to see their personnel files and to insert rebuttals of any information with which they disagree. Employees may take court action to expunge from personnel records any information that the employer knows, or should have known, was incorrect. Mass. Gen. Laws Ann. ch. 149, §52C
Michigan	Employees have the right to see and make a copy of their personnel files and to insert rebuttals of any information with which they disagree. Mich. Comp. Laws §§423.501 through 423.512
Minnesota	Employees of employers with 20 or more employees have the right to see their personnel files and to insert rebuttals of any information with which they disagree. Does not apply to public employers. Minn. Stat. Ann. §181.960
Mississippi	No statute
Missouri	No statute
Montana	No statute
Nebraska	No statute
Nevada	Employees have the right to see and copy any records that the employer used to confirm the employee's qualifications, or as the basis for any disciplinary action. If those records contain incorrect information, the employee may notify the employer of the errors in writing. The employer is required to correct the challenged information if the employer decides it is false. Nev. Rev. Stat. §613.075

New Hampshire	Employees have the right to see and copy their personnel files and to insert rebuttals of any information with which they disagree. Does not apply if disclosure would prejudice law enforcement. N.H. Rev. Stat. §275:56
New Jersey	No statute
New Mexico	No statute
New York	No statute
North Carolina	No statute
North Dakota	No statute
Ohio	No statute
Oklahoma	No statute
Oregon	Employees have the right to see and copy any documents used by the employer in making work-related decisions, such as promotions, wage increases, or termination. Or. Rev. Stat. §652.570
Pennsylvania	Employees and their designated agents have the right to see their personnel files. The files may not be copied or removed. Pa. Cons. Stat. Ann. tit. 43, §§1321 through 1325
Rhode Island	Employees have the right to see their personnel files. The file may not be copied or removed, but the employee may request that specific documents be copied. R.I. Gen. Laws §§28-6.4-1 and 28-6.4-2
South Carolina	No statute
South Dakota	No statute
Tennessee	No statute
Texas	No statute
Utah	No statute
Vermont	No statute
Virginia	No statute
Washington	Employees have the right to see their personnel files, and to insert rebuttals of any information with which they disagree. Does not apply if employee is subject to criminal investigation or if the records have been compiled in preparation of an impending lawsuit. Wash. Rev. Code ¶49.12.240
West Virginia	No statute

Wisconsin	Employees have the right to see their personnel files, and to insert rebuttals of any information with which they disagree. Does not apply if employee is subject to a criminal investigation or to references or recommendations or to records subject to a pending claim in a judicial proceeding. Wis. Stat. §103.13
Wyoming	No statute

2. Criminal Records

According to recent statistics collected by the Bureau of Justice, approximately one-third of the workforce has a criminal record, most commonly including theft. Despite this high proportion of workers with criminal records, many feel they are approached with wariness, or even subjected to abject discrimination, by employers who learn of their histories.

The information is easily found. Arrest and conviction records are kept by a number of agencies—police, prosecutors, courts, the FBI, probation departments, prisons, parole boards.

Most states now have laws that specifically bar employers and prospective employees from getting access to records of arrests that did not lead to convictions. A number of states—including California, Maryland, Michigan and Rhode Island—forbid employers to ask job applicants about such arrests. (See the chart below.)

Still, there are many exceptions to this Don't Ask, Don't Tell rule for specific categories of workers, including most bank employees, securities industry and commodities workers, nuclear power employees and daycare workers.

The reality is that employers customarily bend and trample on the rules against asking about former arrests and convictions. And in most states, private employers can check—and are often duty-bound to check—the conviction records of prospective employees. Since most records of criminal convictions are freely open to the public, there is usually little a job applicant or employee can do to stop an employer from discovering them.[1]

---

[1]For details on how you may be able to keep employers and potential employers from getting access to your criminal records, see *The Criminal Records Book,* by Warren Siegel (Nolo Press).

STATE LAWS ON EMPLOYEE ARREST & CONVICTION RECORDS

Alabama	No statute
Alaska	No statute
Arizona	No statute
Arkansas	No statute
California	Employers may not ask prospective employees to disclose information regarding an arrest or detention which did not result in conviction. They also may not ask regarding a referral to a diversion program. Employers may not seek or utilize as a condition of employment any such information, but may inquire as to an arrest for which a current or prospective employee is out on bail or their own recognizance. Law enforcement and criminal justice agencies are exempt. Cal. Lab. Code §432.7
Colorado	Employers may not require the disclosure of sealed arrest or conviction records. Colo. Rev. Stat. §24-72-308
Connecticut	No statute
Delaware	No statute
District of Columbia	No statute
Florida	No statute
Georgia	No statute
Hawaii	No statute
Idaho	No statute
Illinois	Employers, employment agencies and labor organizations may not inquire about or use arrest information or criminal history record that has been ordered sealed or expunged as a basis to refuse to hire or take any adverse employment action against a current or prospective employee. Ill. Rev. Stat. ch. 68, §2-103
Indiana	No statute
Iowa	No statute
Kansas	No statute
Kentucky	No statute
Louisiana	No statute
Maine	No statute
Maryland	Employers or educational institutions may not require job applicant to disclose information regarding criminal charges that have been expunged. Employers may inquire about charges that either have or have not resulted in conviction or pardon. Md. Code Ann. art. 27, §740

Massachusetts	Prospective employees with sealed criminal record on file need not disclose any information regarding arrest or conviction. Mass. Gen. Laws. Ann. ch. 276, §100A
Michigan	Employers, employment agencies and labor organizations other than law enforcement agencies may not request, make or maintain information regarding arrest or detention that did not result in conviction. This does not apply to felony charges prior to conviction or dismissal. Mich. Comp. Laws §423.303
Minnesota	No statute
Mississippi	No statute
Missouri	No statute
Montana	No statute
Nebraska	No statute
Nevada	No statute
New Hampshire	No statute
New Jersey	No statute
New Mexico	No statute
New York	No statute
North Carolina	No statute
North Dakota	No statute
Ohio	Employers may not question prospective employees regarding criminal record that has been expunged. Ohio Rev. Code §2953.43
Oklahoma	Employers may not question a prospective employee in any application for employment regarding a criminal record that has been expunged. Okla. Stat. Ann. tit. 22 §19
Oregon	Employers seeking criminal offender information must first advise the current or prospective employees that such information is being sought. Or. Rev. Stat. §181.555
Pennsylvania	No statute
Rhode Island	Employers may not inquire of prospective employees whether they have ever been arrested or charged with a crime. They may ask whether they have ever been convicted. R.I. Gen. Laws §28-5-7
	Prospective employees who have had a conviction of a crime expunged may state that they have never been convicted of a crime. Law enforcement applicants are excepted. R.I. Gen. Laws §12-1.3-4
South Carolina	No statute
South Dakota	No statute

Tennessee	No statute
Texas	No statute
Utah	No statute
Vermont	No statute
Virginia	No statute
Washington	Employers may request conviction records from the state of current or prospective employees for these specified purposes only: employee bonding; pre-employment and post-employment evaluation of employees with access to money or items of value; or investigation of employee misconduct which may constitute a penal offense. Employers must notify employee or prospective employee of the inquiry and make the record available. Wa. Rev. Code §43.43
West Virginia	No statute
Wisconsin	No statute
Wyoming	No statute

CHECKING UP ON YOURSELF

The FBI is charged with maintaining complete arrest records—or rap sheets—on every individual who is arrested. It may behoove you to look at the information in your file before an employer does.

You can obtain a copy of your FBI rap sheet by writing to:

Federal Bureau of Investigation
Identification Division
Washington, DC 20537
202/324-3362

Along with your request, you must include: your name, date and place of birth and a set of rolled ink fingerprints obtainable at a local police department—along with a $17 certified check or money order payable to the United States Treasury. It will take about 20 working days to process your request.

You are allowed to correct inaccurate FBI records—although it requires substantial patience and good documentation.

3. Medical Records

Medical information about employees comes into the workplace a number of ways. It is volunteered by an employee who is calling in sick. It becomes general knowledge after filtering through the gossip mill. It is listed on the insurance application for a group policy, which your employer will likely have on file.

As a general legal rule, employers are not supposed to reveal medical information about employees unless there is a legitimate business reason to do so. Again, that nebulous standard, so often used as a fallback in workplace controversies, provides little guidance because it is so poorly defined.

If you are concerned about keeping your medical information confidential and out of the workplace limelight, you must take active steps to do so. If you confide any medical information about yourself to co-workers, ask them not to tell others. Inform all doctors who treat you that they should not reveal anything about your health or treatment to another person without getting a release, or written permission, from you first. (See Section B1 below for more on employee medical exams and records.)

4. Credit Information

This era of the computer is also the era of the ever-present personal credit rating. Credit bureaus—profit-making companies that gather and sell information about a person's credit history—have become a booming business. And the growing power and popularity of the computerized credit rating has found its way into the workplace, as well.

Many employers now use the same credit bureaus used by companies that issue credit cards and make loans to do routine credit checks on employees and job applicants. Unfortunately, there is very little you can do to prevent employers from using your personal credit bureau files in deciding whether to hire, promote or even continue to employ you.

a. Employers' access to your record

A federal law, the Fair Credit Reporting Act (15 U.S.C. §1681 and following) requires credit agencies to share their data only with those who have a legitimate business need for the information, and employers generally qualify. Employers are given broad access to an individual's credit report, which they can see to help in evaluating eligibility for "employment, promotion, reassignment or retention." In short, as far as your employer or prospective employer is concerned, your credit rating is an open book.

Credit bureaus typically track not only your bill-paying habits, but also the companies that have asked to see your credit rating as part of their job applicant screening process. The result is that credit bureaus are increasingly being used by employers to find out whether an employee is seeking a new job with other companies.

b. How to take action

There is nothing you can do to stop an employer from checking your credit, or to stop the credit bureaus from telling one employer whether other employers have checked up on you.

But you do have the right to correct any errors in credit reports compiled about you, and most experts recommend that you check and correct your file every few years.

Call the nearest office of the Federal Trade Commission, listed in the federal government section of the telephone directory, for guidance on how to correct your credit report.[2]

BEWARE OF CREDIT REPORTING SERVICES

TRW, a major credit bureau, is one of several companies that offer what they tout as credit check services. For example, TRW's $44 per year Credentials Program claims to give you unlimited access to your credit file. It sends you a copy of your credit file as often as you want, informs you every time a creditor requests a copy of your credit file and provides you with a quarterly report of negative information reported to your file.

What TRW does not tell you is that the Fair Credit Reporting Act already allows you to see your file as often as you want. You may have to pay a reasonable fee after the first time, but it will not come close to $44. Few people need to see their files more than once a year.

TRW also keeps a financial profile of you—listing your assets and liabilities including your motor vehicles, real estate and deposit accounts. But the truth is that no creditor accepts this information from a credit bureau without having you fill out a separate application.

Mostly, credit check services charge you $44 per year for a service you do not need—or could get for less money.

---

[2]For more detailed information about how credit bureaus operate and how to deal with them, see *Money Troubles,* by Robin Leonard (Nolo Press).

B. Workplace Testing

Ostensibly, prospective employers and employees want the same thing: to match the best person with the most fitting job. But these days, there are a number of tests that purport to take the guesswork out of the process. Ploughing through the Information Age, many employers are quick to welcome outside evaluations of an individual's mental and physical fitness and integrity, and to believe in their results—often at the risk of sacrificing individual privacy rights.

1. Medical Examinations

A number of insurers require employees to undergo medical evaluations before coverage will begin. Beyond that, and often in addition to that, employers may require specific physical and mental examinations to ensure a qualified workforce. However, there are strict rules on when those exams can be conducted—and on who can learn the results.

a. Examining job applicants

Employers may legally give prospective employees medical exams to make sure they are physically able to perform their jobs. However, timing is crucial. Under the federal Americans With Disabilities Act, or ADA (see Chapter 8 Section F), covered employers cannot require medical examinations before offering an individual a job. They are, however, free to make an employment offer contingent upon a person's passing a medical exam. The ADA also requires that your medical history and exam results must be kept in a file separate from your other personnel records. Only a few individuals have the right to see your medical file:

- a supervisor who needs to know whether your medical condition or health requires that you be specially accommodated within the workplace

- First Aid or medical personnel who need to administer emergency treatment, and
- government officials who are checking to be sure your employer is complying with the ADA.

During the course of a medical exam, a company-assigned doctor may ask anything at all about a person's health and medical history. However, his or her final evaluation is supposed to include only a stripped-down conclusion: able to work, able to work with restrictions, not able to work.

b. Examining existing employees

Employees can be required to take a physical or psychological examination after they are hired only if there is a reason to believe the employee is jeopardizing the health and safety of the workplace. For example, several courts have opined that if an employee clearly appears to be homicidal or suicidal, then an employer may have the duty to require a psychological exam, or even inform co-workers of the condition, in the name of workplace safety.

Again, while an examining doctor or psychologist has freer reign to ask questions as part of the examination, the final evaluation revealed to an employer is supposed to be succinct and free of detail: able to work, able to work with restrictions, not able to work.

2. Drug and Alcohol Testing

The abuse of drugs such as alcohol and cocaine has been widely publicized for many years—and many private employers now test for drug and alcohol use. The laws regulating drug abuse in the workplace and testing employees for such abuse, however, are relatively new and still being shaped by the courts. Currently, there are a hodgepodge of legal rules controlling drug testing—some in the Americans With Disabilities Act (see Chapter 8, Section F), some set out in specific state laws (see the chart below), and a number arrived at through court decisions.

Work-related drug tests can take a number of forms. Although analyzing urine samples is the method most commonly used, samples of a worker's blood, hair and breath can also be tested for the presence of alcohol or other drugs in the body.

a. Testing job applicants

In general, employers have the right to test new job applicants for traces of drugs in their systems as long as:

- the applicant knows that such testing will be part of the screening process for new employees
- the employer has already offered the applicant the job
- all applicants for the same job are tested similarly, and
- the tests are administered by a state-certified laboratory.

Today, most companies that intend to conduct drug testing on job candidates include in their job applications an agreement to submit to such testing. If, in the process of applying for a job, you are asked to agree to drug testing, you have little choice but to agree to the test or drop out as an applicant.

b. Testing existing employees

There are a number of employees who, because of their specialized positions or type of work, can be tested more freely for drugs and alcohol use. For example, the Department of Transportation requires drug testing for some critical positions, such as airline pilots. In addition, courts have routinely approved random drug testing for employees with national security clearances, prison officers, employees at chemical weapons and nuclear power plants, and police officers.

But there are some legal constraints on testing existing employees in most private employment jobs for drug usage. Companies cannot usually conduct blanket drug tests of all employees or random drug tests; the testing must usually be focused on an individual. In some cases where employers have tested for drugs without good reason, the employees affected have sued successfully for invasion of privacy and infliction of emotional harm.

However, the courts have generally ruled that companies may test for drugs among employees whose actions could clearly cause human injury or property damage if their performances were impaired by drugs, and in cases where there is good reason to think that the employees are abusing drugs. For example, a bulldozer operator who swerved the machine illogically through a field crowded with workers could probably be the legal target of drug testing.

As an employee, you can always refuse to take a workplace drug test, of course. But if you are fired because of your refusal, you may have little recourse. Your employer needs only to defend that he or she had good reason to believe that you were a safety hazard on the job, or that you seemed unable to perform the work required. You would be placed in the untenable position of proving that your employer knew no such thing. You may, however, be able to win your job back if you can show that you were treated differently than other employees in the same position.

c. State and local drug testing laws

As mentioned, a number of state courts have set out rulings defining when and why drug tests may be given. For example, a New Jersey court held in 1992 that pre-employment testing of employees is an illegal invasion of their privacy (*O'Keefe v. Passaic Valley Water Comm'n*, 602 A. 2d 760). In California, pre-employment testing was given a court's stamp of approval (*Wilkinson v. Times Mirror Corp.*, 215 Cal. App. 3d 1034 (1990)), but not random testing of employees (*Luck v. Southern Pac. RR.*, 265 Cal. App. 3d 618 (1990)).

In addition, a number of states and several municipalities have laws that regulate work-related testing for substance abuse. Many of these laws provide ways of dealing with overbroad or abusive workplace drug testing that are simpler, quicker and less expensive than filing a lawsuit. Some states also require companies to distribute to employees written policies on drug testing and rehabilitation.

Drug and alcohol testing laws vary tremendously and are changing rapidly. The best way to get up-to-date details on laws in your state is to research them at a library near you. (See Chapter 18, Section E.) Your state Labor Department may also have information on current testing laws. (See the Appendix for contact details.)

STATE DRUG AND ALCOHOL TESTING LAWS

Alabama	No statute
Alaska	No statute
Arizona	No statute
Arkansas	No statute
California	Employers with 25 or more employees must reasonably accommodate any employee who enters an alcohol or drug rehabilitation program, unless the employee's current alcohol or drug use prohibits him or her from performing work duties or doing a job safely. Cal. Lab. Code §1025
Colorado	No statute
Connecticut	Employers may require drug or alcohol test when there is a reasonable suspicion that an employee is under the influence and job performance is or could be impaired. Employers may test randomly when authorized by federal law, the employee works in a dangerous or safety-sensitive occupation, or the test is part of an employee assistance program in which participation is voluntary. Job applicants may be required to submit to test. Conn. Gen. Stat. §31-51t
Delaware	No statute
District of Columbia	No statute
Florida	Employers may test for drugs and alcohol upon reasonable suspicion that an employee is under the influence, as a pre-employment screening, during routine fitness-for-duty examinations and as a follow-up to treatment. Fla. Stat. Ann. §440.09
	Employees who voluntarily seek treatment for substance abuse cannot be fired, disciplined, or discriminated against, unless they have tested positive or have been in treatment in the past. Fla. Stat. Ann. §440.102
	State agencies may test job applicants and employees as part of routine fitness-for-duty examinations based upon a reasonable suspicion of substance abuse and as a follow-up to treatment. Fla. Stat. Ann. §112.0455

Georgia	State employees who are involved in dangerous work may be subject to random drug testing. Ga. Code Ann. §45-20-90.
Hawaii	Employers may test employees or job applicants for substance abuse as long as the following conditions are met: they pay all costs; the test is performed by a licensed laboratory; the individuals tested are given a list of the substances they are being tested for and a disclosure form for the medicines and legal drugs they are taking; and the results are kept confidential. Haw. Rev. Stat. §329B-1
Idaho	No statute
Illinois	No statute
Indiana	No statute
Iowa	Employers cannot request random drug testing of employees or require employees or job applicants to submit to a drug test as a condition of employment, pre-employment, promotion or change in employment status, except as part of a pre-employment or regularly scheduled physical examination under certain restrictions. An employer may require a specific employee to submit to a drug test if there is a reasonable suspicion that the employee's faculties are impaired on the job. Iowa Code §730.5
Kansas	No statute
Kentucky	No statute
Louisiana	Employers may require all job applicants and employees to submit to drug testing as long as certain procedural guidelines are followed and the specimens are collected with due regard for the individual's privacy. La. Rev. Stat. Ann. §49:1001
Maine	Employers may require employee to submit to a drug test when there is probable cause to believe the employee is impaired. Random testing is permitted when substance abuse might endanger co-workers or the public or when it is permitted by a union contract. Job applicants may be tested only if offered employment or placed on an eligibility roster. Me. Rev. Stat. Ann. tit. 26, §681
Maryland	Employers may require testing of employees, contractors or other people for job-related reasons for alcohol or drug abuse as long as certain procedural guidelines are followed. Md. Code Ann. Health Law §17-214
Massachusetts	No statute
Michigan	No statute

Minnesota	Employers may require employees to submit to drug or alcohol testing if there is written and posted testing policy and the test is performed by an independent licensed laboratory. Random tests may be given only to employees in "safety-sensitive" positions. Job applicants may be tested if they have been offered the job. Specific individuals may be tested when there is a reasonable suspicion that the employee is under the influence of drugs or alcohol, has violated rule against use, possession or distribution of drugs or alcohol on the job, has caused an injury or accident at work. Minn. Stat. Ann. §§181.950 to 181.957
Mississippi	Employers may require employees to submit to drug or alcohol testing if the policy is posted and certain prescribed procedures are followed. Testing is authorized when there is a reasonable suspicion that an employee is abusing drugs or alcohol. Random testing is also authorized. Employers may also test as part of routine fitness-for-duty examinations or as part of follow-up to a rehabilitation program. Job applicants may be tested if they are warned when they apply for the job. Miss. Code Ann. §71-7-3
Missouri	No statute
Montana	No person may be required to submit to a blood or urine test unless the job involves hazardous work or security, public safety, or fiduciary responsibilities. Mont. Code Ann. §39-2-304
Nebraska	Employers may require employees to submit to drug or alcohol testing unless certain screening procedures are met. Neb. Rev. Stat. §48-1901
Nevada	No statute
New Hampshire	No statute
New Jersey	No statute
New Mexico	No statute
New York	No statute
North Carolina	No statute
North Dakota	No statute
Ohio	No statute
Oklahoma	No statute
Oregon	Employers may not require any employee or job applicant to submit to any breathalyzer alcohol test unless there is a reasonable suspicion that the employee is under the influence of alcohol. Or. Rev. Stat. §659.227
	Employees may be required to be tested for drugs if the laboratory utilized is licensed by the state and certain procedural safeguards are employed. Or. Rev. Stat. §438.435

Pennsylvania	No statute
Rhode Island	Employers may require employees to submit to drug or alcohol testing when there is reason to believe that the use of controlled substances is impairing the employee's ability to do the job, the test sample is provided in private, the testing is part of a rehabilitation program, positive results are confirmed by the most accurate method available, the employee is given reasonable notice that the test will be given, and the employee is given a chance to explain the results. R.I. Gen. Laws §28-6.5-1
South Carolina	No statute
South Dakota	No statute
Tennessee	No statute
Texas	No statute
Utah	No statute
Vermont	Employers may require employees to be tested for drugs or alcohol if there is a probable cause to believe the employee is under the influence on the job, the employer provides a rehabilitation program and the employee who tests positive is given a chance to participate in the rehabilitation program rather than being fired. Employees who have already been through rehabilitation and who again test positive may be fired. Job applicants may be tested when they have been offered the job conditioned upon passing the test, they are given advance notice of the test and the test is given as part of a comprehensive physical examination. Vt. Stat. Ann. tit. 21, §511
Virginia	No statute
Washington	No statute
West Virginia	No statute
Wisconsin	No statute
Wyoming	No statute

3. Psychological Testing

A number of people who label themselves as Workplace Consultants claim they have developed series of written questions—integrity tests—that can predict whether a person would lie, steal or be unreliable if hired for a particular job. And a number of other erstwhile experts claim to have perfected personality tests that allow employers to tell in advance whether an individual is suited by temperament and talent to a particular position.

Psychological tests are not a new idea. They were first developed during World War I to help the military decide how to assign soldiers to various jobs. But legal cutbacks to personality and psychological testing in the workplace began in the 1970s, when employers were banned from questioning prospective employees about age, race or sex.

Today's pre-screening questionnaires usually cover the forbidden topics in round-about ways. For example, employers may glean information about marital and family status by asking applicants to give information about hobbies and other interests. And many employers—about one-fourth of them—use these questionnaires in the process of screening applicants for job openings. But the temptation has been curbed of late by a number of cases sending a clear warning: Psychological tests cannot be used as an excuse to discriminate against prospective employees—and they must be limited to job-related questions. Recently, these tests have been challenged as being discriminatory and as violating employees' rights of privacy.

A few states have enacted laws against some specific forms of psychological testing. In Nebraska, for example, an employer may not require an employee or a prospective employee to submit to a truth and deception exam unless the position involves law enforcement (Neb. Rev. Stat. §81-1901). And in New York, employees may not require that job applicants or employees take psychological stress evaluator tests (N.Y. Lab. Law §§733 to 739).

TARGET LEARNS WHAT NOT TO ASK

The first major case to challenge psychological testing of job applicants recently yielded grand results: a $2 million dollar settlement and a five-year ban on testing.

The settlement came in July 1993, in a class action brought by several people who had applied to the Target Stores chain for work as security guards. As part of the application process, they were asked to respond to over 700 true/false statements including:

- I am very strongly attracted by members of my own sex.
- I have never indulged in unusual sex practices.
- I believe my sins are unpardonable.
- I believe in the second coming of Christ.
- I have had no difficulty starting or holding my urine.

According to one of the attorneys representing the job applicants, about 30% of the 2,500 test takers did not get jobs with Target—either because of the answers they gave or because the results were deemed to be inconclusive. The applicants challenged the test as violating their privacy rights and the state Labor Code, which bans questions about sexual orientation.

They will now share in the $2 million in wealth Target has lost.

4. Lie Detector Tests

For decades, lie detectors, or polygraphs, that purport to measure the truthfulness of a person's statements by tracking bodily functions such as blood pressure and perspiration were routinely used on employees and job applicants.

Employers could—and often did—ask employees and prospective employees questions about extremely private matters such as sexual preferences, toilet habits and family finances while a polygraph machine passed judgment on the truthfulness of the answers. Push the machine's needle too far by reacting to an offensive question and you could be labeled a liar and denied employment.

In 1988, the federal Employee Polygraph Protection Act (29 U.S.C. §2001) virtually outlawed using lie detectors in connection with employment. That law covers all private employers in interstate commerce, which includes just about every private company that uses the U.S. mail or the telephone system to send messages to someone in another state.

Under the Act, it is illegal for all private companies to:

- require, request, suggest or cause any employee or job applicant to submit to a lie detector test
- use, accept, refer to or inquire about the results of any lie detector test conducted on an employee or job applicant, or
- dismiss, discipline, discriminate against or even threaten to take action against any employee or job applicant who refuses to take a lie detector test.

The law also prohibits employers from discriminating against or firing those who use its protections.

a. When lie detector tests can be used

The Employee Polygraph Protection Act allows polygraph tests to be used in connection with jobs in security and handling drugs, or in investigating a specific theft or other suspected crime. However, before you can be required to take such a test as part of an investigation of an employment-related crime, you must be given a written notice stating that you are a suspect at least 48 hours before the test is given. And there must be a provable, reasonable suspicion that you were involved in the theft or other conduct triggering the investigation.

The Act does not apply to employees of federal, state or local government, nor to certain jobs that handle sensitive work relating to national defense.

b. Limitations on the tests

In addition to the strict strictures on when and to whom the tests may be given, there are a number of restrictions on the format of the tests. Before a lie detector test can be administered, your employer must read to you and ask you to sign a statement that includes:

- a list of topics you cannot be asked about, including questions on religious beliefs, sexual preference and political affiliation
- the information that you have the right to refuse to take the test
- the fact that you cannot be required to take the test as a condition of employment
- an explanation of how the test results can be used, and
- an explanation of your legal rights if the test is not given in keeping with the law.

c. How to take action

The Employee Polygraph Protection Act is enforced by the U.S. Department of Labor. If you have questions about whether the Act applies to your job or if you suspect that you have been subjected to illegal polygraph testing, call the office of the U.S. Labor Department's Wage and Hour Division nearest you. It is listed in the federal government section of the telephone directory under Labor Department.

There is no official form for filing a complaint. If, after discussing your situation with a Wage and Hour Division investigator, you decide to file a complaint, do so as soon as possible by writing a letter addressed to your local Wage and Hour Division office. Include such details as the name and address of the employer, when the incident occurred and the address and telephone number where an investigator can reach you. And keep a copy of your letter for your records.

SAMPLE LETTER

October 31, 199X

Wage and Hour Division
U.S. Department of Labor
1234 Main Street
Anycity, USA 34567

Dear Sir or Madam:

As authorized by 29 U.S.C. §2001, the Employee Polygraph Protection Act, I am filing a complaint against the Dine and Dash Restaurant, located at 732 South Street, Anycity, USA.

I had been employed as a cook at Dine and Dash for four-and-one-half years. But this morning, I was told by the restaurant's owner, Henry Hash, that all my co-workers and I would have to take a lie detector test this afternoon because he wants to make sure than none of us eat into his profits by snacking on the job and taking home food.

Because I refused to take the test, I was fired. I will be glad to cooperate in your investigation of this complaint.

Sincerely,

Joe Chef
1244 Linton Lane
Anycity, USA 34567

If the Labor Department finds that your rights under the Act were violated, it can fine the employer up to $10,000 and issue an injunction ordering the employer to reinstate you to your job, promote you, compensate you for back wages, hire you or take other logical action to correct the violation.

If the Labor Department's action on your complaint does not satisfy you, you can file a lawsuit against the employer to obtain whatever compensation or other remedy would be appropriate. Move quickly, because the lawsuit must be filed within three years. You will probably need to hire an attorney to help you if you decide to file a lawsuit under this Act. (See Chapter 18, Section D.) But the law allows the court to grant you attorneys' fees and other costs if you win.

d. State laws on lie detector tests

Some states have laws prohibiting or restricting employers from using lie detectors in connection with employment, but most have been made obsolete by the federal anti-polygraph statute.

However, a few states enforce stricter penalties against employers who illegally use polygraphs than are available under federal law. In New York, for example, an employer who uses polygraph tests illegally may be convicted of a misdemeanor and sentenced to up to one year in jail (N.Y. Lab. Law 189 §§733 to 739).

Some states have also expanded anti-polygraph laws to cover other types of tests that probe bodily functions in connection with employment. For example, it is illegal for employers in Oregon to require employees to submit to brainwave testing (Or. Rev. Stat. §659.227).

STATE LIE DETECTOR TESTING LAWS	
Alabama	No statute
Alaska	Employers cannot require an applicant or employee to submit to a polygraph or lie detection test as condition of employment. Current or prospective police officers are excepted. Alaska Stat. §23.10.037
Arizona	No statute
Arkansas	No statute

California	Employers cannot require employees or applicants to submit to lie detector tests as a condition of employment. Does not apply to public employers. Does not prohibit voluntary testing as long as rights are explained in writing. Cal. Lab. Code §432.2
Colorado	No statute
Connecticut	Employers may not request or require employees or applicants to take a polygraph exam as a condition of employment or dismiss or discipline them for refusing to take the test. Not applicable to police departments except for civilian employees. Conn. Gen. Stat. Ann. §31-51g
Delaware	Employers may not require employees or applicants to submit to a lie detector test and may not fire or discriminate against them for refusing to submit to such a test. Del. Code Ann. tit. 19, §704e
District of Columbia	Employers may not request or require an employee or applicant to submit to a polygraph or any lie detector test as a condition of employment. Does not apply to law enforcement agencies. D.C. Code Ann. §§36-801 to 803
Florida	No statute
Georgia	No statute
Hawaii	Employers cannot require an employee or applicant to submit to lie detector test as a condition of employment. Employers may not terminate or otherwise discriminate against an employee or applicant for refusing to submit to an exam. Does not prohibit voluntary testing as long as the right of refusal is explained in writing. Does not apply to law enforcement agencies. Hawaii Rev. Stat. §378.26.5
Idaho	Employers cannot require employees to take lie detector tests as a condition of employment. Idaho Code §44-903
Illinois	No statute
Indiana	No statute
Iowa	Employers may not request, require or administer a lie detection test as a condition of new or continued employment. Does not apply to law enforcement or corrections agencies. Iowa Code §730.4
Kansas	No statute
Kentucky	No statute
Louisiana	No statute
Maine	Employers cannot request, require, administer or suggest that an employee or applicant submit to a lie detection test as condition employment. Me. Rev. Stat. Ann. title 32, §7166

Maryland	Employers cannot demand or require an employee or applicant to submit to a lie detector test as a condition of employment. Does not apply to law enforcement and correctional agencies. Md. Ann. Code art. 100, §95
Massachusetts	Employers cannot require or request an employee or applicant, including police officers, to submit to a lie detector test as a condition of employment. Employers cannot fire or discriminate against them for refusing to take such a test. Mass. Gen. Laws Ann. ch. 149, §19B
Michigan	Employers cannot require employees or applicants to submit to a polygraph examination as a condition of employment. An employee or applicant may voluntarily request a polygraph examination and, if this is the case, the employer may administer it. Mich. Comp. Laws §§37.201 to 32.209
Minnesota	Employers may not request or require polygraph or any test purporting to test an employee's or applicant's honesty as a condition of employment. Minn. Stat. Ann. §181.75
Mississippi	No statute
Missouri	No statute
Montana	Employers may not require employee to submit to a polygraph or any mechanical lie detection test. Mont. Code §39-2-304
Nebraska	No statute
Nevada	Employers may not request or require employee or prospective employee to take a lie detector test. Employers cannot fire, discipline, discriminate or threaten based on results. Nev. Rev. Stat. §613.447
New Hampshire	No statute
New Jersey	Employers cannot request or require an employee or prospective employee to submit to a lie detector test. N.J. Stat. Ann. §2C:4A-1
New Mexico	No statute
New York	No statute
North Carolina	No statute
North Dakota	No statute
Ohio	No statute
Oklahoma	No statute
Oregon	Employers cannot require lie detector tests (Or. Rev. Stat. §§659.225 and 659.227), although law does not prohibit voluntary administration during a civil or criminal proceeding.

Pennsylvania	Employers cannot require employees or applicants to take lie detector tests as a condition of employment. Does not apply to law enforcement or to dispensers of narcotic or dangerous drugs. Pa. Cons. Stat. Ann. tit. 18, §7507
Rhode Island	Employers cannot request, require or subject any employee to a lie detector test. Written examinations are allowed as long as results are not the primary basis of an employment decision. Does not apply to law enforcement agencies. R.I. Gen. Laws §§28-6.1-1 to 28-6.1-4
South Carolina	Employers may ask employees and applicants to take lie detector tests, but submission must be voluntary. S.C. Code Ann. §40-53-60
South Dakota	No statute
Tennessee	Employers may require employee or applicant to submit to a polygraph test, but no personnel action may be based solely on the results. Tenn. Code Ann. §62-27-128
Texas	No statute
Utah	Employers cannot fire employee for refusing to take a lie detection test. Employers cannot administer such a test without the subject knowing it. Utah Code Ann. §34-37-16
Vermont	Employers cannot request, require or administer a polygraph examination to an employee or applicant, nor fire or discriminate against them, for refusing to submit to such a test. Does not apply to law enforcement agencies and sellers of drugs or precious metals or gems. Vt. Stat. Ann. tit. 494a; 494b
Virginia	No statute
Washington	Employers cannot request or require an employee or applicant to submit to a lie detector test as condition of employment or continued employment. Employers cannot fire, discipline or discriminate in any way for refusal to take such an exam. Wash. Rev. Code Ann. §§49.44.120 to 49.44.135
West Virginia	Employers may not request or require an employee or applicant to submit to a lie detector test as a condition of employment. Employers cannot fire or discriminate against an employee or applicant for refusing to submit to such a test. Lie detector tests are prohibited. W. Va. Code §§21-5-5a to 21-5-5d
Wisconsin	Employers cannot request or require an employee or applicant to submit to a lie detection test as a condition of employment. Employers cannot fire or discriminate against employee or applicant for refusing to submit to such a test. Does not apply to an employee who is suspected of involvement in theft, em-

bezzlement or damage to employer's property, security-type personnel, or manufacturers and sellers of controlled substances. Wisc. Stat. Ann. §111.37

Wyoming   No statute

LEGAL ACTIONS AGAINST PRIVACY VIOLATIONS

There are specific laws that forbid employers from trampling on your right to privacy. However, your most powerful weapon is to file a lawsuit against your employer claiming invasion of privacy. And the most likely way to win such a case is to show that in the process of collecting information on you, the employer was guilty of one or more of the following.

Deception. Your employer asked you to submit to a routine medical examination, for example, but mentioned nothing about a drug test. However, the urine sample that you gave to the examining physician was analyzed for drug traces, and because drugs were found in your urine, you were fired.

Violation of confidentiality. Your employer asked you to fill in a health questionnaire and assured you that the information would be held in confidence for the company's use only. But you later found out that the health information was divulged to a prospective employer that inquired about you.

Secret, intrusive monitoring. Installing visible video cameras above a supermarket's cash registers would usually be considered a legitimate method of ensuring that employees are not stealing from the company. But installing hidden video cameras above the stalls in an employee restroom would probably qualify as an invasion of privacy in all but the highest security jobs.

Intrusion on your private life. Your employer hired a private detective, for example, to monitor where you go in the evening when you're not at work. When the company discovered that you are active in a gay rights organization, you were told to resign from that group or risk losing your job.

5. AIDS Testing

The disease of Acquired Immune Deficiency Syndrome (AIDS) was first identified in 1981. Fairly early on, researchers isolated its viral cause, Human Immunodeficiency Virus (HIV), which suppresses the immune systems of those who carry it, making them easy targets for various other infections and diseases. But beyond that, no great strides have been made in treating AIDS symptoms, or in finding a cure. Many of those who have the HIV infection live a decade or more, nearly symptom-free. But ultimately, the disease is fatal—and spreading fast.

The impact on American workplaces has been, and will continue to be, enormous. Not only have hundreds of thousands of workers died, most of them suffered also from the reactions of others—irrational fear and ostracism—known as the tandem to the AIDS plague: AFRAIDS.

Many workplaces responded to the hysteria with more hysteria, developing intrusive policies of isolating workers suspected to have the disease. (See Chapter 8, Section G for a discussion of discrimination against HIV- and AIDS-infected workers.)

Another offshoot of this hysteria is the practice of testing employees for the HIV virus. While a number of courts have struck down state and local efforts to screen employees for HIV, the practice continues.

a. About AIDS tests

Although medical researchers may develop more methods of testing for the HIV virus, the test first approved for commercial use by the Food and Drug Administration in 1985 is still in use today. Basically, the test measures antibodies in the blood that are stimulated by the HIV virus. If a test is positive, indicating exposure to the deadly virus, a confirmation test is usually performed, which uses a more complicated system of weighing molecular weights found in the blood.

Importantly, there are a number of things the HIV antibody testing does not indicate.

Tests do not identify people who have AIDS. AIDS is defined by the Center for Disease Control (CDC), and the definition is still evolving. Currently, an individual is considered to have AIDS if he or she: has any of the 26 AIDS-related diseases specified by the CDC, and has a T-count—or infection-fighting white corpuscles—of less than 200 in a cubic milliliter of blood.

Also, tests do not identify all blood containing the AIDS virus. The tests are aimed at measuring the antibodies stimulated by HIV, so they do not work effectively on individuals who have been exposed to the virus but have not developed antibodies to it—a period which usually takes about eight weeks, but may take up to a year or more.

OF PLAGUES AND PINSTRIPES: AIDS IN CORPORATE AMERICA

More than a third of major American corporations report dealing with cases of HIV infection or AIDS. From 1991 to 1993, the rate of increase in companies reporting such cases was 58%.

Companies Reporting Cases of HIV Infection or AIDS, by Type of Business

Manufacturer	26.8%
All services	44.7
Wholesale/retail	55.3
Financial services	53.0
Business/professional	23.7
General services	48.9
Public administration	30.0

Source: American Management Association, 1993 Survey on HIV and AIDS-Related Policies

---

b. Legal controls on testing

Originally, HIV blood tests were fashioned to screen blood, not people. But when prospective employees and employees are subjected to testing, the reality is that people are being screened—and sometimes labeled to be unfit workers.

A federal law, the Americans With Disabilities Act (see Chapter 8, Section F), prohibits testing job applicants to screen out people with HIV or AIDS. Once an applicant is offered a job, however, the legal constraints on testing become a bit murkier. To avoid singling out any individual or group, which would be illegal discrimination, an employer would have to test all employees. Even then, to justify giving employees an HIV test, an employer would have to show that the test is necessary to determine fitness to hold a job. This would be nearly an impossible task, as many people infected with HIV show no symptoms of ill health at all.

States are in the infancy of enacting laws regulating employers' uses of HIV tests. Alabama, California, Florida, Hawaii, Iowa, Maine, Massachusetts, Minnesota, Montana, New Jersey, New Mexico, Vermont, Washington and Wisconsin all have laws setting some bounds on employers.

Wisconsin's law is the most restrictive and the most comprehensive, with an interesting qualifier. That law provides that unless the state epidemiologist and Secretary of Health and Social Services declare that individuals with HIV infections provide a "significant risk" of transmitting it to others in the workplace, employers are prohibited from:

• soliciting or requiring as a condition of employment that any employee or applicant take an antibody test

• affecting the terms, conditions, or privileges of employment or terminating the employment of any employee who obtains an antibody test, and

• entering an agreement with an employee or applicant for any pay or benefit in return for taking an antibody test (Wis. Stat. Ann. §103.152a and b).

Test results may not be used to determine suitability for insurance coverage or employment according to the laws in California (Cal. Health & Safety Code §§199.21f) and Florida (Fla. Stat. §381.6065). And Massachusetts bans employers from requiring employees to take a test as a condition of employment (Mass. Gen. Laws ch. 111, §70f).

In addition, a number of cities have enacted ordinances that put additional limits on how and when employers may test for HIV and AIDS. A strict law in San Francisco, for example, states that employers cannot test for AIDS unless they can show that the absence of AIDS is an essential employment qualification (San Francisco Police Code §§3801-16).

This area of the law is changing very rapidly. Doublecheck your local, state and federal law for recent changes. A local clinic, support group or AIDS hotline may also be able to provide you the most up-to-date local information. A number of organizations also offer information on the HIV virus, AIDS and resources on AIDS in the workplace. (See the Appendix for organization contact details.)

C. Surveillance and Monitoring

We long ago arrived at the place we long feared: where technological advances have made it easy for Big Brother to watch us. Most employers cannot properly be painted as paranoid Peeping Toms. And the law does require that most workplace monitoring—listening in on telephone calls, audiotaping or videotaping conversations—must have some legitimate business purpose. Other than that, however, there are very few federal legal controls protecting workers from being watched in the workplace.

Sometimes, states set their own bounds. For example, several states—including Connecticut, Georgia, Ohio, Virginia and Wisconsin—have laws that specifically restrict searches and surveillance of employees, and some of them are quite powerful.

In Connecticut, for example, an employer that repeatedly uses electronic devices such as video cameras or audio tape recorders to monitor employees in restrooms, locker rooms or lounges can be charged criminally and sentenced to jail for 30 days (Conn. Gen. Stat. §31-48b 1987).

1. Telephone Calls

In general, it is legal for employers to monitor business-related telephone calls to and from their own premises—for example, to evaluate the quality of customer service. However, a federal law, the Omnibus Crime Control and Safe Streets Act (18 U.S.C. §§2510 to 2520), states that even if a call is being monitored for business reasons, which is perfectly legal, if a personal call comes in, an employer must hang up as soon as it realizes the call is personal. An employer may monitor a personal call only if an employee knows the particular call is being monitored—and he or she consents to it.

Some state laws have additional twists, requiring for example, that not only the employee but the person on the other end of the phone must know about and consent to the call being monitored.

2. Mail

Whether an employer has the right to expect privacy in the mail he or she receives at work depends for the most part on company custom and policy. In most workplaces, one or more individuals routinely sort and distribute the mail—and most mailings related to work matters range from the boring to the mundane. An employer may inadvertently, or even purposely, open most such mail without incurring any legal liability.

However, sometimes mail arrives addressed to an individual worker that is also marked "Personal" or "Confidential"—or sometimes with the overkilling warning "Personal and Confidential." An employer who opens such mail, or directs or sanctions another person in the workplace to do so, must usually have a compelling business reason to open it. If the employer cannot demonstrate a compelling reason—that there was important, time-sensitive business information in the envelope, for example, and the employee to whom it was addressed was on a month-long vacation—then the employer may be guilty of invading the addressee's privacy.

3. Computer Files

Nearly every workplace in America today conducts some part of its business on computers, and many have become slavish to the machines. While they are hailed by many as timesavers and efficiency-makers, computers have lent a new murkiness to workplace privacy laws. It is unclear whether the files an employee creates on a workplace computer—or the electronic mail written and read on it—has any legal protection from others' snooping eyes.

Some employers have attempted to clear up the question of what is and is not considered private about workplace computers by writing specific policies spelling out that employees are forbidden from using one another's computers. In other places, employers have established elaborate password systems for employees to use to log on to computers and store files on them. It is still unclear, however, whether either of these approaches will create an expectation of privacy in an employee's work computer that will be given credence by the courts.

4. Audiotaping and Videotaping

As the number of lawsuits over workplace disputes has grown, so has an alarming trend: Employers and employees intent on bolstering their claims have begun to record one another in the hope of capturing some wrongdoing on tape. There are a number of legal and practical problems with this approach to evidence gathering, however.

Federal law appears to allow any person involved in a conversation to tape it without the other person's knowledge or permission—as long as the recording is not made for the purpose of committing a crime, such as extortion. A number of state laws, however, have much stricter controls—generally requiring that everyone involved must consent before a conversation or an action can be taped.

Although our guts might tell us the opposite, audiotapes and videotapes also have questionable value as trial evidence. Before any jury would be allowed to hear or see a tape of a workplace scene, it must pass muster of many picky rules set out to qualify and disqualify trial evidence.

Also, in reality, tapes rarely run to script. They often come out garbled or unclear. And they rarely hold up well out of context. What may feel like a damning conversation in which your boss blatantly admits you were fired because of your age may sound very different to those who do not know your boss or you.

D. Searches and Seizures

Most employers would claim a strong motivation to keep workplaces free of illegal drugs, alcohol and weapons. And most employees would claim that they have a right to expect that their personal belongings will remain safe from the groping hands of their employers.

The legal truth lies somewhere between. Employers are generally free to search through an employee's personal items kept at work—unless the employee logically expects that the spot in which those items are stored is completely private.

However, an employer who searches an employee's private belongings such as a purse, briefcase, pockets or car must usually meet a higher standard and have a compelling reason to do so—such as the belief that work property is being stolen and hidden inside.

Example: *Thomas sold household appliances for a department store that provides each employee with a storage cabinet for personal belongings in a room adjacent to the employee lounge. The store's employee manual states that although the company does not provide locks for the cabinets and does not take responsibility for any thefts from the storage area, employees may bring in a lock of their own to secure their individual cabinet.*

One day while at work, Thomas was called to the manager's office, where he was confronted with a letter that had been written to him from his drug rehabilitation counselor. The manager said the letter had been found in his storage cabinet during a routine search by the company's security force, and that he was being fired because he had a history of drug abuse.

Thomas could likely win an invasion of privacy lawsuit against his former employer because, by allowing him to use his own lock to secure his cabinet, the department store had given him a logical expectation of privacy for anything kept in that cabinet. His claim would be somewhat weaker if his former employer had furnished the locks and doled out the keys or combinations to them.

Another fact that weighs heavily in determining whether an employer's search is legal is its reasonableness in terms of length and scope. For example, an employer who suspected an employee of stealing foot-long copper piping might be justified in searching his or her work locker, but not purse or pockets.

E. Clothing and Grooming Codes

In general, employers have the right to dictate on-the-job standards for clothing and grooming as a condition of employment. Codes governing employees' appearance may be illegal, however, if they result in a pattern of illegal discrimination against a particular group of employees or potential employees. This type of violation has most often arisen in companies with different codes for male and female employees.

1. Dress Codes

Many companies have policies about uniforms to keep their employees looking uniform—a legal goal. There is nothing inherently illegal, for example, about a company requiring all employees to wear navy blue slacks during working hours.

Many employers provide workers with some or all of the clothing that they are required to wear on the job. A few companies even rent suits for their employees to assure that they will be similarly dressed. Although generally legal, such systems can violate your rights if the cost of the clothing is deducted from your pay in violation of the Fair Labor Standards Act (FLSA).

For example, it is illegal under the FLSA for an employer to deduct the cost of work-related clothing from your pay so that your wages dip below the minimum wage standard, or so that the employer profits on the clothing. For details on the FLSA and how to file a complaint under it, see Chapter 3.

And sometimes, the legal lines on dress restrictions become blurry. Courts have held, for example, that an employer cannot require female employees to wear uniforms if it allows male employees to wear street clothes on the job. And some differences that seem to be gender-based— such as barring men from wearing earrings but allowing them for women— have been allowed to stand. The courts reason that the differences in dress codes are not discriminatory if they do not put an unfair burden on one gender or the other.

2. Grooming Codes

Most workplace grooming codes simply require that employees must be clean and presentable on the job—a reasonable request. And such codes are rarely challenged.

However, several lawsuits challenging workplace grooming codes have been waged by black men with Pseudofollicullitis Barbae, a race-specific skin disorder making it difficult to shave. Several individuals have successfully challenged companies that refuse to hire men with beards or that fire men who do not comply with no-beard rules.

Example: *Nelson, a black man, was advised by his physician not to shave his facial hair too closely because that would cause his whiskers to become ingrown and infected. Although Nelson took with him to a job interview a note from his doctor attesting to this problem, he was turned down for employment because the company where he had applied had a no-beard policy.*

Nelson filed a complaint against the company under his state's anti-discrimination laws on the basis of racial discrimination. Medical experts testified in his case that the condition which prevented Nelson from shaving usually affected only black men.

The court ruled in Nelson's favor, saying that the company's failure to lift its ban on beards despite Nelson's well-documented medical problem resulted in illegal workplace discrimination against black men. (See Chapter 8 for details on discrimination laws.)

F. Conduct Codes

Some employers have fashioned comprehensive behavior codes for their employees, setting out the bounds of workplace behavior they consider Professional. The dictate that gets caught in many workers' craws is the prohibition against dating others in the workplace, sometimes quaintly referred to as fraternizing.

These days, that attempted control usually flies in the face of reality. Workplace experts posit that as many as 70% of all male and female workers have either dated or married someone they met in the workplace. Those are far better odds than you have of meeting someone at a bar, party or other social gathering specifically engineered to be a meeting place.

But courts have been painfully slow to recognize the social reality of today's workplaces. During the last decade, employees have been fired for having extra-marital affairs, for attending an out-of-town convention with someone other than a spouse, for dating co-workers. There are no clear guidelines but common sense. Where that fails, and an employer's demands truly seem unreasonable, there may be no alternative but a lawsuit for invasion of privacy.

A KISS WAS NOT JUST A KISS

Employees have just begun to fight back against codes they consider to damper and hamper their social lives. In July 1993, a New York couple, Laural Allen and Samuel Johnson, sued the nation's largest retailer, Wal-Mart, after it fired them both for dating one another.

Allen was separated but not yet divorced from her husband when she and Johnson began dating. Wal-Mart lawyers defend that the couple's behavior clearly violated the company handbook reiterating the importance of family values.

Allen and Johnson sought $2 million each, claiming Wal-Mart discharged them wrongfully—and caused them emotional distress in the process.

A number of employers have adopted strict policies prohibiting supervisors from dating people they supervise. While this may be understandable given the relatively low legal threshold for a supervisor's conduct to be considered sexual harassment, it is as unnecessary as it is impossible to enforce. (See Chapter 9.) Far better to remember that since workplace harassment is almost always about an abuse of power—not about romance gone sour—the focus should be on preventing intimidation. ■

CHAPTER

7

HEALTH AND SAFETY

Workers in the past 20 years have pushed strongly for laws to protect their health and safety on the job. And they have been successful. Several laws, notably the Occupational Safety and Health Act (OSHA), now establish basic safety standards aimed at reducing the number of illnesses, injuries and deaths in workplaces. Since most workplace safety laws rely for their effectiveness on employees who are willing to report on the job hazards, most laws also prevent employers from firing or discriminating against employees who report unsafe conditions to proper authorities.

Some of the currently contested workplace health and safety issues are spillovers mirroring our own life choices, such as the debate between workers who smoke and those demanding protection from illnesses caused by secondhand smoke. As more employees establish nonsmoking workplaces, a growing number of states have passed laws prohibiting discrimination against smokers.

A. The Occupational Safety and Health Act

The main federal law covering threats to workplace safety is the Occupational Safety and Health Act of 1970 or OSHA (29 U.S.C. §§651 to 678). That law created the Occupational Safety and Health Administration (also called OSHA), under the U.S. Department of Labor to enforce workplace safety, and the National Institute for Occupational Safety and Health (NIOSH) to research ways to increase workplace safety. (See the Appendix for contact details.)

OSHA broadly requires employers to provide a safe workplace for employees—one that is free of dangers that could physically harm those who work there. The law implements this directive by requiring employers to train employees about potential hazards and to keep records of workplace injuries.

Sometimes, workplace dangers are caught and corrected during unannounced inspections by OSHA. But the vast majority of OSHA's actions against workplace hazards are initiated by complaints from employees or labor unions representing them.

STATE OSHA LAWS

About half the states now have their own OSHA laws. The legal requirements for workplace health and safety in the state laws are generally similar to the federal law. In some cases, the state laws are more strict. (See Section D, below.)

---

1. Who Is Covered

Unlike many other laws which cover only companies with a minimum number of employees, OSHA covers nearly all private employers engaged in interstate commerce. By today's standards, that includes nearly every employer that uses the U.S. Postal Service to send messages to other states, or makes telephone calls to other states. Independent contractors (see Chapter 2, Section A) are not specifically covered by the law. Farms owned and operated by a family are the only significant private employers exempted from OSHA coverage.

2. OSHA Requirements

The Occupational Safety and Health Act requires all private employers to maintain a workplace that is as safe and healthy for employees as is reasonably possible.

Safety regulations are usually concerned with preventing a one-time injury—falling from an unsafe ladder or tripping on an irregular walkway, for example.

The Act's health concerns are in preventing employee illnesses related to potential health dangers in the workplace—toxic fumes, for example, and cumulative trauma such as carpal tunnel syndrome. (See Chapter 13, Section B, for more about carpal tunnel syndrome.)

The law quite simply, but frustratingly, requires that employers protect workers from "recognized hazards." It does not specify or limit the types of dangers covered, so hazards ranging from things that cause simple cuts and bruises to the unhealthy effects of long-term exposure to some types of radiation are covered.

Basically, to prove an OSHA violation, you must produce evidence that:

- your employer failed to keep the workplace free of a hazard, and
- the particular hazard was recognized as being likely to cause death or serious physical injury.

Under OSHA, the definition of a workplace is not limited to the inside of an office or factory. The Act requires that work conditions be safe no matter where the work is performed—even where the workplace is an open field or a moving vehicle.

In addition to the general duty to maintain a safe workplace, employers are required to meet OSHA's safety standards for their specific industries. Depending on the types of hazards and workplaces involved, the employer's responsibility for creating and maintaining a healthy and safe workplace can include such diverse things as informing workers about potentially hazardous substances and labeling them, upgrading or removing machinery that poses a danger, providing employees with special breathing apparatus to keep dust created by a manufacturing process from entering workers' lungs, improving lighting above work areas, providing emergency exits and fire protection systems, vaccinating against diseases that can be contracted at work, or even tracking the effects of workplace conditions on employees' health through periodic medical examinations.

THE DUTY TO POST

OSHA requires employers to display a poster explaining workers' rights to a safe workplace in a conspicuous spot. If the workplace is outdoors, the poster must be displayed where employees are most likely to see it—such as a trailer at a construction site where workers use a timeclock to punch in and out.

These posters are supplied to employers by OSHA and commercial publishers. An employer's failure to display such posters is in itself a violation of OSHA rules.

3. Injury and Illness Reports

Within 48 hours of any workplace accident that results in the death of a worker or requires hospitalization of four or more workers, employers must report complete details to OSHA, including names of injured workers, the time and place of the accident, nature of the injuries and any type of machinery involved in the accident. All employees and former employees must be given access to this report upon request.

Companies employing ten or more people must also keep records of work-related injuries and illness among workers that have caused death or days off work, and post a report on those injuries and illnesses.

THE SAD FATE OF ASBESTOS WORKERS

Workers who have been injured or killed by exposure to the mineral asbestos form a special group of injured workers whose rights are being trampled and exploited by the legal system.

Used primarily as a fire retardant, asbestos causes cancer and several other types of serious illness—including a general weakening of the immune system. The symptoms of asbestos-caused illness often take decades to appear, so many people were routinely exposed to it until the connection between illness and asbestos was established in recent years.

An estimated 3.5 million American workers have been dangerously exposed to asbestos in the workplace, and more than 250,000 of them are expected to die of asbestos-caused illnesses by the year 2015. On average, more than a thousand asbestos-related personal injury suits are filed each month, but many of the plaintiffs die before their lawsuits conclude.

All this litigation has benefited lawyers—and others who make their livings off of lawyers—more than it has the victims of asbestos. For example, in 1991, a committee of federal judges estimated that out of every dollar awarded to asbestos victims who successfully sue their former employers and other parties involved in their exposure to asbestos, only 39 cents ever reaches the plaintiffs. The rest goes to lawyers, physicians, other expert witnesses and related costs.

In one case involving only four plaintiffs, the number of lawyers involved reached a high of 58 at one point in the case—and always involved at least 41 lawyers.

Nevertheless, if you are afflicted with an asbestos-related illness, it is better to pursue your rights than to do nothing at all. If you suspect that you have been exposed to asbestos in the course of your work, get more information by contacting Asbestos Victims of America at 408/476-3646.

B. Enforcing OSHA Rights

If you believe that your workplace is unsafe, your first action should be to make your supervisor at work aware of the danger as soon as possible. If your employer has designated a particular person or department as responsible for workplace safety, inform the appropriate person of the danger.

In general, your complaint will get more attention if it is presented on behalf of a group of employees who all see the situation as a safety threat. And an employer who becomes angry over a safety complaint is much less likely to retaliate against a group of employees than against an individual. (See Section B6.)

1. Filing a Complaint

If you have not been successful in getting your company to correct a workplace safety hazard, you can file a complaint at the nearest OSHA office. Look under the U.S. Labor Department in the federal government section of your local telephone directory.

You can request the proper complaint forms from any OSHA office. You also have the option of telephoning your complaint to your nearest OSHA office, where a compliance officer will complete the paperwork and then send you the completed version for your approval and signature.

If requested to do so, OSHA must keep confidential your identity and that of any other employees involved in the complaint. If you want your identity to be kept secret, be sure to check the section on the complaint form that states: "Do not reveal my name to the employer."

Once you have completed your complaint form, file it with the nearest OSHA office. You can do this in person, but if you send it in by certified mail, you will have proof that OSHA received it should it get mislaid in OSHA's offices. Keep a photocopy of your completed complaint form for your own files.

Upon receiving your complaint, OSHA will assign a compliance officer to investigate your case. The compliance officer will likely talk with you and your employer and inspect the work conditions that you have reported.

PREVENTING ADDITIONAL INJURIES

Workplace hazards often become obvious only after they cause an injury. For example, an unguarded machine part that spins at high speed may not seem dangerous until someone's clothing or hair becomes caught in it. But even after a worker has been injured, employers sometimes fail—or even refuse—to recognize that something that hurt one person is likely to hurt another.

   If you have been injured at work by a hazard that should be eliminated before it injures someone else, take the following steps as quickly as possible after obtaining the proper medical treatment.

- File a claim for workers' compensation benefits so that your medical bills will be paid and you will be compensated for your lost wages and injury. (See Chapter 13.) Workers' compensation claims can cost a company a lot of money, so they tend to quickly focus an employer's attention on safety problems. In addition, in some states, the amount you receive from a workers' comp claim will be larger if a violation of a state workplace safety law contributed to your injury.
- Point out to your employer the continuing hazard created by the cause of your injury. As with most workplace safety complaints, the odds of getting action will be greater if you can organize a group of employees to do this.
- If your employer does not eliminate the hazard promptly, file a complaint with OSHA and any state or local agency that you think may be able to help.

2. How Complaints Are Resolved

A compliance officer who finds that the condition about which you complained poses an immediate danger to you and your co-workers can order your employer to immediately remove the danger from the workplace—or order the workers to leave the dangerous environment.

Where the danger is particularly urgent or the employer has a record of violations, OSHA may get tough by asking the courts to issue an injunction—a court order requiring the employer to eliminate workplace hazards.

Example: *A group of pipeline workers complained to OSHA that the earth walls of the excavation in which they were working were not well supported and could collapse on them. The OSHA compliance officer tried unsuccessfully to talk the employer into improving the situation. OSHA obtained a court injunction forbidding work to continue within the excavation until the walls were shored up with steel supports.*

If the danger is less immediate, the compliance officer will file a formal report on your complaint with the director of OSHA for your region. If the facts gathered by the compliance officer support your complaint, the regional director may issue a citation to your employer.

The citation will specify what work conditions must be changed to ensure safety of the employees, the timetable that OSHA is allowing for those changes to be made—usually known as an abatement plan—and any fines that have been levied against your employer.

Example: *Leslie is a machine operator in an old woodworking shop that is still using lathes that throw a large quantity of wood dust into the air inside the shop. The wood dust appeared to be a hazard to the employees who breath it, and Leslie was unsuccessful in resolving the problem with the shop's owner. She filed a complaint with OSHA.*

OSHA studied the air pollution in the shop and agreed that it was a threat to workers' health. It ordered the shop's owner to install enclosures on the lathes to cut down on the amount of dust put into the air, and filter-equipped fans throughout the shop to capture any wood dust that escapes from the enclosures. Because the lathe enclosures and fans needed to be custom-designed and installed, OSHA allowed the shop's owner six months to correct the situation.

In the meantime, OSHA ordered the shop's owner to immediately provide Leslie and all the other people employed there with dust-filtering masks to wear over their mouths and noses. However, since OSHA regulations generally require employers to make the workplace safe and not just protect workers from an unsafe work situation, the masks are considered merely a temporary part of the long-term abatement plan.

> ### THE IMPORTANCE OF BEING SPECIFIC
>
> Like many other government agencies, OSHA is a huge bureaucracy that operates on computerized file numbers. The best way to get prompt service and accurate information from OSHA is to be as specific as possible. In your dealings with OSHA, be sure to mention the name of the company, the department of that company, the number assigned to the complaint that you are tracking and the date on which it was filed.

3. Contesting an Abatement Plan

You have the right to contest an abatement plan granted to your employer by OSHA to correct a workplace hazard—for example, if you feel the plan is insufficient. To do so, send a letter expressing your intent to contest the plan to your local OSHA director within 15 days after the OSHA citation and announcement of the plan is posted in your workplace. You need not list specific reasons for contesting the plan in this letter; all you need to make clear is that you think the plan is unreasonable.

There is likely to be strength in numbers here. If other employees feel the abatement plan is unfair or insufficient, encourage them to register their protests with OSHA as well.

After it receives your letter, OSHA will refer the case to the Occupational Safety and Health Review Commission in Washington, DC, an agency independent of OSHA. That commission will then send your employer a notice that the abatement plan is being contested.

This notice also will order the employer to post in the workplace an announcement that the plan is being contested. It will also require the employer to send a form that certifies the date on which that announcement was made back to the commission—with copies to OSHA, to you and to other employees who have contested the plan.

Then, everyone involved in the case has ten days from the date the employer posted the contest notice to file an explanation of their viewpoints on the abatement plan with the commission. Copies must also be sent to all others involved in the case.

SAMPLE LETTER

April 10, 199X

Ms. Mary Official
Regional Director
Occupational Safety and Health Administration
321 Main Street
Anycity, USA 12345

Dear Ms. Official:

As allowed by 29 U.S.C. Section 659(e), I wish to contest the abatement plan agreed to by your agency and my employer, the Oldtime Mousetrap Company. This abatement program resulted from a complaint that I filed with your office on April 3, 199X. That complaint was assigned number A-123456 by your office.

I contest this agreement because I believe that it is unreasonable.

Sincerely,

Elmer Springmaker
456 Central Road
Anycity, USA 12340
123/555-5555

4. Administrative Review

When negotiations to reach a resolution are unsuccessful, the commission submits the case to an administrative law judge. These proceedings usually take several months—and sometimes years—depending upon the complexity of the workplace hazards involved.

Hearings before administrative law judges are very much like any other trial. Much time and money can be consumed in gathering evidence, and the hearings are usually scheduled during daytime hours when most employees are at work. You will probably have to hire a lawyer to help if you decide to pursue your safety complaint successfully at this level. (See Chapter 18, Section D.)

You also have the right to appeal a decision by an administrative law judge for the Occupational Health and Safety Review Commission to the full commission or in federal court, but you will probably have to hire a lawyer to help you at these levels, as well.

5. Walking Off the Job

OSHA gives you the right to refuse to continue doing your job in extreme circumstances that represent an immediate and substantial danger to your personal safety.

You cannot walk off the job and be protected by OSHA in just any workplace safety dispute—and this tactic cannot be used to protest general working conditions. But OSHA rules give you the right to walk off the job without being later discriminated against by your employer if the situation fits any of the following definitions of a true workplace safety emergency.

- You asked your employer to eliminate the hazard and your request was ignored or denied. To protect your rights, it would be best to tell more than one supervisor about the hazard, or to call the danger to the attention of the same supervisor at least twice—preferably in front of witnesses.

TIPS ON PRESENTING YOUR VIEWS

The explanation you file on the abatement plan need not be elaborate. It should be as clear, brief and precise as possible. For example, if you have made a list of employee injuries that have already resulted from the hazard in your workplace, list the date, time, location and identity of the worker injured for each incident in your explanation.

Your explanation need not be typewritten, but your odds of communicating your viewpoint effectively will be increased if it is easy to read. If you do not have access to a typewriter or computer, consider having your explanation typed by a commercial typing service. You can usually find them in the Yellow Pages of your local telephone directory.

Send your explanation by certified mail to:

Executive Secretary
Occupational Safety and Health Review Commission
1825 K Street, NW; Room 413
Washington, DC 20006

Be sure to include a cover letter—and to specify in it the name of the company involved, the number assigned to the case by the review commission and OSHA, your mailing address and telephone number. Send a copy to the OSHA office where you filed your original complaint, to your employer and to any people identified in the paperwork the commission sent to you as parties in the case. Also, be sure to save a copy of your cover letter, your explanation and any supporting documents that you send with it for your personal files.

After it has gathered all the statements on the case, the commission will typically turn them over to U.S. Labor Department lawyers who will attempt to meet with everyone who submitted statements and negotiate a resolution that is agreeable to all. The commission tries to negotiate settlements whenever possible, and by this point everyone involved will have had an opportunity to read and think about each other's viewpoints. So the odds are that your complaint will be resolved at this stage.

- You did not have time to pursue normal OSHA enforcement channels. In most cases, this means that the danger must be something that came up suddenly, and is not a safety threat that you allowed to go unchallenged for days, weeks or months.
- Staying on the job would make a reasonable person believe that he or she faced a threat of serious personal injury or death because of the workplace hazard. If the hazard is something that you can simply stay away from—such as a malfunctioning machine in a work area that you do not have to enter—it probably would not qualify as creating an emergency.
- You had no other reasonable choice but to walk off the job to avoid injury.

Example: *Mike is a welder in a truck building plant. Shortly after starting work one day, he noticed that a large electrical cable running along the plant's ceiling had broken overnight, was coming loose from the hardware attaching it to the ceiling, and was dangling closer and closer to the plant floor. He and several of his co-workers immediately told their supervisor about the broken cable, but the supervisor did nothing about it. The group also told the supervisor's boss about the danger, but still nothing was done to correct it.*

By about 11 a.m., the broken cable had dropped to the point where it was brushing against the truck body that Mike was welding. Sparks flew each time the cable and the truck body touched. Because he had a reasonable fear that an electrical shock transmitted from the broken cable could seriously injure or kill him, Mike walked off the job. His supervisor fired him for leaving work without permission. But because the danger fit OSHA's definitions of an emergency, OSHA ordered the company to reinstate Mike to his job with back wages—after first repairing the broken and dangling cable.

If you use the extreme option of walking off a job because of a safety hazard, be sure to contact your nearest OSHA office as soon as you are out of danger. Make a note of the name of the OSHA officer you with whom you spoke—and also note the time that you reported the hazard. That way, you will protect your right to be paid back wages and other losses from the time that the hazard forced you to walk away from work.

> **TRACKING OSHA ACTIONS**
>
> Any citation issued by OSHA must be posted in a conspicuous place within the workplace it affects for at least three days. If the hazard specified in the citation is not corrected within three days after the citation is issued, then the citation must remain posted until it is corrected.
>
> Compliance officers are required to advise those who originally filed a complaint of the action taken on it. If you need more information about the outcome of an OSHA investigation that affects your workplace, call, write or visit your local OSHA office.
>
> If OSHA has given your employer an extended time to remedy a workplace hazard, then you also have a right to request a copy of that abatement plan from your employer. Your other recourse is to obtain a copy from the OSHA compliance officer who handled your complaint.

6. Penalties for Retaliation

Under OSHA, it is illegal for an employer to fire or otherwise discriminate against you for filing an OSHA complaint or participating in an OSHA investigation. OSHA can order an employer who violates this rule to return you to your job and to reimburse you for damages including lost wages, the value of lost benefit coverages and the cost of searching for a new job. Some state laws also protect against retaliation for reporting workplace health and safety violations. (See Section D, below.)

HOW TO FIGHT BACK AGAINST RETALIATION

It is illegal for an employer to fire you or otherwise discriminate against you because you filed an OSHA complaint or assisted in investigating such a complaint. However, the Act does not authorize you to enforce this restriction by going directly into court; you must ask OSHA to intercede.

If you suspect illegal retaliation, you have 30 days from the time the illegal action took place to file a complaint about it with your local OSHA office. The outcome of illegal discrimination complaints filed under OSHA often turns on whether an employee can prove that interacting with OSHA was the reason for firing or other retaliation by the employer. So be sure to back up your complaint with as much documentation for your employer's action as possible. (For details on how to document a dismissal, see Chapter 10, Section C.)

Once you have filed a complaint about illegal job discrimination, OSHA has 90 days to respond. If you have shown that you were fired or otherwise punished because of complaining to OSHA, the compliance officer handling your complaint will attempt to convince your employer to reinstate you to your job with back pay, or whatever other remedy is appropriate.

For example, if you were demoted in retaliation for your OSHA complaint, the OSHA compliance officer would probably ask your employer to reinstate you to your original position. If OSHA is unsuccessful in talking your employer into reversing the effects of the illegal discrimination, it can sue your employer in federal court on your behalf.

C. Criminal Actions for OSHA Violations

As noted, the enforcement arm of OSHA has the power in some situations to pursue criminal prosecutions against employers who fail to maintain a safe workplace, but it rarely does.

However, state prosecutors increasingly are bringing criminal charges such as reckless endangerment and even murder against employers whose behavior seriously endangers workers. This trend was given a boost in 1990 when the New York Court of Appeals ruled that complaints under the Occupational Safety and Health Act do not take the place of criminal actions against employers whose actions cause workers to be injured or killed. Other state courts have ruled differently, however, so the issue may need to be resolved ultimately by the U.S. Supreme Court.

In the meantime, you may want to contact your state's attorney general about the possibility of criminal action if your work conditions pose a serious threat of injury or death to you or your co-workers and you are not able to resolve your concerns through OSHA or other civil actions.

CONVICTIONS RARE IN WORKPLACE DEATH CASES

Although employers can be prosecuted for criminal negligence when an employee dies as a result of violations of OSHA regulations, such convictions are rare. In fact, from 1970 to 1990, only one employer was convicted and sent to jail for such a death.

The main reason for this low conviction rate is that, under OSHA, prosecutors must prove that an employer's violation of workplace safety rules was willful—that is, done on purpose—a subjective standard.

For example, in 1985, a 23-year-old Massachusetts college student who was working a parttime construction job died from electrocution when he grabbed a chain to steer a piece of pipe into a trench. The arm of the backhoe that was holding the chain and pipe aloft had come into contact with a high voltage electrical cable.

OSHA requires that construction equipment such as that backhoe be operated no less than ten feet from live electrical lines. What's more, other workers at the construction site told police investigators that they had warned the employer earlier on the day of the accident to keep the backhoe arm away from the overhead wires. So the employer, who had been operating the backhoe at the time of the electrocution, was charged with criminal negligence.

Nevertheless, the employer was acquitted by a federal jury after a two-day trial because the jury decided that his actions leading to the electrocution were not, in fact, willful.

D. State and Local Health and Safety Laws

Many states and municipalities have laws that can help to ensure a certain level of safety in the workplace. In 1991, California began enforcing the most powerful of these laws: It requires every employer in the state to have a written plan to prevent workplace injuries. State health and safety laws vary greatly in what they require, how they are enforced and even which employers they cover.

1. State OSHA Laws

Nearly half the states now have their own OSHA laws—most with protections for workers that are similar to those provided in the federal law. For example, employers in some low hazard industries, such as retailers and insurance companies with less than ten employees, are exempt from some posting and reporting requirements. Most state laws cover all small employers, regardless of the type of business.

The following states have some form of an occupational health and safety law approved by OSHA: Alaska, Arizona, California, Connecticut, Hawaii, Indiana, Iowa, Kentucky, Maryland, Michigan, Minnesota, Nevada, New Mexico, New York, North Carolina, Oregon, South Carolina, Tennessee, Utah, Vermont, Virginia, Washington and Wyoming.

A number of states are presently considering passing OSHA laws—and many of the states that already have such laws are considering wholesale amendments changing their coverage and content. So check your state's particulars with a local OSHA office—or call the state department of labor to check whether your state has enacted an OSHA law recently. (See the Appendix for contact details.)

A number of state laws specifically forbid employers from firing employees who assert their rights under workplace health and safety rules. (See the chart below.) Alabama is a good example of this. It has one law prohibiting employers from firing employees for filing a written notice of an intentional violation of an employer's specific written safety rule. And another Alabama law bars firing employees for making a report, providing information, filing a lawsuit, or giving testimony in any lawsuit brought under the Toxic Substances in the Workplace statute.

Still another group of state laws extend beyond the workplace to protect employees who report violations of laws and rules that create a specific danger to public health and safety. These laws, commonly referred to as whistleblower statutes, generally protect good eggs—individuals who are attempting to uphold a public policy of the state. For example, typical whistleblower statutes prohibit employees from being fired for reporting toxic dumping or fraudulent use of government funds. (See Chapter 11, Section B for an extensive discussion of these laws.)

STATE HEALTH AND SAFETY LAWS

Alabama	Employees may not be fired for filing a written notice of an intentional violation of an employer's specific written safety rule. Ala. Code §25-5-11.1
	Employees cannot be fired for making a report, providing information, filing a lawsuit, or giving testimony in any lawsuit brought under the Toxic Substances in the Workplace statute. Ala. Code §22-33-1
Alaska	Employees may not be fired or discriminated against for filing a complaint or testifying in any proceeding under the Occupational Safety and Health Act. Alaska Stat. §18.60.089
Arizona	Employers may not discriminate against employees because they have filed complaints about or given testimony in a proceeding about violations of state workplace safety rules. Ariz. Rev. Stat. Ann. §23-425
	Employees may not be fired for filing a complaint or testifying under statutes regulating the control of pesticides. Ariz. Rev. Stat. Ann. §3-376
	Employees cannot be fired for making a complaint regarding workplace health or safety conditions to the Industrial Commission. Ariz. Rev. Stat. Ann. §23-425
Arkansas	No statute
California	Employees cannot be fired for reporting safety violations in the workplace. Cal. Lab. Code §§6310 and 6311
Colorado	No statute

Connecticut	Employees may not be disciplined in any manner for reporting violations of state Occupational Health and Safety laws. Conn. Gen. Stat. Ann. §31-40d
Delaware	No statute
District of Columbia	Employees are protected for disclosing unsafe or unhealthy working conditions. D.C. Code Ann. §1-621.5
Florida	Employees cannot be fired or threatened to be fired for exercising rights under Occupational Safety and Health Act regarding toxic substances. Fla. Stat. §442.116
Georgia	No statute
Hawaii	Employees cannot be fired for reporting Occupational Safety and Health violations or testifying regarding such a violation. Hawaii Rev. Stat. §396-8e
Idaho	Employees cannot be fired or discriminated against for participating in proceedings under the Farm Labor Sanitary Protection Act. Idaho Code §44-1904
Illinois	Employees cannot be fired for assisting in the enforcement of the state's Toxic Substances Act regarding toxic chemical exposure in the workplace. Ill. Ann. Stat. ch. 48, §1414
Indiana	Employees may not be fired for filing a complaint under Occupational Health and Safety Act. Ind. Code Ann. §22-8-1.1-38.1
Iowa	Employees cannot be fired for filing a complaint or participating in a proceeding for violation of Occupational Safety and Health laws. Iowa Code §88.93
Kansas	Employees may not be fired or discriminated against for disclosing information regarding a violation of Occupational Safety and Health laws. Kan. Stat. Ann. §44-636
Kentucky	Employees cannot be fired for exercising rights under an Occupational Safety and Health claim. Ky. Rev. Stat. §338.121
Louisiana	Employees are protected from reprisal for reporting violations of environmental laws or regulations of state, federal or local authorities. La. Rev. Stat. Ann. §30:2027
Maine	Employees cannot be fired for taking action in compliance with state health and safety law (Me. Rev. Stat. Ann. title 26, §570) or assisting in the enforcement of the Toxic Substances Act regarding exposure to toxic substances in the workplace. Me. Rev. Stat. Ann. title 26, §1723
Maryland	Employee cannot be fired for filing an action or complaint under Occupational Safety and Health Act. Md. Ann. Code art. 89, §43

Massachusetts	Employees may not be fired for exercising rights under Toxic Substances law regarding exposure to toxic substances in the workplace. Mass. Gen. Laws Ann. ch. 111F, §13
Michigan	No statute
Minnesota	Employees cannot be fired for being involved in an Occupational Health and Safety case. Minn. Stat. Ann. §182.654
Mississippi	No statute
Missouri	No statute
Montana	Community Hazardous Chemical Information Act prohibits firing or adversely acting against employee who exercises rights under the Act regarding exposure to toxic substances in the workplace. Mont. Code Ann. §50-78-204
Nebraska	No statute
Nevada	Employees may not be fired because of safety and health complaints. Nev. Rev. Stat. §618.445
New Hampshire	Employees cannot be fired for filing complaint or exercising rights under Worker's Right to Know Act regarding toxic substances in the workplace. N.H. Rev. Stat. Ann. §§277-A:7
New Jersey	No statute
New Mexico	Employees cannot be fired because of safety and health complaints. N.M. Stat. Ann. §50-9-25
New York	Employers cannot fire public employees because of Occupational Safety and Health complaints. N.Y. Lab. Law §27-a
North Carolina	Employees cannot be fired for making safety or health complaint under the Hazardous Chemicals Right to Know Act (N.C. Gen. Stat. §95-196) regarding exposure to toxic substances in the workplace or the Occupational Safety and Health Act. N.C. Gen. Stat. §95-1308
North Dakota	No statute
Ohio	No statute
Oklahoma	No statute
Oregon	Employees cannot be fired for reporting safety or health violation in the workplace. Or. Rev. Stat. §654.062
Pennsylvania	Employer may not fire employee for filing a health and safety complaint (Pa. Cons. Stat. Ann. tit. 35, §7313), or exercising rights under Community and Worker Right to Know Act regarding hazardous substances in the workplace.

Rhode Island	Private and public employees are protected for reporting violation of laws regarding toxic waste. R.I. Gen. Laws §§36-15-1 to 36-15-10
	Employees may not be fired for making a complaint regarding toxic substance in the workplace. R.I. Gen. Laws §28-21-8
	Employers may not fire employees for health and safety complaints. R.I. Gen. Laws §28-20-21
South Carolina	Employees may not be fired for making safety and health complaints. S.C. Code Ann. §41-15-510
South Dakota	No statute
Tennessee	Employees may not be fired for making safety and health complaints under Occupational Safety and Health law. Tenn. Code Ann. §50-3-106(7)
Texas	Employees cannot be fired for making Occupational Safety and Health complaints or for exercising rights under Hazard Communication Act regarding toxic substances in the workplace. Tex. Rev. Civ. Stat. Ann. art. 5182b
Utah	Employees cannot be fired for making an Occupational Safety and Health complaint. Utah Code Ann. §35-9-11
Vermont	Employees cannot be fired for making safety and health complaints. Vt. Stat. Ann. tit. 21, §231 and 232
Virginia	Employees cannot be fired for making Occupational Health and Safety complaints. Va. Code §40.1-51.2:1
Washington	Employers cannot fire employees for making a complaint about workplace safety and health under the Worker and Community Right to Know Act (Wash. Rev. Code Ann. §49.70.110) regarding exposure to toxic substances or the Occupational Safety and Health law. Wash. Rev. Code Ann. §49.17.160
West Virginia	No statute
Wisconsin	Employers cannot fire employees for reporting safety and health conditions in the workplace. Wis. Stat. Ann. §101.595
Wyoming	Employers cannot fire employees for reporting safety and health conditions in the workplace. Wyo. Stat. §27-11-109

2. Sanitation Laws

Often, state and local health and building codes offer quick and easy guidance in how to keep your workplace safe. While not intended specifically to ensure workplace safety, these laws often include programs designed to ensure sanitation and public safety in general.

For example, the health department of the city in which you work probably has the power to order an employer to improve restroom facilities that are leaking and causing unsanitary workplace conditions. And your local building inspector typically can order an employer to straighten out faulty electrical wiring that presents a shock or fire hazard to people working near that wiring.

You can usually research state and local health and building codes at your city hall or county courthouse.

E. Tobacco Smoke and the Workplace

OSHA rules apply to tobacco smoke only in the most rare and extreme circumstances, such as when contaminants created by a manufacturing process combine with tobacco smoke to create a dangerous workplace air supply that fails OSHA standards. Workplace air quality standards and measurement techniques are so technical that typically only OSHA agents or consultants who specialize in environmental testing are able to determine when the air quality falls below allowable limits.

But the torturous effects of tobacco smoke on human health have been clearly established and even certified by the government. A recent report by the Environmental Protection Agency, for example, estimated that second-hand tobacco smoke kills about 3,700 Americans per year. And many estimates put the number at several times that amount. So people who smoke cigarettes, cigars or pipes at work are increasingly finding themselves to be an unwelcomed minority—and many employers already take actions to control when and where smoking is allowed.

For example, a recent survey by *Industry Week* magazine found that nearly three-fourths of the 6,000 companies questioned had established a policy that either prohibits smoking in the workplace or restricts it to designated areas that nonsmokers can avoid. And about 15% of the companies surveyed that still did not have a nonsmoking policy were considering adopting one.

The legal issues surrounding tobacco smoke in the workplace are unsettled. Airline flight attendants have secured some indirect protection from secondhand smoke in their workplace from Federal Aviation Administration restrictions on in-flight smoking by passengers. And although there is no federal law that directly controls smoking at work, most states have laws restricting smoking in the workplace. In addition, 400 city and county ordinances restrict smoking in the workplace, but only a handful, including San Francisco, ban it outright. (See the Appendix for contact details for organizations with current information on laws that restrict smoking in your workplace.)

In contrast, about half the states make it illegal to discriminate against employees or potential employees because they smoke during non-working hours. (See the chart in Section E3). And because it has much encouragement and financial support from the tobacco industry, this smokers' rights movement appears to be gaining strength.

So this ongoing legal battle boils down to a question of what is more important: one person's right to preserve health by avoiding co-workers' tobacco smoke, or another's right to smoke without the interference of others.

1. Taking Individual Action

If your health problems are severely aggravated by co-workers' smoking, there are a number of steps you can take.

- *Ask your employer for an accommodation.* Successful accommodations to smoke-sensitive workers have included installing additional ventilation systems, restricting smoking areas to outside or special rooms, and segregating smokers and nonsmokers.

   Example: *Carmelita's sinus problems were made almost unbearable by the smoke created by the people who work with her in an insurance claims processing office. Since her job involves primarily individual work on a computer terminal and no contact with people outside the company, Carmelita convinced her employer to allow her to start her workday at 4 p.m., just an hour before her co-workers leave for home.*

   When Carmelita needs to discuss something with co-workers or her supervisor, she does so via electronic mail or at occasional one-hour staff meetings that begin at 4 p.m.—and at which smoking is not allowed.

- *Check local and state laws.* As mentioned, a growing number of local and state laws prohibit smoking in the workplace. Most of them also set out specific procedures for pursuing complaints. If you are unable to locate local legal prohibitions on smoking, check with a national smokers' rights group. (See the Appendix for contact details.)

- *Consider filing a federal complaint.* While OSHA is handling an increasing number of smoking injuries, most claims for injuries caused by second-hand smoke in the workplace are pressed and processed under the Americans With Disabilities Act. (See Chapter 8, Section F.) In the strongest complaints, workers were able to prove that smoke sensitivity rendered them handicapped in that they were unable to perform a major life activity: breathing freely.

- *Consider income replacement programs.* If you are unable to work out a plan to resolve a serious problem with workplace smoke, you may be forced to leave the workplace. But you may qualify for workers' compensation or unemployment insurance benefits. (For details on unemployment insurance and workers' compensation benefits, see Chapters 12 and 13.)

Example: *Albert has suffered various problems with breathing since birth. The insurance agency where he has worked for five years has no policy on smoking, and his state has no law restricting smoking in the workplace. Albert has complained repeatedly to the management that the smoke-filled air in the office has often caused him to suffer spells of coughing and dizziness.*

One day several of his co-workers puffed up a thick cloud of cigarette smoke, and Albert suffered a particularly bad bout of coughing and dizziness. An ambulance had to be called to take him for emergency medical attention.

Albert's physician advised him that he would be risking serious, permanent damage to his health if he returned to the smoky environment of his job. Albert was able to qualify for unemployment insurance benefits while he looked for a new job, because the cause of his unemployment was beyond his control.

2. Nonsmoking Policies

Because of the potentially higher costs of healthcare insurance, absenteeism, unemployment insurance and workers' compensation insurance associated with employees who smoke, many companies now refuse to hire anyone who admits to being a smoker on a job application or in pre-hiring interviews.

The sentiment against smoking in the workplace and any other space shared with others has grown so strong that many companies now increase their attractiveness to jobseekers by mentioning that they maintain a smoke-free workplace in Help Wanted advertising.

Except in the states that forbid work-related discrimination against smokers and the states where it is illegal for employers to discriminate against employers on the basis of any legal activities during nonwork time (see Section E3), there is nothing to prevent employers from establishing a policy of hiring and employing only nonsmokers.

3. Smokers' Rights Laws

At least eighteen states have laws that prohibit employers from discriminating against smokers. They include: Arizona, Connecticut, District of Columbia, Indiana, Kentucky, Louisiana, Maine, Mississippi, New Hampshire, New Jersey, New Mexico, Oklahoma, Oregon, Rhode Island, South Carolina, South Dakota, Virginia (applies to public employees only) and West Virginia.

Seven states have laws that prohibit employers from discriminating against people on the basis of engaging in any legal activity during nonwork hours. They are: Colorado, Nevada, New York, North Carolina, North Dakota, Tennessee (excludes alcoholic beverages) and Wisconsin.

F. Pesticide Laws

Misused and overused pesticides are one of the greatest safety threats to people who work on farms, in other parts of the food industry and in gardening and lawncare companies, to name just a few. Heavy exposure to some of these chemicals can cause serious health problems and even death. For people with certain types of allergies, even small doses of some pesticides can cause severe illness.

However, in 1975, a federal court ruled that the U.S. Environmental Protection Agency (EPA)—not OSHA—is responsible for making sure that workers are not injured by exposure to pesticides at work (*Organized Migrants in Community Action, Inc. v. Brennan*, 520 F. 2d 1161).

There have been some disputes between the EPA and OSHA over this ruling in recent years—and the question of enforcement responsibility remains unsettled. So if you believe that you or your co-workers are being exposed to dangerous doses of pesticides at work, the best thing to do is to file complaints with both OSHA and the EPA—and let them decide which agency controls your workplace. To find the nearest EPA office, look in the U.S. Government section of the white pages of the telephone book.

G. Hazardous Substances Laws

Most states now have laws that restrict or regulate the use, storage and handling of hazardous substances in the workplace. These laws vary greatly from state to state, and the identification of toxic and otherwise hazardous substances is a very technical matter that most often is the responsibility of the state's labor department.

In some cases, workers detect that they are being exposed to hazardous substance when one or more of them notices that a health problem—a skin rash or eye irritation are common examples—coincides with work hours.

If you think that you are being subjected to hazardous substances in your workplace, follow your complaint to OSHA with a call to your state's labor department. (See the Appendix for contact details.)

Example: *Hanchung took a job as a forklift driver in a metal plating plant. After his first few hours at work, his eyes began to water and became badly reddened. On the way home from work, Hanchung visited a walk-in medical clinic, where the doctor used a cotton swab to take samples of skin residues from his face. A few days later, the doctor told Hanchung that his problem with his eyes was a reaction to sulfuric acid that apparently was in the air where he worked, and had settled on his skin and eyes.*

Hanchung filed a complaint with OSHA and his state's labor department. As a result of the joint investigation, OSHA ordered his employer to construct an enclosure around processing areas that use sulfuric acid, and to provide Hanchung and his co-workers with protective clothing to wear at work while the enclosures were being built.

WORKERS' GREATEST HEALTH THREAT: STRESS

All the evidence points to stress as the most widespread threat to physical well-being in the modern workplace. For example, the Bureau of National Affairs—a business research organization in Washington, DC—has estimated that as many as one million Americans are absent from work on any given day as a result of stress related to their jobs.

According to the National Safe Workplace Institute, a workplace research group, long-term exposure to work-related stress can cause heart attacks, migraine headaches, decreased immunity to viruses, depression, sleep and appetite disorders, high blood pressure and various muscle pains. The job factors most likely to cause such stress, according to the Institute, are repetitive and boring work, excessive monitoring by management, fear of death or injury on the job, sexual harassment, insufficient control over your work situation, lack of recognition for work accomplished, an overly large workload, fear of losing your job or being demoted, insufficient use of your workplace skills and lack of support from supervisors and co-workers.

The courts have been inconsistent in deciding whether employees can file lawsuits for personal injury caused by workplace stress. But in many states, illness caused by work-related stress can be the basis for a workers' compensation claim. (See Chapter 13.) ■

CHAPTER

8

ILLEGAL
DISCRIMINATION

It is almost always illegal for employers to discriminate against workers because of their race, skin color, gender, religious beliefs, national origin, physical handicap—or age, if the employee is at least 40 years old. In most situations, it is also illegal for employers to discriminate against workers on the basis of factors such as testing positive for the HIV virus or being pregnant, divorced, gay or lesbian.

The most powerful anti-discrimination law governing the workplace is Title VII of the federal Civil Rights Act of 1964. It originally outlawed discrimination based on race, skin color, religious beliefs or national origin, and it created the Equal Employment Opportunity Commission (EEOC) to administer and enforce the legal standards it set. (See Section A.)

Today, a number of additional federal laws—several of them amendments to Title VII—are used to fight unfair workplace discrimination.

- The Equal Pay Act of 1963 specifically outlaws discrimination in wages on the basis of gender. (See Section C.)
- The Age Discrimination in Employment Act (ADEA) was passed in 1967 to also outlaw workplace discrimination on the basis of age. The ADEA itself has been amended several times, and now applies only to employees who are at least 40 years old. (See Section D.)
- The Older Workers Benefit Protection Act, enacted in 1990, is an amendment to the ADEA that specifically outlaws discrimination in employment benefit programs on the basis of employees' age, and it too applies only to employees age 40 and older. It also deters employers' use of waivers in which employees sign away their rights to take legal action against age-based discrimination. (See Section E.)
- The Pregnancy Discrimination Act (PDA), which makes it illegal for an employer to refuse to hire a pregnant woman, to terminate her employment or to compel her to take maternity leave, was passed in 1978 as an additional amendment to Title VII. (See Chapter 5, Section C for more on family and medical leaves.)
- In 1986, in *Meritor Savings Bank v. Vinson,* the U.S. Supreme Court held that Title VII also protects against sexual harassment, another form of illegal workplace discrimination. (See Chapter 9.)

- The Americans With Disabilities Act (ADA), enacted in 1990, makes it illegal to discriminate against people because of their physical or mental disability. (See Section F.)
- The Labor Relations Act and amendments, passed as a patchwork of protections, generally make it illegal to discriminate against workers for belonging or refusing to belong to a labor union. (See Chapter 6.)

A. Title VII of the Civil Rights Act

Most of the workplace laws that broadly protect employees against discrimination in the workplace have been enacted through the years as amendments to the Civil Rights Act, also known as Title VII (42 U.S.C. §2000 and following).

1. Who Is Covered

Title VII applies to all companies and labor unions with 15 or more employees. It also governs employment agencies, state and local governments and apprenticeship programs.

Title VII does not cover:

- federal government employees; special procedures have been established to enforce anti-discrimination laws for them, and

- independent contractors (discussed in detail in Chapter 2, Section A).

2. Illegal Discrimination

Under Title VII, employers may not intentionally use race, skin color, age— if at least 40—gender, religious beliefs or national origin as the basis for decisions on hirings, promotions, dismissals, pay raises, benefits, work assignments, leaves of absence or just about any other aspect of employment. Title VII covers everything about the employment relationship—from pre-hiring ads to working conditions, to performance reviews, to giving post-employment references.

3. Remedies Available

There are a number of remedies that the courts or the EEOC can provide under Title VII to an employee who suffers the effects of discrimination on the job.

Reinstatement and promotion. A court can order that the employee be rehired, promoted or reassigned to whatever job was lost because of the discrimination.

Wages and job-connected losses. A court can award any salary and benefits the employee lost as a result of being fired, demoted or forced to quit because of discrimination. This can include loss of wages, pension contributions, medical benefits, overtime pay, bonuses, back pay, shift differential pay, vacation pay and participation in a company profit-sharing plan.

Money damages (limited amount). A court can award damages to compensate for personal injuries. This can include money to cover the actual amount of out-of-pocket losses, such as medical expenses. It can also include other compensatory and punitive damages, but the amount of such damages is limited to between $50,000 and $300,000—depending on the number of people employed by the business.

Injunctive relief. A court can direct the company to change its policies to stop discrimination and to prevent similar incidents in the future.

Attorneys' fees. If the employee wins a case, a court can order the company to pay attorneys' fees.

AFFIRMATIVE ACTION: REQUIRED DISCRIMINATION

Title VII also allows for formal programs, generally known as affirmative action, which intentionally discriminate in employment decisions to counterbalance the effects of past illegal discrimination against a particular group.

For example, companies with records of nondiverse employee rolls are sometimes required by court order to abide by a racial ratio for new hires—such as one black employee hired for every two white employees hired—until the company's workforce resembles the racial mix of the community.

Affirmative action programs often generate resentment among employees who are not members of minority groups—usually white males—who see the programs as blocking their paths to improved employment opportunities. But since lawsuits challenging affirmative action rarely succeeded, very little of that resentment found its way into court until 1989.

What changed the prospects of such lawsuits that year was a U.S. Supreme Court decision in a case involving a court-approved affirmative action program at the Birmingham, Alabama, Fire Department. The court ruled that a person injured by an affirmative action program may file a lawsuit in federal court challenging the legality of that program (*Martin v. Wilks*, 490 U.S. 755). Since then, a number of lawsuits challenging affirmative action programs have been filed and reopened.

---

4. Filing a Complaint With the EEOC

Compared to most other government agencies, the EEOC has very well-defined procedures for filing complaints. But the EEOC also operates through a complex hierarchy of offices and has strict time limits for filing complaints. Pay particular attention to timing if you decide to take action against what you believe is illegal workplace discrimination.

a. Where to file

Title VII complaints can be filed at:

- Local Equal Employment Opportunity agency offices. These are not federal offices, but agencies that have been designated as representatives of the EEOC. (See Chapter 9, Section C for contact information.)
- State and regional offices of the EEOC. (See the listing below.)

There are EEOC offices throughout the United States. Normally, it is best to file a complaint at the office nearest to you or your place of employment. But if there is no office nearby or in your state, you can legally file a complaint in any office. For assistance in locating the nearest office, call 800/669-3362.

EEOC DISTRICT OFFICES

Alabama	Birmingham District Office 1900 Third Avenue, North, Suite 101 Birmingham, AL 35203 205/731-0082
Arizona	Phoenix District Office 4520 North Central Avenue, Suite 300 Phoenix, AZ 85012-1848 602/640-5000
Arkansas	Little Rock Area Office 425 West Capitol Avenue, Suite 625 Little Rock, AR 72201 501/324-5060
California	Fresno Local Office 1265 West Shaw, Suite 103 Fresno, CA 93711 209/487-5793
	Los Angeles District Office 255 East Temple, 4th Floor Los Angeles, CA 90012 213/894-1000

	Oakland Local Office 1301 Clay Street, North Tower, Suite 1170 Oakland, CA 94612 510/637-3230
	San Diego Area Office 401 B Street, Suite 1550 San Diego, CA 92101 619/557-7235
	San Francisco District Office 901 Market Street, Suite 500 San Francisco, CA 94103 415/744-6500
	San Jose Local Office 96 North Third Street, Suite 200 San Jose, CA 95112 408/291-7352
Colorado	Denver District Office 303 East 17th Avenue, Suite 510 Denver, CO 80203 303/866-1300
District of Columbia	Washington Field Office 1400 L Street, NW, Suite 200 Washington, DC 20005 202/663-4264
Florida	Miami District Office 1 Northeast First Street, 6th Floor Miami, FL 33132 305/536-4491
	Tampa Area Office 601 E. Kennedy Tampa, FL 33602 813/272-5969
Georgia	Atlanta District Office 75 Piedmont Avenue, NE; Suite 1100 Atlanta, GA 30335 404/331-6093
	Savannah Local Office 410 Mall Boulevard, Suite G Savannah, GA 31406 912/652-4234

Hawaii	Honolulu Local Office 677 Ala Moana Boulevard, Suite 404 Honolulu, HI 96813 808/541-3120
Illinois	Chicago District Office 500 West Madison Street, 28th Floor Chicago, IL 60661 312/353-2713
Indiana	Indianapolis District Office 101 West Ohio Street, Suite 1900 Indianapolis, IN 46204 317/226-7212
Kentucky	Louisville Area Office 600 Dr. Martin Luther King Jr. Place Room 268 Louisville, KY 40202 502/582-6082
Louisiana	New Orleans District Office 701 Loyola Avenue, Suite 600 New Orleans, LA 70130 504/589-2329
Maryland	Baltimore District Office 10 South Howard Street, 3rd Floor Baltimore, MD 21201 410/962-3932
Massachusetts	Boston Area Office 1 Congress Street, 10th Floor Boston, MA 02114 617/565-3200
Michigan	Detroit District Office 477 Michigan Avenue, Room 1540 Detroit, MI 48226 313/226-7636
Minnesota	Minneapolis Local Office 330 2nd Avenue South, Suite 430 Minneapolis, MN 55401-2141 612/335-4040
Mississippi	Jackson Area Office Cross Roads Building Complex 207 West Amite Street Jackson, MS 39201-9996 601/965-4537

Missouri	Kansas City Area Office 911 Walnut Street, 10th Floor Kansas City, MO 64106 816/426-5773
	St. Louis District Office 625 North Euclid Street, 5th floor St. Louis, MO 63108 314/425-6585
New Jersey	Newark Area Office 1 Newark Center, Suite 2132 Newark, NJ 07102 201/645-6383
New Mexico	Albuquerque Area Office 505 Marquette, NW; Suite 900 Albuquerque, NM 87102-2189 505/766-2061
New York	Buffalo Local Office 6 Fountain Plaza, Suite 350 Buffalo, NY 14202 716/846-4441
	New York District Office 7 World Trade Center, 18th Floor New York, NY 10007 212/748-8500
North Carolina	Charlotte District Office 5500 Central Avenue Charlotte, NC 28212 704/567-7100
	Greensboro Local Office 801 Summit Avenue Greensboro, NC 27405 910/333-5174
	Raleigh Area Office 1309 Annapolis Drive Raleigh, NC 27608 919/856-4064
Ohio	Cincinnati Area Office 525 Vine Street, Suite 810 Cincinnati, OH 45202 513/684-2851

Cleveland District Office
Skylight Office Tower
1660 West 2nd Street, Suite 850
Cleveland, OH 44113
216/522-2001

Oklahoma

Oklahoma City Area Office
531 Couch Drive
Oklahoma City, OK 73102
405/231-4911

Pennsylvania

Philadelphia District Office
1421 Cherry Street, 10th Floor
Philadelphia, PA 19102
215/656-7020

Pittsburgh Area Office
1000 Liberty Avenue, Room 2038-A
Pittsburgh, PA 15222
412/644-3444

South Carolina

Greenville Local Office
15 South Main Street, Suite 530
Greenville, SC 29601
803/241-4400

Tennessee

Memphis District Office
1407 Union Avenue, Suite 621
Memphis, TN 38104
901/722-2617

Nashville Area Office
50 Vantage Way, Suite 202
Nashville, TN 37228
615/736-5820

Texas

Dallas District Office
207 South Houston Street
Dallas, TX 75202
214/655-3355

El Paso Area Office
The Commons Building C, Suite 100
4171 North Mesa Street
El Paso, TX 79902
915/534-6550

Houston District Office
1919 Smith Street, 7th Floor
Houston, TX 77002
713/653-3320

San Antonio District Office
5410 Fredericksburg Road, Suite 200
San Antonio, TX 78229
210/229-4810

Virginia   Norfolk Area Office
252 Monticello Avenue, 1st Floor
Norfolk, VA 23510
804/441-3470

Richmond Area Office
3600 West Broad Street, Room 229
Richmond, VA 23230
804/771-2692

Washington   Seattle District Office
909 1st Avenue, Suite 400
Seattle, WA 98104
206/220-6883

Wisconsin   Milwaukee District Office
310 West Wisconsin Avenue, Suite 800
Milwaukee, WI 53203-2292
414/297-1111

b. When to file

If your state has its own equal employment opportunity laws (see Section
B), you will typically be allowed 300 days after the act of discrimination
occurred to file a complaint. But at EEOC offices, the time limit for filing a
complaint is 180 days. The safest way to proceed is to assume that 180 days
is the limit in your case and file your complaint as soon as possible.

In some cases, you will not be able to recognize illegal discrimination
from a single action by an employer. If you discern a pattern of illegal
discrimination that extends back more than 180 days, the safest way to
proceed is to assume that the EEOC time limit began with the event that
caused you to recognize the pattern and file a complaint as soon as possible.

Example: *A woman who worked with Jan in a pharmaceutical lab was fired in
January. Two months later, the lab fired another woman. In June, a third woman
was fired.*

*When the third woman was fired, Jan began to notice that the firings seemed
to have nothing to do with job performance. Although the lab employed several*

men with less experience and whose job performance was not as good as the three women who had been fired, no men had been fired.

After consistently receiving positive performance reviews, Jan's supervisor informed her the lab staff was being reduced and she should start looking for another job. Jan took a few weeks to gather evidence to support her belief that the company was illegally discriminating against women on the basis of gender, and then filed a complaint with the EEOC in September.

c. Organizing your evidence

Because illegal discrimination rarely takes the form of one simple event, it is important to organize your evidence of incidents of illegal discrimination before contacting the EEOC to file a complaint.

Whenever possible, keep a log of the date, time, location, people involved and nature of actions that demonstrate any pattern of illegal discrimination. Keep a file of any documents that your employer gives you, such as written performance reviews or disciplinary notices. (See Chapter 1.)

If you present your evidence to the EEOC in an organized way—without yielding to the temptation to vent your displeasure with your employer's policies and practices—you will raise the chances of your complaint getting full attention and consideration from the EEOC investigators.

d. How the EEOC handles complaints

When you file a complaint, typically an EEOC staff lawyer or investigator will interview you and initially evaluate whether or not your employer's actions appear to violate Title VII. Theoretically, the EEOC has 180 days to act on your complaint. If the interviewer does not feel that the incident warrants a complaint, he or she will tell you so. You may have to think about other options, such as pursuing a complaint through your company's established complaint procedure.

If the interviewer feels you should pursue your complaint with the EEOC, he or she will fill out an EEOC Charge of Discrimination form describing the incident and send it to you to review and sign. After receiving your complaint, the EEOC is supposed to interview the employer that is the subject of the complaint and then try to mediate a settlement of the complaint between you and that employer.

That is what the EEOC's operating regulations provide. And for the most part, the EEOC does what it is supposed to do. But do not expect every claim to proceed as described. EEOC offices differ in caseloads, local procedures and the quality of their personnel. Investigations are usually slow, sometimes taking three years or more. The EEOC takes only a small portion of its cases to court—as few as 1% of those that are filed with it. These and other factors can have an impact on how a case is actually handled.

Some things to keep in mind:

- *Stay alert.* Do not assume that the EEOC will do everything and that you don't have to monitor what is going on. Check periodically with the EEOC to find out to what is happening with your case.

- *Be assertive.* If some EEOC action—or, more likely, inaction—is causing you serious problems, call that to the attention of the people handling your case.

- *Keep your options open.* Filing a claim with the EEOC does not prevent you from taking other action to deal with your case. You still have a right to try to solve the problem on your own or use a company complaint procedure. You also have the right to hire an attorney to file a lawsuit, if that is appropriate for your situation.

e. Penalties for retaliation

It is illegal for your employer to retaliate against you either for filing a Title VII complaint, or for cooperating in the investigation of one. But to take advantage of this protection, you must be able to prove that the retaliation occurred because you filed a complaint.

More often than not, an employer that wants to retaliate against you for filing a Title VII complaint will cite substandard job performance.

Example: *Hector filed a Title VII complaint because he observed that his employer never promotes anyone of his race above a certain level. To investigate Hector's complaint, the EEOC reviewed documents related to the company's hiring practices to determine whether it is, in fact, using race as the basis for hiring decisions.*

Two weeks later, Hector was dismissed from his job because, the company claimed, his performance was below its standards. If Hector decides to file an additional complaint charging the company with illegal retaliation, he will probably have to prove that his performance satisfied or exceeded the company's standards—and that the real reason he was fired was because he filed a Title VII complaint.

5. Filing a Title VII Lawsuit

In the very likely event that the EEOC does not act on your complaint within 180 days, you then have the right to request a right to sue letter that authorizes you to file a lawsuit in federal court against the offending employer. This type of suit is complex, and in cases involving an employee dismissal is often packaged with other claims. (See Chapter 11, Section D.) You will probably need to hire a lawyer to help you file a lawsuit under Title VII. (See Chapter 18, Section D.) A number of specialized organizations offer legal referrals and advice on workplace discrimination. (See the Appendix for contact details.)

Once you receive a right to sue letter, you have only 90 days to file a lawsuit, so deadlines are very important at this point of the Title VII process, as well. The EEOC has the right to file a lawsuit on your behalf, but do not expect that to happen unless your case has a very high political or publicity value—a very small percentage of the claims filed. The EEOC's out-of-pocket expenses are limited by law to $5,000 per lawsuit—many thousands of dollars less than it typically costs to take an employment discrimination case to court.

a. Class actions

For some employees, the most likely way to succeed in a Title VII case is to become part of a class action lawsuit. The courts allow lawsuits to be pursued as class actions when it is shown that a number of people have been injured by the same unlawful act. Because the potential damages from a Title VII class action lawsuit are much larger than in an individual lawsuit, some attorneys will take those cases on a contingency basis—which means that their fees will not be paid upfront but will be taken as a percentage of the amount recovered. (See Chapter 18, Section C.) The amount recovered will be divided among those certified as class members.

b. State and local laws

In general, employment-related lawsuits filed under state or local laws are easier to win than those filed under Title VII. And, unlike most Title VII cases, state and local anti-discrimination laws often offer the possibility of a larger judgment in favor of the worker who files the lawsuit. (See Section B.)

BFOQS: JOBS THAT REQUIRE DISCRIMINATION

Under Title VII and many state and local anti-discrimination laws, an employer may intentionally use gender, religious beliefs or national origin as the basis for employment decisions only if the employer can show that the job has special requirements that make such discrimination necessary.

When an employer establishes that such a special circumstance exists, it is called a bona fide occupational qualification (BFOQ).

Example: A religious denomination that employs counselors who answer telephone inquiries from those interested in becoming members of that religion would typically be allowed to limit its hiring of counselors to people who believe in that religion. Being a member of that denomination would be a BFOQ.

In general, the courts, the EEOC and state equal employment opportunity agencies prohibit the use of BFOQs except where clearly necessary. They typically require any employer using a BFOQ in employment decisions to prove conclusively that the BFOQ is essential to the successful operation of the company or organization.

You are most likely to encounter a BFOQ on a job application, in which case the employer must state on the application that the employment qualification covered by the questions would otherwise be illegal, but has been approved by the EEOC.

B. State and Local Anti-Discrimination Laws

Nearly all state and local laws prohibiting various types of discrimination in employment echo federal anti-discrimination law in that they outlaw discrimination based on race, color, gender, age, national origin and religion. But the state and local laws typically tend to go into more detail, creating categories of protection against discrimination that are not covered by federal law.

In Louisiana, for example, it is illegal to discriminate in employment matters on the basis of a worker's political activity. In Minnesota, it is illegal to discriminate against people who are collecting public assistance. And in several states, the age range for workers protected against age-based discrimination is broader than under the federal ADEA.

Many state anti-discrimination laws also provide faster and more effective procedures for pursuing complaints about illegal workplace discrimination than the EEOC process. An employee in New Jersey, for example, may go directly into superior court with a lawsuit based on age discrimination without first complaining to the EEOC.

State laws prohibiting discrimination in employment, along with agencies responsible for enforcing anti-discrimination laws in those states, are listed in the chart below. (See Section B3.) Municipal anti-discrimination laws can usually be researched at the headquarters of your community's government, such as your local city hall or county courthouse.

1. How to Take Action

If you wish to consider filing a complaint under your state's employment discrimination laws, you must first find out if your state has an agency empowered to process such a complaint. (The chart in B3 provides this information.) There are several states that have discrimination laws, but no state agency to enforce them. In these states, you must rely on the federal law or a private lawsuit to enforce your rights.

2. Time Limits for Filing

Ordinarily, a charge with the EEOC must be filed within 180 days of the date of the action about which you are complaining. State laws have their own separate time limits. And if your state has an agency that enforces its own age discrimination law, you must file your EEOC complaint within 30 days of notice that the state is no longer pursuing your case, even if the normal 180-day period is not up.

These time limits are counted from the date you get notice from your employer or union of the action—demotion, layoff, retirement—you think is discriminatory. If there is no specific date you can pinpoint, file your charge as soon as you have gathered enough information to convince yourself that you have been subjected to discrimination.

3. State Laws and Enforcing Agencies

This is a synopsis of factors that may not be used as the basis for employment discrimination under state laws. Keep in mind that it is only a synopsis, and that each state has its own way of determining such factors as what conditions qualify as a physical disability. Many state anti-discrimination laws apply only to employers with a minimum number of employees, such as five or more.

In states where no special agency has been designated to enforce anti-discrimination laws, your state's labor department or Attorney General's office or the closest office of the federal Equal Employment Opportunity Office should direct you to the right agency or person with whom to file a complaint over illegal discrimination in employment.

In certain states or circumstances, you may have no way to pursue your complaint over illegal discrimination other than to file a lawsuit or to hire an attorney to file one for you.

STATE LAWS PROHIBITING DISCRIMINATION IN EMPLOYMENT	
Alabama	No true anti-discrimination law, but employers are encouraged to employ people who are blind or otherwise physically disabled. (Ala. Code §21-71-1)
	Enforcing agency: None
Alaska	Race, religion, color, national origin, age, physical disability, gender, marital status, changes in marital status. Alaska Human Rights Law (Alaska Stat. §18.80.110)
	Pregnancy or parenthood. (Alaska Stat. §18.80.220)
	Mental illness. (Alaska Stat. §47.30.865)
	Enforcing agency: Human Rights Commission 800 A Street, Suite 204 Anchorage, AL 99501 907/274-4692

Arizona	Race, color, religion, gender, age, physical disability (excluding current alcohol or drug use), AIDS, national origin. Arizona Civil Rights Act (Ariz. Rev. Stat. Ann. §41-1401)
	Enforcing agency: Civil Rights Division 1275 West Washington Street Phoenix, AZ 85007 602/542-5263
Arkansas	No general discrimination law.
	Prohibits discrimination in wages on the basis of gender. (Ark. Code Ann. §11-4-601-12)
	For state employees only: physical disability (Ark. Code Ann. §20-14-303) and age if 40 years old or older. (Ark. Code Ann. §21-3-201
	Enforcing agency: None
California	Race, religion, color, national origin, ancestry, physical disability, medical condition, marital status, gender, pregnancy, childbirth or related medical conditions. (Cal. Gov't. Code §12900)
	AIDS/HIV condition. (Cal. Health & Safety Code §§199.20 and 199.30)
	Age if age 40 or over. (Cal. Govt. Code §1241)
	Sexual orientation. (Cal. Lab. Code §§1101 and 1102)
	Enforcing agency: Department of Fair Employment and Housing 2014 T Street, Suite 210 Sacramento, CA 95814 916/445-9918
Colorado	Race, religion, color, age, gender, national origin, ancestry. Fair Employment Practices Act (Colo. Rev. Stat. §24-34-401)
	Physical or mental disability. (Colo. Rev. Stat. §27-10-115)
	Enforcing agency: Civil Rights Commission 1560 Broadway, Suite 1050 Denver, CO 80202-5143 303/894-2997

Connecticut	Race, color, religion, age, gender, pregnancy, marital status, sexual orientation, national origin, ancestry, present or previous mental or physical disability. Fair Employment Practices Act (Conn. Gen. Stat. Ann. §46a-60)
	Enforcing agency: Commission on Human Rights and Opportunities 1229 Albany Avenue Hartford, CT 06112 203/566-7710
Delaware	Race, color, religion, gender, national origin, marital status, refusal to grant sexual favors, age (if between ages 40 and 70), or physical disability as long as the cost to the employer of accommodating the employee's physical disability doesn't exceed 5% of that employee's annual compensation. Fair Employment Practices Act (Del. Code Ann. tit. 19, §710)
	Enforcing agency: Department of Labor Labor Law Enforcement Section State Office Building, 6th Floor 820 North French Street Wilmington, DE 19801 302/577-2900
District of Columbia	Race, color, religion, national origin, age (if between ages 18 and 65), gender, personal appearance, marital status or family responsibilities, sexual orientation, political affiliation, matriculation or physical disability. Human Rights Act (D.C. Code Ann. §1-2502)
	Enforcing agency: Human Rights Commission 441 4th Street, NW Washington, DC 20001 202/724-1385
Florida	Race, color, religion, gender, national origin, age, marital status, physical disability, political activity. Human Rights Act (Fla. Stat. Ann. §760.01)
	AIDS/HIV condition. (Fla. Stat. Ann. §760.50)
	Enforcing agency: Commission on Human Relations 325 John Knox Road, Bldg. F, Suite 240 Tallahassee, FL 32303-4149 904/488-7082

Georgia	In public employment:
	Race, color, national origin, religion, sex, disability (excluding alcohol or drug use). Fair Employment Practices Act (Ga. Code Ann. §45-19-20)
	In private employment:
	Mental or physical disability (excluding the use of alcohol or any illegal or federally controlled drug). (Ga. Code Ann. §66-501)
	Age, if between 40 and 70 years old. (Ga. Code Ann. §§54-1102 and 54-9927)
	Enforcing agency: None
Hawaii	Race, religion, color, ancestry, gender, sexual orientation, age, marital status, mental or physical disability, pregnancy, childbirth or related medical conditions. Fair Employment Practices Law (Haw. Rev. Stat. §378-1)
	Enforcing agency: Hawaii Civil Rights Commission 888 Mililani Street, 2nd Floor Honolulu, HI 96813 808/586-8640
Idaho	Race, color, religion, national origin, gender, age (if age 40 or older), or physical or mental disability. Fair Employment Practices Act (Idaho Code §67-5901)
	Enforcing agency: Commission on Human Rights 450 West State Street Boise, ID 83720 208/334-2873
Illinois	Race, color, gender, national origin, ancestry, age, marital status, physical or mental disability. Human Rights Act (Ill. Ann. Stat. ch. 68, ¶ 1-101)
	Enforcing agency: Department of Human Rights James R. Thompson Center 100 West Randolph Street, 10th Floor Chicago, IL 60601 312/814-6245
Indiana	Race, color, gender, national origin, ancestry, religion, age if between 40 and 70 years old or physical disability. Civil Rights Law (Ind. Code Ann. §22-9-1-1)
	Enforcing agency: Civil Rights Commission 100 N. Senate Avenue, Room N-103 Indianapolis, IN 46204 317/232-2600

Iowa	Race, color, religion, age, gender, national origin or physical disability. Civil Rights Act (Iowa Code Ann. §601A.1)
	Enforcing agency: Civil Rights Commission 211 East Maple Street, 2nd Floor Des Moines, IA 50319 515/281-4121
Kansas	Race, color, religion, gender, age (if over age 18), national origin or ancestry, or physical disability. Act Against Discrimination (Kan. Stat. Ann. §44-1001)
	Enforcing agency: Civil Rights Commission Landon State Office Building 900 SW Jackson, Suite 851 South Topeka, KS 66612-1258 913/296-3206
Kentucky	Race, color, religion, national origin, gender, age (if between ages 40 and 70). Civil Rights Act (Ky. Rev. Stat. §344.040)
	Physical disability. (Ky. Rev. Stat. §207.130)
	Enforcing agency: Human Rights Commission 332 West Broadway, 7th Floor Louisville, KY 40202 502/595-4024
Louisiana	Race, color, religion, gender, national origin, pregnancy, sickle cell traits. Discrimination in Employment Act (La. Rev. Stat. Ann. §23:1001)
	Physical or mental disability. (La. Rev. Stat. Ann. §46:2251)
	Age (40 to 70 years old). (La. Rev. Stat. Ann. §23:972)
	Participation in investigations relating to state's employment laws (La. Rev. Stat. Ann. §23:964)
	Enforcing agency: none
Maine	Race, color, gender, religion, national origin, ancestry, age, or physical or mental disability. Human Rights Act (Me. Rev. Stat. Ann. tit. 5, §4572)
	Enforcing agency: Human Rights Commission Statehouse, Station 51 Augusta, ME 04333 207/624-6050

Maryland	Race, color, religion, gender, national origin, age, marital status (including a prohibition of company policies forbidding marriage between two employees or setting different benefit levels for employees designated as heads of their households), past or current physical or mental illness or disability as long as the disability does not prevent the worker from performing the job. Human Relations Commission Act (Md. Code Ann. art. 49B, §1)
	Enforcing agency: Commission on Human Relations 20 East Franklin Street Baltimore, MD 21202 301/333-1700
Massachusetts	Race, color, religion, gender, sexual orientation, national origin, ancestry, age or physical or mental disability. Fair Employment Practices Act (Mass. Gen. Laws Ann. ch. 151B, §1)
	Enforcing agency: Commission Against Discrimination One Ashburton Place Boston, MA 02108 617/727-3990
Michigan	Race, color, religion, gender, national origin, height, weight, marital status, or age. Elliot Larsen Civil Rights Act (Mich. Comp. Laws Ann. §37.2202)
	Physical disability. (Mich. Comp. Laws Ann. §37.1103)
	Mental disability. (Mich. Comp. Laws Ann. §37.1202)
	Enforcing agency: Department of Civil Rights 1200 6th Street, 7th Floor Detroit, MI 48226 313/256-2615
Minnesota	Race, color, religion, gender, marital status, sexual orientation, national origin, age, physical disability or receipt of public assistance. (Minn. Stat. Ann. §363.03)
	Enforcing agency: Department of Human Rights Bremer Tower 7th Place and Minnesota Streets St. Paul, MN 55101 612/296-5663
Mississippi	State employer cannot discriminate based on race, color, religion, sex, national origin, age or physical disability. (Miss. Code Ann. §25-9-149)

	Enforcing agency: None
Missouri	Race, color, religion, gender, national origin, ancestry, age (between ages 40 and 70) or physical or mental disability. Human Rights Act (Mo. Ann. Stat. §213.055)
	AIDS condition. (Mo. Ann. Stat. §191.650)
	Enforcing agency: Commission on Human Rights 3315 West Truman Boulevard Jefferson City, MO 65102-1129 314/751-3325
Montana	Race, color, religion, gender, age, national origin, marital status, or physical or mental disability. Human Rights Statute (Mont. Code Ann. §49-2-303)
	Enforcing agency: Human Rights Commission 1236 Sixth Avenue Helena, MT 59624 406/444-2884
Nebraska	Race, color, religion, gender, national origin, age (between ages 40 and 70), marital status or disability (excluding addiction to alcohol, other drugs or gambling). Fair Employment Act (Neb. Rev. Stat. Ann. §48-1104)
	Enforcing agency: Equal Opportunity Commission 301 Centennial Mall South Lincoln, NE 68509-4934 402/471-2024
Nevada	Race, color, religion, gender, age (if over 40 years old), national origin, physical disability, AIDS/HIV condition. Fair Employment Practices Act (Nev. Rev. Stat. Ann. §613.30)
	Enforcing agency: Equal Rights Commission 2450 Wrondel Way, Suite C Reno, NV 89502 702/688-1288
New Hampshire	Race, color, religion, gender, age, national origin, marital status, or physical or mental disability. Law Against Discrimination (N.H. Rev. Stat. Ann. §354-A:1)
	Enforcing agency: Human Rights Commission 163 Loudon Road Concord, NH 03301 603/271-2767

New Jersey	Race, color, religion, gender, national origin, ancestry, age (between ages 18 and 70), marital status, sexual or affectional orientation, atypical hereditary cellular or blood trait, past or present physical or mental disability or draft liability for the armed forces. Law Against Discrimination (N.J. Stat. Ann. §10:5-12)

Enforcing agency:
Division of Civil Rights
31 Clinton Street, 3rd Floor
Newark, NJ 07102
201/648-2700 |
| New Mexico | Race, color, religion, gender, age, national origin, medical condition, or physical or mental disability. Human Rights Act (N.M. Stat. Ann. §28-1-7)

Enforcing agency:
Human Rights Commission
1596 Pacheco Street
Aspen Plaza
Santa Fe, NM 87505
505/827-6838 |
| New York | Race, color, religion, gender, age (if age 18 or older), national origin, marital status, or physical disability. Human Rights Law (N.Y. Exec. Law §296)

Enforcing agency:
Division of Human Rights
55 West 125th Street
New York, NY 10027
212/961-8400 |
| North Carolina | Race, color, religion, gender, age, national origin. Equal Employment Practices Act. (N.C. Gen. Stat. §143-422.2)

Sickle cell or hemoglobin C traits. (N.C. Gen. Stat. §95-28.1)

Physical or mental disability. (N.C. Gen. Stat. §168A-1)

AIDS/HIV condition. (N.C. Gen. Stat. §130A-148)

Enforcing agency:
Human Relations Commission
121 West Jones Street
Raleigh, NC 27603
919/733-7996 |
| North Dakota | Race, color, religion, gender, national origin, age (if between ages 40 and 70), marital status, status with regard to public assistance or physical or mental disability. (N.D. Cent. Code §14.02.4-03)

Enforcing agency: None |

Ohio	Race, color, religion, gender, national origin, ancestry, age or physical or mental disability. Civil Rights Act (Ohio Rev. Code Ann. §4112.02)
	Age, if 40 years old or over. (Ohio Rev. Code Ann. §4107.17)
	Enforcing agency: Civil Rights Commission 220 Parsons Avenue Columbus, OH 43266-0543 614/466-5928
Oklahoma	Race, color, religion, gender, national origin, age (if age 40 or older) or physical disability. Civil Rights Act (Okla. Stat. Ann. tit. 25, §1302)
	Enforcing agency: Human Rights Commission 2101 North Lincoln Boulevard, Room 480 Oklahoma City, OK 73105 405/521-2360
Oregon	Race, color, religion, gender, national origin, marital status or age (if age 18 or older). Fair Employment Act (Or. Rev. Stat. §659.030)
	Physical or mental disability. (Or. Rev. Stat. §659.400)
	Enforcing agency: Civil Rights Division Bureau of Labor & Industry 800 NE Oregon Street, Box #32 Portland, OR 97232 503/731-4075
Pennsylvania	Race, color, religion, gender, national origin, ancestry, age (if between ages 40 and 70), or physical or mental disability. Human Relations Act (43 Pa. Cons. Stat. Ann §954)
	Enforcing agency: Human Relations Commission Uptown Shopping Plaza 2971-E North 7th Street Harrisburg, PA 17110-2123 717/787-4410
Rhode Island	Race, color, religion, gender, ancestry, age (if between ages 40 and 70), or physical or mental disability. Fair Employment Practices Act (R.I. Gen. Laws §28-5-7)
	AIDS condition. (R.I. Gen. Laws §23-6-22)
	Enforcing agency: Commission for Human Rights 10 Abbott Park Place Providence, RI 02903-3768 401/277-2661

South Carolina	Race, color, religion, gender, age (if age 40 or older), national origin. Human Affairs Law (S.C. Code §1-13-20)
	Physical or mental disability. (S.C. Code §43-33-530)
	Enforcing agency: Human Affairs Commission 2611 Forest Drive, Suite 200 Columbia, SC 29204 803/253-6336
South Dakota	Race, color, religion, gender, national origin, ancestry or physical and mental disability. Human Relations Act (S.D. Codified Laws Ann. §20-13-10)
	Enforcing agency: Commission on Human Relations 224 West 9th Street Sioux Falls, SD 57102 605/339-7039
Tennessee	Race, creed, color, religion, gender, age (if age 40 or older), national origin. Fair Employment Practices Act (Tenn. Code Ann. §4-21-401)
	Physical or mental disability. (Tenn. Code Ann. §8-50-103)
	Enforcing agency: Human Rights Commission 531 Henley Street, Suite 701 Knoxville, TN 37902 615/594-6500
Texas	Race, color, religion, gender, age (if between ages 40 and 70), national origin, or physical or mental disability. Commission on Human Rights Act (Tex. Rev. Civil Stat. Ann. art. 5221k, §5.01)
	Enforcing agency: Commission on Human Rights 8100 Cameron Road, #525 Austin, TX 78754 512/837-8534
Utah	Race, color, religion, gender, age (if over age 40), national origin; pregnancy, childbirth or related medical conditions; or physical or mental disability. Anti-Discrimination Act (Utah Code Ann. §34-35-1)
	Enforcing agency: Anti-Discrimination Division of the Industrial Commission 160 East Third, South, 3rd floor Salt Lake City, UT 84111 801/530-6801

Vermont

Race, color, religion, gender, national origin, ancestry, age (if age 18 or older), place of birth, AIDS or HIV condition or physical or mental disability. Fair Employment Practices Act (Vt. Stat. Ann. tit. 21, §§495 and 495a)

Enforcing agency:
Attorney General's Office
Civil Rights Division
109 State Street
Montpelier, VT 05609
802/828-3657

Virginia

Race, color, religion, gender, national origin, age, marital status or physical or mental disability. Human Rights Act (Va. Code Ann. §2.1-714)

Enforcing agency:
Council on Human Rights
1100 Bank Street
Richmond, VA 23219
804/225-2292

Washington

Race, color, religion, gender, age (if between age 40 and 70), national origin, marital status, or physical or mental disability. (Wash. Rev. Code Ann. §49.60.180)

Enforcing agency:
Human Rights Commission
1511 Third Avenue, Suite 921
Seattle, WA 98101
206/464-6500

West Virginia

Race, religion, color, national origin, gender, age (if age 40 or older), physical or mental disability. Human Rights Act (W.V. Code §5-11-9)

Enforcing agency:
Human Rights Commission
1321 Plaza East, Room 106
Charleston, WV 25301
304/348-6880

Wisconsin

Race, color, religion, gender, age (if age 40 or older), national origin, sexual orientation, marital status, arrest or conviction record, or physical disability. Fair Employment Practices Act (Wis. Stat. Ann. §111.31)

Enforcing agency:
Department of Industry, Labor and Human Relations
Equal Rights Division
201 East Washington Avenue, Room 402
Madison, WI 53708
608/266-6860

Wyoming

Race, color, religion, gender, national origin, ancestry, age (if between ages 40 and 69), or physical or mental disability. Fair Employment Practices Act (Wyo. Stat. §27.9-101)

Enforcing agency:
Fair Employment Commission
6101 Yellowstone, Room 259C
Cheyenne, WY 82002
307/777-7262

C. The Equal Pay Act

A federal law, the Equal Pay Act (29 U.S.C. §206), requires employers to pay all employees equally for equal work, regardless of their gender. It was passed in 1963 as an amendment to the Fair Labor Standards Act. (See Chapter 3, Section B.)

While the Act technically protects both women and men from gender discrimination in pay rates, it was passed to help rectify the problems faced by women workers because of sex discrimination in employment. And in practice, this law almost always has been applied to situations where women are being paid less than men for doing similar jobs.

The law's biggest weakness is that it is strictly applied only when men and women are doing the same work. Since women have historically been banned from many types of work and had only limited entree to managerial positions, the Equal Pay Act in reality affects very few women.

To raise a valid claim under the Equal Pay Act, you must show that two employees of the opposite sex:
- are working in the same place
- are doing equal work, and
- are receiving unequal pay.

You must also show that the employees in those jobs received unequal pay because of their sex.

1. Who Is Covered

The Equal Pay Act applies to all employees covered by the Fair Labor
Standards Act, which means virtually all employees are covered. (See
Chapter 3, Section A.) But in addition, the Equal Pay Act covers professional employees, executives and managers—including administrators and
teachers in elementary and secondary schools.

2. Determining Equal Work

Jobs do not have to be identical for the courts to consider them equal. In
general, the courts have ruled that two jobs are equal for the purposes of
the Equal Pay Act when both require equal levels of skill, effort and
responsibility and are performed under similar conditions.

There is a lot of room for interpretation here, of course. But the general
rule is that if there are only small differences in the skill, effort or responsibility required, two jobs should still be regarded as equal. The focus is on
the duties actually performed. Job titles, classifications and descriptions
may weigh in to the determination, but are not all that is considered.

The biggest problems arise where two jobs are basically the same, but
one includes a few extra duties. It is perfectly legal to award higher pay for
the extra duties, but some courts have looked askance at workplaces in
which the higher-paying jobs with extra duties are consistently reserved for
workers of one gender.

EQUAL PAY V. COMPARABLE WORTH

The Equal Pay Act covers only situations where men and women are performing jobs that require equal skill, effort and responsibility and are performed under similar circumstances. Often, however, men and women are doing different jobs at different payrates, despite the fact that the value of their work is equal. Disputes over this type situation are typically lumped under the term comparable worth.

When Congress passed the Equal Pay Act, it tried to choose its words carefully. Representative Goodell (R—NY), one of the Act's sponsors, explained: "We went from 'comparable' to 'equal,' meaning that the jobs should be virtually identical—that is, that they would be very much alike or closely related to each other."

A comparable worth case typically is not covered by the Equal Pay Act. Because they are broader in scope, Title VII or the state anti-discrimination laws (discussed in Section B), are better routes to use for pursuing comparable worth complaints.

3. Determining Equal Pay

In general, pay systems that result in employees of one gender being paid less than the other gender for doing equal work are allowed under the Equal Pay Act if the pay system is actually based on a factor other than gender, such as a merit or seniority system.

Example: *In 1960, the Ace Widget Company was founded and initially hired 50 male widgetmakers. Many of those men are still working there. Since 1980, the company has expanded and hired 50 more widgetmakers, half of them female. All of the widgetmakers at Ace are doing equal work, but because the company awards raises systematically based on seniority or length of employment, many of the older male workers earn substantially more per hour than their female co-workers. Nevertheless, the pay system at Ace Widget does not violate the Equal Pay Act because its pay differences between genders doing equal work are based on a factor other than gender.*

4. How to Take Action

The Equal Pay Act was passed one year before Title VII of the Civil Rights Act. Both laws prohibit wage discrimination based on sex, but Title VII goes beyond ensuring equal pay for equal work, as it also bars discrimination in hiring, firing and promotions. In addition, Title VII broadly prohibits other forms of discrimination, including that based on race, color, religion and national origin. (See Section A for a detailed discussion of how to take action under Title VII.)

Example: *Suzanne works as a reservations agent for an airline, answering calls on the company's toll-free telephone number. About half of the other reservations agents in her office are men, who are typically paid $1 per hour more than Suzanne and the other female agents. What's more, the company has established a dress code for female reservations agents, but not for the male agents.*

If Suzanne decides to file a discrimination complaint against her employer, the Equal Pay Act would apply to the pay difference between females and males. Title VII would apply to both the pay difference and the fact that only the female employees in her office are held to a dress code.

In cases where both Title VII and the Equal Pay Act apply, the Equal Pay Act offers two potential advantages:

* You can file a lawsuit under the Equal Pay Act without first filing a complaint with the EEOC.
* Unlike Title VII, the Equal Pay Act does not require proof that the employer acted intentionally when discriminating. That can make an Equal Pay Act case much easier to win in court.

D. The Age Discrimination in Employment Act

The federal Age Discrimination in Employment Act, or ADEA (29 U.S.C. §§621 to 634), is the single most important law protecting the rights of older workers. Basically, it provides that workers over the age of 40 cannot be arbitrarily discriminated against because of age in any employment decision.[1] Perhaps the single most important rule under the ADEA is that no worker can be forced to retire.

The Act also prohibits age discrimination in hiring, discharges, lay-offs, promotion, wages, healthcare coverage, pension accrual, other terms and conditions of employment, referrals by employment agencies and membership in and the activities of unions.

There has to be a valid reason, not related to age, for all employment decisions, but especially firing—for example, economic reasons or poor job performance.

The ADEA is enforced, along with other discrimination complaints, by the EEOC. (See Section A for more on procedure.) A number of national organizations will also provide legal referrals and help in evaluating age discrimination complaints. (See the Appendix for contact information.)

---

[1]For a more extensive discussion of the ADEA, its protections and how to pursue a complaint under it, see *Social Security, Medicare and Pensions: The Sourcebook for Older Americans,* by Joseph L. Matthews with Dorothy Berman Matthews (Nolo Press).

THE END OF MANDATORY RETIREMENT

No one fought so hard or did so much to shape the law for the poor and the elderly as Claude Pepper, the Democratic Congressman from Florida. He promoted, and many say created, legal rights for the elderly—backing legislation to fight crime in housing projects for the elderly, to cut Amtrak fares for senior citizens and to provide meals for homebound older Americans. He was also widely recognized as the primary congressional advocate of Social Security and Medicare.

Elected to the House of Representatives for 14 terms, Pepper was appointed chair of the Select Committee on Aging in 1977. In that role, he orchestrated dramatic parades of witnesses to testify about the plight of the aging elderly, some of them wheeled in on hospital beds and hooked to oxygen tanks.

But the legislative reform of which Pepper was proudest was the 1978 bill abolishing the federally mandatory retirement age of 65. True to form, Pepper packed the congressional hearing room when the bill was being debated. This time, he filled it with vibrant and able-bodied septuagenarians—politicians, actors and businesspeople, including Colonel Harlin Sanders, the fried chicken magnate. That bill did away with the mandatory retirement limit for federal government workers; the retirement age for nonfederal employees was raised from 65 to 70 years old.

Pepper died on May 30, 1989. He was 88 years old.

1. Who Is Covered

The ADEA applies to employees age 40 and older—and to workplaces with 20 or more employees. Unlike several other federal workplace laws, the ADEA covers employees of labor organizations and local, state and federal governments.

There are also a number of exceptions to the broad protection of the ADEA in addition to workers employed by companies which have less than 20 employees.

- Executives or people "in high policy-making positions" can be forced to retire at age 65 if they would receive annual retirement pension benefits worth $44,000 or more.
- There are special exceptions for police and fire personnel, tenured university faculty and certain federal employees having to do with law enforcement and air traffic control. If you are in one of these categories, check with your personnel office or benefits plan office for details.
- The biggest exception to the federal age discrimination law is made when age is an essential part of a particular job—referred to by the legal term of bona fide occupational qualification (BFOQ). An employer that sets age limits on a particular job must be able to prove the limit is necessary because a worker's ability to adequately perform that job does in fact diminish after the age limit is reached.

2. State Laws

Most states have laws against age discrimination in employment. (See Section B.) An individual working in a state with such a law can choose to file a complaint under either state law or the federal law (ADEA), or both.

In many cases, the state law can provide greater protection than the federal law. For example, several states provide age discrimination protection to workers before they reach age 40, and other states protect against the actions of employers with fewer than 20 employees. Even if the protection offered by your state law is the same as that provided by the federal law, you may get better results pursuing your rights under state law. A state agency entrusted with investigating and enforcing its own age discrimination law may provide easier, quicker and more aggressive prosecution of your complaint than the overburdened Equal Employment Opportunity Commission does in enforcing the ADEA. (See Section B for specific information on how to enforce your rights under state law.)

E. The Older Workers Benefit Protection Act

The main purpose of the Older Workers Benefit Protection Act (29 U.S.C. §§623, 626 and 630) is to make it clearly illegal:

- to use an employee's age as the basis for discrimination in benefits, and
- to discourage companies from targeting older workers for their staff cutting programs.

The law was passed in 1990, after a controversial U.S. Supreme Court ruling (*Public Employees Retirement Sys. v. Betts,* 109 U.S. 2854 (1989)), confused the question of when and how the Age Discrimination in Employment Act applied to benefit programs. (See Section D.)

Most of the effects of this law are very difficult for anyone but a benefits administrator who is immersed in the trendy lingo to understand. However, one provision of the law that you are most likely to use—regulating the legal waivers that employers are increasingly asking employees to sign in connection with so-called early retirement programs—is relatively clear and specific.

By signing a waiver—often called a release or covenant not to sue—an employee agrees not to take any legal action against the employer, such as an age discrimination lawsuit. In return for signing the waiver, the employer gives the employee an incentive to leave voluntarily, such as a severance pay package that exceeds the company's standard policy. (See Chapter 3, Section C.)

This type of transaction was very popular in the early 1990s among large corporations that wanted to reduce their payroll costs. Because older workers who have been with a company a long time typically cost more in salary and benefits than younger workers, most staff-cutting programs were directed at older workers. But cutting only older workers constitutes illegal age discrimination, so companies typically induced the older workers to sign away their rights to sue their former employers. In colloquial parlance, these deals are often referred to as Golden Handshakes—as in Thank-You-Very-Much-for-Your-Hard-Years-of-Service-and-If-You-Retire-Right-Now-This-Grand-Bunch-of-Benefits-Will-Be-Yours. This cruel, squeeze play technique is no longer legal.

Under the Older Workers Benefit Protection Act, you must be given at least 21 days to decide whether or not to sign such a waiver that has been presented to you individually. If the waiver is presented to a group of employees, each of you must be given at least 45 days to decide whether or not to sign. In either case, you have seven days after agreeing to such a waiver to revoke your decision.

1. Who Is Covered

The Older Workers Benefit Protection Act applies to nonunion employees in private industry who are at least 40 years old.

2. Restrictions on Agreements Not to Sue

There are a number of other key restrictions the Older Workers Benefit Protection Act places on agreements not to sue.

- Your employer must make the waiver understandable to the average individual eligible for the program in which the waiver is being used.
- The waiver may not cover any rights or claims that you discover are available after you sign it, and it must specify that it covers your rights under the ADEA.
- Your employer must offer you something of value—over and above what is already owed to you—in exchange for your signature on the waiver.
- Your employer must advise you, in writing, that you have the right to consult an attorney before you sign the waiver.
- If the offer is being made to a class of employees, your employer must inform you in writing how the class of employees is defined; the job titles and ages of all the individuals to whom the offer is being made; and the ages of all the employees in the same job classification or unit of the company to whom the offer is not being made.
- You must be given a fixed time in which to make a decision on whether or not to sign the waiver.

3. Negotiation Rights

The Older Workers Benefits Protection Act gives additional legal protections, if your employer offers you the opportunity to participate in a staff reduction program. The Act indirectly puts you in a position to negotiate the terms of your departure.

The fact that your employer has offered an incentive tells you that the company wants you gone and is worried that you might file a lawsuit for wrongful discharge. (See Chapter 11, Section A.) So, although the company may say that you have only two choices—accept or reject the offer—there is nothing preventing you from making a counteroffer.

For example, after taking a week or two to think, you might go back to your employer and agree to leave voluntarily if your severance pay is doubled. There is power in numbers, so this type of negotiating is even more likely to be effective if done on behalf of a group of employees who are considering the same offer.

As in all employment transactions, it is wise to advise your employer of your decision in writing, and to keep a copy of that letter—along with copies of all documents given to you by your employer as part of the staff reduction program. If you refuse to accept such an offer and are later dismissed, you may be able to allege illegal age discrimination as a basis for challenging your dismissal.

4. How to Take Action

If you believe that an employer has violated your rights under the Older Workers Benefit Protection Act, you can file a complaint with the EEOC just as you would against any other workplace discrimination prohibited by Title VII. (See Section A4.) If the EEOC does not resolve your complaint to your satisfaction, you may decide to pursue your complaint through a lawsuit. (See Section A5.)

F. The Americans With Disabilities Act

The Americans With Disabilities Act (ADA) prohibits employment discrimination on the basis of workers' disabilities. While debated, haggled over and honed by both employees and employers before it was passed, the law is not a panacea for either group. It is widely criticized as poorly drafted.

Generally, the ADA prohibits employers from:

- discriminating on the basis of virtually any physical or mental disability
- asking job applicants questions about their past or current medical conditions
- requiring job applicants to take pre-employment medical exams
- creating or maintaining worksites that include substantial physical barriers to the movement of people with physical handicaps.

The Act requires that an employer must make reasonable accommodations for qualified individuals with disabilities, unless that would cause the employer undue hardship. But those dictates are frustrating. It is unclear what disabilities qualify individuals for coverage under the law. (See Section 2, below.) And the meanings of "qualified workers," "reasonable accommodations" and "undue hardship" remain elusive. (See Sections 1 and 4, below.)

A precursor of the ADA, the Vocational Rehabilitation Act (29 U.S.C. §794) prohibits discrimination against handicapped workers in state and federal government. Its narrow protections are generally thought to be usurped by the more inclusive ADA.

1. Who Is Covered

Effective July 1994, the ADA covers companies with 15 or more employees. Its coverage broadly extends to private employers, employment agencies and labor organizations. Some of its requirements were phased in earlier, beginning with larger employers.

The Act protects workers who, although disabled in some way, are still qualified for a particular job—that is, they would be able to perform the essential functions of a job, either with or without some form of accommodation. Whether a disabled worker is deemed qualified for a job seems to depend on whether he or she has appropriate skill, experience, training or education for the position.

To determine whether a particular function is considered essential for a job, look first at a written job description. If a function is described there, it is more likely to be considered an essential part of the job. But an employer's discretion and the reality of an individual workplace enter the fray, too. For example, if other employees would likely be available to take over some tangential part of a job, or if only a small portion of the workday is spent on the function, or if the work product will not suffer if the function is not performed—then that function may not be deemed essential to the job.

2. Definition of Disabled

The ADA's protections extend to the disabled—defined as a person who:

* has a physical or mental impairment that substantially limits a major life activity
* has a record of impairment, or
* is regarded as having an impairment.

This list makes clear why the new law provides just cause for consternation. Many of the terms used in the Act are broad—and not well-defined. Some of their intended meanings were hinted at during the congressional debates on the legislation, but many will simply have to be hammered out in the courts over time.

a. Impairments limiting a life activity

Impairment includes both physical disorders, such as cosmetic disfigurement or loss of a limb, and mental and psychological disorders.

Many of the conditions the ADA is intended to cover are specifically listed—a list that is sure to grow over time. In fact, the ADA requires that every year, the Secretary of Health and Human Services must provide a list of infectious and communicable diseases, as well as information on how they are transmitted.

Note, however, that several state and local public health departments have passed regulations that allow some forms of discrimination in the food handling industry. For example, several state laws provide that if a communicable disease can be transmitted through handling food, and if the risk cannot be eliminated by reasonable accommodation, then an employer may refuse to hire an individual for a food handling job. For more information on these types of laws, contact your local public health department.

In addition, testing applicants and employees for the possibility of infectious diseases raises a number of privacy issues, commonly addressed in local and state laws. (See Chapter 6.)

The ADA specifically protects workers with: Acquired Immunodeficiency Syndrome (AIDS) and Human Immunodeficiency Virus (HIV) (see Chapter 6, Section B), alcoholism, cancer, cerebral palsy, diabetes, emotional illness, epilepsy, hearing and speech disorders, heart disorders, learning disabilities such as dyslexia, mental retardation, muscular dystrophy and visual impairments.

A number of other conditions can be protected under the ADA upon proper proof that they are limiting in some way. To be covered, an individual's condition must restrict a life activity—broadly defined as the ability to walk, talk, see, hear, speak, breathe, sit, stand, reach, reason, learn, work or care for himself or herself. However, the ADA does not cover conditions that impose short-term limitations, such as pregnancy or broken bones.

b. Records of impairment

Because discrimination often continues even after the effects of a disability have abated, the ADA prohibits discrimination against those who have had impairments in the past—including rehabilitated drug addicts and recovering alcoholics.

c. Regarded as impaired

In recognition of the fact that discrimination often stems from prejudice or irrational fear, the ADA protects workers who have no actual physical or mental impairment, but may be viewed by others as disabled—for example, someone who is badly scarred, deaf or epileptic. An employer cannot refuse to hire a person because of the perception that others will react negatively to him or her.

3. Illegal Discrimination

The ADA prohibits employers from discriminating against job applicants and employees who have disabilities in a number of specific situations.

a. Screening tests

Employers may not use pre-employment tests or ask interview questions that focus on an applicant's disabilities rather than skills related to the job. Although these questions used to be routine, employers can no longer ask, for example: Have you ever been hospitalized? Have you ever been treated for any of the following listed conditions or diseases? Have you ever been treated for a mental disorder? (See Chapter 6, Section B for a discussion of privacy issues related to testing.)

However, in screening applicants to find the best match to fill a job opening, employers are free to ask questions about an individual's ability to perform job-related tasks, such as: Can you lift a 40-pound box? Do you have a driver's license? Can you stand for long periods of time?

b. Insurance benefits

Employers cannot deny health coverage or other fringe benefits to disabled workers. Before the ADA was passed, many employers railed that their insurance costs would skyrocket if they were forced to provide coverage for the special medical needs of disabled workers. The ADA does not require that all medical conditions be covered; workplace policies can still limit coverage for various treatments or limit exclusions for pre-existing conditions. However, employers must provide the same coverage for workers with disabilities as they do for workers without disabilities. (See Chapter 4 for a discussion of health insurance.)

c. Disabled relatives and friends

The ADA also attempts to clamp down on the invidious effects of taint by association. Employers are banned from discriminating against people who are not disabled, but are related to or associated with someone who is disabled. For example, an otherwise qualified worker cannot be denied employment because a brother, roommate or close friend has AIDS.

d. Segregation

On the job, employers cannot segregate or classify disabled workers in a way that limits their opportunities or status—for example, by placing them in jobs with different pay, benefits or promotion opportunities than workers who are not disabled.

IS OBESITY A DISABILITY? TOO SOON TO TELL

Courts that have been called upon to decide whether overweight people are disabled within the meaning of state disability laws and the ADA have split on the issue.

Some courts have held that all overweight workers are physically impaired—and entitled to be protected from discrimination under disability laws. Some courts have opined that overweight workers are protected by disability laws only if there is some medical evidence showing that the weight gain is due to a physiological condition. And a third line of legal reasoning holds that only morbidly obese workers—those 100% or more over normal weight—are entitled to the laws' protections.

When asked to provide some guidance, the EEOC was noncommittal—stating only that obesity claims would be considered "on a case by case basis."

4. Accommodations by Employers

The core of the ADA is what initially got employers up in arms over its passage; some of them felt the law wrested important workplace decisions from them. It requires employers to make accommodations—changes to the work setting or the way jobs are done—so that disabled people can work. The law also specifies what employers must do in the sticky situation where two equally qualified candidates, one of whom is disabled, apply for a job. An employer cannot reject the disabled worker solely because he or she would require a reasonable accommodation—a reserved handicapped parking space, a modified work schedule, a telephone voice amplifier—to get the job done.

In reality, a disabled individual who wants a particular job must become somewhat of an activist. Since the law does not require an employer to propose reasonable accommodations—only to provide them—the onus of suggesting workable and affordable changes to the workplace that would allow him or her to perform a job is on the employee who wants the accommodation.

a. What is a reasonable accommodation

The ADA points to several specific accommodations that are likely to be deemed reasonable—some of them changes to the physical set-up of the workplace, some of them changes to how or when work is done. They include:

- making existing facilities usable by disabled employees—for example, by modifying the height of desks and equipment, installing computer screen magnifiers or installing telecommunications for the deaf
- restructuring jobs—for example, allowing a ten-hour/four-day work-week so that a worker can receive weekly medical treatments
- modifying exams and training material—for example, allowing more time for taking an exam, or allowing it to be taken orally instead of in writing
- providing a reasonable amount of additional unpaid leave for medical treatment (see also, Chapter 5)
- hiring readers or interpreters to assist an employee, and
- providing temporary workplace specialists to assist in training.

These are just a few possible accommodations. The possibilities are limited only by an employee's and employer's imaginations—and the reality that might make one or more of these accommodations financially impossible in a particular workplace.

b. What is an undue hardship

The ADA does not require employers to make accommodations that would cause them an undue hardship—a weighty concept defined in the ADA only as "an action requiring significant difficulty or expense." To show that a particular accommodation would present an undue hardship, an employer would have to demonstrate that it was too costly, extensive or disruptive to be adopted in that workplace.

The Equal Employment Opportunity Commission (EEOC), the federal agency responsible for enforcing the ADA, has set out some of the factors that will determine whether a particular accommodation presents an undue hardship on a particular employer:

- the nature and cost of the accommodation
- the financial resources of the employer—a large employer, obviously, may reasonably be asked to foot a larger bill for accommodations than a mom and pop business
- the nature of the business, including size, composition and structure of the workforce, and
- accommodation costs already incurred in a workplace.

It is not easy for employers to prove that an accommodation is an undue hardship, as financial difficulty alone is not usually sufficient. Courts will look at other sources of money, including tax credits and deductions available for making some accommodations and the disabled employee's willingness to pay for all or part of the costs.

5. How to Take Action

Title I of the ADA is enforced by the Equal Employment Opportunity Commission. (See Section A4 for specifics on how to file a complaint.) How efficient and responsive the agency will be and what kinds of lines it will draw in the cases it investigates remain to be seen as the new law makes its presence felt in workplaces and courts.

In addition, many state laws protect against discrimination based on physical or mental disability. (See Section B for a list of laws and enforcing agencies.) An individual working in a state with such a law can choose to file a complaint under either state law or the federal law (ADA), or both.

6. Where to Get More Information

For additional information on the ADA, contact:

Office on the Americans With Disabilities Act
Civil Rights Division
U.S. Department of Justice
P.O. Box 66118
Washington, DC 20035-6118
202/514-0301 (voice) or 202/514-0381 (TDD)

There are also a number of national organizations that offer guidance and referrals in dealing with ADA problems. (See the Appendix for contact details.)

THEY DON'T HAVE THAT EXCUSE TO KICK AROUND ANYMORE

Recent tallies of the cost to employers of making reasonable accommodations to disabled workers shows that the workplace investments are surprisingly inexpensive.

Percent of accommodations that cost nothing:	31
Percent that cost less than $50:	19
Percent that cost $50 to $500:	19
Percent that cost $500 to $1,000:	19
Percent that cost $1,000 to $5,000:	11
Percent that cost more than $5,000:	1

Source: Job Accommodation Network, 1993

G. Discrimination Against Workers With HIV or AIDS

According to the Center for Disease Control (CDC), more than 200,000 cases of AIDS in the U.S. were reported in the decade since the first case was diagnosed in 1981. Half of those—100,000 people—had been diagnosed since 1989. And half of them—100,000 people—had died of the disease. Public health authorities estimate that about one million people are now infected with HIV.

A growing number of employers have attempted to smooth over real and perceived problems with HIV- and AIDS-infected workers by holding training sessions and adopting written policies specifically prohibiting discrimination. The efforts, however, have lagged far behind the devastation the plague has wrought.

THE ALARMING RISE IN INFECTED WORKERS

According to early researchers, HIV, the viral cause of AIDS , was at first present in a relatively small segment of certain identifiable populations: homosexuals, intravenous drug users, Haitian immigrants and sexual partners of people in these groups. At that time, many people believed it did not threaten the wider population.

Twelve years later, more than a third of major American corporations report dealing with real or perceived cases of HIV infection or AIDS. From 1991 to 1993, the rate of increase in companies cumulatively reporting such cases was 58%.

Major American Corporations Reporting Cases of HIV Infection or AIDS

1991	22.8%
1992	28.0%
1993	35.9%

Source: Research report published by the American Management Association, 1993

1. How the Virus Is Spread

Contrary to early notions which served to fan the flames of hysteria and prejudice against those infected, the HIV virus is not spread through the kind of casual contact with other human beings that typically takes place at work.

Extensive medical research has shown that the HIV virus is spread primarily through sexual intercourse and the exchange of blood by intravenous drug users—not by everyday workplace interactions with someone who is infected such as:

- sharing a workspace or office
- shaking hands or using the same telephone, computer or furniture, and
- sharing bathroom or kitchen facilities.

Nevertheless, some employers and employees have reacted to the spread of AIDS with panic—and a strong prejudice against working with people who are infected with the HIV virus. Some insurance companies have made that panic worse by restricting healthcare coverage or dramatically raising premiums for those infected. (See Chapter 6, Section B, for a discussion of privacy rights connected with AIDS testing.)

A number of organizations offer specific information on the HIV virus, AIDS and resources on AIDS in the workplace including sources of counseling and legal referrals. (See the Appendix for contact details.)

2. Rights of Infected Workers

In recent years, the courts have generally, but not always, held that being infected with the HIV virus or having AIDS is a type of physical handicap. Also, federal and many state and local anti-discrimination laws make it illegal to discriminate in employment-related matters on the basis of HIV infection or AIDS. (See Section B.)

A number of states and municipalities have also passed AIDS-specific laws in recent years in attempts to deal with injustices arising from panicked reactions to AIDS in the workplace. Most of these laws limit the testing of employees and job applicants for the HIV virus to positions such as those in hospital laboratories, where the virus might conceivably be passed accidentally from an employee to a patient. (See Chapter 6, Section B.)

These inconsistent, piecemeal approaches to dealing with AIDS in the workplace have been expensive, time-consuming and often frustrating for those infected with the HIV virus.

But the legal picture for workers with HIV and AIDS is becoming more clear since the recent passage of the Americans With Disabilities Act or ADA. (See Section F, above.) Under the ADA, it is clearly illegal for any company employing 15 or more people to discriminate against workers because they are HIV-infected or have AIDS. Employers covered by the ADA must also make reasonable accommodations to allow employees with AIDS to continue working. Such accommodations include extended leave policies, reassignment to vacant positions within the companies that are less physically strenuous and flexible work schedules.

H. Discrimination Against Gay and Lesbian Workers

There is no federal law that specifically outlaws workplace discrimination on the basis of sexual orientation. However, laws that do outlaw discrimination on that basis have been enacted by the several states—including California, Connecticut, the District of Columbia, Hawaii, Massachusetts, Minnesota, New Jersey, Vermont and Wisconsin. (See the chart in Section B.)

In addition, over 100 cities prohibit discrimination based on sexual orientation. They include: Tucson, Arizona; Sacramento, California; Aspen, Colorado; Hartford, Connecticut; Atlanta, Georgia; Chicago, Illinois; Iowa City, Iowa; Boston, Massachusetts; Detroit, Michigan; Minneapolis, Minnesota; Buffalo, New York; Raleigh, North Carolina; Columbus, Ohio; Portland, Oregon; Philadelphia, Pennsylvania; Austin, Texas; Seattle, Washingto; and Milwaukee, Wisconsin.

In states and cities that do not have laws forbidding workplace discrimination on the basis of sexual orientation, you can often take action against an employer who fires or otherwise discriminates against you because you are gay or lesbian by filing a lawsuit claiming invasion of privacy.

Example: *Raymond's employer fired him because he was quoted in a local newspaper as a spokesperson for a gay organization that was trying to raise funds for charity. Raymond was able to win a lawsuit against the employer based on invasion of privacy, because the firing amounted to the employer exerting undue control over his private life.*

With sufficient documentation, you may also be able to prove in specific instances that your firing was due to:

- illegal discrimination under the ADA (discussed in Section F) based on a perceived fear of HIV virus infection, or
- one of the other wrongful discharge strategies (discussed in Chapter 11, Section A). ■

CHAPTER

9

SEXUAL HARASSMENT

In legal terms, sexual harassment is any unwelcome sexual conduct on the job that creates an intimidating, hostile or offensive working environment. Simply put, sexual harassment is any offensive conduct related to an employee's gender that a reasonable woman or man should not have to endure while at work.

The laws prohibiting sexual harassment are gender-blind; they protect women from harassing men, men from harassing other men, and women from harassing other women. However, the vast majority of cases involve women workers being harassed by male co-workers or supervisors.

The forms that sexual harassment can take range from offensive sexual innuendoes to physical encounters, from misogynist humor to rape. An employee may be confronted with sexual demands to keep a job or obtain a promotion, known as a quid pro quo form of harassment—literally, do this for that. In other forms of sexual harassment, the threat—or the trade-off— is not as blunt. When sexually offensive conduct permeates the workplace, an employee may find it difficult or unpleasant to work there. The term hostile environment is frequently used in the cases and literature to describe this form of sexual harassment.

The definition of sexual harassment is likely to evolve and be refined by courts and legislatures. Recently, the U.S. Supreme Court held that a worker need not show psychological injury to prove a case of sexual harassment; it also intimated that one or two offensive remarks are not enough to make a case (*Harris v. Forklift Sys., Inc.,* 114 S. Ct. 367 (1993)).

A. The Effects of Sexual Harassment

Sexual harassment on the job can have a number of serious consequences, both for the harassed individual, and for other workers who experience it secondhand and become demoralized or intimidated at work. (See Section B for a discussion of legal remedies.)

1. Loss of Job

Sometimes the connection between sexual harassment and the injuries it causes is simple and direct: A worker is fired for refusing to go along with the sexual demands of a co-worker or supervisor. Usually the management uses some other pretext for the firing, but the reasons are often quite transparent.

Sometimes the firing technically occurs because of some other event, but it is still clearly related to sexual harassment. For example, if a company downgrades an employee's job and assignments because of a harassment incident and then fires him or her for complaining about the demotion, that injury is legally caused by sexual harassment.

If an employee is temporarily unable to work as a result of the harassment and the management uses that as an excuse to fire him or her, this is considered part of the harassment.

2. Loss of Wages and Other Benefits

An employee who resists sexual advances or objects to obscene humor in the office may:

- be denied a promotion
- be demoted, and
- suffer various economic losses.

That employee may also suffer harm to his or her standing within the company and have future pay increases jeopardized.

A loss of wages usually entails a loss of other job benefits as well, such as pension contributions, medical benefits, overtime pay, bonuses, sick pay, shift differential pay, vacation pay and participation in any company profit-sharing plan.

3. Forced Reassignment

Sometimes a company responds to a complaint of sexual harassment by transferring that employee somewhere else in the company and leaving the harasser unpunished. This forced reassignment is another form of job-connected injury, and it may be compounded if it results in a loss of pay or benefits, or reduced opportunities for advancement.

4. Constructive Discharge

Sometimes the sexual harassment is so severe that the employee quits. If the situation was intolerable and the employee was justified in quitting, sexual harassment caused him or her to be constructively discharged—that is, forced to leave. This is the same as an illegal firing.

Example: *A woman who worked for a film editing company received frequent threats as well as blatant sexual solicitations from the owner of the company, which culminated when he posed the ultimatum: "Fuck me, or you're fired." The owner told the woman he was leaving for a brief business trip, but his parting words were: "I'll see you when I get back." A federal court hearing the case ruled that the sexual ultimatum, combined with the explicit threat, made her working conditions so intolerable that a reasonable person in her position would be compelled to resign—the very definition of a constructive discharge. (Stockett v. Tolin, 791 F. Supp. 1536 (S.D. Fla. 1992)).*

5. Penalties for Retaliation

Employees are frequently fired or penalized for reporting sexual harassment, or otherwise trying to stop it. This is called retaliation. In such cases, the injury is legally considered to be a direct result of the sexual harassment.

6. Personal Injuries

In addition to job-connected losses, a sexually harassed worker often suffers serious and costly personal injuries—ranging from stress-related illnesses to serious physical and emotional problems.

Sexual harassment also causes a great many other types of physical, mental and emotional injuries. Some of these injuries are stress-related, but others are caused by physical pranks or violent acts directed at the harassed worker.

B. Federal Law

Sexual discrimination in employment became illegal in the United States when the Civil Rights Act of 1964 was adopted. That Act established the Equal Employment Opportunities Commission (EEOC), which later issued regulations and guidelines on the subject of sexual harassment. (See Chapter 8, Section A, for a discussion of the EEOC.)

For several years, the EEOC took no action against sexual discrimination in employment. It was not until a long time later, however, that the agency began enforcing the law as written. In late 1991, in the wake of the well-publicized hearings to confirm Clarence Thomas as a U.S. Supreme Court Justice, Congress amended the Civil Rights Act to allow employees to sue for damages for sex discrimination, including harassment.

1. Who Is Covered

The Civil Rights Act extends protection against sexual harassment to employees of all public and private employers in the United States, including U.S. citizens working for a U.S. company in a foreign country. The Act also applies to labor unions—both to the workers they employ and to their members.

However, there is one major exception: The Civil Rights Act does not apply to any company that has fewer than 15 employees.

2. Remedies Available

Remedies that the courts or the EEOC can provide under the Civil Rights Act to a sexually harassed employee include: reinstatement and promotion in job, an award of wages and job-connected losses, money damages and injunctive relief—including a court order to fashion a written sexual harassment policy and attorneys' fees to the harassed employee.

BEHIND OPEN DOORS: HOW THE BATTLE WAS ACCIDENTALLY WAGED

As introduced in Congress, the Civil Rights Act of 1964 only prohibited employment discrimination based on race, color, religion or national origin. Discrimination on the basis of sex was not included. It was attached to the bill at the last moment by conservative, Southern opponents of the bill. They hoped that adding sexual equality was so obviously preposterous that it would scuttle the entire bill when it came to a final vote.

The very idea of prohibiting sex-based discrimination engendered mirth on the floor of the Congress and on the editorial pages of major newspapers: Men, it was laughingly argued, could now sue to become Playboy bunnies. The Lyndon Johnson administration, however, wanted the Civil Rights Act passed badly enough that it decided not to oppose the amendment. The Civil Rights Act, including the ban on sex discrimination, became law. Only one of the Congressmen who had proposed the sex discrimination amendment actually voted for the bill.

C. State Laws

Some states have passed their own laws and regulations making sexual harassment illegal—usually called Fair Employment Practices (FEP) laws. But whether a harassed worker has good protection under state law depends on where he or she lives.

Some states, like Alabama and Arkansas, have no statute at all. Others, like Louisiana, adopted a law prohibiting sexual discrimination but established no agency to enforce it. Still others, like Georgia, set up an enforcement agency but enacted a law that only applied to public employees. Most states have done somewhat better, giving their enforcement agency or the courts the power to reinstate a sexually harassed worker who was fired or forced out of a job, as well as being able to make the employer pay any lost wages.

On the key issue of compensation for personal injuries, some states, like New York and Massachusetts, have enacted relatively good remedies that allow an employee to recover full compensation. Unfortunately, most state laws have no provision for awarding compensatory damages for personal injuries suffered by the employee.

The following list includes citations of statutes on sexual harassment. In most cases, the state organization responsible for administering and enforcing the law against sexual harassment is the same as the state agency charged with enforcing state anti-discrimination laws. (See Chapter 8, Section B.) Call the state agency for information on how and where to file a claim. Where no state law or agency is available, contact the local EEOC office. (See Chapter 8, Section A.)

STATE FAIR EMPLOYMENT PRACTICES LAWS	
Alabama	No state FEP law.
Alaska	Alaska Stats. §§18.80.010-300
Arizona	Arizona Rev. Stats. §41-1461 to 1465, 1481 to 1484
Arkansas	No state FEP law.
California	Cal. Gov't Code §§12900 to 12996

Colorado	Colorado Rev. Stats. §§24-34-301 to 406
Connecticut	Conn. Gen. Stats. §46a-51 to 99
Delaware	19 Del. Code Ann. §§710 to 718
District of Columbia	D.C. Code §1-2501 to 2557
Florida	Fla. Stats. Ann. §760.01 to .10
Georgia	Code of Georgia Ann. §45-19-20 to 45
	Applies only to employees of the State of Georgia
Hawaii	Hawaii Rev. Stats. §368-1 to 17, §378-1 to 9
Idaho	Idaho Code Ann. §67-5901 to 5912
Illinois	Ill. Ann. Stats., chapter 68, §§1-101 to 2-105, §7A-101 to 104, §8-101 to 105, §8A-101 to 104
Indiana	Indiana Stats. Ann. §22-9-1-1 to 13, §22-9-4-1 to 6
Iowa	Iowa Code Ann. §601A.1 to .19
Kansas	Kan. Stats. Ann. §44-1001 to 1311
Kentucky	Ky. Rev. Stats. §344.010 to .450
Louisiana	La. Rev. Stat. Ann. §23-1006
Maine	Maine Rev. Stats. Ann., tit. V, §4551-4632
Maryland	Ann. Code of Md. article 49B, §1 to 39
Massachusetts	Ann. Laws of Mass. chapter 151B, §§1 to 10
Michigan	Mich. Compiled Laws Ann. §37.2101 to .2804
Minnesota	Minn. Stats. Ann. §363.01 to .15
Mississippi	Miss. Code Ann. § 25-9-149
	Although there is a state law prohibiting discrimination against state employees, no damages, exclusions or other specifics are mentioned in the statute.
Missouri	Vernon's Ann. Missouri Stats. §213.010 to .130
Montana	Montana Code Ann. §§49-1-101 to 49-2-601
Nebraska	Nebraska Rev. Stats. §48-1101 to 1126
Nevada	Nev. Rev. Stats. Ann. §613.310 to .430
New Hampshire	N.H. Rev. Stats. Ann. §354-A:1 to A:14
New Jersey	N.J. Stats. Ann. §10:5-1 to 38.
Nw Mexico	N.M. Stats. Ann. §28-1-1 to 15
New York	N.Y. Executive Law §§290 to 301
North Carolina	Gen. Stats. of N.C. §143-422.1 to .3
North Dakota	N.D. Century Code Ann. §14-02,4-01 to 21
Ohio	Page's Ohio Rev. Code Ann. §4112.01 to .99
Oklahoma	25 Oklahoma Stats. §§1101 to 1802

Oregon	Or. Rev. Stats. §659.010 to .990
Pennsylvania	43 Penn. Stats. Ann. §§951 to 962.2
Rhode Island	Gen. Laws of R.I. §28-5-1 to 40
South Carolina	Code of S.C. title 1, §1-13-10 to 110
South Dakota	S.D. Codified Laws chapter 20-13
Tennessee	Tenn. Code Ann. §4-21-101 to 408
Texas	Tex. Stats. Ann., Article 5221(k) §§1.01 to 10.05
Utah	Utah Code Ann. §34-35-1 to 7.1
Vermont	21 Vermont Stats. Ann. §495
Virginia	Code of Virginia §§2.1-714 to -725
Washington	Rev. Code of Wash. Ann. §49.60.010 to .330
West Virginia	W. Va. Code §5-11-1 to 19
Wisconsin	Wis. Stats. Ann. §11.31 to .39
Wyoming	Wyoming Stats. Ann. §27-9-101 to 108

D. Taking Steps to End Sexual Harassment

The alternatives described here can be viewed as a series of escalating steps in stopping sexual harassment. If a particular tactic does not end the objectionable behavior, you can switch to an increasingly formal strategy until you find one that is effective.

1. Confront the Harasser

Often the best strategy for the employee sounds the simplest: Confront the harasser and persuade him or her to stop. This is not appropriate or sensible in every case, particularly when you have suffered injuries or are in some physical danger. But surprisingly often—most workplace experts say up to 90% of the time—it works.

Confronted directly, harassment is especially likely to end if it is at a fairly low level: off-color jokes, inappropriate comments about appearance, repeated requests for dates, sexist cartoons tacked onto the office refrigerator. Clearly saying no does more than assert your determination to stop the behavior. It is also a crucial first step if you later decide to take more formal action against the harassment.

Tell the harasser what you don't want. It is best to deal directly with the harassment when it occurs. But if your harasser surprised you with an obnoxious gesture or comment that caught you completely off-guard—a common tactic—you may have been too flabbergasted to respond at once. Or if you did respond, you may not have expressed yourself clearly. Either way, talk to the harasser the next day.

- Keep the conversation brief. Try to speak privately, out of the hearing range of supervisors and co-workers.
- Do not use humor to make your point. Joking may be too easily misunderstood—or interpreted as a sign that you don't take the situation seriously yourself.
- Be direct. It is usually better to make a direct request that a specific kind of behavior stop than to tell your harasser how you feel. For example, saying "I am uncomfortable with this," may be enough to get the point across to some people, but the subtlety may be lost on others. And of course, making you uncomfortable may be just the effect the harasser was after.
- Offer no excuses. Keep in mind that you're not the one whose behavior is inexcusable. Simply make the point and end the conversation. There is no need to offer excuses, such as: "My boyfriend wouldn't like it if we met at your apartment to discuss that new project."

Put it in writing. If your harasser persists, write a letter, spelling out what behavior you object to and why. Also specify what you want to happen next. If you feel the situation is serious or bound to escalate, make clear that you will take action against the harassment if it does not stop at once. If your company has a written policy against harassment, attach a copy of it to your letter.

2. Use a Company Complaint Procedure

A court sometimes requires a company to write a comprehensive policy if it finds there has been a problem with sexual harassment. Many businesses are also adopting sexual harassment policies on their own, to foster a better atmosphere for employees.

If you are harassed at work, a sexual harassment policy can help you determine what behavior you can take action against and how to ensure the harassment is stopped.

Find out whether or not your employer has a sexual harassment policy by contacting the human resources department or the person who handles employee benefits. If there is no policy, lobby to get one.

3. File a Complaint With a Government Agency

If the sexual harassment does not end after face-to-face meetings or after using the company complaint procedure, consider filing a complaint under the U.S. Civil Rights Act with the U.S. Equal Employment Opportunities Commission (EEOC) (see Chapter 8, Section A), or filing a complaint under a similar state law with a state or fair employment practices (FEP) agency. (See Section C, above.)

Contacting these agencies does two important things:

- It sets in motion an investigation by the EEOC or the state FEP agency that may resolve the sexual harassment complaint, and

- It is a necessary prerequisite under the U.S. Civil Rights Act and under some state FEP laws if you want to file a lawsuit with the help of an attorney under the Civil Rights Act or under a state FEP law.

Sometimes an EEOC or a state FEP agency can resolve a sexual harassment dispute at no cost to the employee and with relatively little legal involvement. Almost all of these agencies provide some sort of conciliation service—a negotiation between the employer and employee to end the harassment and restore peace in the workplace. And most agencies protect the employee against retaliation for filing the complaint. Most agencies have the power to expand their investigation to cover more widespread sexual harassment within the company. A few state FEP agencies also provide an administrative hearing panel that can award money to compensate a harassed employee for personal injuries, although the EEOC and most state agencies do not have this important power.

The EEOC and state FEP agencies can resolve a lot of cases, but not all of them. Investigations sometimes drag on longer than the harassed employee is prepared to wait. Not all cases will yield to the conciliation efforts of such agencies; this is particularly true in severe cases of sexual harassment with significant personal injuries.

4. File a Private Lawsuit

If investigation and conciliation by the EEOC or a state FEP agency does not produce satisfactory results, your next step may be to file a lawsuit under the U.S. Civil Rights Act or under one of the state FEP statutes.

Even if you intend right from the beginning to file such a lawsuit, you frequently must first file a claim with a government agency, as described above. An employee must file a claim with the EEOC before bringing a lawsuit under the U.S. Civil Rights Act. Some states also require that the employee first file a claim with the state FEP agency before suing under state law. At some point after such claims are filed and investigated, the agency will issue you a document—usually referred to as a right to sue letter—that allows you to take your case to court. Going to court in such lawsuits requires getting legal advice from an attorney who is experienced in these types of cases. (See Chapter 18, Section D.)

Generally speaking, suing under the U.S. Civil Rights Act is better than relying on state law. Most state FEP laws allow you to win lost wages and benefits, not compensation for physical and mental injuries, such as stress and anxiety caused by the harassment. By contrast, the Civil Rights Act allows the employee to recover some money—out-of-pocket losses plus $50,000 to $300,000, depending upon the number of employees in the company. Its coverage, however, is limited to employers with 15 or more employees.

However, some states, such as New York and California, do better. They allow an employee to be compensated up to the full amount of damages proven without any artificial limits. Employees in those states will probably want to pursue their rights under state law or maybe a combination of state and federal law.

5. File a Tort Lawsuit

Bringing a tort action is often the last legal resort for sexually harassed workers. These legal actions provide a wider range of possible remedies than those available under the Civil Rights Act. You can sue for both compensatory damages for the emotional and physical distress suffered because of the workplace harassment and potentially large punitive damages aimed at punishing the wrongdoer.

These lawsuits, which will usually require help from a lawyer, are based on traditional legal theories such as assault and battery, intentional infliction of emotional distress, interference with contract and defamation. These actions, called torts, are civil wrongs—and are filed in state courts like any other lawsuit based on a personal injury.

Tort actions allow, at least in theory, unlimited dollar verdicts for some of the most severe injuries wrought by the harassment: emotional and physical harm. These tort actions are particularly appropriate where a worker has suffered severe trauma from the psychological remnants of harassment—embarrassment, fright, humiliation—which can cause a permanent loss of self-esteem and take a heavy toll on emotional and physical health.

While a tort lawsuit action may be the best option for some harassed workers, it is the only possible remedy for others. As mentioned, if your employer has 14 or fewer employees, you are not covered by the U.S. Civil Rights Act and cannot file an EEOC complaint or a federal lawsuit for money.

E. Where to Get More Information

Contact the local office of the EEOC and your state FEP agency. Many will send you written materials on sexual harassment, and can provide information on local training programs, support groups and attorneys.

Some states and larger cities also have a Commission on the Status of Women, or a state or local agency dealing specifically with women's issues—and offer help to sexually harassed workers. The services these groups provide range from referrals to local groups, to advice and counseling, to legal referrals. Check your telephone book to see if there is such a group in your area.

Many unions and groups for union members are especially active in the fight against sexual harassment. Contact your local to find out if it offers any special services or guidance.

Also, some law schools have clinics that deal with sexual harassment or employment law. These clinics are usually staffed by students, who are assisted by experienced attorneys. Many provide in-person or telephone counseling and legal advice, and some will even represent you in court. Their services are low-cost, often free. Call law schools in your area and ask if they have such a clinic.

Finally, a number of organizations offer specialized information and guidance on evaluating sexual harassment in the workplace and many also offer legal referrals. (See the Appendix for contact details.)

SPECIAL MENTION: 9TO5

One group is doing so much to end sexual harassment that it deserves special mention.

9to5, National Association of Working Women, is a national nonprofit membership organization for American office workers that has local chapters throughout the country. It maintains a toll-free confidential telephone hotline, staffed by trained job counselors, and provides information and referrals on how to deal with sexual harassment and other problems on the job. Books and reports on sexual harassment are also available at a discount to members; members also get legal referrals to attorneys specializing in sexual harassment. A newsletter is published five times a year. Some 9to5 local chapters offer sexual harassment support groups and referrals to training resources.

9to5, National Association of Working Women
614 Superior Avenue, NW
Cleveland, OH 44113
216/566-9308 (General information)
800/522-0925 (Hotline) ◼

CHAPTER 10

LOSING OR LEAVING A JOB

The truth will surprise you: No law gives you an automatic right to keep your job. In fact, most of the legal principles and practices of the workplace are indisputably on the side of the employer who fires you.

You can be fired for a host of traditional and obvious reasons: incompetence, excessive absences, violating certain laws or company rules, sleeping or taking drugs on the job. And other reasons are gaining in popularity—most notably, firing employees because of economic need occasioned by a downturn in company profits or demands. In most cases, an employer does not need to provide any notice before giving an employee walking papers.

Still, there are limits. The laws do guarantee you some rights on the way out the door. And because of the grand importance of job security to the majority of Americans, employees are increasingly fighting for and slowly garnering more rights in the workplace.

Employers do not have the right to discriminate against you illegally (see Chapter 8) or to violate state or federal laws, such as those controlling wages and hours. (See Chapter 3.) And there are a number of other more complex reasons that may make it illegal for an employer to fire you—basically boiling down to the Golden Rule that an employer must deal with you fairly and honestly.

If you lost your job—or have good reason to think you are about to lose it—it may behoove you to become familiar with the various situations in which it may be illegal to fire an employee. (See Chapter 11.)

A. The Doctrine of Employment at Will

Once again, for the value of its shock: People employed in private industry have no automatic legal right to their jobs.

That is because of the long-established legal doctrine of employment at will—a term you are most likely to hear cited by your boss or your company's lawyers if you speak up and protest your dismissal. An employer's right to unilaterally determine whether or not you should stay on the payroll stems from a 1894 case (*Payne v. Western & Atlantic RR*, 81 Tenn. 507) in which the court ruled that employers do not need a reason to fire employees—they may fire any or all of their workers at will. Even if the reason for dismissal is morally wrong, the court held, no legal wrong has occurred and the government has no basis to intervene.

The management of America's factories was still in the experimental stage in the 1890s when that case was decided. The business community successfully argued then, and in cases that followed, that factories could not be operated profitably unless employers were free to hire and fire as they chose. The employment at will doctrine has been reinforced over and over again by subsequent court rulings—and expanded to include not only factories but also virtually all other types of private industry jobs.

But the doctrine has been weakened a bit since the 1970s by rulings in wrongful discharge suits in which former employees question the legality of their firings (discussed in Chapter 11, Section A)—and by some new laws that are more favorable to employees. For example, some states have made it illegal to fire employees for taking time off to care for a sick child (discussed in Chapter 5, Section B) or because they are gay or lesbian (discussed in Chapter 8, Section H).

1. Exceptions to the Rule

There are a few exceptions to the employment at will doctrine—scarce and becoming scarcer. Most often, a strong written statement is required, signifying that an employee is to be excepted from the employment at will doctrine.

For example, most collective bargaining agreements that set out union members' rights state that union members can be fired only "for good cause." So while union members are still technically employees at will, their agreements often make them exceptions to the general rule, requiring that employers point to a specific reason before firing them. (See Chapter 16.)

And some employees enter detailed contracts with their employers—contracts which set out the specifics terms of their employment, including salary and relocation rights. Employment contracts are rare—usually reserved for only the uppermost company executives and other notables such as professional athletes. Those holding employment contracts are usually not subject to the employment at will doctrine; their contracts spell out the length of their employment and specifically note when and how the employment relationship can end.

Finally, some former employees have successfully contested their dismissals by pointing to the promising words found in the employee manuals they were handed when they signed on at a particular workplace. A few courts held, for example, that where manuals stated that employees became permanent after a certain time, or that they must be given a hearing before being fired, employers must deliver on those promises. However, most savvy businesses these days are well-acquainted with this legal loophole, so few of them now include such easily misconstrued promises in their employee manuals.

2. Employees' Rights

The other side of the employment at will logic is that employees are also free to leave a job at any time; an employer cannot force you to stay in a job you no longer wish to keep. And while it is customary to give an employer notice before leaving a job, it is not usually required by law. The right to leave a job at any time feels like small recompense for most workers. Obviously, most legal battles are fought by former employees who want their jobs back, not employers demanding that employees stay on.

B. Finding Out Why You Were Fired

Few job losses come as complete surprises. Unless you are the unfortunate heir to a sudden unforeseen cutback in the workforce, you are likely to have seen the end of your employment coming well before it arrived. This is particularly true if you are fired because your employer claims your work was below par or that you violated a particular workplace rule.

STABBING AT EMPLOYMENT AT WILL: THE BOMBSHELL THAT WASN'T

The California Supreme Court recently dealt a blow to employers that cling to the employment at will doctrine. The court held that an employer violated an implied contract when it fired an employee who worked there nearly seven years. The court was persuaded by the facts that the employer:

- made repeated oral assurances that the job was secure
- gave the employee consistent promotions, salary increases and bonuses
- did not follow a mandated pre-termination discipline procedure before firing the employee, and
- required that the employee sign an agreement vowing not to compete with the employer one year after termination (*Foley v. Interactive Data Corp.*, 765 P. 2d 373 (1988)).

Although the California Supreme Court is traditionally regarded as The Legal Trendsetter, few other courts have jumped on the bandwagon to weaken the employment at will doctrine. Many employers, however, have acted to give the doctrine stronger roots by changing their employee handbooks to include an employment at will policy along the following lines: "The K Company and its officers have the right to hire, dismiss, direct and schedule employees in any way that does not violate federal, state or municipal law. As an employee, you have the right to end your employment at the K Company at any time and for any reason."

Courts have generally upheld this practice, even when it represents a complete about-face from former workplace policy. However, the employer must inform all employees and must not make the change in bad faith—for example, to ease firing a particular employee. (*Bankey v. Storer Broadcasting Co.*, 443 N.W. 2d 112 (1989)).

1. If You Have Been Disciplined

Although an employer has the right to fire you on the spot for substandard performance or stealing from the company coffers, most proceed more gingerly these days—beginning with a verbal warning and progressing to a written warning to probation to suspension, then to dismissal.

WHAT TO DO WHEN THE END IS NEAR

You are not legally entitled to any progressive warning system. But if you find yourself on the receiving end of a disciplinary notice, there are several steps you should take to avoid losing your job.

- Be sure you understand exactly what work behavior is being challenged. If you are unclear, ask for another specific meeting with your supervisor or human resources staff to discuss the issue more thoroughly.

- If you disagree with allegations that your work performance or behavior is poor, ask for the assessment in writing. You may want to add a written clarification to your own personnel file—but should do so only if you feel your employer's assessment is inaccurate. First take some time to reflect and perhaps discuss your situation with friends. If not, your words could be twisted against you as evidence of your inability to work as a team player, take constructive criticism or some other convenient company slang.

- Look for written company policy on discipline procedures in the employee handbook or a separate document. If the policy says certain measures "must," "will" or "shall" be followed before an employee will be dismissed, then you have more clout in demanding that the steps be followed. That may help buy you more time so that you can change your work habits, you can wait until a workplace controversy dies down, or the situation improves in some other way.

- Read behind the lines to see whether your disciplining or firing may be discriminatory or in other ways unfair. Look particularly at the timing: Were you put on probation shortly before your rights in the company pension plan vested? Look also at uneven applications of discipline: Are women more often given substandard performance reviews or fired before being elevated to supervisor?

---

2. Finding Out the Reason

Before any holes had been punched in the employment at will doctrine, companies often refused to give employees any reason for being fired. Since a company had the legal right to hire and fire without any justification, most opted not to invite trouble by stating a reason for firing.

Today, many companies have reversed their policies on giving reasons for dismissals. Because courts throughout the country are gradually establishing more rights for fired employees (discussed in Chapter 11), many companies, particularly large corporations that are attractive targets for wrongful discharge lawsuits, now are careful to provide at least the appearance of fair and evenhanded treatment of employees who are fired. Company owners and managers typically do this by carefully documenting the employee's allegedly unacceptable work performance. Then, the employer can provide the employee—and a court, should it come to that—with specific and tangible documentation of the cause of firing.

If you are fired, make your best effort to obtain a clear statement of the employer's reasons for doing so. Office or factory rumors, your suspicions or your spouse's hunches just will not suffice. If you eventually decide to challenge your dismissal (discussed in Chapter 11, Section D), the reasons that your former employer stated for firing you will almost certainly become a major point in any legal battle that may develop.

C. Documenting Your Dismissal

Even if you decide not to challenge the legality of your firing, you will be in a much better position to enforce all of your workplace rights if you carefully document the circumstances. For example, if you apply for unemployment insurance benefits and your former employer challenges that application, you will typically need to prove that you were dismissed for reasons beyond your control. (See Chapter 12, Section D.)

There are a number of time-tested ways to document the circumstances leading to your firing.

LABELS MAKE NO DIFFERENCE

People tend to think that getting fired means that you did something wrong on the job, and that when other terms are used—such as dismissal, discharge, layoff, staff cut and downsizing—it somehow means something less onerous. In hopes of preventing bad community relations and wrongful discharge lawsuits, many companies use these gentler words to describe firings.

Some companies have gone so far as to announce the firing of large groups of employees by using sterile, institutional terms such as Reorganizational Incentives or Activity Analysis and Review. Still other companies have described the process of firing groups of employees as early retirement—even where the people being dismissed are not being given anywhere near enough money to continue to live the rest of their lives without working.

Whenever you are permanently dismissed from a job without being given sufficient income to continue living without working, all these terms mean the same thing: You've been fired. (For more information on layoffs, see Section G.)

1. Keeping a Paper Trail

Long before being fired, you may sense that something has gone wrong in the relationship between you and your employer, even if there has been no formal disciplinary action against you. Perhaps your first clue will be that your pay has been stuck at one level with no raises for an unusually long time. Or you may notice that none of your work assignments extend more than a few weeks. Whatever the sign that your job may be in jeopardy, use it as a reason to begin keeping a log of your interactions with your employer.

Record and date each work-related event such as performance reviews, commendations or reprimands, salary increases or decreases and even informal comments that your supervisor makes to you about your work. Note the date, time and location for each event; which members of management were involved; and whether or not there were witnesses. Whenever possible, back up your log with materials issued by your employer, such as copies of the employee handbook, memos, brochures and employee orientation videos.

In addition, ask to see your personnel file. (See Chapter 6, Section A, for a discussion of privacy concerns.) Make a copy of all reports and reviews in it. Because personnel administrators are notoriously covetous of employee files, you may have to make repeated requests to see your file or pay a certain amount of money to copy each page in the file. It will be money well spent. Many former employees are startled to learn that their personnel files have been tampered with by unscrupulous former employers. If you fear this might happen, make an additional copy of your file or of relevant reports or performance reviews and mail them to yourself by certified mail. Then, should matters heat up later—or should a court battle become necessary—you will have dated proof of how the documents looked before any tampering took place.

2. Getting Written Explanations

There are a number of reasons why you might want to get a written explanation from a former employer of why you were fired: to see whether the reason your former employer gives mesh with your own hunches, and in the hardest situations, to use as documentation if you feel your dismissal was discriminatory or otherwise illegal. Written explanations may also help you in a later job search, as you will be better able to assess whether a soon-to-be-former employer is likely to give a good recommendation to your prospective employers.

a. Service letter laws

Several states have laws, commonly known as service letter laws, that require employers to provide former employees with letters describing work histories. (See the chart below.)

Service letter laws vary greatly from state to state. In Minnesota, for example, an employer must provide a written statement of the reasons for an employee's dismissal within five days after the employee requests such a statement in writing. Kansas also has a service letter law, but it does not require an former employer to list a reason for your dismissal. Employers in Kansas must state only your length of employment, job classification and wage rate.

STATE SERVICE LETTER LAWS

Kansas	Upon written request, an employer must provide a former employee with a letter stating the former employee's length of employment, job classification and wage rate. Kan. Stat. Ann. §44-808
Maine	Upon written request, an employer must provide a discharged employee with a written listing of the reasons for that employee's firing. Me. Rev. Stat. Ann. 26 §630
Minnesota	Employers must provide a discharged employee with a written listing of the reasons for the employee's dismissal. However, the former employee must request that listing in writing within five working days after the discharge. Minn. Stat. Ann. §181.933
Missouri	Employers with seven or more employees must provide a discharged employee with a letter stating the length of the former employment, the nature of the job held and the reasons for the discharge. This letter must be provided to the former employee within 45 days after the company receives a request for it. Mo. Ann. Stat. §290.140
Montana	Upon request from a discharged employee, an employer must provide that employee with a written statement of the reasons for the discharge. Mont. Code Ann. §39-2-801
Nebraska	Law applies to public service corporations and contractors doing business in the state. Upon request by a discharged or quitting employee, an employer must provide a statement of the nature and duration of the services rendered by the employee and the reasons for the termination. Neb. Rev. Stat. §§48-209 to 48-211
Nevada	Former employees who held a job for 60 days or more may demand from the former employer a written statement of the reason for their departure from the job. Nev. Rev. Stat. §613.210

Oklahoma	Employees of public service corporation and their contractors are entitled to a statement of the nature of service, duration, cause of discharge or quitting. No form letters are allowed. Okla. Stat. Ann. tit. 40 §171
Texas	Employees who are discharged or voluntarily quit are entitled to a true statement of the reason upon written request. Tex. Civ. Stat. Art. 5196
Washington	Upon request of a discharged employee, former employers must furnish a signed statement of the reason for the discharge. Wash. Admin Code R. §296-126-050

If you live in a state that has a service letter law requiring explanations of dismissals, and the employer who fired you does not provide you with one, request one in writing.

SAMPLE LETTER

June 10, 199X

Ellen Ullentine
President
Tasteless Frozen Pizzas Inc.
123 Main Street
Anywhere, MO 54321

Dear Ms. Ullentine:

As required by Missouri Statutes Section 290.140, I request from you a letter stating the length of my employment with Tasteless Frozen Pizzas Inc., the nature of my work there and the reason I was dismissed from employment.

Please note that this law requires you to provide me with such a letter within 45 days of when you receive this request.

Sincerely,

Paul Smith
321 Front Street
Anywhere, MO 54321
234/555-6666

Some laws specify a time limit for requesting service letters. But if possible, it is usually wise to make your request within a day or two of your dismissal to make sure that you meet any such deadlines and to prevent the passing of time from affecting people's memories. Send your request for a service letter by certified mail so that you can prove, if necessary, that you made your request within any time limits specified.

ASK AND YOU MAY RECEIVE

If you live in a state that does not have a service letter law, there is a chance that your employer will not offer you any written explanation for your firing. This is particularly likely if the company dismissing you is small or does not know much about workplace law and current legal techniques for firing employees. If no written explanation of your dismissal is given, ask the person who officially informs you of your firing for a written explanation of the company's decision to dismiss you. Be firm but polite; keep in mind that having to fire someone is an extremely stressful assignment for even the most experienced managers.

Companies usually want dismissed employees to be out of their buildings and away from the remaining employees as quickly as possible to prevent vengeful sabotage or spreading anti-company sentiment. Therefore, a person being fired exercises a substantial amount of negotiating power by merely sitting in place in front of the person doing the firing, quietly insisting on written documentation, until the request is satisfied. Remember, however, that in some companies, using your posterior as a negotiating tool can get you escorted out forcibly by the corporate security force or local police if pushed too far.

b. Letters of understanding

If you have done everything within the limits of civility, but your employer still refuses to give you written documentation of its reasons for your dismissal, you may be in for a wait—and some extra work—before you get it. If your state is among the majority that have no laws requiring such documentation, there is not much else you can do to force the issue at the time of your dismissal. Later, you may obtain documentation through some of the laws granting employees access to their personnel files (see Chapter 6, Section A), or by filing a wrongful discharge lawsuit (see Chapter 11, Section A), and demanding the company's internal documents concerning your employment.

But before that, you might want to write a letter of understanding to the person who fired you. This is especially important if you received some mixed messages upon being fired. Of course, it is to your advantage to get your employer to specify the reason for your firing that makes you seem the least culpable—and the most attractive to prospective employers.

SAMPLE LETTER

August 2, 199X

Aggie Supervisor
XYZ Company
2222 Lake Street
Anytown, CA 12345

Dear Ms. Supervisor:

I'm writing to clarify the reasons for my dismissal from employment at XYZ Company on July 29, 199X.

My understanding is that I was dismissed because there was a sharp decline in the market for our product, seamless rolled rings, due to the recent cutback in government military spending.

If you feel that my understanding is incorrect, please advise me in writing by August 16, 199X.

Sincerely,

John Employee

123 Any Street
Anytown, CA 12345
234/555-6666

Although you should mail your letter of understanding promptly, it is usually best to let it sit for a day or two after writing it. Then, read it over again to make sure you have kept it businesslike and to the point. Getting fired is a very emotional event—one that often generates more than a little anger and desire for revenge in even the most saintly people.

Correspondence between you and your former employer may eventually become the basis of future negotiations or even courtroom evidence, and you don't want its credibility to be tainted by ink from a poison pen. Send your letter of understanding by certified mail so that you will be able to prove that the company received it. Using certified mail in this case may also help drive home to your former employer that you are serious about enforcing your rights concerning your dismissal.

If the company responds to your letter, you have obtained at least one piece of documentation of its reason for firing you. If the company does not respond to your letter after a month or so, you can probably assume that the reason stated in your letter of understanding is correct.

3. Additional Documentation

Other important forms of documentation for your firing may come your way in the weeks following your dismissal. For example, if you file a claim for unemployment compensation, your former employer will have to respond to that claim. That response will eventually be translated into a document that the local unemployment insurance office will provide to you.

Store all such documents in a file folder, shoebox, or some safe place where they will not get lost or destroyed—and where you can find and organize them easily.

D. Waiving Your Right to Sue

In large companies, the firing process may work like this: A member of the human resource management staff hands you a formal written notice that you are fired. You are then asked to sign a statement indicating that you have read the documents and that you accept what is in them. You are given a check for a few extra months of severance pay, although this is beyond the company's legal obligations. (See Section F.) You will then be told that the check will be released to you immediately if you sign a waiver of any rights to take legal action against the company as a result of your dismissal.

This method of firing can seem cruel or unfair. But in the past, it was effective for some companies in discouraging wrongful discharge lawsuits.

It is no longer a foolproof tactic. An increasing number of employees who have signed waivers of their rights to file a lawsuit over their firing have later succeeded in having the courts throw out the waivers by arguing, for example, that the waivers were signed under duress. Whether or not signing such a waiver will prevent you from suing your former employer depends on the circumstances of each individual case, however, so there is no way of predicting the power of a waiver in advance.

Going along with the firing will typically give you immediate severance pay. However, if you have doubts about the validity of your dismissal, withhold your signature on any waiver of your right to sue while you think over the company's offer, obtain more information and perhaps hire a lawyer. (See Chapter 18.) You take the chance of not getting the money and documentation that the company waves in front of you, but you will lower your risk of signing away essential rights.

BEWARE OF THE EARLY RETIREMENT WAIVER

If you are asked to sign a waiver of your right to sue in return for participation in an early retirement program offered by your former employer, the Older Workers Benefit Protection Act may give you the right to consider the company's offer for 45 days before you accept or reject it, and seven more days to revoke a decision to accept the company's offer. (See Chapter 8, Section E.)

E. Your Right to a Final Paycheck

Most state laws specify when a final paycheck must be issued to employees who are fired or resign, and some of those laws are quite powerful. (See the listing below.) For example, Wyoming law requires that an employee who is fired be paid in full within 24 hours. If not, the employee may sue for additional wages and interest on them, plus attorneys' fees and costs of the lawsuit.

STATE LAWS THAT CONTROL YOUR FINAL PAYCHECK

The laws listed here specify how soon your final paycheck must be given to you under the laws of the state in which you work.

Alabama	No applicable law.
Alaska	Within three days. (Alaska Stat. §23.05.140)
Arizona	If you are fired: within three days or next scheduled payday. If you quit: next scheduled payday. (Ariz. Rev. Stat. Ann. §23-353)
Arkansas	If you are fired: within seven days after your demand. If you quit: no applicable law. (Arkansas Code §11-4-405)
California	If you are fired: immediately—or within 72 hours for employees of the seasonal industries. If you quit: within 72 hours, or immediately if you have given 72 hours notice. (Cal. Labor Code §§201 and 202)
Colorado	If you are fired: immediately. If you quit: next scheduled payday. (Colo. Rev. Stat. Ann. §8-4-104)
Connecticut	If you are fired: next business day. If you quit: next scheduled payday. (Conn. Gen. Stat. Ann. §1-71c)
Delaware	Next scheduled payday. (Del. Code Ann. §19-1103)
District of Columbia	If you are fired: next business day. If you quit: next scheduled payday or seven days, whichever is sooner. (D.C. Code §36-103)
Florida	No applicable law.
Georgia	No applicable law.
Hawaii	If you are fired: next business day. If you quit: next scheduled payday. (Hawaii Rev. Stat. §388-3)

Idaho	Next scheduled payday or within ten business days, whichever is sooner. If written request made for earlier payment, within 48 hours. (Idaho Code §45-606)
Illinois	Next scheduled payday. (820 Ill. Cons. Stat. 115/5)
Indiana	Next scheduled payday. (Ind. Code §§22-2-9-2 and 22-2-5-1)
Iowa	Next scheduled payday. (Iowa Code Ann. §91A.4)
Kansas	Next scheduled payday. (Kan. Stat. Ann. §31-315)
Kentucky	If you are fired: next scheduled payday or within 14 days, whichever is later. If you quit: no applicable law. (Ky. Rev. Stat. Ann. §337.055)
Louisiana	Within three days of your date of discharge or resignation. (La. Rev. Stat. Ann. §§23-631)
Maine	Next scheduled payday or within two weeks after demand, whichever is earlier. (Me. Rev. Stat. Ann. tit. 26 § 626)
Maryland	Next scheduled payday. (Md. Labor & Employment Code Ann. §3-505)
Massachusetts	If you are fired: immediately. If you quit: next scheduled payday. (Mass. Ann. Laws ch. 149 §148)
Michigan	As soon as amount can be determined with due diligence. (Mich. Stat. Ann. §17.277(5))
Minnesota	If you are fired: within 24 hours of demand. If you quit: within five days, or within 24 hours if you have given at least five days' notice. (Minn. Stat. §§181.13 and 181.14)
Mississippi	No applicable law.
Missouri	If you are fired: within seven days after you make a written demand. If you quit: no applicable law. (Mo. Ann. Stat. §290.110)
Montana	If you are fired for cause: immediately; otherwise, within three days. An extension of three additional days is given to the employer if its payroll checks come from outside the state. (Mont. Code Ann. §39-3-205)
Nebraska	If you are fired: next scheduled payday or within two weeks, whichever is sooner. If you quit: no applicable law. (Neb. Rev. Stat. §48-1230)
Nevada	If you are fired: immediately. If you quit: next scheduled payday or within seven days, whichever is earlier. (Nev. Rev. Stat. §608.020 and 608.030)
New Hampshire	If you are fired: within 72 hours. If you quit: next scheduled payday; or if you give at least one pay period's notice, within 72 hours of end of work. (N.H. Rev. Stat. Ann. §275:44)

New Jersey	Next scheduled payday. (N.J. Stat. Ann. §34:11-4.3)
New Mexico	If you are fired: within 5 days. If you quit: no applicable law. (N.M. Stat. Ann. §§50-4-4 and 50-4-5)
New York	If you are fired: next scheduled payday. If you quit: no applicable law. (N.Y. Labor Laws §191)
North Carolina	Next scheduled payday. (N.C. Gen. Stat. §95.25.7)
North Dakota	If you are fired: within 24 hours of the time of separation at employer's place of business or within 15 days or on the next scheduled payday, whichever comes first. If you resign: next scheduled payday by certified mail to an address designated by the employee. (N.D. Cent. Code §34-14-03)
Ohio	No applicable law.
Oklahoma	Next scheduled payday. (Okla. Stat. Ann. tit. 40, §165.3)
Oregon	If you are fired: immediately. If you quit: within 48 hours. (Or. Rev. Stat. §652.140)
Pennsylvania	Next scheduled payday. (Pa. Stat. Ann. tit. 43, §260.5)
Rhode Island	Next scheduled payday under normal circumstances; within 24 hours if the employer is going out of business, merging or moving out of state. (R.I. Gen. Laws §28-14-4)
South Carolina	Within 48 hours or next scheduled payday, which may not be more than 30 days after written notice is given. (S.C. Codified Laws §41-11-170)
South Dakota	If you are fired: within five days after you have returned anything belonging to the employer. If you quit: next scheduled payday after you have returned anything belonging to the employer. (S.D. Codified Laws §§60-11-10 and 60-11-11)
Tennessee	No applicable law.
Texas	If you are fired: within six days. If you quit: next regularly scheduled payday. (Tex. Civ. Stat. Art. 5155)
Utah	If you are fired: within 24 hours. If you quit: within 72 hours, or immediately if you have given at least 72 hours notice. (Utah Code Ann. §34-28-5)
Vermont	If you are fired: within 72 hours. If you quit: next scheduled payday or, if no scheduled payday exists, the next Friday. (Vt. Stat. Ann. tit. 21, §342)
Virginia	Next scheduled payday. (Va. Code §40.1-29)
Washington	Next scheduled payday. (Wash. Rev. Code §49.48.010)
West Virginia	If you are fired: within 72 hours. If you quit: next regular payday. (W. Va. Code §21-5-4)
Wisconsin	If you are fired: within three days. If you quit: within 15 days. (Wis. Stat. Ann. §109.03)

Wyoming — If you are fired: within 24 hours. If you quit: within 72 hours. (Wyo. Stat. Ann. §27-4-103)

F. Severance Pay

Many people assume that when they leave a job, they have a legal right to severance pay. This is yet another bit of workplace lore that builds false hope in the newly unemployed.

Most employers do offer severance in the form of a month or two worth of salary to employees who are laid off or let go for some reason other than misconduct. But no law requires it. And whether it is given at all varies drastically from employer to employer, region to region, industry custom to industry custom.

However, an employer may be legally obligated to pay you some severance pay if you had good reason to believe you had it coming, as evidenced by:

- a written contract stating that severance will be paid
- a promise that employees would receive severance pay as documented in an employee handbook
- a history of the company paying severance to other employees in your position, or
- an oral promise that the employer would pay you severance—although you may run into difficulties proving the promise existed.

If your employer refuses to pay you severance or offers an amount that you find unacceptable, you have nothing to lose by asking, or asking again. Request a meeting with a company representative to discuss the issue. Remain calm and polite; do not threaten. Explain why you need the money—support while securing another job is the usual reason. Fear of lawsuits in the last few years has meant that more employers are willing to grant severance pay to departing employees and to be flexible in the amount they will award.

If you meet with no success, take another hard look at the reasons listed above that may entitle you legally to severance pay. If you feel you may have a valid claim, collect as much evidence as you can to back up your position. (See Section C.)

Then think again. A breach of contract action, which is what you can bring against an employer that has reneged on a promise to pay severance, will likely require the help of an attorney. If the amount involved is not substantial, you could be facing more in legal fees than you would stand to gain by collecting the severance money.

G. Temporary Job Losses

We tend to speak in euphemisms around difficult and painful events—like the death of a person or the loss of a job. This lack of directness may make it easier to get words out, but it also makes it easy to get confused when talking.

Historically, the word layoff typically was used to describe situations in which factory production workers were told not to report to work until their help was needed again on the production lines. But over time, the word has also been applied to other types of job losses—even those that obviously are permanent.

The confusion over the meaning of layoff became even worse in the early 1990s, when economic downturns meant that some companies needed to cut costs. Some of these companies decided that it was more equitable to make all of their employees take a week off from work without pay every once in a while than to fire a few employees. Ironically, many of these plans, which clearly fit the traditional definition of layoff, were euphemistically called Job Security Programs.

Ignore the name that your employer assigns to a temporary loss of employment. If you become involved in an employment cut that appears to be temporary, the strategies discussed in the preceding sections of this chapter and in Chapter 11 will not be relevant. These strategies are intended for people who have lost their jobs permanently. Typically, the only legal action available to deal with a temporary loss of employment is to file an application for unemployment insurance benefits (discussed in Chapter 12, Section D) and then wait to be recalled to your job.

However, if you believe that temporary employment cuts imposed by your employer form a pattern of illegal discrimination (discussed in Chapter 8, Section A), you may want to file what is usually called an abusive layoff complaint under anti-discrimination laws. You will probably need to hire a lawyer to help you with that kind of case. (See Chapter 18, Section D.)

Example: *John is employed as a production worker at a nonunion steel foundry in Pennsylvania, where about two-thirds of the workers are white and one-third are black. For the past three years, business has been slow for the foundry, so some employees were told not to report to work for six weeks at a time every few months.*

The employees who were laid off were allowed to collect unemployment insurance benefits, which replaced about one-half of the income they would receive if they were working.

But all the workers who have been put out of work temporarily, John notices, were black. All the white workers have been employed steadily for 40 hours or more per week. Even black workers who have been employed there longer and have more work skills were told to stay home while the white workers continue to work.

It appears that the foundry is treating its white workers better than those who are black, so John can take action against the abusive layoffs under Title VII of the Civil Rights Act of 1964 or under his state's anti-discrimination laws on the basis of racial discrimination.

H. Collecting Fringe Benefits

A number of workplace benefits, formerly known by the quaint title of fringe benefits, need not be provided by employers, although most employers provide them—at least to fulltime employees. Fringe benefits include retirement plans, group health insurance and paid days off for vacations, holidays, personal and medical leave. (See Chapters 3, 4 and 5 for a more in-depth discussion of these topics.)

Keep in mind, however, that if your employer does have a policy of offering some or all of these job benefits, it cannot discriminate in offering them. The question that most often arises about these discretionary benefits when employees quit or are fired from a job is whether they are entitled to be paid for time that was accrued—or earned and owing—but not taken.

There is no easy answer.

First of all, just as the benefits are discretionary with each employer, so is the policy of how and when they accrue. Employers are free to apply conditions on fringe benefits. For example, it is perfectly legal for an employer to require a certain length of employment—six months or a year are common—before an employee is entitled to any fringe benefits. It is perfectly legal for fringe benefits to be prorated for parttime employees, or denied them completely. Employers are also free to set limits on how much paid time off employees may accrue before it must be lost or taken.

1.   Getting the Benefits You Are Due

In evaluating whether your former employer has given you all accrued fringe benefits you are due, you have two allies: documentation and history. First, search for any written policy on benefit accrual: in an employee manual, personnel package or company memo. If the rights have been promised to you, you can enforce them just like any other contract. If the promise is in writing, you have an even better chance of succeeding in enforcing it.

Look, too, to the history of how other employees were treated. If it has become company custom to pay other employees accrued fringe benefits when you leave, you may be legally entitled to them, too. You must compare apples with apples. Look to other employees who worked in jobs similar to yours and who worked the same hours. Finding out what they were paid when they left may take some brave sleuthing on your part: You may have to hunt down past employees and ask them some uncomfortable questions, point blank. But the effort may be worth it. If other former workers with jobs similar to yours were given benefits you were denied, you may be able to claim that your employer discriminated against you when it denied them. (See Chapter 8.)

2. Continuing Healthcare Coverage

Most workplace disputes and misunderstandings over fringe benefits concern healthcare coverage. Ironically, workers have more rights to healthcare insurance coverage after they lose their jobs than while employed because of a 1986 law, the Consolidated Omnibus Budget Reconciliation Act (COBRA). Under COBRA, employers must offer former employees the option of continuing to be covered by the company's group healthcare insurance plan at the workers' own expense for some time after employment ends. Family coverage is included.

In general, COBRA gives an employee who quits or is dismissed for reasons other than gross misconduct the right to continue group healthcare coverage for 18 months. In some other circumstances, such as the death of the employee, that employee's dependents can continue coverage for up to 36 months. (See Chapter 4, Section C.)

I. Outplacement Programs

If asked to name a major industry that grew up in the 1980s, most people would probably guess it would be computers. But, in fact, the industry known as outplacement—services that smooth the movement of employees off of corporate payrolls—expanded with similar vigor during that decade.

Until corporate staff cutting became an epidemic during the early 1980s, the outplacement profession was economically insignificant. Today, the American outplacement industry bills its clients more than $350 million each year. And more than 2,000 people are employed as Outplacement Professionals.

Each year, many thousands of workers are permanently dismissed by corporations that are shrinking or dying. Most management experts agree that long-term job security is obsolete. Yet the outplacement industry continues to be regarded much as the funeral industry is: Most people avoid taking the time to understand how it works until they find themselves participating in it under duress.

Outplacement services are not employment agencies. They are not executive search firms. They are not employee leasing companies. They do not find a new job for you, but they do help and encourage you in finding one for yourself.

Although some outplacement firms offer packages of services that can be purchased by individuals, outplacement counselors are most often brought in and paid for by employers who want to diminish their risks of being sued for wrongful discharge. Outplacement benefits have even been negotiated into union contracts.

The theory underlying the popularity of outplacement in the corporate world is that fired employees who move quickly and smoothly into a new job typically do not sustain grudges against the company that fired them. Nor do they experience the kind of financial problems that can inspire job-related lawsuits. In cases where a person goes through outplacement, still cannot find a replacement job and decides to file a wrongful discharge lawsuit, the company can show a court that it has done all it can to limit the damage done to the employee by the firing.

An outplacement program typically begins with classes or individual counseling on how to take an inventory of your marketable job skills. Then, you are assigned a furnished office space from which to launch your search for a new employer. These offices are usually equipped with a telephone and an extensive library of business directories, and they have a central typing service that will pump out resumes and letters for you.

Many outplacement firms even provide the people passing through them with business cards that carry only the person's name and a daytime telephone number, but no business title. Outplacement offices are frequently equipped with a switchboard operator to answer telephone calls in a corporate style, but without indicating any company affiliation. These props typically get a lot of use because many outplacement participants are required to turn in daily or weekly logs of potential employers they have contacted to inquire about possible job openings.

Periodic counseling and encouragement sessions with the outplacement firm's staff continue until you have found a new job, or until your former employer's willingness to pay for the outplacement services runs out. There is no standard duration for outplacement services. Some people spend only a few days in outplacement, but some stay for a year or more. Because some people have a difficult time finding a new job even with the support of an outplacement firm, some of these firms now offer programs that teach new work-related skills.

An employer cannot force you to participate in an outplacement program. However, most large employers will continue to pay your salary and benefits for at least a few weeks or months after you are fired on the condition that you actively participate in the outplacement services provided. Drop out—and you are on your own financially.

Refusal to participate in an outplacement program might also weaken any lawsuit you might later file against your former employer because you could be depicted as contributing to your loss of employment income. Your participation in outplacement might, on the other hand, provide additional verification that you were competent and professional while at the job from which you were fired.

HELP AND COMFORT FOR THE JOBLESS

Losing a job—particularly one you have held for a long time—can feel wrenching and traumatic. But you need not brave the battle alone. A number of groups—university organizations, churches, community centers, hospitals and even health clubs—now offer support services to those out of work.

While services differ, typical programs provide workshops in writing resumes and honing interviewing techniques, building self-esteem and acquiring job contacts—along with the support and camaraderie that group meetings can offer.

You may have to do a little investigative work to find a local group that meets your needs. Check community newspapers, neighborhood bulletin boards, local social groups and alumni offices of nearby schools and universities.

J. Replacing Your Income

When your employment is interrupted, it is important to act quickly to replace as much of your income as you can. Each day that passes without money earned puts you and those who rely on you for financial support in greater risk of running into money troubles. In some states, for example, the gap between the time that a person files for unemployment insurance and the time he or she receives the first unemployment check averages six weeks. And applying for the wrong income replacement program can waste many more precious days, weeks or even months.

Here is a brief breakdown of what is covered by each of the three major income replacement programs.

• Unemployment insurance. This program may provide some financial help if you lose your job, temporarily or permanently, through no fault of your own. (See Chapter 12.)

• Workers' compensation. When you cannot work because of a work-related injury or illness, this is the program that is most likely to provide you with replacement income promptly. It may also pay the medical bills resulting from a workplace injury or illness; compensate workers for a permanent injury, such as the loss of a limb; and provide death benefits to the survivors of workers who die from a workplace injury or illness. (See Chapter 13.)

• Social Security disability insurance. This is intended to provide income to adults who, because of injury or illness, cannot work for at least 12 months. Unlike the workers' compensation program, it does not require that your disability be caused by a workplace injury or illness. (See Chapter 14.)

Once you have decided which of these program fits your situation, read the more detailed description of that program in the chapters noted and then apply for the appropriate benefits.

DUAL PAYMENTS FOR DISABLED WORKERS

Many disabled employees qualify for benefits under both workers' compensation and Social Security disability insurance. There is nothing illegal about collecting from both at the same time if the claims you file are valid.

However, if you qualify for benefits from both programs, the total benefits you receive from both programs cannot equal more than 80% of your average earnings prior to becoming disabled.

Some states also allow disabled workers to collect both unemployment and workers' compensation benefits at the same time. When in doubt, file truthful claims for any program for which you might logically qualify and let the system decide if you are eligible for benefits.

K. Other Income Replacement Options

Although the government insurance programs covering unemployment, workplace injuries and permanent disability are the most substantial sources of replacement income for people who are out of work, there are other options.

1. Private Disability Insurance

While you were working, you or your employer may have been paying into a private disability insurance program. If you were paying for it through payroll withholdings, or if all the premiums were being paid by your employer, you may have forgotten that you have this coverage.

Coverage and eligibility for benefits differ among policies and companies. Review the employee policy manual or packet that your employer gave you when you took the job to see whether any private disability coverage is described there. If not, the people who handle benefits for your employer should be able to help you determine whether you have such coverage.

2. State Disability Programs

A few states—including California, New Jersey, Rhode Island, New York and Hawaii—offer disability benefits as part of their unemployment insurance programs. Typical program requirements mandate that you submit your medical records and show that you requested a leave of absence from your employer. Some may also require proof that you intend to return to your job when you recover. Call the local unemployment insurance and workers' compensation insurance offices to determine whether your state is one that maintains this kind of coverage. (See Chapters 12 and 13.)

3. Withdrawals from Pension Plans

Some pension programs allow withdrawals prior to retirement for emergency purposes. The administrator of your pension plan can advise you on whether you have this option. (For more on pensions, see Chapter 15, Section B.)

4. Food Stamps

Although many people incorrectly think that the federal food stamp program is a form of welfare, it is actually financed by the U.S. Department of Agriculture as a way of increasing the demand for food products. You do not have to be receiving welfare to qualify for food stamps. In fact, the eligibility formula for food stamps makes them available to many people who are not all that poor. If your income is eliminated or significantly reduced for several months because you are not working, check on whether you are eligible for food stamps.

To locate the agency in your area that issues food stamps, scan the county government offices listings in the telephone directory. Typically, you will find a listing for food stamp information under a category such as Human Services. If not, call your local office of the U.S. Department of Agriculture.

5. Veterans' Benefits

There are programs that provide income to veterans of the U.S. military who become unable to work because of a disability, even if that disability is not a result of military service. Your local Veterans' Administration office, listed in the federal government agency section of the telephone directory, can give you details.

6. Supplemental Social Security Income

Usually known as SSI, this program provides money to disabled people who have low incomes and very few assets. Unlike Social Security disability insurance, it does not require you to have worked under and paid into the Social Security program. If the circumstances surrounding your inability to earn income are so unusual that you have fallen between the cracks of the larger programs, SSI may be the one program that provides you with some income.

You can get details and file a claim at your local Social Security Administration office. Look in the federal government section of the telephone directory for contact details.

7. Black Lung Benefits

The Social Security Administration also runs a federal program that provides money benefits to victims of anthracosilicosis—an occupational disease often suffered by miners. Typically known as Black Lung, the disease is caused by long exposure to coal particles in the air. It frequently leaves miners unable to work because they cannot breath properly.

The benefits under this program are also payable to dependents of Black Lung victims, so the best way to research your eligibility for those benefits is to investigate details of the program at your local Social Security office.

8. Disaster Benefits

When a flood, earthquake, hurricane or other natural disaster tears through an area, the president or governor will often declare it a disaster area and special unemployment benefits will become available to people who lost their jobs because of the disaster. These special unemployment benefits are usually handled by the same offices that handle regular unemployment claims.

9. Medicare

Like Social Security, Medicare is usually thought of as being for elderly people. But, in fact, it also covers disabled people, and can be a good way of coping with medical bills when an injury or illness prevents you from working. For more details on this program, call the Medicare information line: 800/952-8627.

However, you should be aware that the federal government has been tightening the restrictions for Medicare for those less than 65 years old, so this type of coverage may be difficult to secure. ■

The legal doctrine of employment at will rules the workplace, so the dire truth remains that your employer can fire you.

On the spot.

Any time.

Without notice.

And the odds are that you will not be able to use the legal system to completely reverse your firing and return to your job. (See Chapter 10, Section A for a detailed discussion of employment at will.)

However, if you have lost your job or think you may soon lose it, do not despair. There are some laws that may protect you against suddenly joining the ranks of the unemployed without money or other help to ease the impact.

Depending on your situation, you may have the legal right to:

- protection from being denied a promotion, demoted or fired from your current job
- fair treatment during and after you are fired
- a positive reference from your former employer to help in future job hunting, or
- continuing coverage under your former employer's benefit programs.

You may even be able to get some compensation if the firing causes you severe damage, or to win a court judgment against your former employer in a wrongful discharge lawsuit.

At the very least, understanding how and when laws may protect job security and other workplace rights should help you determine whether your dismissal may justify taking legal action, in which case you may want to consult a lawyer. (See Chapter 18, Section D.)

A. When a Firing Is Illegal

There are no hard and fast limits on what legal arguments can be used to challenge an employee's dismissal. New legal theories challenging firings are being developed constantly. In general, these actions are lumped under the label of wrongful discharge.

The most common ground for a wrongful discharge claim is that there has been some form of discrimination in hiring, employing or firing an individual worker. A number of local, state and federal laws prohibit discriminating against an individual worker because of race, gender, age, national origin or sexual orientation. (See Chapter 8 for a thorough discussion of discrimination in employment and how to take action against it.)

There are also strong state and federal protections prohibiting individuals from being fired in violation of public policy—or for a reason most people would find morally wrong, such as for reporting mishandling of government funds. (See Section B.)

Several additional legal theories are frequently used in challenging employee firings:

- breach of good faith and fair dealing
- breach of contract, and
- defamation.

In some situations, more than one of these theories may be used in the same legal action. (See Section D.)

1. Breach of Good Faith and Fair Dealing

The most flexible way to challenge a job dismissal is to show that there has been a breach of good faith and fair dealing—simply that the employer did not follow that Golden Rule about doing unto others and should now be required to do the right thing.

This type of claim is based on the legal principle that an employer has an inherent responsibility to deal with employees fairly and in good faith. However, employers often commit breaches of good faith and fair dealing by:

- firing or transferring employees to prevent them from collecting sales commissions
- misleading employees about their chances for future promotions and wage increases
- contriving reasons for firing an employee on the basis of on-the-job performance when the real motivation is to replace that employee with someone who will work for lower pay

- misleading employees about the bad aspects of a particular job, such as the need to travel through dangerous neighborhoods late at night, and
- repeatedly transferring an employee to remote, dangerous or otherwise undesirable assignments to coerce him or her into quitting without collecting the severance pay and other benefits due.

The legal claim of breach of good faith and fair dealing is so broad and flexible that, no matter what other claims you use as a basis for a wrongful discharge action, you will probably want to include a claim of breach of good faith and fair dealing as well. (See Section D.)

2. Breach of Contract

If you have a written employment contract setting out the terms of your work, pay and benefits, you may be able to get it enforced against an employer who ignores any one of its terms. But written employment contracts are rare—reserved mostly for top level executives and professional athletes. (See Chapter 10, Section A.)

A legal contract—covering employment or anything else—is created when three things occur:
- an offer is made by one party to another
- that offer is accepted, and
- something of value is exchanged based on the agreement.

To bring a breach of contract action, most employees must allege they had an implied contract with a particular employer. But that is not easy. An implied contract assumes that words and things of value exchanged between a former employer and employee created a legal contract governing their relationship.

Until legal challenges to employee dismissals began to gain popularity in the early 1980s, many employers used terms such as permanent employment in their employee manuals, on job application forms, or orally when offering a position to a prospective employee.

Today, employees who challenge their firings sometimes argue that when an employer referred to permanent employment in the hiring process, that created an implied contract between them. They claim that an implied employment contract requires the company to employ the worker for life—and that anything less than lifetime employment is a breach of contract.

In determining whether an implied employment contract exists, courts will look at a number of factors that might have led you to believe your employment was rooted in solid ground, including:

* the duration of your employment
* whether you have received regular promotions
* whether you have consistently received positive performance reviews
* whether you were assured that you would have continuing employment
* whether your employer violated a usual employment practice in firing you—such as neglecting to give a warning, or
* whether promises of permanence were made when you were hired.

Example: *In 1979, Marguerite took a job as an accountant with EZ Ink Printing. EZ Ink's employee manual stated that employees were not considered permanent until they completed a 90-day probationary period.*

For more than 15 years, Marguerite built her life around EZ Ink—assuming that she would be able to keep her job there until she reached retirement age. However, in 1993, EZ Ink decided to completely computerize its accounting operations—and to fire Marguerite.

Marguerite would likely be able to win a lawsuit against EZ Ink on the basis of a breach of an implied contract. The three elements required to create an implied employment contract were there:

1. *an offer—the employee manual's implication that all employees who remained with the company more than 90 days were permanent employees*
2. *an acceptance of that offer—Marguerite's more than 15 years of employment by the company*
3. *an exchange of value—the wages that EZ Ink had paid Marguerite and her labor for them.*

BEWARE OF JOB LOSS INSURANCE POLICIES

As the concept of long-term job security fades, some businesses are trying to exploit employees' fears of job loss by offering insurance policies that claim to cover certain bills during periods of unemployment.

Flyers urging you to buy job loss insurance are often included with your monthly credit card statement. The glitzy ads usually offer to make the payments on that credit card account should you lose your job. And mortgage companies frequently offer job loss insurance as a part of the process of closing the purchase of a home, arguing that your mortgage payments would be made by the insurance company should you become unemployed.

Such insurance usually is not a wise buy for most people. Look closely at the fine print of most job loss insurance policies and you will see a long list of situations which would disqualify you for benefits. Typical exceptions: you are out of work for less than several weeks, you volunteered for an early retirement program, you were fired because of something you did at work, or you are involved in a labor dispute.

Most job loss policies only provide coverage in limited situations—for example, if your employer suddenly went bankrupt.

---

3. Defamation

Defamation is a legal action with the chivalrous-sounding intent of protecting a person's reputation and good standing in the community. There are a lot of opportunities in the typical firing process for an employer to do just that, so it is increasingly common for former employees to use defamation to challenge a firing.

A defamation claim is not a challenge to the legitimacy of an employee's dismissal as much as it is a way of getting monetary revenge on the employer who was sloppy, insensitive or downright mean in firing you or in dealing with your need for references in obtaining a new job.

But defamation is usually difficult to prove. Typically, you must show that, in the process of dismissing you from your job or subsequently providing references to potential new employers, your former employer significantly damaged your good name and reduced your chances for gaining new employment. This commonly entails much legal hair-splitting over the facts surrounding a firing, to whom the employer may communicate the facts surrounding an employee's dismissal and whether or not the distribution of the damaging information was intentional and malicious—that is, meant to harm you.

To sue for defamation, you must show that your former employer:

- made a false or damaging statement about you
- told or wrote that statement to at least one other person
- was negligent or intentional in communicating the statement, and
- harmed you in some way by communicating the statement, such as by causing others to shun you, or resulted in your losing a job or a promotion.

To win a case of defamation, you must prove that the hurtful words were more than malicious watercooler gossip. The words must also be more than a personal opinion. It is ordinarily legal for anyone to voice an opinion, no matter how unflattering.

Statements that have been ruled to sufficiently harm a worker and qualify as defamation are false claims that he or she:

- committed a crime
- performed job duties incompetently
- improperly used drugs or alcohol, or
- acted in some other way that clearly implied unfitness for a particular job.

Because a few unflattering comments or even a small dose of mean-spiritedness do not usually qualify as defamation, it is extremely important to scrupulously document cases where false or damaging statements are made. You can do this by recording not only the exact offensive words that were said and who said them, but when and where they were said and whether there were any witnesses. Securing this type of documentation may be even more difficult if you have lost your job and are no longer in the workplace.

Keep in mind that courts will generally be most persuaded by words that clearly damaged your work reputation. For example, a false statement that you stole money from your former employer would probably qualify as defamation because most people would lower their opinions of you because of it. But a false statement that you had stayed on your last job only two months would probably be defamatory only if you could prove that it damaged you, such as by preventing you from getting a new job, causing a landlord to refuse to rent an apartment to you, or otherwise causing you social embarrassment and emotional distress.

PLEASE DON'T TALK ABOUT ME WHEN I'M GONE

Employers contacted for references about former employees often find themselves on a slippery precipice—as a number of costly defamation lawsuits have been filed over negative references.

These days, conventional lawyer wisdom cautions all employers to stick to the barest bones. Many companies now have steel-clad policies that they give out only the dates of employment, job title and final salary to prospective employers. Some cautious companies even require that employees who leave must sign releases allowing them to give out reference information in the future.

The broad warning for employers giving references is that they should give out only easily documented facts—your attendance record or production record, for example.

But many employers that perceive an employee has done a poor job or blatantly violated company rules feel that they have the mission to let other prospective employers know of the problem. There is nothing inherently illegal about this, unless you can prove that an employer told a bald-faced lie about you—for example, that you raided the company till when you did not. However, gathering positive proof of that is nearly impossible. And even a noncommittal "no comment" in response to a prospective employer's probe about your strengths and weaknesses may sound damaging.

If you suspect your former employer would give a negative review of your work, it is best to have a strategy on hand. Try to secure a letter of recommendation from someone in the company who would praise your work. Perhaps you can persuade your employer to keep certain employment matters confidential—like the reason for your dismissal. If not, it might be best not to list the employer as a reference. And have a ready reason to explain the circumstances that has no acrimonious ring to it—for example, you believe it was time to move on to a new challenge.

B. Violations of Public Policy

An employer may not violate public policy when he or she fires you—that is, fire you for a reason that most people would find morally or ethically wrong.

Deciding what is morally wrong, of course, can be a murky exercise. Many state and federal laws that take some of the guessing out of this issue by specifying employment-related actions that clearly violate public policy, such as firing an employee for:

• taking time off work to serve on a jury (see Chapter 3, Section E2)
• taking time off work to vote (see Chapter 3, Section E3)
• serving in the military or National Guard (see Chapter 3, Section E4), or
• notifying authorities about some wrongdoing harmful to the public—generally known as whistleblowing (see the listing below).

In addition, a number of state laws protect employees from being fired for asserting a number of more arcane rights—including serving as an election officer, serving as a volunteer firefighter, having certain political opinions, appearing as a witness in a criminal case or even being elected to the general assembly. Many of these laws, passed as kneejerk reactions to assuage particular workplace disputes, have become all but dead letters. Few people know they exist, they are seldom violated. And very few attempt to claim their protections. Still, if you feel there is the possibility that your firing may have violated one of these prohibitions, doublecheck the law in your state. (See Chapter 18, Section E, for guidance on how to do your own legal research.)

THE HIGH COST OF WHISTLEBLOWING

The story of one of the most famous whistleblowers, Karen Silkwood, was the inspiration for hundreds of articles, several books—and a heavily-bankrolled motion picture.

In the early 70s, Silkwood worked as a lab analyst in an Oklahoma Kerr-McGee plant which manufactured plutonium pins used as fuel for nuclear reactors. Plutonium is a radioactive chemical element, known to be highly toxic and carcinogenic. Silkwood, an elected union official and outspoken critic of Kerr-McGee's health and safety practices, began collecting and recording information to substantiate her charges that employees at the plant were dangerously exposed.

In early November 1974, Silkwood was found to be contaminated with the chemical. Nine days later, while enroute to meet with a *New York Times* reporter and union leader to turn over her documentation of Kerr-McGee's unsafe work conditions, Silkwood was killed in a car accident with suspicious overtones. The damning documentation she was alleged to have with her was not recovered from the accident scene.

Silkwood's estate sued Kerr-McGee for the injuries caused by the escaping plutonium. After several appeals involving arcane issues of state and federal legal authority, the U.S. Supreme Court affirmed the award to the Silkwood estate of $10 million in punitive damages— damages designed to punish the wrongdoer and act as a deterrent—and an additional $5,000 in property damages to cover the cost of sanitizing her contaminated apartment (*Silkwood v. Kerr-McGee*, 464 U.S. 238 (1984)).

Courts have also held that it violates public policy for an employer to fire you because you took advantage of some legal remedies or exercised a legal right. For example, it is illegal for your employer to fire you because you:

- file a workers' compensation claim (see Chapter 13, Section F)
- file a complaint under the Fair Labor Standards Act (see Chapter 3, Section H)

- report a violation of the Occupational Safety and Health Act or state safety law (see Chapter 7, Section B)
- claim your rights under Title VII of the Civil Rights Act (see Chapter 8, Section A and Chapter 9, Section D), or
- exercise your right to belong or not to belong to a union (see Chapter 16)
- exercise your right to take a leave from work that was available under state or federal law (see Chapter 5)
- refuse to take a lie detector test (see Chapter 6, Section B)
- refuse to take a drug test given without good reason (see Chapter 6, Section B2), or
- have your pay subject to an order for child support or a wage garnishment order (see Chapter 3, Section F).

1. State Whistleblower Laws

While states differ, whistleblowing laws generally protect individuals who report to proper authorities unlawful activity or any activity that is against the public interest. One unique feature about whistleblowing is that it has an objective foul-crying kind of aspect to it. The whistleblower is protected for doing his or her civic duty by pointing out the misdeeds of powers that be. Many of the whistleblower statutes apply only to public employees.

STATE WHISTLEBLOWER LAWS

Alabama	No statute
Alaska	State and local employees are protected for reporting any violation of a law, regulation, danger to public health and safety, gross mismanagement, waste, abuse of authority or a matter for investigation by the office of the ombudsman to a public body. Employer may require employee to give notice prior to making a report, but notice is not required if employee believes it would not result in prompt action, the employer already knows about the activity, the situation is an emergency or the employee fears discrimination or reprisal. Alaska Stat. §39.90.100 through 39.90.150

Arizona	Public employees are protected against reprisal for reporting violations of law, mismanagement, abuse of authority or gross waste of funds to attorney general, legislature, governor, county attorney or federal, state or local law enforcement agency. Ariz. Rev. Stat. Ann. §38-532
Arkansas	No statute
California	State employees are protected from reprisal for reporting violations of state or federal law or regulation, economic waste, gross misconduct, incompetence or inefficiency to the Joint Legislative Audit Committee, Auditor General or university officers. Cal. Gov't. Code §§10540 to 10549
	Employees are protected from reprisal for reporting violations of federal or state statute or regulation to a government or law enforcement agency. Cal. Lab. Code §1102.5
Colorado	State employees are protected from reprisal for disclosing information to any person or testifying before any committee of the general assembly regarding any practice, including waste of public funds, abuse of authority or mismanagement). Employees must make good-faith effort to provide information to their supervisor before disclosure. Colo. Rev. Stat. §§24-50.5-101 through 24-50.5-107
Connecticut	Employees are protected from reprisal for reporting or testifying to a public body about a violation of federal, state or local statutes, regulations or ordinances. Conn. Gen. Stat. Ann. §31-51m
	State government employees are protected from reprisal for reporting corruption, unethical conduct, violation of state or federal law, gross waste of funds, mismanagement, abuse of authority, danger to public health and safety to a public body. Conn. Gen. Stat. Ann. §4-61dd
Delaware	State employees protected from reprisal for reporting to the state Office of Auditor of Accounts violations of state or federal law or regulation. Del. Code Ann. tit. 29, §5115
District of Columbia	District employees are protected against reprisal for disclosing information concerning illegal or unethical conduct that threatens public health or safety or involves the unlawful use of public funds. D.C. Code Ann. §§1-616.2 and 1-616.3
Florida	State employees and independent contractors for the state are protected against reprisal for reporting violations of law or regulations that create danger to the public. Fla. Stat. §112.3187
Georgia	No statute

Hawaii	Employees are protected against reprisal for disclosing violations of state or local laws or rules to public bodies. Hawaii Rev. Stat. §§378-61 through 378-69
Idaho	No statute
Illinois	State employees are protected from reprisal for disclosing waste, mismanagement, abuse of authority, substantial and specific danger to public health and safety, or violation of law, rule or regulation. Ill. Ann. Stat. ch. 127, §63b119c.1
Indiana	State employees are protected from reprisal for reporting in writing violation of state or federal laws or regulations, or misuse of public resources. Employee must disclose to supervisor and give reasonable time to correct before reporting. Ind. Code Ann. §4-15-10-4
Iowa	State employees protected against reprisal for disclosing information regarding violation of law or rule, mismanagement, gross abuse of funds, abuse of authority, or substantial and specific danger to public health and safety to a member of the General Assembly, legislative service bureau, legislative fiscal bureau or caucus staff of General Assembly. Iowa Code §79.28
Kansas	Employees may not be fired or discriminated against for disclosing any matter of controversy between the employer and the employee. Kan. Stat. Ann. §44-615
	State employees are protected from reprisal for reporting violations of state or federal law, or rules or regulations to any person, agency, or organization. Statute specifically prohibits any requirement of notification of supervisor prior to reporting. Kan. Stat. Ann. §75-2973
Kentucky	State government employees protected against reprisal for reporting violations of any state or federal law or regulation, or mismanagement, waste, fraud, or endangerment of public health or safety to judicial, legislative, or law enforcement agencies. Ky. Rev. Stat. §§61.102 through 61.103
Louisiana	Employees are protected from reprisal for reporting violations of environmental laws or regulations of state, federal or local authorities. La. Rev. Stat. Ann. §30:2027
	Public employees may not be subject to reprisals for reporting acts of impropriety within any government entity. La. Rev. Stat. Ann. §42:1169

Maine	Private sector employees are protected from reprisal for reporting information concerning violations of state or federal law or regulation. To be protected, the employee must first disclose the violation to a supervisor and give an opportunity to correct, unless such notice is futile. State employees are protected for giving any information to legislative committees. Me. Rev. Stat. Ann. 26, §§831 to 840
Maryland	State employees are protected against reprisal for disclosing violation any law, rule or regulation, gross mismanagement, gross waste of funds, abuse of authority, substantial and specific danger to public health and safety. Md. Ann. Code art. 64A, §12G
Massachusetts	No statute
Michigan	Employees are protected against reprisal for reporting violations of federal, state, or local statute or regulation. Mich. Comp. Laws §§15.361 and 17.428
Minnesota	Employees are protected for reporting violations of any federal or state law or rule to the employer or to any governmental body or law enforcement official. Employee's identity must be kept confidential. Employers must give written notice of reason for employee's termination. Minn. Stat. Ann. §§181.931 through 181.935
Mississippi	No statute
Missouri	State employees are protected from reprisal for disclosing violations of any law, rule or regulation, gross mismanagement, gross waste of funds, abuse of authority, substantial and specific danger to public health and safety to the state auditor or member of the legislature. Mo. Rev. Stat. §105.0550
Montana	The Wrongful Discharge From Employment Act (Mont. Code Ann. §§39-2-901) provides that a discharge is wrongful if: 1. It is in retaliation for employee's reporting of a violation of public policy or refusal to violate public policy; 2. Employee has completed probation and discharge was not for good cause; or 3. Employer violated provisions of personnel policy. Mont. Code Ann. §39-2-904
Nebraska	Employees of private employers with 15 or more employees are protected against reprisal for opposing an unlawful practice or refusing to carry out unlawful action under federal or state law. Neb. Rev. Stat. §48-1114
Nevada	No statute

New Hampshire	Employees are protected from reprisal for reporting violations of any state or federal law or rule or for participating in an investigation. Employees may refuse to participate in any unlawful activity or any activity which is fraudulent or incompatible with public policy concerning public health, safety and welfare, and the protection of the environment. The employee is required to give prior notice to the employer and reasonable time to correct unless such notice is futile. N.H. Rev. Stat. Ann. §275-E:1 to 275-E:7
New Jersey	Public and private sector employees are protected from reprisal for reporting violation of any law or regulation to a supervisor, a public body, or to another employer with whom there is a business relationship. Employees are required to give written notice to supervisors, unless violation is known to supervisors, the situation is an emergency, or the employee fears physical harm. N.J. Stat. Ann. §34:19.1 to 34:19.8
New Mexico	No statute
New York	Employees are protected from reprisal for reporting to a public body violations of state, federal or local statutes or regulations which create a substantial and specific danger to the public health and safety. Written notice to supervisors with reasonable opportunity to correct must be given. Employees may refuse to participate in the violation. N.Y. Lab. Law, §740
North Carolina	State employees are protected from reprisal for reporting violations of state or federal law or regulation, fraud, misappropriation of state funds, or danger to public health and safety to a supervisor or other appropriate authority. Notice of intention to report must be given to a supervisor or other appropriate authority. N.C. Gen. Stat. §126-84
North Dakota	Public employees are protected from reprisal for reporting violations of state or federal laws or rules or misuse of public resources. N.D. Cent. Code §34-11.1-04
Ohio	Employees are protected against reprisal for disclosing to supervisors or any appropriate public officials violations of any federal or state law or regulation which is either criminal or likely to cause imminent risk of physical harm to persons or a hazard to public safety. Employee must give employer immediate oral notice of the violation followed by a written report. Employer has 24 hours to remedy the situation. If the violation is not corrected, the employee may report to the appropriate public officials. Ohio Rev. Code Ann. §§4113.51 through 4113.53

Oklahoma	State employees are protected from reprisal for disclosing any information to any member of legislature, legislative committee, administrative hearing, or court of law. Okla. Stat. tit. 74, §841.7
Oregon	Public employees are protected from reprisal for disclosing violations of laws, rules or improper actions, or inefficiency of superior officers or fellow employees, gross waste of funds, abuse of authority, specific danger to public health and safety. Or. Rev. Stat. §659.510
Pennsylvania	State and local government employees are protected against reprisal for disclosing to superiors or appropriate federal, state or local agencies violations of any federal or state law or regulation, or of a code of ethics designed to protect the public's or employer's interest. Pa. Cons. Stat. Ann. tit. 43, §§1421 to 1428
Rhode Island	State and local government employees are protected from reprisal for reporting violations of state, federal or local statute or regulation. R.I. Gen. Laws §§36-15-1 to 36-15-10
South Carolina	State and local government employees are protected from reprisal for disclosing violations of any federal or state law or regulation, or criminality, corruption, waste, fraud, gross negligence or mismanagement to an appropriate public body. S.C. Code Ann. §§8-27-10 through 8-27-50
South Dakota	No statute
Tennessee	Private sector employees are protected from reprisal for reporting or refusing to participate in an activity in violation of a state or federal law or regulation that is intended to protect public health and safety. Tenn. Code Ann. §50-1-304
Texas	State employees are protected against reprisal for reporting violations of state or federal statute or rule, or local ordinance or rule to an appropriate law enforcement agency. Tex. Rev. Civ. Stat. Ann. art. 6252-16a
Utah	State or local government employees are protected from reprisal for reporting in any fashion, including verbal, written, broadcast or otherwise, violation of federal, state or local law or rule, or waste of public funds, property or human resources. Employee must give the employer formal notice of the situation and allow reasonable time for correction. Utah Code Ann. §§67-21-1 through 67-21-9
Vermont	No statute
Virginia	No statute

Washington	State government employees are protected from reprisal for reporting to the State Auditor any violation of state law or rule, abuse of authority, waste of public funds, or a substantial and specific danger to public health and safety. Wash. Rev. Code Ann. §42.40.010
West Virginia	State or local government employees are protected from reprisal for reporting violations which are not technical or minimal of any federal or state law or regulation, or of a code of ethics designed to protect the public's or employer's interest. W. Va. Code §6C-1-1
Wisconsin	State employees are protected from reprisal for disclosure of violations of any state or federal statute, rule or regulation, mismanagement, abuse of authority, substantial waste of public funds, or a danger to the public health and safety to the appropriate law enforcement agency or to any person. Employee must disclose the information in writing to a supervisor. Wis. Stat. Ann. §§230.80 through 230.89
Wyoming	No statute

2. Using Other State Laws

Even if the reason for your dismissal is not specifically outlawed by a public policy law in your state or a provision within another workplace law, employers' conduct that is considered to violate public policy in other states would probably be considered morally or ethically wrong in your state, too.

Example: *Horatio, a salesperson in a clothing store in Nevada, was fired because he reported to police that the manager of the store was buying stolen wristwatches and selling them to customers on the sly. Nevada does not have a law that specifically prohibits firing an employee who reports a crime. Nevertheless, Horatio might be able to argue successfully in court that his firing violated public policy because other states, such as South Carolina, have laws that specifically forbid such firings.*

TIPS FOR TELLING WHETHER YOU ARE PROTECTED

Whistleblower statutes attempt to protect against the too-common occurrence of employees who are fired just after speaking up to authorities about some wrongdoing.

Coincidence? Maybe.

What makes the firing questionable—and possibly covered by a whistleblower statute—is often the timing. Pay strict attention to when you were fired. Was it soon after your employer found out that you reported the wrongful behavior? The shorter the time, the more likely you are protected by a whistleblower statute.

There are also a number of other questions you should ask to help determine whether you may be covered by a whistleblower statute.

- Did you complain to anyone at your own workplace about the wrongful behavior before going outside? If so, what was the response? Were you threatened? Were you offered special benefits for not filing a complaint?
- If your company has a policy of progressively disciplining employees—reprimand, probation, suspension, dismissal—was it speeded up or ignored in your case?
- Were your whistleblowing activities specifically mentioned to you by your supervisor? By company management? By other employees?
- Have other employees been fired for whistleblowing?
- Did you notice management or co-workers treating you differently after you complained about the illegal behavior? Were you suddenly ostracized or ignored, passed over for promotions, given a less attractive job assignment?

The more documentation you can produce—memos from management, dated notes summarizing conversations with co-workers, signed statements from other former employees—the stronger your case will be. (For other advice on documenting your dismissal, see Chapter 10, Section C.)

C. Blacklisting

As archaic and barbaric as it may seem, there are still some companies, labor unions and people working within them that are not content to merely fire you or force you out of your job. They seem unwilling to rest until they have squelched all hope that you will work again.

The danger of losing a defamation lawsuit does not seem to dissuade some vengeful people from trying to put former employees on a list of people that no one else will hire. So some states have passed laws that expressly allow former employees to take legal action—criminal, civil or both—against those who try to sabotage efforts to secure new employment. (See the chart below for state blacklisting laws.)

1. Detecting Blacklisting

The mere fact that you have to work hard at finding a new job usually is not sufficient evidence to suggest blacklisting. But a strong signal would be a series of situations in which potential new employers seem to be on the verge of hiring you, then suddenly lose all interest. This indicates that, when a prospective employer checks your references just before hiring you, the blacklister is tipped off to where you have applied for work and is able to ding you.

2. Conducting Your Own Investigation

You can hire a lawyer or a private detective to investigate whether or not you are being blacklisted. But it is easier and cheaper to conduct your own investigation by establishing an imaginary business and using that business to inquire about your own employment record with former employers. You can create your imaginary business through the creative use of inexpensive printing services, private postal boxes and telephone answering services— and enlisting a little help from your friends.

Typically, you can create for a few months the illusion of a business that has classy letterhead stationery, a suite number for a mailing address and a business telephone line. Even large corporations now use voice mail and other answering systems, making telephone receptionists nearly obsolete. So it is virtually impossible for anyone to tell from any distance how large and established any company is unless they spend a lot of time and money checking corporate credit reports.

Pretend that you have applied for a job at the imaginary company that you create, and have it go through the ritual of checking your work history with previous employers by mail. Ask a friend to use his or her name and signature to sign the reference—checking letters as your imaginary company's human resources manager.

What comes back in the mail may give you all the evidence you need to prove blacklisting. But some people who do this type of thing are smart enough not to write down the defamatory information that they are spreading. So if the written materials that are sent to your imaginary company do not jibe with the reactions you have been getting from potential new employers, ask a friend to pose as a human resources manager and to telephone your former employers to discuss your work history. This is not quite as strong evidence as it would be to have something incriminating in writing from your former employer. But ask your friend to write and sign a statement attesting to the conversation and setting out the details of the discussion.

If you uncover evidence that you are, in fact, being blacklisted, you will probably need to get some advice on the problem from a lawyer. (See Chapter 18, Section D.) You may be able to have the blacklister arrested and prosecuted—and then be able to win a large judgment based on the blacklisting.

3. State Laws on Blacklisting

This is a synopsis of state laws prohibiting blacklisting. Note also that nearly half the states—including Alabama, California, Colorado, Florida, Georgia, Idaho, Kansas, Louisiana, Michigan, Minnesota, Montana, Nevada, New Hampshire, New Mexico, North Carolina, North Dakota, South Carolina, Tennessee, Utah, Washington and Wisconsin—have additional laws that specifically make it illegal for an employer to defame an employee in words or writing.

STATE BLACKLISTING LAWS

Alabama	Employers may not keep or use blacklist to prevent any person from gaining employment. Violations are punishable as misdemeanors. Ala. Code §13-A-11-123
Alaska	No statute
Arizona	Blacklisting is forbidden by state constitution. Ariz. Const. Art. XVIII, §9
	Employer may provide information on former employee's education, training, experience, qualifications, and job performance if another employer requests it. A copy of any written communication must be sent to the employee. Ariz. Rev. Stat. Ann. §23-1361
Arkansas	Employers may not distribute writing containing false statement or any other information about the employee for the purpose of getting that employee fired or to prevent a hiring. Violations are punishable as a misdemeanor by fines of $100 to $500 and/or jail for up to one year. (Ark. Stat. Ann. §11-3-202)
California	Employers may not make a false statement to prevent a former employee from getting a new job. However, an employer may make true statements about a former employee in response to an inquiry from a prospective employer. Cal. Lab. Code §§1050, 1052, 1054
Colorado	Employers may not blacklist or cause to be blacklisted a discharged employee. Violators are subject to fine, imprisonment, or both. This prohibition does not apply to banks and other financial institutions. Colo. Rev. Stat. §§8-2-110 and 8-2-111
	An employer may give another person "fair and unbiased information" about a current or former employee as long as it is not knowingly false, misleading or disclosed for a malicious purpose. Colo. Rev. Stat. §8-2-114
Connecticut	Employers may not blacklist, publish employee's name with intent of preventing employee from getting employment, or conspiring to prevent employee from getting other employment. Employers may make truthful statement to prospective employers. Violations are punishable by fines of from $50 to $200. Conn. Gen. Stat. Ann. §31-51
Delaware	No statute

District of Columbia	No statute
Florida	Agreement or conspiracy to prevent any person from procuring work or to cause firing is prohibited. Communications threatening injury to life, property, or business for the purpose of procuring the firing of any person or to prevent a person from getting hired is also prohibited. Violations are punishable as misdemeanors. Fla. Stat. §448.045
Georgia	No statute
Hawaii	No statute
Idaho	No statute
Illinois	No statute
Indiana	Employers may not prevent a fired employee from obtaining another job, but may state the correct reason for a former employee's dismissal to prospective employers. Ind. Code Ann. §§22-5-3-1 and 22-5-3-2
Iowa	Employers may not prevent or try to prevent a fired employee from obtaining other employment either by oral or written communication of any kind, blacklisting or making false charges concerning the employee's honesty. Iowa Code §§730.1 through 730.3
Kansas	Employers may not prevent a discharged employee from obtaining employment except by furnishing in writing, upon request, the cause of such discharge. Kan. Stat. Ann. §§44-117 through 44-119
Kentucky	No statute
Louisiana	No statute
Maine	A person may not prevent a wage earner from gaining employment by intimidation, force or a blacklist. Violators may be fined up to $500 and jailed for up to two years. Me. Rev. Stat. Ann. title 17, §401
Maryland	No statute
Massachusetts	No statute
Michigan	No statute
Minnesota	Employers may not prevent former employees from obtaining employment elsewhere. Violations are punishable as misdemeanors. Minn. Stat. §179.60
Mississippi	No statute
Missouri	No statute
Montana	Employers may not blacklist a discharged employee or an employee who voluntarily left the company's service. Employ-

ers may give a prospective employer a truthful statement regarding the reason for discharge. Mont. Code Ann. §§32-2-801 through 32-2-803

Nebraska	No statute
Nevada	Employers may not prevent former employees from engaging in or securing other employment. Violations are punishable as misdemeanors. However, when employees are discharged, employers may give truthful written reasons for the discharge. Nev. Rev. Stat. §613.210
New Hampshire	No statute
New Jersey	No statute
New Mexico	Employers may not prevent or try to prevent a former employee from obtaining other employment. However, employers may give accurate report or honest opinion of the qualifications or performance of a former employee upon request. N.M. Stat. Ann. §30-13-3
New York	No statute
North Carolina	Employers may not prevent, attempt to prevent or conspire to prevent a discharged employee from obtaining other employment. N.C. Gen. Stat. §14-355
North Dakota	No person may interfere or hinder another in obtaining or enjoying employment. N.D. Cent. Code §34-01-06
Ohio	No statute
Oklahoma	Employers may not blacklist or require a "letter of relinquishment"—basically, a letter of resignation—for the purpose of preventing the employee from obtaining other employment. Okla. Stat. Ann. tit. 40 §§172 and 173
Oregon	Employers may not prevent former employees from engaging in or securing other employment. Or. Rev. Stat. §659.230
Pennsylvania	No statute
Rhode Island	No statute
South Carolina	No statute
South Dakota	No statute
Tennessee	No statute
Texas	Employers may not blacklist a discharged or voluntarily quitting employee to prevent the former employee from getting similar or other employment. Tex. Code Ann. Art. 5196d
Utah	Employers may not blacklist someone who is fired or voluntarily quits to prevent that person from obtaining similar employment. Violations are punishable as felonies by a fine of

	up to $1,000 and imprisonment for 60 days to one year. Utah Code Ann. §§34-24-1 and 34-24-2
Vermont	No statute
Virginia	Blacklisting is prohibited, but the employer may tell other employers the true reason for a discharge or give true statement regarding the character and ability of a employee who voluntarily quit employment. Va. Code §40.1.27
Washington	Employers may not blacklist employees or former employees to prevent their employment or cause their discharge. Violations are misdemeanors and punishable by a fine of from $100 to $1,000 or imprisonment for 90 days to one year. Wash. Rev. Code Ann. §49.44.010
West Virginia	No statute
Wisconsin	Employers are prohibited from blacklisting discharged or voluntarily quitting employees to prevent them from obtaining other employment. Violations are punishable by fines of from $100 to $500. Wis. Stat. §134.02
Wyoming	No statute

D. Taking Action Against Your Dismissal

Once you become familiar with how employee dismissals are successfully challenged, compare those legal strategies to your firing and decide:
- which legal principle used to challenge a job loss best fits your situation
- whether you are willing to expend the effort, money and time it usually takes to fight a firing, and
- whether or not you will need a lawyer to help you challenge your firing.

Look first to local specialized resources for affordable help. For this, your telephone book can be a godsend. Check the topic index in the yellow pages under Community Services, Employment or similar headings. You are likely to find a number of listings for groups that deal with specialized workers—younger workers, older workers, immigrants, blue collar workers. Steel your nerves and give them a call. Many organizations now offer legal counseling or referrals. A growing number also offer the invaluable help of support groups or workplace counselors—people in like situations or with specialized training who can help you discover what your options might be.

Also check the Appendix; it lists a number of resources that may offer help or referrals.

If you were fired for reasons that appear to violate public policy (see Section B), or were discriminated against in some way (see Chapter 8), you may be able to get government help in challenging your dismissal. For example, if you were fired for filing a complaint under the Fair Labor Standards Act, you can ask the Labor Department to help you fight that dismissal. But be forewarned. These agencies are swamped with complaints—and are able to pursue only a fraction of the claims that have merit.

Look into possibilities less drastic than going to court—such as arbitration or mediation. (See Chapter 18, Section A.) Finally, consider getting a lawyer's help in filing a lawsuit to challenge your dismissal. (See Chapter 18, Section D.)

If you do consult a lawyer, he or she will likely urge you to package two or more legal claims in a single lawsuit. This may be your strongest bet in wrongful discharge cases because contract law and many of the laws prohibiting employee dismissals as violations of public policy offer little chance of winning a large judgment.

For example, damages awarded in a lawsuit based only on a breach of an implied employment contract would typically be limited to:

• reinstatement to the job—not a desirable thing, in many cases, because there are often bad feelings between the employee and employer, and

• lost wages, which do not often amount to much—particularly if you find a new job soon after being fired.

In contrast, a breach of good faith and fair dealing is a tort—an intentional or careless act of a person or institution that directly harms another person or institution. And in tort actions, you typically can ask for actual damages based on such things as emotional suffering, and for punitive damages—an amount of money that the wrongdoer is ordered to pay as a form of punishment and as a deterrent to repeating the behavior that gave birth to the lawsuit.

Punitive damages are usually based not on the size of the injury, but on the court's estimate of how large a financial penalty would be needed to make a former employer feel the sting. In the case of many large corporations, the size of the penalty needed to make the company hurt can be quite large.

Example: *Elmer was a salesperson for a building supply company whose employee manual stated that employees were considered permanent after completing a 90-day probation period. Elmer had been employed by the company for 14 years, and was about to qualify for more than $50,000 in commissions from accounts he had sold years before.*

He was fired just a week before qualifying for those commissions—but he found an equivalent new job just a few weeks later. Elmer sued the company that had fired him for breach of implied contract (the employee manual's statement on permanent employment) and breach of good faith and fair dealing (the company's use of dismissal as a way to avoid having him qualify contractually for the commissions).

On the breach of implied contract count, the court awarded him only the wages he lost while unemployed—which, because he quickly found a replacement job, totaled less than $5,000. But on the breach of good faith and fair dealing claim, the court awarded Elmer the $50,000 in commissions that he would have qualified for had he not been fired, $250,000 for the emotional stress he suffered because of the ordeal of being fired and another $250,000 in punitive damages to deter his ex-employer from using that commission-avoidance trick again.

E. Plant Closing Laws

The statutes typically known as plant closing laws apply only to mass dismissals of employees. They are the poor cousins of wrongful discharge lawsuits.

These laws sometimes offer a way to challenge a job loss that is much quicker, easier and less expensive than filing a lawsuit. But the amount of money and other relief that workers can seek under plant closing laws typically is minuscule compared with the remedies available via the wrongful discharge lawsuit route.

Also, keep in mind that neither the federal plant closing law nor the state and local laws in the same category actually forbid closing worksites and dismissing the people who work there. All these laws really do is to give employees a little advance notice that their jobs are going to go away, like it or not.

At most, plant closing laws can provide some income between jobs for employees of companies that fail to provide a warning that they're going to make a mass staff cut—and some punishments that might persuade a company that does not comply with the advance notice requirements of the plant closing laws not to repeat that behavior.

1. Federal Law

The federal plant closing law—more properly, the Worker Adjustment and Retraining Notification Act (29 U.S.C. §§2101, 2102 to 2109)—requires employers with 100 or more fulltime employees to provide 60 days' advance written notice that they are going to lose their jobs before closing a facility—and before putting into effect any other mass staff reduction that will last six months or more.

Employers are also required to provide 60 days' notice of the staff reduction to the chief local elected official, such as the mayor of the city in which the cut will take place, and to the Dislocated Worker Unit of the state in which the cut will occur. The agency designated as the Dislocated Worker Unit varies from state to state, but your state's labor department should be able to direct you to the agency responsible for assisting workers who lose their jobs in mass dismissals. (See the Appendix for contact information.)

2. Exceptions

The federal plant closing law does not apply if:
- less than 50 workers are cut from the payroll
- the cut takes away the jobs of less than 500 workers and represents less than one-third of the employer's workforce
- the workers affected are parttime; this law defines parttime workers as those who average less than 20 hours of work per week, or who have

been employed by the company for less than six of the 12 months preceding the staff cut

- the employees left voluntarily or were discharged for good cause, such as performance that does not meet the company's standards
- the staff cut is the result of a natural disaster
- the employees affected were working on a project that was considered temporary and were told that when they were hired
- waiting 60 days to let the workers go would put the company in danger of going out of business
- the employer could not have foreseen the circumstances that make the staff cut necessary
- the employer offers the workers being cut new jobs at another site within reasonable commuting distance, and the new jobs start within six months of when the old ones ended, or the workers being cut are offered new jobs at another site anywhere and they agree to the transfers within 30 days of when the employer offers them
- the employer voluntarily offers severance pay, not required under any contract or other agreement, that is equal to or greater than the number of days that the company is short on the 60-day notice requirement, or
- more than 90 days pass between two mass dismissals which would require advance notice if added together but which fall under the minimum size rules when counted separately.

3. Penalties for Violations

Obviously, the plant closing law has almost as many holes as fabric. But employers who manage to violate it despite all the exceptions can be made to pay the following penalties:

- backpay to each employee affected by the violation, up to a maximum of 60 days' pay
- reimbursement of the employees' benefit costs that would have been paid by the company had the illegal staff cut not occurred
- a fine of up to $500 per day for each day of the violation, up to a maximum of $30,000, and
- any attorneys' fees incurred.

This last penalty—requiring that legal fees be paid—is important because, if you have received your walking papers as part of a mass firing that violates the federal plant closing law and the government refuses to go to bat for you, you and your co-workers will probably have no recourse but to file a lawsuit to enforce your rights.

HELP FROM THE GOVERNMENT

Before you hire a lawyer to take action under the federal plant closing law, you may want to write or call the highest elected official of the municipality where the staff cut took place and ask him or her to pursue your complaint. The federal plant closing law specifies that a unit of the local government aggrieved may sue the employer involved in the federal district court when the incident occurred, or in any district where the employer does business.

In general, governmental bodies are not very aggressive in pursuing complaints against businesses. But because largescale staff cutting may be a high profile political issue, your local mayor may surprise you by suddenly becoming your legal advocate.

---

4. State and Local Plant Closing Laws

A growing number of states have their own plant closing laws. (See the chart below.) Even a few cities, such as Vacaville, California, and Philadelphia, Pennsylvania, have laws restricting companies that order mass dismissals. Most of these laws merely add a minor restriction or two to the rules of the federal plant closing law, such as requiring that the corporation planning a mass staff cut notify another level of government of its plans in advance.

However, some of the state plant closing laws do provide substantial benefits for the workers they cover. For example, Hawaii's version requires an employer to make up the difference between a worker's regular pay and the unemployment compensation the worker will receive for up to four weeks after the staff cut, under certain conditions.

Each of these laws specifies different restrictions, penalties and methods of enforcement. You can usually learn the details of any state or local law governing mass dismissals by calling your state's labor department.

STATE PLANT CLOSING LAWS

Alabama	No statute
Alaska	No statute
Arizona	No statute
Arkansas	No statute
California	No statute
Colorado	No statute
Connecticut	When employer with 100 or more workers closes or relocates, the employer must continue to pay for employee's health insurance for 120 days after the closing or relocation, or until the employee becomes eligible for replacement group coverage. Conn. Gen. Stat. Ann. §31-51
Delaware	No statute
District of Columbia	No statute
Florida	No statute
Georgia	No statute
Hawaii	Employers with 50 or more employees must give at least 45 days notice of impending job loss due to mass dismissal or business relocation. (Haw. Rev. Stat. §394B-9)
	Employers must pay each former employee an allowance for the difference between the former wage and unemployment benefits for four weeks after termination. Haw. Rev. Stat. §394B-1
Idaho	No statute
Illinois	No statute
Indiana	No statute
Iowa	No statute
Kansas	The state Secretary of Human Resources must give prior approval to mass dismissals within certain industries such as public utilities and public transportation companies. Kan. Stat. Ann. §44-616
Kentucky	No statute
Louisiana	No statute

Maine	Employers with 100 or more employees at a single location must pay employees at least one week's wages when company closes. Me. Rev. Stat. tit. 26, §625B
Maryland	Employers should follow voluntary guidelines covering issues such as advance notice to employees when planning a mass dismissal or relocation. Md. Code Ann. art. 83A, §§3-301 through 3-304
Massachusetts	Employers who receive assistance from certain state agencies are required to make a good faith effort to give advance notice to employees who will lose their jobs in a mass dismissal. Mass. Gen. Laws Ann. ch. 149, §182
Michigan	No statute
Minnesota	Employers are to provide advance notice of plant closing, relocation or substantial layoffs to the state, affected employees and local government. Minn. Stat. Ann. §268.975
Mississippi	No statute
Missouri	No statute
Montana	No statute
Nebraska	No statute
Nevada	No statute
New Hampshire	No statute
New Jersey	No statute
New Mexico	No statute
New York	No statute
North Carolina	No statute
North Dakota	No statute
Ohio	No statute
Oklahoma	No statute
Oregon	No statute
Pennsylvania	No statute
Rhode Island	No statute
South Carolina	Employer must give employees two weeks notice of a closing. S.C. Code Ann. §41-1-40
South Dakota	No statute
Tennessee	Employers with 50 or more fulltime employees within the state must notify state labor officials of a mass dismissal after notifying those employees who will lose their jobs. Tenn. Code Ann. §50-1-602
Texas	No statute

Utah	No statute
Vermont	No statute
Virginia	No statute
Washington	No statute
West Virginia	No statute
Wisconsin	Employers with 50 or more employees within the state must give at least 60 days notice of a business closing or mass dismissal in which ten or more fulltime employees lose their jobs. Wis. Stat. §109.07
Wyoming	No statute ■

CHAPTER

12

UNEMPLOYMENT INSURANCE

Unemployment insurance, often called UI or unemployment compensation, is intended to provide you with regular financial support when you are out of work.

The unemployment insurance program is run jointly by the federal government and the states, and is paid for primarily by a tax on employers. There are differences among the states in how the programs are administered, in who qualifies to receive benefits—and, importantly, in how much is available in benefits.

This chapter discusses unemployment insurance in general and explains some specific state nuances. For more information on your state's program, check with the nearest Unemployment Insurance Office or Employment Security Division, usually part of the state department of labor. (See the Appendix for contact details.)

A. Who Is Covered

Unemployment insurance covers employees of all stripes, including parttimers and temporaries.

To be covered, you must meet a number of qualifications.

- You must have worked as an employee for a substantial period and earned a minimum amount of wages before becoming unemployed. In most states, you must have been employed for at least six months during the year before your job loss. The amount you.are required to have earned to qualify for unemployment insurance benefits varies by state, and is frequently changed to reflect inflation and the cost of living.

- You must be a U.S. citizen or have the documents required by the U.S. Immigration and Naturalization Service to legally work in the United States. (See Chapter 17.)

- You must be available to be recalled to your old job or to work in a similar one. For example, you may become ineligible if you take a new job or if you take a long vacation during which you cannot be reached by your former employer or a new one.

- You must be physically and mentally able to perform your old job or a similar one. The requirement that workers be physically able to work can be confusing when applied to pregnant women. In general, the courts have ruled that unemployment insurance benefits cannot be denied simply because an employee is pregnant, but can be denied if the pregnancy makes the employee physically unable to perform her normal job or one similar to it.

Workers who are physically unable to perform their jobs usually have to apply for the workers' compensation or Social Security disability insurance programs. (See Chapters 13 and 14.) However, a few states pay unemployment insurance benefits during periods of temporary disability. Your local unemployment insurance agency should help you determine whether your state is one of them.

The requirement that a worker must be mentally able to work has reduced the number of unemployment claims filed because a job was too stressful.

B. Being Disqualified for Benefits

A few categories of employees are specifically listed as ineligible to receive unemployment insurance benefits. And a great many more employees are disqualified because of their own behavior or actions—such as quitting a job without a legally recognized reason.

1. Employees Excluded

The categories of employees not covered by unemployment insurance usually include people employed by small farms, those who are paid only through commissions, casual domestic workers and babysitters, newspaper carriers under age 18, children employed by their parents, adults employed by their spouses or their children, employees of religious organizations, some corporate officers and elected officials.

2. Disqualifying Behavior

Even if you are covered by unemployment insurance and otherwise eligible to receive it, you may be disqualified from receiving benefits. The reasons for disqualification vary from state to state, but the most common ones are discussed here.

- You were fired from your job for deliberate and repeated misconduct. That includes chronic absence or tardiness without a good explanation, sleeping on the job or violating clear and reasonable workplace rules. Note that it is not enough that you were careless or negligent on the job—that you arguably used poor judgment or that you accidentally damaged some of your employer's property. Your misconduct must have been purposeful and, unless it is very serious, must usually have happened more than one time.

- You refused to accept a similar job without good reason. In these economically strapped times, courts have been especially hard-pressed to find legally sufficient grounds for you to reject a valid job offer. The few reasons that have succeeded are that you are not physically able to do the work required, that the job is too far from your home and family or would require you to violate a firmly held religious belief, such as working on days your religion prohibits working.

- You are unemployed because you went on strike or are not working because you refused to cross a picket line. In some states, you will be entitled to unemployment benefits if there is a lockout at work—that is, your employer closes down because there is a contract dispute or refuses to let you work until you agree to accept changed work conditions.

- You quit your job without a good reason. (See the discussion below.)

INDEPENDENT CONTRACTORS: A GRAY AREA

Independent contractors are not usually eligible for unemployment insurance. But in some cases, people treated as independent contractors by companies are found to be legal employees—and therefore eligible for unemployment benefits. (See Chapter 2, Section A.)

In fact, the legal controls are somewhat relaxed in allowing independent contractors to be covered by unemployment benefits. If your employment status is somewhat uncertain, you may need to provide proof that you qualified as an employee of a company rather than an independent contractor before you can collect benefits from your state's unemployment system.

Persuasive proof would be that:

* your work was supervised by employees of the company
* your work was considered a normal part of the company's course of business—for example, an integral part of the quarterly financial review, rather than a one-time consulting job
* you worked in the company office, rather than from your own home, workshop or studio, or
* you used company-owned equipment—computers, machining tools, construction equipment—to get the work done.

3. Acceptable Reasons for Quitting

The last reason to be shut off from benefits—quitting your job—is particularly troublesome. Disputes over unemployment insurance claims often occur when the employee believes that his or her reason for quitting a job was a good one, and the employer disagrees.

Of course, the definition of a good reason to quit a job varies with each person and each circumstance. In most situations, you must first have informed your employer that there was a change in the job or working conditions that make it impossible for you to stay on. A number of reasons are usually considered good enough for you to quit your job and still be eligible for unemployment insurance.

- Some form of fraud was involved in recruiting you for the job. For example, employers sometimes offer a certain level of wages and benefits, but then try to cut back on that offer once the employee shows up for work.

- Your life or health was endangered by the employer's failure to maintain workplace safety. You will need to have some evidence that a doctor has examined you and confirmed that your health was jeopardized by the chemical discharge or other condition in the workplace. (See Chapter 7 for additional workplace safety concerns.)

- The nature of your work was changed dramatically from what you had originally been hired to do, or your wages and benefits were substantially reduced without your consent. Keep in mind that you may have to tolerate small changes in your job duties or conditions due to work restructuring or simple economics. However, if your job changes so substantially that it begins to look and feel different from the position you were offered originally, that may mean you are legally allowed to quit and still collect unemployment benefits.

- You were subjected to some intolerable or illegal condition on the job, such as discrimination or sexual harassment, and your employer refused to correct the situation after learning of it.

- A change in the location of your work made it impractical for you to continue in the job. A change of only a few miles would not likely be sufficient. But if the move is so far that it adds a substantial increase to your commuting time—several hours—or the company relocates to another state, that may be considered sufficient reason for you to leave the job and collect unemployment benefits.

- Your spouse had to relocate to take a new job. This reason, however, will not hold up in all states. In a number of cases, former employees argued that because women most often leave their jobs when a spouse gets transferred, it is discriminatory to deny unemployment benefits to them. The courts so far have disagreed and held that because men could be affected, too, there is no sex discrimination in denying benefits to workers who must move to stay with their mates.

Several states may also award you unemployment benefits if you can prove you quit for a compelling personal reason. But beware that you must usually back such claims with substantial evidence. For example, if you quit your job to care for a sick spouse, you will probably be asked to show that no alternative care arrangements were feasible, and that your employer was unwilling to grant you a paid or unpaid leave of absence.

If you have the luxury, do a little research on your eligibility for benefits before you leave your job. You can quit your job for other reasons and still file a claim for unemployment insurance benefits. True—filing for unemployment benefits requires perseverance, time, wading through paperwork and waiting in lines to speak with—and sometimes be berated by—unemployment office personnel. Still, you have little to lose by filing a claim you consider to be valid and hoping for a favorable decision. As the system is set up, employees who file for unemployment benefits are presumed to be entitled to them. But if your former employer challenges your claim, you will need to prove through the appeal process described below that your reason was good enough.

C. Calculating Your Benefits

Each state sets its own maximum and minimum limits on the amount of benefits you can collect. Massachusetts, for example, has one of the highest maximum rates—$444 weekly if you have dependents; Hawaii has one of the lowest minimum benefits of only $5 a week. Whether you are entitled to the high end or the low end of the benefit amount allowed depends on the amount of money you earned in your last position.

Under normal circumstances, unemployment insurance benefits are limited to 26 weeks. However, this period is extended by legislative whim—especially during periods of high unemployment. In most states during most times, you will be entitled to an additional 13 weeks of benefit payments on top of the 26 weeks you already have coming.

To calculate your benefits, the unemployment insurance office will typically use one of three rather complicated formulas premised on the wages you recently earned. Then, depending on your state's law, you will be given more or less than half that amount. In addition, each state has minimum and maximum benefit limits with which it must abide.

SEVERANCE PAY: IT MAY NOT COMPUTE

As protection against wrongful discharge lawsuits, employers increasingly offer an unearned severance payment—usually several months' worth of the employee's normal pay—to get an employee to quit a job rather than be fired. (See Chapter 10, Section F.) In such situations, severance pay can delay the start of unemployment insurance benefits—or even make a worker ineligible for them.

Example: Raj worked for a company that wanted to economize by cutting 500 employees. He accepted the company's offer of six months' severance pay—four months more than the two months' severance pay he had earned through the benefits program—in return for a signed statement that he had not been dismissed, but had volunteered to quit his job.

When Raj filed a claim for unemployment insurance benefits, he was shocked and disappointed when it was turned down. His former employer contested the claim, arguing that Raj had made a decision to quit voluntarily.

Raj appealed the denial of his claim, and he won because he proved that he was coerced into quitting. But the appeal office also ruled that Raj could not begin collecting unemployment insurance benefits until the four months covered by the unearned severance package had expired.

Regulations and rulings covering the effects that severance pay has on unemployment insurance vary greatly from state to state, and are changing rapidly. In some cases, groups of workers who have been cut from company payrolls through offers of severance packages have created enough political pressure to have the rules in their state changed in their favor.

If you quit your job in exchange for severance pay, protect your rights by filing a claim for unemployment insurance benefits. If that claim is denied, you will then have the right to explain during the appeals process what really happened—or to benefit from any changes in your state's unemployment insurance rules covering severance pay.

1. Average Weekly Wages

In Florida, Michigan, New Jersey, New York and Ohio, benefits are based on the average weekly wage, which is then cut in half to determine the weekly unemployment benefit amount.

Example: *Marika worked as a sales clerk, earning a weekly salary of $600, which was increased to $800 mid-year. Her average weekly wage was $700 ($600 + $800 divided by 2). The weekly unemployment benefit to which she is entitled is $350—$700 divided in half.*

2. Total Wages

In Alaska, Kentucky, Montana, New Hampshire, Oregon and West Virginia, unemployment benefits are computed by taking the annual wage and multiplying it by a set percentage, which varies by state and with time.

Example: *Blaine earned an annual wage of $36,500 as an assistant furniture buyer at a department store in Lexington, Kentucky. Multiplying his total annual wages by the state multiplier—.01185—yields a weekly unemployment benefit amount of $433.*

3. Highest Quarter of Earnings

All other states compute unemployment benefits using a slightly more complicated formula—based on the highest earnings you made during a certain period. In most states, this is calculated by quarters, or three-month periods. The period in which an employee had the highest wages is the one most states use to calculate the amount of weekly unemployment insurance benefits. And the crucial quarters in most states are the first four of the last five quarters you worked before losing your job, but the period varies.

Example: *Bart worked for 26 weeks as a mechanic in an auto repair business, earning $350 per week. He then got a raise to earn $400 weekly—and worked an additional 26 weeks before being laid off. Bart's benefits will be based on the $5,200 ($400 x 13 weeks) that he earned during the quarter of his highest* *earnings. That amount will then be divided by 26, to get the $200 in weekly unemployment benefits Bart will be allowed.*

Some states also pay partial benefits to people whose workhours slip below their normal level for a substantial period. These programs vary widely, so when in doubt, it is wise to inquire at the unemployment insurance office if you think you may qualify for coverage.

PARTTIME WORK: THROWING IT INTO THE MIX

The bottom line is that unemployment benefits are based on the amount you used to earn. If your former job was parttime, you still may be eligible to collect unemployment benefits if you lose that job. This is true even if you hold down several parttime jobs—and lose only one of them. Keep in mind, however, that the amount to which you are entitled in unemployment benefits will be offset by the amount you still earn—and by any amounts you receive from workers' compensation and other sources.

The same is true if you secure a parttime job after losing other work. Your unemployment benefits will be reduced by the amount of income you earn in the new parttime job. You will have to weigh the drawbacks of this income loss against the benefits the parttime work may afford: a boost to your confidence, camaraderie of co-workers, increased visibility and contacts in the work world, added work experience.

D. Filing a Claim

Claims for unemployment insurance benefits are accepted and paid by the states through thousands of offices throughout the country. Tales of difficult dealings with the unemployment office are legion—long waits, surly officeworkers, piles of paperwork—all coming your way at what is likely to be an emotionally shaky time for you. Keep in mind that you are merely pursuing your legal right. And arm yourself with the mantle of patience.

Finding the right office is the first hurdle. The names for the agencies that handle the claims vary, but are typically something that sounds more upbeat than unemployment—such as Bureau of Employment Security, Job Service Office or State Employment Service.

Whatever your local version is called, you can locate the office closest to you by checking the state government section of your local telephone directory. Because of the varying names used and the fact that there are many other government programs relating to jobs, it is wise to call to confirm that you have the right place.

In most states, there is a waiting period of one week between the time you lose your job and the time you can collect unemployment insurance benefits. But it is a good idea to visit the nearest unemployment office as soon after you lose your job as possible. You can then present your documentation, complete the required paperwork and convince agency representatives to begin investigating your claim—all the initial steps needed to get the bureaucratic ball rolling.

THE TAXMAN WILL COMETH

Unlike workers' compensation benefits (discussed in Chapter 13), unemployment insurance benefits are taxed as income. Because the benefit amounts paid are often below the taxable annual earning level, however, many states will not take the automatic step of deducting any taxes from your unemployment benefit check.

However, the state will—almost unfailingly—take the leap of reporting the unemployment benefit amount you were paid to the Internal Revenue Service and to your state taxing authority.

If you were receiving unemployment benefits during part of the year during which you got a new job, you may want to increase the amount your employer withholds in taxes from your paycheck. Otherwise, you may be unpleasantly surprised at tax time when you either owe more or receive less of a refund than anticipated.

1. Required Documentation

You claim will get processed more quickly if you bring the proper documentation when you visit the local office. You will need a number of documents, including:

- a detailed work history covering at least a few years prior to your unemployment, including accurate names, addresses, telephone numbers and IRS employer identification numbers of your previous employers. You should find these numbers on your paystubs or on employment-related IRS forms, such as your W-2 or 1099-Miscellaneous

- recent pay stubs and other wage records, such as the W-2 form on which your employer reports your income to the Internal Revenue Service

- your Social Security card, or another document that shows your Social Security number, and

- any documentation you have of why you are unemployed, such as a layoff or dismissal notice from your employer, and your employer's unemployment insurance account number, if it has been provided to you. (For more on how to document a job loss, see Chapter 10, Section C.)

Typically, your first visit to the unemployment insurance claims office will include some type of orientation—ranging from simple instructional signs hanging from the ceiling to explanatory pamphlets to sophisticated video productions. In any case, you will be required to fill out forms explaining your unemployment. This is where your documentation will be especially useful.

WHAT TO SAY—AND WHAT NOT TO SAY

When completing your unemployment forms, one of the first questions posed will be something like: Explain in your own words the reason for leaving your last job. You will see first that there is little room for long-worded explanations. Take the clue and keep your responses simple and non-committal.

Unless you were clearly dismissed from your job because of something you did wrong, avoid using the word "fired" in filing out any forms or answering any interview questions at the unemployment insurance office. There are many unspecified words thrown around concerning the end of employment, but fired is the one most often taken to mean that you did something wrong and were dismissed because of it.

If you lost your job because business was slow, note that you were laid off. "Laid off" is an equally vague term, but it is less likely to raise questions about the validity of your claim.

If you were discharged by your employer, take pains to note: "Discharged without any misconduct," or "Quit for good cause personal reason." Leave out any qualifying details, such as: "My supervisor never liked me from the first day I walked in, so naturally, I was the first to be laid off."

2. The Investigation

Once you have handed in your completed forms, the rituals that follow vary somewhat from state to state. You may be interviewed the same day or told to come back for an interview. If a second visit is required, be sure to take your employment document collection with you.

Whatever the ritual in your locale, the goal of the unemployment insurance claim filing process is to determine whether you are entitled to benefits, and what the amount of those benefits should be. The interviewer will likely concentrate on why you left your last job. Keep your explanations helpful but as brief and objective as possible.

In some states, you may be approved to receive benefits immediately. If your employer later challenges the award, you should continue to get those benefits during the time the appeal is processed.

But in most states, the clerks at the unemployment insurance office will use your first interview to launch an investigation of your claim by sending inquiries to your former employers. The employers then must respond, either verifying or disputing your version of the circumstances surrounding your unemployment, the wages you received and other relevant information. The process usually takes at least a few weeks, and sometimes more.

While waiting for your claim to go through this verification process, you will probably be required to visit the unemployment insurance office once each week or two to sign a statement affirming that you still meet all the legal requirements of the program—and that you are looking for a new job. It is important to comply with this reporting requirement even before receiving unemployment insurance checks. If you have not yet received a cent in unemployment benefits, once your claim is verified, you will usually be paid after the fact for all the weeks for which you did qualify.

If your claim is approved, you will typically receive your unemployment benefit check in the mail every two weeks after your claim is verified and your benefit level is determined.

3. Continuing Your Benefits

Once you have qualified for unemployment insurance benefits, you are not free to simply sit back and welcome the checks each week. You must continue to comply with the state program's rules and rituals to keep them coming.

You must visit the unemployment insurance office as frequently as your state requires it. During each visit, you must verify that you remain unemployed but available for work, that you remain physically able to work and that you are actively looking for work. The documents you sign on your visits to the unemployment insurance office will typically ask you to certify that you continue to meet these requirements, and it is usually a criminal offense to lie about any of your answers.

In some states, you are also required to list a minimum number of potential employers to whom you have applied for work since the last time you signed for benefits. This requirement may vary according to economic conditions. If the lines at the unemployment insurance offices get too long in your area, for example, you may be allowed to merely mail in your information every two weeks.

The unemployment insurance program cannot require you to take a job that varies much from your normal field of work and your normal wage level. But these ranges are subject to interpretation, so exercise care in deciding where to apply for a new job. Some unemployment insurance offices maintain and post listings of jobs that are available locally. Apply only for jobs that are similar to your normal type of work and wage levels so that you will not run the risk of having your unemployment insurance claim discontinued because you refused to accept substitute employment.

WHERE TO FILE IF YOU MOVE

If you become unemployed in one state and then move to another, you can file your claim in your new state, but your benefits will be determined by the rules used by your former state. Although your new state administers your claim, the cost of your benefits is charged back to the state in which you became unemployed. A move will also add time to processing your claim—usually increasing the delay by several weeks.

Keep in mind that even when you relocate, you still must meet all the requirements of the unemployment insurance program to qualify for benefits. Your new location must be one to which you were required to move by family circumstances, or in which it is logical for you to expect to find a new job. For example, you cannot decide to move to a small seacoast town with virtually no business activity because you like the lifestyle there, quit your old job for no other reason, and then expect to be eligible for unemployment insurance when you get to your new home and cannot find work.

E. Appealing Benefit Decisions

If your claim is approved, your former employer will have the right to appeal it. If you are denied benefits, you are legally entitled to appeal the decision.

1. If Your Employer Appeals

There are cases, of course, where some former employees begin to collect unemployment insurance benefits to which they are not legally entitled—and the employer justifiably appeals the decision.

However, some employers have an outrageous policy of appealing all unemployment insurance claims filed against them. Typically, they use tactics such as claiming that workers quit when, in fact, they were fired because business became slow.

These employers often hire lawyers or agencies that specialize in frustrating unemployment insurance claims—hired gunslingers who make a living by fighting employees' claims until the employees find new jobs and drop their complaints. Money is usually their motivation: the higher turnover a company has, the higher the company's unemployment premiums.

If your claim is approved but your employer appeals it, you will be notified of that appeal in writing. In general, an appeal by your former employer of an approved claim will be conducted in the same way as your appeal of a denied claim. (See Section 2, below.)

You will be able to continue collecting your benefits until a decision is issued on your former employer's appeal. You may, however, be required to repay all or part of the benefits if your ex-employer wins the appeal. Typically, your ability to repay is the deciding factor in such circumstances.

2. Appealing a Denied Claim

If your claim is denied, you will be notified in writing of why that decision was made, and informed of the procedure and time limits for filing an appeal. Depending on your state, you will have from one to four weeks to file an appeal from the time that the notice of denial of an unemployment insurance claim is mailed to you.

A hearing will likely be scheduled within a few weeks after you advise the unemployment insurance office of your intention to appeal its decision, and you will have the option of representing yourself or having a lawyer do it. If you want a lawyer but cannot afford one, check with your local Legal Aid Society or a clinic at a nearby law school to see if someone there can represent you. If you are unemployed and without benefits, chances are good that they will help. (See Chapter 18, Section D.)

Your former employer also has the option of being represented by a lawyer or an agency that specializes in challenging unemployment insurance claims. Typically, the appeal hearing will be conducted informally before a hearing examiner, referee or administrative law judge. At the hearing, you and your former employer will be allowed to bring witnesses, such as co-workers and medical experts—and most of the formal rules of evidence that apply to formal courtroom proceedings will not apply or will be only loosely enforced.

REPRESENTING YOURSELF

If you can clearly document the reasons that you are unemployed and present them in an organized manner, you can do a good job of representing yourself in all but the most complex situations. At this level, the appeal process is intended to resolve disputes rather than to take on the look of a formal court action, so do not be afraid to ask questions at the unemployment insurance office or at your hearing.

Well before the hearing is scheduled to begin, write down the reasons that you feel you are entitled to unemployment insurance benefits in as few words as possible, then practice presenting those reasons to a friend or family member. Don't give in to the human temptation to use the hearing as an opportunity to insult or get revenge on your former employer.

Do a thorough and thoughtful job of researching, organizing, documenting and presenting your case. Keep your argument focused, because it is at this level that you are most likely to win a decision that will quickly start your benefit checks flowing. (For details of how to document your job loss, see Chapter 10, Section C.)

If you win this appeal, you will soon begin receiving benefits, typically including back payments from the date on which you first became eligible.

Both you and your former employer will have the option of appealing the ruling on your appeal to the state courts. However, only a tiny percentage of unemployment insurance cases continue up into the state courts or higher. Those that do typically require help from a lawyer. (See Chapter 18, Section D.) ■

CHAPTER

13

WORKERS' COMPENSATION

The workers' compensation system provides replacement income and medical expenses to employees who are injured or become ill as a result of their jobs. Financial benefits may also extend to workers' dependents and to the survivors of workers who are killed on the job. In most circumstances, workers' compensation also protects employers from being sued for those injuries or deaths.

OTHER LAWS ON WORK-RELATED ILLNESS AND INJURY

Workers' compensation covers some aspects of work-related injuries, illnesses and deaths. But injured workers should be aware of other laws that may give them rights or entitle them to compensation. Some laws work in tandem, providing individuals with different options; some may provide the exclusive remedy for a workplace wrong.

- Social Security disability insurance provides some income for people who are unable to work because of a physical or mental disability. (See Chapter 14.)
- Unemployment compensation provides individuals with some financial benefits when they are out of work. (See Chapter 12.)
- The Americans With Disabilities Act prohibits discrimination against workers who have some types of physical limitations or illnesses. (See Chapter 8, Section F.)

Other lawsuits for injuries or job loss may help redress some additional workplace injuries, particularly where workers have lost their jobs. For example, workers' comp claims filed by workers who have been fired are often paired with wrongful termination actions. (See Chapter 11, Section A.)

The benefits paid are almost always limited to the relatively modest amounts available under the workers' compensation system. The system is financed primarily by insurance premiums paid by employers. In some states, employers may opt to self-insure—meaning that they can pay for any claims themselves.

Contrary to popular misconception, filing a workers' comp claim does not involve suing the employer. Unless the employer has committed some serious wrong or is illegally uninsured or underinsured, filing a claim is more like submitting a claim to a car insurer following an accident.

The idea behind the workers' comp system is that employers and employees can settle their potential differences over money and liability privately and quickly. Injured employees are compensated for the costs of workplace injuries and illnesses. In return, employers can run their businesses free from the constant threat of negligence lawsuits filed by their employees. In reality, however, the system is fraught with difficulties—high premiums for employers and grindingly slow claim processing for injured employees. Doctors and lawyers are often thrown into the fray to make the system painfully costly and complicated.

Like unemployment insurance (discussed in Chapter 12) and Social Security disability insurance (discussed in Chapter 14), the workers' compensation system is national, but is administered by the states. The laws and court decisions governing it follow a pattern throughout the country, but vary significantly from state to state on everything from eligibility for benefits to the proper process for filing claims.

THE RISING COST OF DOING BUSINESS

For the last two decades, insurance premiums that employers must pay for workers' compensation have increased more every year than the Consumer's Price Index.

Note these recent estimates of the raging annual cost to employers of workers' comp claims.

1970	$4.9 billion
1976	$11 billion
1980	$22.3 billion
1988	$43.3 billion
1991	$62 billion
1994	$70 billion

A. Who Is Covered

In general, anyone who qualifies as a parttime or fulltime employee under the Internal Revenue Service guidelines (discussed in Chapter 2, Section A) is covered by workers' compensation insurance. There are a few exceptions to this rule—notably harbor workers, seafarers, railroad employees and federal employees—all of whom must file lawsuits to get disputed compensation rather than use the workers' comp system.

But coverage details vary from state to state, so certain categories of employees may be excluded from coverage in some locales. For example, in some states, companies with fewer than five employees are not required to carry workers' compensation coverage, and many states exclude volunteers, farm workers and domestic workers from coverage.

Workers who are not covered by workers' comp but who suffer work-related illnesses or injuries are usually relegated to getting compensation from their employers through:

• a company-backed policy, such as paid time off for sick days
• a settlement reached through arbitration or mediation (see Chapter 18, Section A), or
• a lawsuit filed against an employer or former employer—for negligence or breach of contract, for example.

Many states require employers to post an explanation of workers' compensation coverage in a prominent place within the work area. So if your employer keeps such a notice on your workplace bulletin board, you are probably covered. If you are unsure whether your employer is covered, your state workers' compensation agency should tell you. (See the listing in Section G for contact details.)

Independent contractors are not covered under the workers' comp systems in most states. However, workers who are categorized as independent contractors may in reality be employees. (See Chapter 2, Section A.) If you are unclear about your status as a worker, file a workers' comp claim for your injuries, anyway. It will then be up to your employer to prove that you are not eligible because you qualify legally as an independent contractor rather than an employee.

HOLDING DOWN THE HIGH COST OF COMPENSATION

The nation's tab for handling workers' comp cases has nearly tripled since 1980—up to $70 billion a year, according to the Workers' Compensation Research Institute, an insurance industry group. Where the cost crisis is the most pronounced—California, Florida and Maine—many insurers have fled the state, taking with them the possibility of startup business ventures. That bottom line has sounded the wake-up call to other states that they need to trim the fat from their workers' comp systems. Most often, that means reclaiming the system from lawyers and doctors, who stand to profit the most from lengthy litigation and high awards.

Washington and Oregon have been among the early listeners—with dramatic results.

In 1990, Oregon set up a medical arbitration system that bypasses courts and relies on independent panels to rule on workers' comp cases. Two years later, injury claims in Oregon had fallen by 17% and the cost of employer premiums dropped by nearly 30%. The savings allowed the state to double benefits for serious injuries.

In Washington, private insurers were banned from writing policies in 1985. By studying its data base of 1.3 million insured workers to target trends in injuries, the state focused on preventing workers' compensation claims. In doing so, the state turned a $225 million workers' comp deficit into a $342 surplus.

Private companies are following suit, using innovation to save money and build trust and efficiency into flagging workers comp systems.

For example, Steelcase Inc., in Grand Rapids, Michigan, fosters trust in staff doctors by including an employee advocate on its medical review board. As a result, its average claim cost has been cut in half.

And Rockwell International Corporation in Seal Beach, California, saves an estimated $2 million annually by using a computer program to check for doctors who double-bill through both workers' comp and other insurance.

Source: *Business Week*, October 19, 1992

B. Conditions Covered

Workers' compensation provides a claim and benefit system for workers who become ill, are injured or who die on the job.

1. Injuries

To be covered by workers' compensation, an injury need not be caused by a sudden accident such as a fall. Equally common claims are for injury due to repeated use of a body part—backstrain from lifting heavy boxes, for example. Also covered may be a physical condition that was aggravated by workplace conditions—such as emphysema made worse by airborne chemicals. And increasingly, workers are being compensated for the effects of psychological stress caused by the job.

With a few exceptions, any injury that occurs in connection with work is covered. The legal boundary is that employees are protected by workers' comp as long as they are "in the course of employment." For example, a computer repair technician would be covered by workers' comp while making service calls on customers, but not while traveling to and from work or going to a purely social dinner later that evening.

From the employee's standpoint, workers' comp is a no-fault system. It does not matter whether a worker was careless while injured—although claims from employees hurt while drunk or fighting have traditionally been rejected as outside the bounds of "work-related activity." Some states restrict coverage for injuries caused by employees' own "willful misconduct"—a term given differing spins by differing courts. And a number of states expressly restrict or eliminate benefits when an employee's claim is based on injuries caused by non-prescription, illegal drugs. These states include Alaska, Connecticut, Florida, Georgia, Idaho, Iowa, Kansas, Louisiana, Maryland, Missouri, North Dakota, Ohio, Oklahoma, Oregon, Rhode Island, South Dakota, Virginia and Wyoming.

Injuries that can be shown to have been intentionally self-inflicted by the employee, or to have been caused by substance abuse, generally are not covered. However, the courts have often sided with the injured worker when such cases are disputed—ruling that the injury is covered as long as the employee's behavior was not the only thing that caused the injury.

The legal definition of when you are working for workers' compensation purposes also has expanded in recent years so that a great number of injuries are covered. For example, employees who were injured playing baseball or football on a company-affiliated team have been allowed to collect workers' compensation benefits for those injuries.

AVOIDING INJURIES CAUSED BY REPETITIVE MOTION

In a typical year, more than six million work-related injuries and illnesses occur in the United States. The most rapidly growing and widely publicized category of workplace injuries is caused by repetitive motions of the human body.

Carpal Tunnel Syndrome—which primarily afflicts the wrists, hands and forearms—is the bane of a growing number of office workers who spend their days in front of computer terminals. And many other parts of the body are susceptible to injury from being used repeatedly to perform motions that exceed the specifications for which nature designed them. People working on auto factory and meat processing production lines, for example, often suffer repetitive motion injury to their elbows, fingers, shoulders, backs, knees, ankles and feet.

Typical symptoms of repetitive stress injuries include swelling and redness near bone joints; extreme sensitivity of the affected body part to movement and external touch; pain, both sharp and dull, in the overused area that may radiate into other parts of the limb, abdomen, head or back; and numbness of the affected body part or those near it. If detected early, injuries caused by repeated motions can often be cured by a short period of rest, light medication and rehabilitative exercise. The most serious and neglected cases, however, can escalate to a lifelong physical disability.

Work-related cumulative motion injuries are typically covered by workers' compensation insurance. But the best workers' compensation claim is the one that you never have to file, so here are a few of the steps that health experts recommend to avoid becoming afflicted with a work-related repetitive motion injury:

(continued)

- Take frequent, short breaks from repetitive, physically stressful work whenever possible. This allows your muscles and joints to recover a bit from unnatural tensions that may result from your work.
- Do gentle stretching exercises at work regularly, paying particular attention to the parts of your body that are likely to be used most often. This reduces the muscle tightening that is believed to contribute to the illness.
- Watch for early symptoms, such as stiffness or other discomfort in heavily used body parts. Quick and complete recovery is much more likely if the symptoms are recognized early.
- Redesign your work tools or your typical work position and movements—or ask your employer to help do so. Good examples of redesigning are wrist supports for use with personal computer keyboards and ergonomic lines of office furniture.
- Remember that heart-pounding physical exertion is not necessary for dangerous body stress to occur. Just as you can wake up with a sore shoulder after sleeping all night in an awkward position, you can subject yourself to the dangers of muscle and tendon injury even in jobs that involve very limited exertion. (For more on preventing workplace injuries, see Chapter 7, Section B.)

2. Illnesses

An illness becomes an occupational illness—and so, covered under the workers' compensation system—when the nature of a job increases the worker's chances of suffering from that disease. In fact, in some states, certain illnesses such as heart attacks and hernias are presumed to be covered for high stress jobs such as police work and firefighting. There must, however, be a clear connection between the job and the illness. Also, in examining a claim, investigators will look into nonwork factors, such as diet, exercise, smoking and drinking habits, and hobbies, that may affect or aggravate a particular condition.

Illnesses that are the gradual result of work conditions—for example, emotional illness and stress-related digestive problems—increasingly are being recognized by the courts as covered by workers' compensation insurance. Perhaps not coincidentally, such stress injury claims are on the rise, too.

The American medical profession, traditionally slow to acknowledge the interworkings of mind and body, no longer ignores the effects of job-related stress on general health. According to the American Institute for Preventative Medicine, stress is at the root of nearly two-thirds of all office visits and plays a major role in heart disease and cancer. Currently, only about half the states recognize stress as a valid basis for workers' comp claims. But in every state, if you show that stress has disabled you from doing your job, employers must accommodate your work to your condition—by reducing work hours or providing a quieter atmosphere, for example. (See Chapter 8, Section F.)

3. Deaths

Dependents of workers who are killed on the job or die as a result of a work injury or illness are almost always eligible to collect workers' compensation benefits.

Even if an employee is found dead in the workplace, no one witnessed the death and no cause of death is obvious, the death is usually covered by workers' compensation. The possibilities of suicide or murder are usually ignored by courts unless there is strong evidence that the death qualifies as one or the other.

THE EXPANDING AND SHRINKING COMPENSATION WORLD

One of the most dramatic expansions of the definition of illness caused by work occurred in a 1990 Michigan appeals court ruling. In that case, a brewery worker was found eligible for workers' compensation benefits because his tendency toward alcoholism—he typically drank 15 to 20 bottles of beer at work each day, and more at home—had been made worse by the fact that his employer gave employees free beer to drink during their breaks (*Gacioch v. Stroh Brewery Co.*, 466 N.W. 2d 302).

However, the courts have begun to set limits, as demonstrated by a 1991 California case. There, a workers' compensation claim was filed by a lawyer who fell off his bicycle while pedaling to a weekly meeting of workers' compensation attorneys. He argued that because he is a lawyer, much of his work involves thinking and analyzing. And because "his office is in his head," he claimed he should remain covered by workers' comp around the clock.

In rejecting the claim, the workers' comp board referee injected a bit of common sense: "Would claimant be covered if he woke in the middle of the night with an idea regarding a case and injured himself falling out of bed to write it down?" he asked. "Common sense tells me that the employment relationship, no matter how all-consuming it may appear to the claimant, must have limits. When claimant fell from his bicycle . . . while thinking of client calls to be made, he was pedaling beyond those limits" (WCB Case No. 90-18674).

C. The Right to Medical Care

When you are injured at work, the workers' comp system usually entitles you to receive immediate medical care.

1. Treating Physician

If you have a regular doctor, inform your employer in writing that if you are injured at work, you wish to be treated by that doctor. Keep a copy of that letter should problems arise later.

If you make no such written request—and you intend to have an injury claim handled under the workers' comp system—either your employer or the insurance company will usually be free to dictate which doctor will treat you for the first 30 days after your injury or work-related illness. After that time, you may be free to receive treatment from the doctor of your choice. But by that time, the company-referred doctor, who is likely to give a conservative diagnosis of the extent of your injury, may have already jeopardized your benefit claim.

2. Continuing Treatment

The insurance company is responsible for paying for all treatment you are diagnosed to require, even if that treatment must continue after you return to work. Your ongoing treatment should be paid for life, but you can trade away future medical payments for cash when you settle your case.

If you are uncertain about whether settling makes good financial sense for you—and that uncertainty is more likely if your work-related illness or injury is quite severe—than you may want to consult an experienced workers' comp attorney. (See Chapter 18, Section D.)

D. Filing a Workers' Compensation Claim

Get immediate medical care if your injury requires it. You must then inform your employer of your injury as soon as possible. This is a tricky part of processing a workers' comp claim, since states have wildly different limits on the number of days you have to notify your employer; in most states, the limit is one month, but the range is from a few days to two years.

In the unlikely event that your employer refuses to cooperate with you in filing a workers' compensation claim, a call to your local workers' compensation office will usually remedy the situation.

Typically, your employer will have claim forms for you to fill out and submit, or can obtain a form quickly. It then becomes your employer's responsibility to submit the paperwork to the proper insurance carrier. Depending on state law, you—rather than your employer—may need to file a separate claim with your state's workers' compensation agency. There is a time limit on this, too—often a year after injury. But your state may have a shorter limit.

If your claim is not disputed by your employer or its insurance carrier, it will be approved and an adjuster for the insurance company will typically contact you or your employer with instructions on how to submit your medical bills for payment. But be prepared. Things do not always go smoothly. The employer, in an attempt to keep workers' comp rates from skyrocketing, may fight your right to benefits. The best way you can counteract such disputes is by producing good documentation, including complete medical records, of your injury and treatment.

If your injury is not permanent and does not cause you to lose income, the payment of your medical bills will probably be the extent of your claim and there will not be much else for you to do. If you are temporarily unable to work because of your injury, you will also begin receiving checks to cover your wage loss—typically within a week or two after your claim is approved. Your employer will notify the insurance company to stop sending you wage-replacement checks as soon as you recover and return to work.

E. Calculating Benefits

Your workers' compensation benefits may take several forms. The following are most common, although some states may provide additional benefits.

1. Costs of Medical Care

The bills for medical care you required because of your workplace injuries will be paid. Theoretically, at least, there is no limitation on medical coverage for illnesses and injuries that are covered. Medical coverage includes costs of:

- doctors
- hospitals
- nursing services, including home care
- physical therapy
- dentists
- chiropractors, and
- prosthetic devices.

2. Temporary Disability

This is the most common disability compensation paid under workers' compensation, awarded if you are unable to work, but are expected to recover and return to work.

You will receive tax-free temporary disability payments that substitute for the income you would have earned had you not been injured. If you cannot work at all, typically you will be paid two-thirds of your average wages, with state-set minimums and maximums. People with unusually low incomes may actually experience an income increase while receiving workers' compensation—and those with high incomes will probably experience an income cut.

In most states, workers become eligible for wage loss replacement benefits as soon as they have lost a few days of work because of an injury covered by workers' compensation. The number of days required to qualify varies by state—and some states allow the payments to be paid retroactively to the first day of wage loss if the injury keeps the employee out of work for an extended period.

3. Vocational Rehabilitation

If your injury prevents you from returning to your job, but you are physically able to do some work, you may be entitled to vocational rehabilitation, which may include additional job training or schooling. Since the early 90s, when workers' comp costs skyrocketed, most states have put severe limits on the sensible benefit of rehabilitation. At a minimum, your treating physician and a workers' comp board staffer or judge must agree to your need for vocational rehabilitation. Injured workers who qualify for state-sponsored rehabilitation programs will usually be entitled to receive temporary disability payments—at a somewhat reduced rate.

4. Permanent Disability

If you have a partial or complete disability, you may receive a lump sum payment in workers' compensation benefits. The lump sum payments that you are eligible to receive will vary greatly with the nature and extent of your injuries. If your injuries fall into one of the following categories, you may qualify for lump sum benefits.

- *Permanent total disability:* You are unable to work at all, and you are not expected to be able to work again.
- *Permanent partial disability:* Although you are able to perform some types of work, you are not expected to be able to fully regain your ability to earn money. This type of disability is usually divided into two groups, schedule and nonschedule injuries.
- *Schedule injuries* are those for which a set lump sum payment has been prescribed by law in your state. It is the injury that is assigned a value, not the employee, so former earnings levels are irrelevant. For example, in New Mexico, an employee who loses a foot in a work-related accident is entitled to $32,626.
- *Nonschedule injuries* are those for which no such lump sum amount has been specified, so a settlement must be negotiated. In Florida, for example, there is no law specifying the benefit to be paid to an employee who loses a foot in a work-related accident.

5. Death Benefits

Weekly compensation benefits are paid to surviving dependents—typically children and spouses—of workers who are killed in the course of employment or as the result of a work-related injury or occupational disease. The amounts paid typically equal about two-thirds of the deceased worker's weekly salary. About a third of the states limit the total amount of the death award given; a few states limit the number of weeks or years survivors may receive death benefits.

Death benefits to surviving spouses usually come to an end if they remarry—and some states provide for a lump sum to a former spouse upon remarriage. Death benefits for surviving children usually end when they reach majority—or somewhat later for fulltime students.

In addition, if an employee dies from a workplace accident, then the employee's estate receives burial expenses in the amount specified by law in the state where the accident occurred.

COMPLEX CASES REQUIRE EXPERTISE

If your workers' compensation claim is denied, you have the right to appeal it at several levels. If your work-related injury is a permanent or long-term one, then pursuing your claim for workers' compensation benefits to its fullest extent will likely be a complicated task.

And there may be added complications: If you have previously filed another workers' compensation claim, the cost of your benefits may have to be distributed between your current employer's insurance carrier and a special state fund that covers workers' compensation injuries beyond the first one.

If your claim falls into any of these categories, you will probably need to hire a lawyer who specializes in workers' compensation cases to help you. (See Chapter 18, Section D.)

F. Penalties for Retaliation

In many states, employers may not retaliate against an employee for filing a worker's compensation claim. Some states prohibit all forms of retaliation—for example, firing, disciplining, discriminating in any way; other statutes mention only discharge.

STATE RETALIATION LAWS	
Alabama	Employees may not be fired for filing a workers' compensation claim. Ala. Code §25-5-11.1
Alaska	No statute
Arizona	Employees cannot be fired for filing a workers' compensation claim. Arizona Constitution, Article 18, Section 3, as interpreted by *Daniel v. Magma Copper Co.,* 620 P.2d 699 (Ariz. Ct. App., 1980)
Arkansas	Employers may not discriminate in hiring, tenure of work or any term or condition of work of any employee on account of a workers' compensation claim or because of testifying in such a proceeding. Ark. Stat. Ann. §11-4-608
California	Employees cannot be fired for filing a workers' compensation claim. Cal. Lab. Code §132a
Colorado	No statute
Connecticut	Employees cannot be fired or discriminated against for filing a workers' compensation claim. Conn. Gen. Stat. Ann. §31-290a
Delaware	No statute
District of Columbia	Employees may not be fired for claiming workers' compensation benefits. D.C. Code Ann. §36-342
Florida	Employees cannot be fired for filing a workers' compensation claim. Fla. Stat. §440.205
Georgia	No statute
Hawaii	Employees cannot be fired, suspended or discriminated against for filing a workers' compensation claim. Hawaii Rev. Stat. §378-32(2)
Idaho	No statute
Illinois	Employees cannot be fired for exercising rights under Workers' Compensation Act. (Ill. Ann. Stat. ch. 48, §138.4)
Indiana	No statute

Iowa	No statute
Kansas	No statute
Kentucky	Employees cannot be fired or discriminated against for filing a workers' compensation claim. Ky. Rev. Stat. §342.197
Louisiana	Employees may not be fired for filing workers' compensation claim. La. Rev. Stat. Ann. §23:1361
Maine	Employees cannot be fired or discriminated against for filing a workers' compensation claim. Me. Rev. Stat. Ann. 39, §111
Maryland	Employees cannot be fired for filing a claim under workers' compensation. Md. Code Ann. Lab. & Emp. Law §9-1105
Massachusetts	Employees cannot be fired or discriminated against for filing workers' compensation claim. Mass. Gen. Laws Ann. ch. 152, §75B
Michigan	No statute
Minnesota	Employees cannot be fired for filing a workers' compensation claim. Minn. Stat. Ann. §176.82
Mississippi	No statute
Missouri	Employees cannot be fired or discriminated against for filing a workers' compensation claim. Mo. Ann. Stat. §287.780
Montana	No statute
Nebraska	No statute
Nevada	No statute
New Hampshire	No statute
New Jersey	No statute
New Mexico	No statute
New York	Employees cannot be fired or otherwise discriminated against for filing a workers' compensation claim. N.Y. Work. Comp. Law §120
North Carolina	Employees cannot be fired or demoted for filing a workers' compensation claim. N.C. Gen. Stat. §97-6.1
North Dakota	No statute
Ohio	Employees cannot be fired or disciplined for filing a workers' compensation claim. Ohio Rev. Code Ann. §4123.90
Oklahoma	No statute
Oregon	Employee cannot be fired or discriminated against for filing a workers' compensation claim. Or. Rev. Stat. §659.410
Pennsylvania	No statute
Rhode Island	No statute
South Carolina	No statute

South Dakota	No statute
Tennessee	No statute
Texas	No statute
Utah	No statute
Vermont	No statute
Virginia	No statute
Washington	No statute
West Virginia	No statute
Wisconsin	No statute
Wyoming	No statute

G. State Workers' Compensation Offices

Alabama	Workers' Compensation Division Department of Industrial Relations Industrial Relations Building Montgomery, AL 36131 205/242-2868
Alaska	Alaska Department of Labor Alaska Workers' Compensation Board P.O. Box 25512 Juneau, AK 99802-5512 907/465-2790
Arizona	The Industrial Commission of Arizona 800 West Washington P.O. Box 19070 Phoenix, AZ 85005-9070 602/542-4661
Arkansas	Arkansas Workers' Compensation Commission 4th & Spring Streets P.O. Box 950 Little Rock, AR 72203-0950 501/682-2781
California	There are 20 offices throughout the state. To find the one nearest you, look in the telephone book under: State of California, Industrial Relations Department or Workers' Compensation, or phone 800/573-4636 for assistance.

Colorado	Colorado Department of Labor and Employment Division of Worker's Compensation 1120 Lincoln Street, Suite 1200 Denver, CO 80203 303/764-2929
Connecticut	Workers' Compensation Commission 1890 Dixwell Avenue Hamden, CT 06514 203/230-3400
Delaware	Industrial Accident Board 820 North French Street, 6th Floor Wilmington, DE 19801 302/577-2884
District of Columbia	D.C. Department of Employment Services Office of Workers' Compensation 1200 Upshur Street, NW P.O. Box 56098 Washington, DC 20011 202/576-6265
Florida	Department of Labor & Employment Security Division of Workers' Compensation Employees' Assistance Office 2728 Centerview Drive, Suite 131 Tallahassee, FL 32399-0684 904/488-5201
Georgia	State Board of Workers' Compensation Claims Assistance Office 1 CNN Center #1000 South Tower Atlanta, GA 30303-2788 404/656-3818
Hawaii	State of Hawaii Department of Labor & Industrial Relations Disability & Compensation Division 830 Punchbowl Street, Room 209 P.O. Box 3769 Honolulu, HI 96812 808/586-9161
Idaho	Industrial Commission of Idaho 317 Main Street Boise, ID 83720 208/334-6000

Illinois	Illinois Industrial Commission 100 West Randolph, Suite 8-200 Chicago, IL 60601 312/814-6611
Indiana	Workers' Compensation Board of Indiana 402 West Washington Street, W-196 Indianapolis, IN 46204 317/232-3808
Iowa	Industrial Commission 1000 East Grand Avenue Des Moines, IA 50319 515/281-5934
Kansas	State of Kansas Department of Human Resources Division of Workers' Compensation Claims Advisory Office 800 S.W. Jackson, Suite 600 Topeka, KS 66612-1227 913/296-2996; 800/332-0353
Kentucky	Department of Workers' Claims Perimeter Park West 1270 Louisville Road, Building C Frankfort, KY 40601 502/564-5550
Louisiana	Department of Employment & Training Office of Workers' Compensation 1001 N. 23rd P.O. Box 94040 Baton Rouge, LA 70804-9040 504/342-5658
Maine	Workers' Compensation Board Station 27, Deering Building Augusta, ME 04333 207/287-3751
Maryland	Workers' Compensation Commission 6 N. Liberty Street Baltimore, MD 21201 410/333-4700
Massachusetts	Department of Industrial Accidents 600 Washington Street, 7th Floor Boston, MA 02111 617/727-4900

Michigan	Department of Labor
	Workers' Disability Compensation Office
	7150 Harris Drive
	Box 30016
	Lansing, MI 48909
	517/373-3480
Minnesota	Minnesota Department of Labor & Industry
	Workers' Compensation Division
	443 Lafayette Road
	Street Paul, MN 55155
	612/296-2432; 800/342-5354
Mississippi	Mississippi Workers' Compensation Commission
	P.O. Box 5300
	Jackson, MS 39296-5300
	601/987-4200
Missouri	Department of Labor
	Division of Workers' Compensation
	3315 West Truman Boulevard
	P.O. Box 58
	Jefferson City, MO 65102
	314/751-4231
	Info: 800/775-2667
Montana	Department of Labor & Industry
	Division of Workers' Compensation
	5 South Last Chance Gulch
	P.O. Box 4759
	Helena, MT 59604
	406/444-6500
Nebraska	State of Nebraska
	Workers' Compensation Court
	Capitol Building
	Lincoln, NE 68509-8908
	402/471-2568
Nevada	State Industrial Insurance System
	515 E. Musser Street
	Carson City, NV 89714
	702/687-5220
New Hampshire	New Hampshire Department of Labor
	95 Pleasant Street
	Concord, NH 03301
	603/271-3176

New Jersey	Division of Workers' Compensation Department of Labor 135 East State Street, CN 381 Trenton, NJ 08625-0381 609/292-2515
New Mexico	Workers' Compensation 1820 Randolph, SE P.O. Box 27198 Albuquerque, NM 87125-7198 505/841-6000
New York	New York Workers' Compensation Board 180 Livingston Street Brooklyn, NY 11248 718/802-4900
North Carolina	North Carolina Industrial Commission Workers' Compensation Dobbs Building 430 North Salisbury Street P.O. Box 26387 Raleigh, NC 27611 919/733-4820
North Dakota	Workers' Compensation Bureau 500 East Front Avenue Bismarck, ND 58504-5685 701/224-3800
Ohio	Ohio Bureau of Workers' Compensation 30 West Spring Street Columbus, OH 43266-0581 614/466-1238
Oklahoma	Workers' Compensation Court 1915 North Stiles Oklahoma City, OK 73105 405/557-7600
Oregon	Department of Consumer & Business Services Workers' Compensation Division Benefits Section 21 Labor and Industries Building Salem, OR 97310 503/945-7585 Injured worker hotline: 800/452-0288
Pennsylvania	Bureau of Workers' Compensation 1171 South Cameron Street, Room 103 Harrisburg, PA 17104-2501 717/783-5421

Rhode Island	Department of Workers' Compensation Dr. John E. Donley Rehabilitation Center 249 Blackstone Blvd. Providence, RI 02906-5899 401/277-3994 Fax: 401/277-3887
South Carolina	Workers' Compensation Commission 1612 Marion Street Columbia, SC 29201 803/737-5700
South Dakota	Division of Labor and Management South Dakota Department of Labor 700 Governors Drive Pierre, SC 57501-2291 605/773-3681
Tennessee	Department of Labor Division of Workers' Compensation 710 James Robertson Parkway Gateway Plaza, 2nd Floor Nashville, TN 37243 615/532-4812
Texas	Workers' Compensation Industrial Accident Board 4000 South I-H 35, Southfield Building Austin, TX 78704-7491 512/448-7900
Utah	Industrial Commission of Utah Industrial Accidents Division P.O. Box 146610 Salt Lake City, UT 84114-6610 801/530-6800
Vermont	Division of Workers' Compensation Department of Labor and Industry National Life Building, Drawer 20 Montpelier, VT 05620-3401 802/828-2286
Virginia	Virginia Workers' Compensation Commission 1000 DMV Drive Richmond, VA 23220 804/367-8600
Washington	Department of Labor and Industries P.O. Box 44850 Olympia, WA 98504

	206/956-5800
West Virginia	Workers' Compensation Fund
	601 Morris Square
	Box 3151
	Charleston, WV 25332
	304/558-2580
Wisconsin	Workers' Compensation Division
	Department of Industry, Labor and Human Relations
	201 E. Washington Avenue
	P.O. Box 7901
	Madison, WI 53707
	608/266-1340
Wyoming	Wyoming Workers' Compensation Division
	Office of the State Treasurer
	Herschler Building
	122 West 25th Street
	Cheyenne, WY 82002
	307/777-7441

H. Related Lawsuits for Work Injuries

The workers' compensation system is the normal remedy for work-related injuries and illness. But in a growing number of situations, an injured worker will have the option of filing a lawsuit against another responsible person or company in addition to filing a claim for workers' compensation. For example, an injured worker might sue the manufacturer of a defective machine for negligence.

Employers who fail to maintain the workers' compensation coverage required in their state, or who otherwise violate the laws of the workers' compensation system, generally can be sued over work-related injuries. You will probably need to hire a lawyer to help with this type of lawsuit. (See Chapter 18, Section D.)

Nearly half the states also allow employees to sue employers who fired them in retaliation for filing a workers' compensation claim, or for testifying on someone else's behalf in a workers' compensation case. (See Section F.) ■

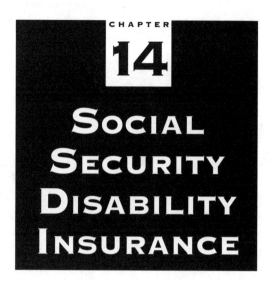

CHAPTER

14

SOCIAL
SECURITY
DISABILITY
INSURANCE

Social Security disability insurance is one component of the federal Social Security system. The benefits it provides are intended to prevent people from becoming paupers because an injury or illness has left them completely unable to earn a living—something that affects a surprisingly large portion of the population. In fact, one out of every four regularly employed workers in America can expect to become disabled for at least a year before reaching age 65. And three-and-one-half million workers and their families currently draw Social Security disability benefits.

When you and your employer pay into the Social Security program, you are buying long-term disability insurance coverage. Once you have paid into the program for a period specified by the Social Security program, you are eligible for benefits should you become unable to earn a living.[1]

Disability program payments are not intended to cover temporary, short-term or partial disability. The benefits were sanctioned by Congress with the assumption that working families have other support resources during short-term disabilities—such as workers' compensation, insurance, savings and investment income.

---

[1]For a complete explanation of the Social Security system and more detail on filing and appealing Social Security disability insurance claims, see *Social Security, Medicare and Pensions*, by Joseph L. Matthews with Dorothy Matthews Berman (Nolo Press).

WORKERS' COMP AND SOCIAL SECURITY: SEPARATE AND UNEQUAL

In contrast to the workers' compensation program (see Chapter 13), the Social Security disability insurance system does not recognize degrees of wage-earning capability. Under Social Security eligibility rules, you are either able to work—in which case you do not qualify for its benefits. Or you are not able to work—in which case you may qualify. Also, unlike workers' comp eligibility requirements, a disability need not be work-related under the Social Security benefit system.

However, if you receive workers' comp payments, your Social Security benefit may be reduced. The law states that the sum of all your disability payments cannot exceed 80% of your earnings averaged over a period of time shortly before you became disabled. (See Section F3, below.)

A. Who Is Covered

Disability benefits are only paid to workers and their families when the worker has enough work credits to qualify.

The definition of what is required for a work credit changes over time. Currently, workers accumulate one quarter of work credit for each $570 per year earned in covered employment—up to a maximum of four quarters per year. The number of work credits needed to qualify for disability benefits depends on your age when you become disabled.

In addition, you must have earned at least 20 quarters of the required credit within the ten years immediately preceding the time you became disabled—unless you qualify under one of the special rules explained below. The amount of your monthly disability check is based on your age and earnings record. (See Section D2.)

AGE OF DISABILITY AND WORK CREDITS REQUIRED

If you were born before 1930,
and you became disabled before age 62 in:

You need this many
quarters of work credit:

1980	29
1981	30
1982	31
1983	32
1984	33
1985	34
1987	36
1989	38
1991 or later	40

If you were born after 1929,
and you became disabled at age:

You need this many
quarters of work credit:

42 or younger	20
44	22
46	24
48	26
50	28
52	30
54	32
56	34
58	36
60	38
62 or older	40

1. Young Workers

If you were disabled when still young, you are required to have fewer work credits. This is because you obviously did not have the opportunity to acquire many quarters of work.

So, if you were disabled between the ages of 24 and 31, you only need work credits for half of the quarters between age 21 and the time you became disabled. In other words, if you became disabled at age 29, there were eight years between age 21 and the time you became disabled; you would need credit for half that time—four years (16 quarters). If you were disabled before age 24, you only need credit for six quarters in the three-year period immediately before you became disabled.

2. Blind Individuals

If your vision is not better than 20/200 even with glasses, or if your field of vision is limited to 20 degrees or less, you are considered "blind" under Social Security rules.

If you are disabled by blindness, there is no requirement that any of your work credits must be earned within the years immediately preceding your disability. Your work credits can be from any time after 1936—the year the Social Security law went into effect. The only requirement is that you have enough cumulative work credits, based on your age, as shown in the chart above.

3. Widows and Widowers

If you are a widow or widower, age 50 or over, and disabled, you may receive disability benefits even though you do not have enough work credits of your own to qualify—as long as your deceased spouse had enough work credits for his or her age at the time of death.

The rules are as follows.

- You must be disabled. Your age, work experience and training are not considered in whether you are disabled.
- You must be age 50 or older.
- Your spouse must have been fully insured at death—meaning he or she had enough work credits considering his or her age.
- Your disability must have begun before your spouse's death or within seven years after the death.
- If you already receive Social Security benefits as a surviving widow or widower with children, you will be eligible for disability benefits if you are age 50 or older and you become disabled before those payments end

or within seven years after they end.

- Even if you were divorced before your former spouse died, you may still be eligible for these benefits if you had been married to him or her for ten years or more.

The amount of these benefits will depend entirely upon your spouse's work record and average earnings. And these special disability benefits may end if you remarry.

B. Disabilities Covered

Many injuries and illnesses are obviously disabling. There are others, however, such as chronic illnesses which become acute with age, or residual conditions which deteriorate over time, that become disabling even though they were not initially too severe. For example, a worker may have had a previous injury that is aggravated through the years to the point where work is extremely difficult or impossible. He or she may become eligible for disability benefits even though the original illness or injury was not disabling.

Social Security disability is a government program—and so it carries with it a grand amount of qualifying rules and regulations. To receive Social Security disability benefits:

- You must have a physical or mental impairment
- The impairment must prevent you from doing any substantial gainful work, and
- The disability must be expected to last, or has lasted, at least 12 months, or must be expected to result in death.

Of course, these terms are subject to different interpretations. There are guidelines developed by Social Security and the courts regarding qualifications for disability. But proving a disability is often a difficult task. In preparing your claim for a disability, examine these guidelines carefully, discuss the matter with your doctor or doctors, and plan your claim thoroughly.

LISTING OF IMPAIRMENTS SOCIAL SECURITY CONSIDERS DISABLING

To simplify things a bit, the Social Security Administration has developed a list of conditions which it usually considers disabling without giving much of an argument. In other words, if you prove, through medical records or doctors' reports, that you have one of the conditions on Social Security's Listing of Impairments—paralysis of an arm and a leg, for example—you will probably be considered disabled without having to convince Social Security that you cannot perform substantial gainful work. But each claim for disability is considered separately; having a condition on this list does not automatically qualify you for disability benefits.

Impairments certified by Social Security include:

- diseases of the heart, lung or blood vessels which have resulted in a serious loss of heart or lung reserves as shown by X-ray, electrocardiogram or other tests; and, in spite of medical treatment, there is breathlessness, pain or fatigue
- severe arthritis which causes recurrent inflammation, pain, swelling and deformity in major joints so that the ability to get about or use the hands is severely limited
- mental illness resulting in marked constriction of activities and interests, deterioration in personal habits and seriously impaired ability to get along with other people
- damage to the brain or brain abnormality which has resulted in severe loss of judgment, intellect, orientation or memory
- cancer which is progressive and has not been controlled or cured
- diseases of the digestive system which result in severe malnutrition, weakness and anemia
- progressive diseases which have resulted in the loss of a leg or which have caused it to become useless
- loss of major function of both arms, both legs, or a leg and an arm
- serious loss of function of the kidneys, and
- total inability to speak.

1. Physical or Mental Impairments

The basic rule regarding disability is that the condition preventing you from working must be a medical one—meaning that it can be discovered and described by doctors. To prove this, when you file your disability claim, you should bring with you letters from doctors, or from hospitals or clinics where you have been treated, describing the medical condition that prevents you from doing any substantial gainful work. The letters should also state that your disability is expected to last for 12 months or is expected to result in death.

2. Substantial Gainful Work

Social Security will first consider whether your condition prevents you from doing the job you had at the time you became disabled, or the last job you had before becoming disabled. If your disability prevents you from performing your usual job, Social Security will next decide whether you are able to do any other kind of substantial gainful work—defined as any job that pays $500 per month or more.

Your age, education, training and work experience will be considered in making this determination—as will the practicality of learning new job skills for another work position. Social Security will evaluate whether you are able to perform any kind of work for pay, whether or not there are actually any such jobs available in the area in which you live. However, it is up to Social Security to prove that there is gainful employment you can perform. You need not prove there is no work you can do.

Example: *Arnold has been a longshoreman for 40 of his 58 years. Weakened by an early injury, Arnold's back has grown slowly but steadily worse over the past decade, causing him to miss several months of work in the past two years. His doctor has told him that his back will not get better, and Arnold decides to apply for disability benefits.*

As Arnold's back prevents him from standing for long periods of time, and restricts the movement of his arms, Social Security determines he is unable to do any physical labor. The next question would be whether he is able to do any other kind of work. It's possible that his back would be too bad for him to do even a job which required him to sit at a desk; if so, and Arnold proved this to Social Security through his doctor or by trying and being unable to do a desk job, he would probably get his disability payments. On the other hand, if his back were not quite that bad, he might be forced at least to try other work.

3. Disability Must Be Lasting

No matter how serious or completely disabling your illness or injury is, you will not qualify for disability benefits unless your condition has lasted, or is expected to last, for 12 months—during which time you are unable to perform substantial gainful work. The disability will also qualify if it is expected to result in death. Even though the disability must be expected to last 12 months, you do not have to wait for 12 months to apply.

As soon as the condition is disabling and a doctor can predict that it is expected to last a year, you may qualify for disability benefits. And if, after you begin receiving benefits, it turns out that your disability does not last 12 months, Social Security cannot ask for its money back. You are not penalized for recovering sooner than expected, as long as the original expectation that the illness would last 12 months was a legitimate one.

TIMING MAY BE EVERYTHING

Social Security disability benefits may be discontinued if you are able to earn your own living. If you are legally disabled but are earning too much money to qualify for Social Security benefits, you may still be able to claim something if your earnings are significantly lower than they were before the onset of your disability.

You may qualify because in some circumstances, the Social Security Administration can put a disability freeze on your earnings record.

The amount of your ultimate retirement benefits or of your disability benefits if you later qualify is determined by your average income over the years. If, after your disability, you are earning considerably less than you were before, the years of those earnings would pull your average income lower, which could result in a lower ultimate Social Security payment. The disability freeze permits you to work and collect your lower income without having it figured into your lifetime average earnings.

C. Dependents Entitled to Benefits

If you are disabled, your spouse and children under age 18 may also be eligible for dependents' benefits. If so, your combined family benefits—the total amount you, your spouse and your children receive—will be limited to a maximum of either 85% of what you were earning before you became disabled, or to 150% of what your monthly individual benefit would have been, whichever is lower. (See Section D2 for an explanation of how monthly individual benefits are calculated.)

Example: *Juan Menendez was making $2,200 a month when he was disabled. At the time he became disabled, Juan's total Social Security earnings record would have given him an individual disability benefit of $600 a month. But Juan's wife, Theresa, and their two teenage children, Angela and Bobby, were also eligible to collect dependents' benefits. Their total family benefits would be the lower of 85% of Juan's $2,200 monthly salary, which comes out to $1,870, or 150% of what Juan's individual disability benefit ($600) would be, which comes out to $900. The Menendez family would receive $900 a month, the lower of the two amounts.*

In addition, certain family members may qualify for benefits if a disabled worker dies. They include:

- a disabled widow or widower 50 or older, and
- a disabled ex-wife or ex-husband who is 50 or older if the marriage lasted ten years or longer.

D. Filing a Social Security Claim

It is extremely important to file your claim for Social Security disability benefits as soon as you become disabled, because there is a waiting period of five months after filing before you can begin receiving payments. If you wait a long time to file, you may be disappointed to learn that back payments are limited to the 12 months before the date on which you file.

You must file your claim at one of the Social Security Administration offices located in most cities, listed in the government section of the telephone book. If your disability prevents you from visiting a Social Security office, you can usually file your claim by mail or over the telephone.

1. Documentation Required

Social Security staff will complete the forms and other paperwork necessary to file a disability claim. You will need to provide documentation, including:

- a copy of your birth certificate
- your Social Security number
- names, addresses and telephone numbers of doctors, clinics and hospitals—and the dates on which they treated you
- a summary of your work history for the past 15 years, and
- dates of any military service.

If you have dependents who may be eligible for benefits under your Social Security disability insurance claim, you will have to present similar documentation for them when filing a claim.

The Social Security Administration will then investigate your claim—and will pay for any examinations and reports it requires to verify your claim. The Social Security staff will also help you with the paperwork and procedures required for payment.

The results of those examinations and reports will usually be sent to your state's vocational rehabilitation agency, which is responsible for determining whether or not you are considered sufficiently disabled to qualify for benefits. In some cases, the vocational rehabilitation office will conduct its own examination, tests and personal interviews as well, before providing the Social Security Administration with a decision on your case.

The Social Security Administration provides emergency funds for disabled people who need financial help during the long waiting period during which their claims are being processed. The Social Security employees handling your claim can give you details of how to qualify for emergency funds.

TRIAL RUNS AT RETURNING TO WORK

Social Security disability insurance is more friendly than other income-replacement programs because it allows you to try going back to work without canceling your claim. You can participate in a total of nine months of trial work without losing any benefits—and the nine months need not be consecutive or in one job. Of course, you must still technically qualify as disabled to take advantage of this trial period.

You could, for example, continue to receive Social Security disability checks while trying different jobs for a week or two every few months, until you find one you can do with your disability. Any months in which you do not earn more than $200—or spend more than 40 hours in self-employment—do not count as trial months.

After a trial work period, Social Security will review your case to see whether you have become able to work gainfully. The first key is whether you are able to earn $500 per month in gross wages. (See Section F1.)

If you succeed in returning to work after qualifying for Social Security disability benefits, the checks will keep coming for two months after your period of disability has ended to help ease your transition back into the workforce.

2. Calculating Benefits

Like other Social Security benefits, the amount of your monthly disability check is determined by your age and earnings record. The amount of your benefits will be based upon your average earnings for all the years you have been working—not just on the salary you were making most recently. Although the amount will be substantial, it alone will not equal your pre-injury income.

Monthly payments for individuals qualifying for disability benefits average about $625. The average disability payment for a disabled worker with a spouse and child is about $1,050. There is also a yearly cost-of-living increase—if the Consumer Price Index rises over 3% for the year. For those who first become disabled in 1982 or later, there is no minimum benefit amount.

Some people—generally only those with high total incomes—may have to pay federal income taxes on their Social Security disability benefits. At the end of the year, you will receive a Social Security Benefit Statement showing the amount of benefits you received. Contact the Internal Revenue Service's toll-free number for forms and publications, 800/829-3676, and ask for IRS Publication 915 if you need additional information on the tax.

Your monthly check will be based entirely on your earnings record, with no consideration given to a minimum amount needed to survive. If you receive only a small disability benefit, however, and you do not have a large amount of savings or other assets, you may be eligible for some other benefits in addition to your Social Security disability benefits. (See Section F.)

GETTING HELP WITH ESTIMATING BENEFITS

The best way to determine your specific benefit level is to file a copy of the Social Security Administration's Form SSA-7004-PC-OP1, entitled Request for Earnings and Benefit Estimate Statement. You can obtain one at your local Social Security Administration office. You need not be planning to file a claim to do this—you can file the form any time you are merely curious. The Social Security staff will calculate benefits to which you are entitled and notify you by mail of its determination.

3. Continuing Your Claim

Although many people who suffer total disabilities remain disabled for life, that is not always the case. So the Social Security disability insurance program includes various efforts to rehabilitate workers and get them back to work.

THEY'LL BE KEEPING TABS

If your medical condition improves and you go back to work, your disability eligibility will end. Even if you do not go back to work voluntarily, Social Security will review your case periodically—or at least once every three years—to determine whether, in its opinion, your condition has improved enough for you to go back to work. From time to time, therefore, Social Security may ask for updated medical evidence from your doctor, or may even require that you be examined by another doctor, or undergo additional medical tests—arranged and paid for by Social Security.

You must cooperate with these periodic reviews or run the risk of losing your disability benefits. You have the right, however, to insist on being given enough time to gather necessary information from your doctor, and enough notice to meet the appointment for the examination or test. If you are unable to keep an appointment scheduled for you by the Social Security office, do not hesitate to ask for a rescheduling.

E. Appealing a Denied Claim

The greatest number of Social Security disability claims are denied because an individual is deemed to be able to do some kind of work, in spite of a disability. If your claim is denied, there are four levels of appeal available to you. At each step of the appeal process, you have 60 days from the date of the previous decision to take action to move up to the next appeal level.

With the exception of the fourth option, filing a lawsuit in federal court, the staff at the Social Security Administration office will supply you with the proper forms for pursuing an appeal, and will assist you in completing them.

Request for reconsideration. You ask to see the Social Security Administration's files concerning your claim, and then submit corrections or additional information that you hope will cause the agency to reconsider your claim and approve it.

Administrative hearing. You request a hearing by an administrative law judge who has never looked at your case before. You can ask to have the judge issue a ruling based on the evidence you have already submitted, or you can ask for a ruling without a hearing but with consideration of additional written evidence. You can also request a hearing at which new or more detailed evidence can be presented. These hearings are usually informal and held in the same locale where you filed your claim.

Review by appeals council. You ask to have the Social Security Appeals Council, based in Washington, DC, consider your claim. If the council decides to hear your appeal, you can submit a written argument in support of your evidence. Or you can elect to appear before the council to argue your case.

Federal court. If you do not win approval of your claim at any of the previous levels, or if the appeals council refuses to hear your appeal, you can file a lawsuit in federal court to try to get the courts to order the Social Security Administration to approve your claim. You will probably have to hire a lawyer to help you at this appeal level. (See Chapter 18, Section D.)

F. Collecting Other Benefits

Since disability payments are often not enough to live on, it is important for you to collect all the other benefits to which you may be entitled, and even try to supplement your income by working a little if you are able.

1. Earned Income

If you earn any regular income, you might not be considered disabled any longer and you could lose your disability eligibility altogether. You are only officially disabled if you are unable to perform any substantial gainful work.

However, Social Security usually permits you to earn up to about $500 a month before you will be considered to be performing substantial gainful work—its buzzword for disability eligibility. But this $500 is not a fixed rule, and other facts will be considered—your work duties, the number of hours you work and, if you are self-employed, the extent to which you run or manage your own business. In deciding how much you are earning, the Social Security office can deduct from your income the amounts of any impairment-related work expenses such as medical devices or equipment—a wheelchair, for example—attendant care, drugs or services required for you to be able to work.

2. Other Social Security Benefits

You are not permitted to collect more than one Social Security benefit at a time. If you are eligible for more than one monthly benefit—disability and retirement, for example, or disability based on your own work record and also as the disabled spouse of a retired worker—you will receive the higher of the two benefit amounts, but not both.

For the purposes of this rule, though, Supplemental Security Income (SSI)—a program jointly run by federal and state governments to guarantee a minimum income to elderly, blind and disabled people—is not considered a Social Security benefit. You may collect SSI in addition to a Social Security benefit.

3. Other Disability Benefits

You are permitted to collect Social Security disability payments and, at the same time, private disability payments from an insurance policy or coverage from your employer. You may also receive Veterans' Administration disability coverage at the same time as Social Security disability benefits. And you may collect workers' compensation benefits at the same time as Social Security disability benefits.

However, the total of your disability and workers' compensation payments cannot be greater than 80% of what your average wages were before you became disabled. If they are, your disability benefits will be reduced to the point where the total of both benefits is 80% of your earnings before you became disabled. If you are still receiving Social Security disability benefits when your workers' compensation benefits run out, you can again start receiving the full amount of your Social Security benefits.

Example: *Minnie became disabled while working for the telephone company in the computer analysis department. At that time she was making $1,400 a month. Her Social Security disability benefits were $560 a month; she also applied for and began receiving workers' compensation benefits of $625 a month. Because the total of the two benefits was more than 80 percent of her prior salary (80% of $1,400 is $1,120, and she would be getting $1,185), her disability benefits were reduced by the extra $65 down to $495 a month.*

If Minnie were still disabled when her workers' compensation benefits ran out, her Social Security disability benefits would go back up to $560 a month, plus whatever cost of living increases had been granted in the meantime. If Minnie also had private insurance which paid disability benefits, she could receive those benefits as well as all of her Social Security.

4. Medicare

After you have been collecting disability benefits for 24 months—not necessarily consecutive months—you become eligible for Medicare coverage even though you are not old enough to be covered by Medicare under the regular rules of the program. Medicare Part A hospitalization coverage is free after you pay a deductible. Like everyone else, though, you must pay a monthly premium if you want to be covered by Medicare Part B medical insurance that partially covers doctor bills, lab work, outpatient clinic care and some drugs and medical supplies.

For more information on Medicare, contact the Medicare information line: 800/952-8627. ■

CHAPTER

15

RETIREMENT PLANS

There is no law requiring private employers to offer their employees retirement plans. In fact, only about half of the country's total private workforce—about 40 million people—are employed by companies that have some kind of pension plan.

Those employers that do offer pension plans are not required to pay any minimum amount of money—and an increasing number of individuals who invested in saving for their futures are disappointed and disillusioned to learn their retirement plans simply do not deliver what they promised.

The old standby, Social Security—the government's income system for people 55 and over created by the passage of the Social Security Act in 1935—was not meant to be a pension program as much as insurance against extreme poverty in the later years of life. Although Social Security benefit checks for retirees have increased some in recent years, they still do not provide enough income for most people to maintain their preretirement lifestyles. Consequently, many people rely on some form of private pension—however small—to enhance their incomes after they retire.

This chapter cannot begin to cover all aspects of pension law, which has evolved into a complex morass of legal exceptions, exemptions and loopholes and is controlled by individual plan agreements. It discusses the most important laws concerning your right to collect the pension benefits you have earned and provides resources for more help.

A. Social Security Retirement Benefits

There are many ins and outs to the Social Security retirement benefit system—most of them dependent on factors such as the type of job you work, the length of time you work and the age at which you retire.[1]

---

[1]For more detailed information on Social Security programs and benefits, complete with detailed instructions on how to file for them, see *Social Security, Medicare and Pensions: The Sourcebook for Older Americans* by Joseph L. Matthews with Dorothy Matthews Berman (Nolo Press).

1. Who Is Qualified

As with other Social Security benefits, to be eligible for any amount of retirement benefits, you must have accumulated enough work credits. Work credits are measured in quarters (January through March, April through June, and so on) in which you earned more than the required amount of money. The number of work credits you need to be eligible for benefits depends on your age when you apply.

WORK CREDITS REQUIRED FOR SOCIAL SECURITY RETIREMENT BENEFITS	
If you reach age 62 in:	*You need this many quarters of employment:*
1980	29
1981	30
1982	31
1983	32
1984	33
1985	34
1990	39
1991 or later	40

In addition, certain dependents of retired workers are eligible for monthly benefits if the worker has amassed enough work credits to qualify for benefits. Dependents who may qualify for these derivative benefits include:

- a spouse age 62 or older
- a spouse under age 62 who cares for the worker's young or disabled children
- a divorced spouse age 62 or older, if the marriage lasted ten years and if two years have passed since the divorce
- unmarried children under 18 or who are severely disabled, and
- grandchildren under the care and custody of the worker.

2. Calculating Your Benefits

Note that when the term retire is used by the Social Security Administration, it only refers to the time you claim your retirement benefits. It does not necessarily mean you have reached a particular age or that you have stopped working.

The average benefit for a person who retires at age 65 is about $650 per month; for a couple, the monthly average is about $1,000. Whatever the amount of your retirement benefit, you will receive an automatic cost of living increase on January 1 of each year. This increase is tied to the rise in the Consumer Price Index—the cost of basic goods and services.

HELP WITH ESTIMATING BENEFITS

Even if you have not worked for many years, and you did not make much money in the few years you did work, check your earnings record. You may be surprised to find you have quite a few quarters of credit from years gone by. If you want to estimate the amount of Social Security benefits you are entitled to receive after you have retired from your job, complete and submit the Social Security Administration's Form SSA-7004-PC-OP1, Request for Earnings and Benefit Estimate Statement. You can obtain one from the Social Security Administration office closest to you.

---

3. Taxes on Your Benefits

Most Social Security retirement benefits are not considered taxable income by the Internal Revenue Service—although you do have to pay income tax on any interest you earn from saving your benefits. But if your adjusted gross income—from a parttime job, for example—plus one-half of your year's Social Security benefits adds up to $25,000 or more, then you must pay income tax on one-half of your Social Security benefits. The income and benefit limit is about $32,000 for a couple. In January of each year, you will receive a statement from the Social Security Administration showing the amount of benefits you received in the previous year and an IRS form explaining how to report this income, if necessary.

> ### MEDICARE AND DISABILITY: NOT-SO-DISTANT COUSINS
>
> The Social Security system wears many hats.
>
> Another one of them is Medicare—a federal government program run by the Department of Health and Human Services, set up to assist senior and some disabled people in paying for some hospital and medical costs. If you become sick or disabled and unable to work, you and your dependents may qualify for additional benefits that are part of the broader Social Security system. (See Chapter 14, Section F.)

4. Working After Retirement

In addition to the need for more income, many people keep their jobs or take new ones after a planned retirement so that they can stay active and involved in the world of work. But if you do plan on working after retirement, be aware that your earnings may cause a reduction in the amount of your Social Security retirement benefits.

Until you reach age 70, the Social Security Administration will subtract money from your retirement check if you have a substantial earned income from work you are currently doing. Social Security does not count as earned income any money you receive from such things as interest on savings, insurance premiums, investments, royalties, rental income or pensions.

Example: *In 1993, if you were under 65, you were allowed about $7,680 per year of earned income before Social Security retirement benefits are reduced by one dollar for every two dollars earned over this limit. If you were age 65 to 69, you could earn up to $10,560; for every three dollars of earned income over this limit, you lose one dollar in retirement benefits. After you reached age 70, there was no limit on the amount you can earn without penalty.*

RETIREMENT BENEFITS: KEY AN EYE ON THE CALENDAR

The Social Security law permits you to retire and claim benefits as early as age 62. If you do, you will receive a lower monthly amount—one that Social Security figures will total, over your lifetime, the same amount you would have received if you retired at 65.

Monthly benefits for retirement at age 62 are about 20% less than if you wait until age 65—about 13% less if you retire at 63, 6.6% less at age 64. The reduction in monthly benefits is permanent. They do not increase to the full amount when you turn 65.

Not only do you have the option of claiming early retirement, you can also wait until after age 65 and claim a higher delayed retirement benefit. For example, if you wait until age 72 to claim retirement, your benefits would permanently be 7% higher than if you retired at age 65.

B. Private Pensions

Jargon dominates the pension industry. However, these definitions of some of the common terms involving plans and benefits will get you on the road to understanding your pension rights and wrongs.

Since the passage of a federal law, the Employee Retirement Income Security Act of 1974—commonly called ERISA—at least some of the worst sorts of disappearing pension acts have been halted. ERISA sets minimum standards for pension plans, guaranteeing that pension rights cannot be unfairly denied or taken from a worker. ERISA also provides some protection for workers in the event certain types of pension plans cannot pay all the benefits to which workers are entitled. But while ERISA does provide the protection of federal law for certain pension rights, its scope is limited.

PENSION TERMS DEFINED

Defined benefit plan. The employer promises to pay the employee a fixed amount of money, usually monthly, after the employee retires. Although a defined benefit plan is what usually comes to mind when people think about pensions, this plan has become less common than the defined contribution type.

Defined contribution plan. The employer promises to pay a certain amount into the employee's retirement account while the employee is working, but does not promise a specific amount of income for the employee after retirement. Your employer may promise to pay $50 per month per employee into the company's pension plan, for example, but the size of the monthly pension check you would receive after retirement would vary according to the interest rate paid on your pension account and other economic factors.

Defined contribution plans can take several different forms, such as 401(k) plans through which your employer and you can contribute jointly to retirement savings. For the most part, defined contribution pension plans are individual savings accounts that have some tax advantages—but also some limitations on withdrawals and reinvestment—that regular savings accounts do not have.

Employee Retirement Security Act (ERISA). The most important federal law governing pensions and other employee benefit programs. Administered by the U.S. Department of Labor, the Internal Revenue Service and the Securities and Exchange Commission, ERISA sets minimum standards for pensions and attempts to guarantee that pension rights cannot be unfairly taken from or denied to workers.

Pension Benefit Guaranty Corporation. An organization that insures many pension plans in the United States, the PBGC is half private and half public. It is supposed to get its money from insurance premiums paid by the pension plans it covers, but it regularly turns to the federal government for money when it runs short.

Plan administrator. The person or organization with the legal authority and responsibility for managing your pension program.

Vesting. Getting a legal right to collect from a benefit program. For example, some pension plans require you to work a certain number of years for a company before you have any right to a pension. Once you are vested, you continue to have rights to the pension plan even if you no longer work there.

1. Legal Controls on Pensions

Pensions, according to many workplace experts, are a good idea run amok.

Pension plans became popular during the Second World War at a time when there were more jobs than workers. Employers used fringe benefits, such as pensions, to attract and keep workers without violating the wartime wage freeze rules. Since the early 1950s, unions and employers have both recognized pension plans as crucial elements in labor negotiations. But until the mid-1970s, having a pension plan and collecting a pension benefit check were two different animals. Many people were promised a pension as part of the terms of their employment, and many workers contributed to pension funds through payroll deductions, but relatively few actually received much in the way of benefits at retirement. There were several reasons for the failure of pensions to deliver what they promised: people changed jobs and had to leave their pension rights behind; workers were not-so-mysteriously let go just before they reached retirement age; and pension plans, or whole companies, went out of business.

Since the passage of a federal law, the Employee Retirement Income Security Act of 1974—commonly called ERISA—at least some of the worst sorts of disappearing pension acts have been halted. ERISA sets minimum standards for pension plans, guaranteeing that pension rights cannot be unfairly denied or taken from a worker. ERISA also provides some protection for workers in the event certain types of pension plans cannot pay all the benefits to which workers are entitled. But while ERISA does provide the protection of federal law for certain pension rights, its scope is limited.

> ## THE INCREDIBLE SHRINKING PENSION CHECK
>
> Inflation is an old enemy of your right to receive a decent retirement pension. The figures an employer shows you as your potential pension benefit may seem decent when you are hired, and may even pay a reasonable amount when you first retire. But because few private pension plans are indexed to the rising cost of living, an amount sufficient at the time you retire will seem smaller and smaller as inflation cuts into the value of your pension dollar. In other words, the cost of living will go up, but your pension check will not. Unfortunately, ERISA does not require pension plans to respond to inflation's bite into your retirement benefits.

2. Eligibility for Pension Coverage

There is no law that requires an employer to offer a pension plan. However, if a company chooses to do so, ERISA requires that the pension plan spell out who is eligible for coverage. Pension plans do not have to include all workers, but they cannot legally be structured to benefit only the top executives or otherwise discriminate—for example, by excluding older workers. The plan administrator for your company's pension program can tell you whether or not you are eligible to participate.

If you are eligible to participate in your employer's pension program, the administrator must provide you with several documents needed to understand the plan.

- *A summary plan description.* Explains the basics of how your plan operates. ERISA requires that you be given the summary plan within 90 days after you begin participating in a pension plan, and that you must be given any updates to it.

  This document will also tell you the formula for vesting in the plan—if it is a plan that includes vesting—the formula for determining your defined benefits or the defined contributions that your employer will make to the plan, and whether or not your pension is insured by the

Pension Benefit Guaranty Corporation or PBGC. (See Section 7, below.)

- *A summary annual report.* A yearly accounting of your pension plan's financial condition and operations.
- *Survivor coverage data.* A statement of how much your plan would pay to any surviving spouse should you die first.

Your plan administrator is also required to provide you with a detailed, individual statement of the pension benefits you have earned, but only if you request it in writing or are going to stop participating in the plan because, for example, you change employers. Note, however, that ERISA gives you the right to only one such statement from your plan per year.

INTEGRATED PLANS: INNOVATION OR DEVIATION?

In the past few years, the popularity of integrated plans, a somewhat devious form of pension plan, has grown among employers. When a pension plan is integrated with Social Security retirement benefits, your actual monthly or yearly pension benefit is reduced by all, or some percentage of, your Social Security check. One type of integrated plan operates by setting up what is called a benefit goal for your retirement. This means the plan sets a goal for the amount of money you should have from a combination of pension and Social Security retirement income. The figure the plan arrives at as your benefit goal is usually a percentage of your average pre-retirement income. Your pension amount is then only what is needed to make up the difference between your Social Security benefits and this pre-determined benefit goal.

One small—very small—consolation about integrated plans is that once they have reduced your pension to fit it into the benefit goal along with Social Security benefits, they cannot further reduce your pension amount when Social Security benefits rise because of cost of living increases.

3. Early Retirement and Pension Benefits

Each pension plan has its own rules on the minimum age for filing benefits. Most private pension plans consider 65 to be the normal retirement age. However, some private pensions also offer the option of retiring early, usually at age 55. If you elect early retirement, however, expect your benefit checks to be much smaller than they would be if you waited until the regular retirement age.

Many corporations now use the early retirement option of their pension plans to cut staff. By making a temporary offer to increase the benefits available to those who opt to retire early, these corporations create an incentive for employees to voluntarily leave the company's payroll before turning age 65. Sometimes companies make the early retirement offer even more attractive by throwing in a few months of extra severance pay.

Some early retirement offers are very lucrative, and some are not. Before accepting one, study the details carefully, keeping in mind that the offer you accept may have to serve as your primary income for the rest of your life. (See Chapter 8, Section E, on the Older Workers Benefit Protection Act.)

Because pension law is so specialized and complex, you may also consider consulting a lawyer who specializes in it if the terms of your employer's early retirement offer to you are not clear. (See Chapter 18, Section D.)

4. Filing for Benefits

Although ERISA does not spell out one uniform claim procedure for all pension plans, it does establish some rules which must be followed when you retire and want to claim your benefits. All pension plans must have an established claim procedure and all participants in the plan must be given a summary of the plan which explains the plan's claim procedure. When your claim is filed, you must receive a decision on the claim, in writing, within a "reasonable time." The decision must state specific reasons for the denial of any claimed benefits and must explain the basis for determining the benefits which are granted.

From the date you receive a written decision on your pension claim, you have 60 days to file a written appeal of the decision. The details for where and how this appeal is filed must be explained in the plan summary. In presenting your appeal, the claim procedures must permit you to examine the plan's files and records and to submit evidence of your own. ERISA does not, however, require the pension plan actually give you a hearing regarding your appeal. Within 60 days of filing, the pension plan administrators must file a written decision on your appeal. If your claim is still denied, in whole or in part, you then have a right to press your claim in either state or federal court.

WHEN RETIREMENT DOES NOT MEAN RETIREMENT

If your benefits have vested when you reach the retirement age established by your pension plan—usually 65—you're free to leave a job with the employer who pays your pension and work for someone else, or open your own business, while collecting your full pension. However, if you return to work for the employer that is paying your pension benefits, ERISA permits the employer to suspend payment of your pension for as long as you continue working for that employer. Some workers are covered by a multi-employer pension plan, such as those through an industry-wide union contract. Those your pension benefits can be suspended if you return to work for a different employer whose employees are covered by the same pension plan.

---

5. Appealing a Denial of Benefits

Each pension plan has its own system for appeals. If your pension plan denies you benefits to which you're entitled, its administrator is required to advise you about how to appeal that decision. You will have 60 days to request such an appeal, and the group that reviews your appeal will, in most cases, have 120 days after you file it to issue its decision. ERISA requires that you be given a plain English explanation of the decision on your appeal.

If your pension plan's internal review system also rules against you, you are entitled to appeal that decision by contacting:

Pension and Welfare Benefits Administration
1730 K Street, NW; Suite 556
Washington, DC 20006
202/254-7013

In addition, the rules of ERISA permit you to file a specific ERISA-enforcement lawsuit in federal court to enforce any rule or provision of the ERISA law or of a pension plan covered by ERISA rules. In particular, you may file a federal court lawsuit under ERISA to:

- recover benefits which have been unfairly denied
- change a ruling made by the pension plan that would affect your future benefits —such as a ruling regarding eligibility, accrual, vesting
- force the plan to provide information required by ERISA
- correct improper management of the plan or its funds, and
- protect any other right established by the rules of your particular pension plan or by ERISA itself.

6. Terminated Plans

If your employer terminates your pension plan, your plan administrator is required to notify you in writing of the approaching termination at least 60 days before the plan ends.

If the termination is a standard one, that means that your plan has enough assets to cover its obligations. Your plan's administrator is required to notify you in such cases of how the plan's money will be paid out, and what your options are during the pay-out period.

If the termination is being done under distress, the Pension Benefit Guaranty Corporation may become responsible for paying your pension benefits. (See Section 7, below.) If your plan is not insured by the PBGC and it is terminated, your pension rights may be reduced—or you may lose them.

7. Mismanaged Plans

In recent years, a number of pension funds have gone broke, either through mismanagement, fraud or over-extension of resources. The future is likely to bring with it an increasing number of pension plan failures. Under ERISA, there is some insurance against pension fund collapses. ERISA established the Pension Benefit Guaranty Corporation, a public, non-profit insurance fund, to provide coverage against bankrupt pension funds. Should a pension fund be unable to pay all its obligations to retirees, the PBGC may, under certain conditions, pick up the slack and pay much of the pension fund's unfulfilled obligations.

However, the PBGC does not cover all types of pension plans and does not guarantee all pension benefits of the plans it does cover. Only defined-benefit plans are covered—through insurance premiums they pay to the PBGC—and only vested benefits are protected by the insurance. Also, PBGC insurance normally only covers retirement pension benefits; other benefits, such as disability, health coverage and death benefits, are not usually covered.

If you have a question about termination of benefits because of failure of your pension plan, contact:

Pension Benefit Guaranty Corporation
Case Operations and Compliance
1200 K Street, NW
Washington, DC 20005
202/326-4000

If you think you can prove that the people managing your pension plan are not handling your pension money in your best interests—for example, they are making questionable investments—ERISA gives you the right to file a lawsuit against them in federal court. You will probably need to hire a lawyer to help you with this type of lawsuit. (See Chapter 18, Section D.)

C. Where to Get More Information

If you want more detail on your rights to receive benefits from a private pension plan, there are a number of free brochures available from:

American Association of Retired Persons (AARP)
601 E Street, NW
Washington, DC 20049
202/434-2277

Another organization that offers a number of publications relating to pensions is:

The Pension Rights Center
918 16th Street, NW; Suite 704
Washington, DC 20006
202/296-3778 ■

CHAPTER

16

LABOR UNIONS

L abor unions are organizations that deal collectively with employers on behalf of employees. Their best-known role is negotiating group employment contracts for members that spell out workplace essentials such as mandatory procedures for discipline and firing. But unions also often perform other workplace chores such as lobbying for legislation that benefits their members and sponsoring skill training programs.

Today, less than 15% of all American workers are union members—half as many as belonged in 1946 when membership was at a fever pitch. If you belong to a union, the specifics of your work relationship are covered in a collective bargaining agreement. That means nearly everything—work schedules, wages and hours, time off, discipline, safety rules, retirement plans—is spelled out in that contract. If you have a workplace problem, the process available to resolve it is spelled out in your collective bargaining contract, too. Usually, you are required to discuss your problem first with a designated union representative, who will then take it up with union officials. If your complaint is found to be a reasonable one, the union reps will guide you through a complaint or grievance procedure. If you disagree with the union's assessment of your situation, you can follow the steps provided for appealing the decision.

Some labor unions also operate benefit programs, such as vacation plans, healthcare insurance, pensions and programs that provide members with discounts on various types of personal needs, such as eyeglasses and prescription drugs.

Most unions are operated by a paid staff of professional organizers, negotiators and administrators, with some help from members who volunteer their time. In general, the money to pay unions' staffs and expenses comes from dues paid by their members—which typically total about $50 per member per month. There is no law that specifically regulates the amount of money that unions can charge their members—but they may not be excessive. Courts have provided little guidance in defining this, but have held that a union initiation fee equal to one month's salary by a starting worker would likely be considered excessive.

The laws and court decisions governing labor unions and their relationships with employers are so complex and separate from the rest of workplace law that this chapter can give you only an overview.

If you are already a member of a labor union and want to continue as one, the information provided here can help you to doublecheck on the performance of your union's leaders.

If you are not represented by a union and would like to be, or if you are a member of a union and want out, this chapter will help you become familiar with the basic laws labor unions must follow and alert you to your rights in dealing with unions.

A. Federal Laws

The federal laws broadly regulating unions—and the copious amendments to those laws—have dramatically changed the look and function of unions over time. The changing laws have also acted as political mirrors—alternately protecting employees from unfair labor practices and protecting employers from unfair union practices as unions' influence in the workplace has ebbed and flowed. Several of the most important federal controls are discussed here.

1. The National Labor Relations Act

Labor unions secured the legal right to represent employees in their relationships with their employers when the National Labor Relations Act, or NLRA, (29 U.S.C. §§151 and following) was passed in 1935. That federal Act also created the National Labor Relations Board (NLRB) to police the relationships among employees, their unions and their employers.

Under the NLRA, an employer may not:

* interfere with or restrain employees who are exercising their rights to organize, bargain collectively and engage in other concerted activities for their own protection

- interfere with the formation of any labor organization—or contribute financial or other support to it
- encourage or discourage membership in a labor organization by discriminating in hiring, tenure or employment conditions
- discharge or discriminate against employees who have filed charges or testified under the NLRA, or
- refuse to bargain collectively with the employees' majority representative.

a. Who is covered

The NLRA requires most employers and unions to negotiate fairly with each other until they agree to a contract that spells out the terms and conditions of employment for the workers who are members of the union. The NLRB enforces this requirement by using mediators, negotiators, administrative law judges, investigators and others.

b. Who is excluded

Certain groups of employees are not covered by the NLRA. They include:

- managers, supervisors and confidential employees such as company accountants
- farm workers
- the families of employers
- government workers
- most domestic workers, and
- certain industry groups, such as railroad employees, whose work situations are regulated by other laws.

The NLRA also contains some special exemptions for specific groups of workers within industries that are otherwise covered. Contact your local NLRB office for more information on whether your job is covered by the NLRA.

2. The Labor Management Relations Act

In the dozen years following enactment of the NLRA, Congress was progressively bombarded with pleas to rein in the unions' power in the workplace. Both employers and employees contended they needed protection from union overreaching, such as coercing workers to join by using threats and violence. The public joined in the outcry—complaining about work stoppages that increasingly threatened health, safety and food supply.

In 1947, the Labor Management Relations Act, popularly known as the Taft-Hartley Act, was passed (29 U.S.C. §141 and following). It was aimed at preventing unfair union practices and banned unions from:

- restraining or coercing employees who were exercising their rights under the NLRA, including the right to select a bargaining representative
- causing or influencing an employer to discriminate against an employee because of membership or nonmembership in a union
- refusing to bargain in good faith with an employer if a majority of employees have designated a union bargaining agent
- inducing or encouraging employees to stop work to force special treatment of union matters, and
- charging excessive fees to employees and employers.

3. The Labor Management Reporting and Disclosure Act

In a third attempt to right the balance among employees, employers and unions, Congress passed the Labor Management Reporting and Disclosure Act of 1959 (29 U.S.C. §153 and following). The most important contribution of that law is that it imposes a code of conduct for unions, union officers, employers and management consultants—holding each to a standard of fair dealing.

4. Enforcing Your Rights

You can sue unions and employers over violations of the National Labor Relations Act (NLRA), and many people have won such lawsuits. However, you will probably need a lawyer's help to file a lawsuit under the NLRA. (See Chapter 18, Section D.)

Also, there are a number of organizations that may provide free or low-cost helping in pursuing union problems and complaints. (See Section H and the Appendix for contact information.)

B. State Laws

Section 14(b) of the NLRA authorizes each state to pass laws that require all unionized workplaces within their boundaries to be open shops—and nearly half the states have passed such laws. (See the chart below.) In each of these states, you have the right to hold a job without joining a union or paying any money to a union, so they are usually called right to work laws.

One boon for employees in right to work states is that the NLRA requires that a union give fair and equal representation to all members of a bargaining unit, regardless of whether they are union members. If you are employed in a right to work state and are a member of a bargaining unit represented by a labor union, you can refuse to join the union or to pay any money to it—and the union still must represent you the same as your union co-workers.

If the union representing your bargaining unit fails or refuses to represent you in such situations, you can file an unfair labor practices charge against it with the NLRB.

The states listed below have right to work laws—which prohibit making union membership or nonmembership a condition of employment.

STATE RIGHT TO WORK LAWS

Alabama	Ala. Code §25-5-11.1
Alaska	No statute
Arizona	Ariz. Rev. Stat. Ann. §23-1302
Arkansas	Ark. Stat. Ann. §11-3-303
California	No statute
Colorado	No statute
Connecticut	No statute
Delaware	No statute
District of Columbia	No statute
Florida	Fla. Stat. Ann. §447.17
Georgia	Ga. Code Ann. §34-6-21
Hawaii	No statute
Idaho	Idaho Code §44-2003
Illinois	No statute
Indiana	No statute
Iowa	Iowa Code §736A.2
Kansas	Kan. Stat. Ann. §44-808
Kentucky	No statute
Louisiana	La. Rev. Stat. Ann. §23:983
Maine	No statute
Maryland	No statute
Massachusetts	No statute
Michigan	No statute
Minnesota	No statute
Mississippi	Miss. Const. Art. 7, §198-A
Missouri	No statute
Montana	No statute
Nebraska	Neb. Rev. Stat. §48-217
Nevada	Nev. Rev. Stat. §613.230
New Hampshire	No statute
New Jersey	No statute
New Mexico	No statute
New York	No statute
North Carolina	N.C. Gen. Stat. §§95-78 to 95-84
North Dakota	N.D. Cent. Code §34-0914

Ohio	No statute
Oklahoma	No statute
Oregon	No statute
Pennsylvania	No statute
Rhode Island	No statute
South Carolina	S.C. Code Ann. §41-7-30
South Dakota	S.D. Codified Laws Ann. §60-8-3
Tennessee	Tenn. Code Ann. §50-1-201 to 204
Texas	Tex Rev. Civ. Stat. Ann. art. 5207a, §2
Utah	Utah Code Ann. §§34-34-8 to 34-34-10
Vermont	No statute
Virginia	Va. Code §§40.1-60 to 40.1-62
Washington	No statute
West Virginia	No statute
Wisconsin	No statute
Wyoming	Wyo. Stat. §27-7-109

C. The Bargaining Unit

The basic union building block under the NLRA is the bargaining unit: a group of employees who perform similar work, share a work area and who could logically be assumed to have shared interests in such issues as pay rates, hours of work and workplace conditions.

A bargaining unit may be only a part of a larger union, or it may constitute a whole union itself. And a bargaining unit is not always limited to people who work in one building or for one company. For example, the workers in several small, independent sheet metal shops in a specific city will often be members of the same union bargaining unit.

On the other hand, a bargaining unit may include only part of a company. So it is possible—and quite common—for only a small portion of a company's workforce to be unionized, or for various departments in one company to be represented by different unions.

Something that is frequently misunderstood about bargaining units is that they are composed of jobs or job classifications—not of individual workers. For example, if Wilda Samano retires, and her former position as machinist is then filled by Sam Alvarez, the bargaining unit does not change—only the personnel.

D. Types of Union Work Situations

If you take a job that is covered by a contract between the employer and a labor union, a representative of the union will typically approach you about membership requirements shortly after you are hired.

Unionized work situations generally fall into one of three categories: open shop, agency shop and union shop. The type of shop that exists within a unionized bargaining unit will be spelled out in the contract between the union representing that unit and the employer. Ask the union representative for a copy of the contract governing your job before you sign up for union membership.

1. The Open Shop

Here, a union represents the bargaining unit of which you are a member—but you are not required to join the union or pay dues to it. Open shops are most commonly found in states that have passed right to work laws. (See Section B.)

2. The Agency Shop

You can make your own decision about whether or not to join the union. But, whether you join or not, you will have to pay the union the same dues and other fees that other members of your bargaining unit are required to pay. In return for your dues, the union must represent you if labor problems develop, just as it protects members of a bargaining unit. However, you will not be able to take advantage of the broader protections and disciplinary processes included in union contracts. This type of arrangement is legal in any state that has not passed a right to work law. (See Section B.)

3. The Union Shop

Although you are not required to be a union member when you take the job, you will be forced to join after a specified grace period —usually within 30 days after starting your new job—if a union shop clause is included in the contract covering your bargaining unit. Whether or not union shops are legal is a matter of controversy because the controlling law, Section 8(a)(3) of the NLRA, seems to contradict itself.

First, the law specifies that it is legal for a contract to require an employee to join a union within 30 days of starting a job. But it also states that an employer may fire you because of your lack of union membership only if the union rejected or expelled you for not paying the union's regular fees and dues.

In 1963, the U.S. Supreme Court ruled that the second clause is the one that controls. That decision, widely considered to be the landmark on the legality of union shops, is *NLRB v. General Motors* (373 U.S. 734).

If you take a job in a company in which the union contract calls for a union shop but you refuse to join the union, the employer and the union will usually overlook your refusal to join as long as you pay the union's fees and dues. You can, however, expect to be subjected—at the very least—to cold shoulder treatment by union officials and members.

E. Union Elections

When a union files a petition with the NLRB to be recognized as the representative of a bargaining unit, the petition includes the union's description of what group of workers it would like to have included in that bargaining unit. The employer usually contests these descriptions and tries to have the size of the bargaining unit trimmed down. Negotiations follow, and if the union and the employer cannot agree on the exact shape and size of a bargaining unit, the NLRB decides.

Bargaining units are little democracies, in which the majority rules and the minority must comply. For example, if you work in an office and more than half of the people who work there with you vote to be represented by a union, the entire office is likely to be designated as a bargaining unit. You will be represented by that union. Even if you do not want to be.

Except in a few circumstances, the NLRB generally will conduct an election for a bargaining unit to decide whether or not it wants to be represented by a certain union whenever at least 30% of the members of that bargaining unit indicate they want an election to be held. The members of the bargaining unit may express their wishes for an election by signing a group petition—or by signing individual cards that state, in essence, the same thing—and presenting that evidence of their wishes to their local NLRB office.

1. Types of Union Elections

NLRB-supervised elections generally fall into three categories:
- Certification elections, in which the employees who make up a bargaining unit vote on whether to have a union begin representing them.
- Decertification elections, in which the employees who make up a bargaining unit vote on whether to end their representation by a specific union.
- Situations where the employees who make up a bargaining unit want to switch unions. The existing union must be voted out through a decertification election and the new union voted in through a certification vote.

UNION-FREE POLICIES MAY VIOLATE YOUR RIGHTS

In companies where the employees are not represented by unions, it is common practice for the employer to openly state its wish to remain union-free. In general, companies have the right to make such statements under Section 8(c) of the National Labor Relations Act, as well as under the freedom of speech provisions of the First Amendment to the U.S. Constitution.

However, recent rulings by the National Labor Relations Board indicate that employers must be very careful about where and how they express their wishes for a workplace free of unions. They run the risk of violating the employees' right to unionize under the National Labor Relations Act.

One of the most significant rulings restricting union-free statements was issued by the NLRB in 1989, after a union that hoped to organize the employees of a hotel chain filed an unfair labor practices charge against the chain.

The hotel company's management had violated the NLRA, the NLRB ruled, by positioning a union-free statement in the policy manual that it gave to all new employees. The page following the one on which the union-free statement appeared asked employees for their signatures, verifying that they accepted the terms of employment set out in the manual.

The sequence of those pages in the employee manual, the NLRB decided, could lead employees to believe that adhering to the company's union-free policy was a condition of continued employment. And making employees believe that would violate Section 8(a) of the NLRA, which makes it illegal for an employer to coerce employees away from pursuing their rights to union representation (293 NLRB No. 6, 130 LRRM 1338 (1989)).

2. Restrictions on Union Elections

The courts have reached different conclusions about whether a union-related election can be held. But there are three NLRB policies on union-related elections that you can usually count on. The NLRB will not conduct an election:

- during the first year that a bargaining unit is represented by a particular union
- within a year of the last election held for that bargaining unit, or
- during the period covered by a union contract.

If the contract lasts more than three years, the NLRB will conduct an election at the end of the first three years of the contract if that is what the bargaining unit's members want.

RELIGIOUS OBJECTIONS TO UNIONS

Some employees are members of religions with beliefs that conflict with membership in a labor union. If your religion prohibits you from taking oaths, for example, having to swear allegiance to a labor union might force you to violate your religious beliefs.

In general, the courts have recognized an employee's right to refuse to join a union on religious grounds. However, you can still be required to pay union dues and fees if you work in an agency or union shop in a state that has not passed a right to work law. (See Section B.)

F. The Right to Unionize

Sections 7 and 8 of the National Labor Relations Act guarantee employees the right to create, join and participate in a labor union without being unfairly intimidated or punished by their employers.

1. Employee Rights

Generally, the courts have ruled that Section 7 of the NLRA gives employees the right to:
- discuss union membership and read and distribute literature concerning it during nonwork time in nonwork areas such as an employee lounge
- sign a card asking your employer to recognize your union and bargain with it, to sign petitions and grievances concerning employment terms and conditions and to ask your co-workers to sign petitions and grievances, and
- display your pro-union sentiments by wearing message-bearing items as hats, pins and T-shirts on the job.

2. Employer Limitations

Most courts have also ruled that Section 8 of the NLRA means that an employer may not:
- grant or promise employees a promotion, pay raise, a desirable work assignment or other special favors if they oppose unionizing efforts
- close down a worksite or transfer work or reduce benefits to pressure employers not to support unionization, or
- dismiss, harass, reassign or otherwise punish or discipline employees— or threaten to—if they support unionization. (See Chapter 11, Section C, for a related discussion of blacklisting laws.)

3. Deducting Union Dues From Paychecks

One thing on which labor unions and the government agree is that it is easier to get money from people who never get to touch that money in the first place. To ease their operations, many union contracts include a check-off clause.

Much like income tax withholding, the check-off clause requires your employer to withhold your union dues from your pay and then forward the money to the union. By voting to approve a contract between your union and your employer, you also signify approval of any check-off clause in that contract. So unions' practice of having employers withhold dues from a paycheck is generally legal.

HOW UNIONS ARE BORN

If a group of employees wishes to campaign for unionization of their jobs, the best place to begin is by contacting a union they think would be interested and propose the idea.

Unions are usually listed in the Yellow Pages of your local telephone directory under Labor Organizations. Don't let their names discourage you. It is not unusual for meatpackers to belong to the United Steel Workers, for example, or for office workers to belong to the Teamsters union that originally represented freight drivers. The only practical way to determine which unions might be interested in unionizing your workplace is to call and ask.

If the union you approach is interested, it will assign professional organizers who will guide you through the rest of the process. If it is not interested—perhaps because your employer is too small or because you work in an industry with which it is not comfortable—that union should be able to suggest another one that would be more appropriate for you to contact. If not, contact:

The American Federation of Labor and Congress of Industrial Organizations (AFL-CIO)
815 16th Street, NW
Washington, DC 20006
202/637-5000

The National Labor Relations Act allows you to form your own, independent union to represent only the workers at your place of employment without affiliating with any established union. Such unions exist, but the complexities of labor law and the cost of running an independent union typically make them infeasible in all but the largest companies

G. The Right to De-Unionize

Just as it gives employees the right to unionize, the NLRA gives them the right to withdraw from union membership.

1. How to De-Unionize

There are two basic ways to de-unionize.

One way is to conduct a campaign among the members of your bargaining unit to get them to petition the NLRB to conduct a de-certification election. If you are able to bring about an election, you will probably also have to campaign hard against the union for the votes of other members of the bargaining unit.

Another way to de-unionize is simply to resign your individual membership. The courts have ruled that informing your employer that you want check-off deductions for union dues and fees stopped is not sufficient to quit a union; you must advise the union in writing of your decision to quit.

In right to work states, such a resignation leaves you free and clear of the union altogether—no membership, no dues, no fees. In other states, you may be required to continue paying fees and dues to your bargaining unit's union if the contract there calls for a union or agency shop, as described in Section D.

2. Limitations on Unions

The NLRA also prohibits unions from interfering with your right to reject or change union membership. Unions may not:

- restrain or coerce employees from exercising their rights under the NLRA. This includes the violence and threats of violence that some unions use against people who reject union membership
- cause or encourage an employer to discriminate against an employee or group of employees because of their de-unionization activities
- interfere in any way with an employee's right to freely express opinions on union membership

- fail or refuse to bargain in good faith with an employer on behalf of a
  bargaining unit that has designated the union as its bargaining agent,
  even if the union and the bargaining unit are at odds, or
- prevent you from going to work by using such tactics as mass picketing.

H. Where to Get More Help

It is easier to get free legal advice and help with labor union matters than on
any other aspect of workplace law.

The place to start is your local office of the National Labor Relations
Board (NLRB), listed in the Federal Government section of your telephone
directory. If the NLRB considers your union-related problem to be a serious
one, it will pay for all the costs of the investigations and hearings required
to take your complaint through the legal process.

If the NLRB cannot or will not help, you can turn to several other
sources. If you consider yourself to be pro-union, contact AFL-CIO headquarters:

The American Federation of Labor and Congress
of Industrial Organizations
815 16th Street, NW
Washington, DC 20006
202/637-5000

If you consider yourself to be anti-union, contact:

The National Right to Work Committee
8001 Braddock Road
Springfield, VA 22160
703/321-9820

If you are unsure about what your opinion on unions is, call both
places. These organizations maintain legal staffs to answer union-related
questions. They may even provide you with free legal representation. (See
the Appendix for contact information.) ■

CHAPTER

17

IMMIGRATION ISSUES

Many immigrants, even those with the documentation required to stay in the United States, may incorrectly believe they have fewer legal rights than American-born citizens. In fact, the Constitution of the U.S. protects everyone, regardless of citizenship or immigration status. It guarantees the same freedoms—to practice religion, to say what you want, to due process of law, to live and work free from discrimination.

A. Federal Law

The Immigration Act and Naturalization Act of 1990, or the Immigration Act (8 U.S.C. §§1323a and b), marked the most comprehensive overhaul of immigration law since legal controls were passed in the early 1900s. It sets out a complex system of quotas and preferences for determining who will be allowed to permanently live and work in the United States.[1]

The Immigration Act covers all employers and all employees hired since November 6, 1986, except employees who provide occasional, irregular domestic services in private homes. Independent contractors are not covered. (See Chapter 2, Section A for details on independent contractor status.)

Under the Immigration Act, it is illegal for an employer to:

- hire or recruit a worker who the employer knows has not been granted permission by the Immigration and Naturalization Service (INS) to be employed in the United States
- hire any worker who has not completed an INS Form I-9, the Employment Eligibility Verification Form, proving the worker's identity and legal right to work in the United States, or

---

[1]For a complete explanation of immigration laws, including step-by-step guidance on how to enter and stay in the United States legally, see *How to Get a Green Card: Legal Ways to Stay in the U.S.A.*, by Loida Nicolas Lewis with Len Madlansacay (Nolo Press).

- continue to employ an unauthorized worker—often called an illegal alien or undocumented alien.

    Employers may continue to employ workers who were on their payrolls before November 6, 1986—regardless of their immigration status—as long as those workers continue in essentially the same jobs they had before the law went into effect.

    Your employer is not required under the Immigration Act to fire you if you lack employment authorization from the INS but have been in the same job since before the law took effect. However, this provision does not exempt employees from complying with other requirements of U.S. immigration law.

B. Documentation Required to Work in the U.S.

Only legally authorized employees may work in the United States. When you take a new job, you are required to fill out the employee's section of INS Form I-9 by the end of your first day on the job. You then have three business days to present your new employer with documents that prove:
- that you are who you say you are, and
- that you are legally authorized to work in the United States.

    If you use forged, counterfeit or altered documents to prove your identification or authorization to work, you may be fined from $250 to $2,000—and up to $5,000 for each false document if there is a second offense (8 U.S.C. §1324c).

1. When One Document Is Sufficient

The INS considers a current U.S. passport sufficient to prove both your identity and your eligibility to be employed in the United States. It may also accept as appropriate proof:
- a certificate of United States citizenship
- a certificate of naturalization

- an unexpired foreign passport if it has the Attorney General's endorsement that an individual is entitled to work in the United States, or
- a resident alien or other alien registration card.

2. When Two Documents Are Required

If you do not have any of these, you are required to produce two documents: one establishing that you are authorized to work in the U.S., and another verifying your identity.

As documents proving your employment authorization, the INS will accept:
- a Social Security card
- a U.S. birth or nationality certificate, or
- other documentation that specifically shows the U.S. Attorney General has authorized you to work in the United States.

As documents proving your identity, the INS will accept:
- a current driver's license, or
- a state identification card with your photograph on it.

For workers 16 and under, the INS considers a school report card or a hospital record such as a birth certificate acceptable as proof of identity.

3. Time Requirements

New employees have three days in which to complete the I-9 Form. However, when you require some extra time to pull together the documents proving your identity and authorization—for example, if you need to obtain a certified copy of a birth certificate from another state—your employer can give you an additional 18 business days to produce the required documents. To get an extension of time, however, you must show proof that you have applied for the documents by producing, for example, a receipt for fees charged for a certified birth certificate.

Your new employer is required to note the type of documents you produce and any expiration dates on your Form I-9. Although employers are not required to photocopy such documents, they have the right to do so. If they do, the copies must be kept on file with your Form I-9. Employers who do not keep completed forms on file can be fined $100 for a first violation—and more if the violations persist.

C. Illegal Discrimination

The Immigration Act makes it illegal for an employer with three or more employees to:

- discriminate in hiring and firing workers—other than unauthorized immigrant workers, of course—because of their national origin
- discriminate in hiring and firing workers because of their citizenship, or
- retaliate against employees for exercising any rights under immigration laws.

To be successful in charging an employer with a violation of the Immigration Act, you must prove that the employer knowingly discriminated against you because of your citizenship or national origin, or that the employer had a pattern of committing the same offense against others.

1. Enforcing Your Rights

If a prospective or current employer violates your rights under the Immigration Act, you have 180 days from when the violation occurred to file a complaint with the Office of the Special Counsel for Unfair Immigration-Related Employment Practices. The most common violation of the anti-discrimination laws protecting immigrants occurs when employers refuse to hire someone because they suspect—incorrectly—that the person is not legally authorized to work in the United States.

2. The Complaint Process

To begin the complaint process, you can write a letter summarizing the situation to the following address:

> Special Counsel
> Immigration-Related Employment Practices
> P.O. Box 27728
> Washington, DC 20038-7728

If you need legal advice, call the special counsel office to discuss your situation with a staff attorney: 202/514-2000.

The special counsel has 120 days from the day it received your complaint to investigate and decide whether it will pursue a charge against the employer before an administrative law judge.

If the special counsel does not bring a charge against the employer within the 120 days, or notifies you that it has not found sufficient evidence to support your charges, you have the right to plead your case directly before an administrative law judge. But you must request your hearing within 90 days of the end of the original 120-day period allowed for the special counsel to take action.

Immigration law is a world all its own. You will probably need the help of an attorney with experience in immigration law if you decide to pursue an anti-discrimination complaint after the special counsel has failed to do so. (See Chapter 18, Section D.)

The Appendix also contains contact information for a number of groups that may provide advice and legal referrals. Since the Immigration Act specifically outlaws immigration-related discrimination only in hiring and firing decisions, but not in other employment-related actions such as promotions and wage increases, you may want to file your immigration-related complaint under Title VII of the Civil Rights Act or your state's anti-discrimination laws. (For details on those laws and how to take action under them, see Chapter 8, Sections A and B.)

D. English-Only Rules

Workplace rules that require employees to speak only English are generally illegal.

The Equal Employment Opportunity Commission and the courts regard English-only rules in the workplace to be wrongful discrimination on the basis of national origin under the Civil Rights Act of 1964. (See Chapter 8, Section A.) In most situations, employees must be allowed to speak among themselves in their own language while working or during breaks. In fact, EEOC guidelines, issued to clarify the suspiciousness with which courts must approach English-only rules, expound that such rules are presumed to be illegal—unless there is a clear business necessity for doing so. The same skepticism applies to workplace screening tests that seem to exclude or disqualify a disproportionate number of applicants of a specific national origin.

Exceptions have been allowed only in cases where there is a clear business necessity, such as for air traffic controllers or for those who must deal with company customers who speak English. And even these exceptions are becoming progressively more limited, as a growing number of courts have ruled that the business necessity occurs only during certain times of a workday.

Whenever there is some stricture requiring that employees speak only English on the job, employers must first:

- notify all employees of the rule
- inform all employees of the circumstances under which English is required, and
- explain the consequences of breaking the rule. ■

CHAPTER

18

LAWYERS
AND
LEGAL
RESEARCH

In workplace disputes, more than any other area of possible legal dispute, there are specialized agencies to advise and assist you with legal problems. If your problem is a matter of wage and hour law, for example, you can call the Labor Department's investigators directly for assistance. If your problem involves illegal discrimination, you can call the Equal Employment Opportunity Commission and talk over your case with a compliance officer or staff attorney. A number of specialized agencies are noted throughout the book—and a list of additional resources and contact information is contained in the Appendix.

With some types of workplace problems, however, you are on your own. If you need help getting your former employer to continue your healthcare benefits after you have lost your job, for example, no one is quite sure where to call. If you have been denied workers' compensation benefits, you may want to doublecheck your rights before deciding whether to file an appeal. In some unsettled legal areas, you may need to decide the best course of action: an alternative to court such as mediation, a small claims court claim, hiring a lawyer to help you through or doing some of your own legal research. This chapter gives you guidance in using and choosing among your options.

A. Mediation and Arbitration

At least partly because of how the legal world is portrayed on television and in movies, some people think that a courtroom is the best—and only—place to resolve any legal dispute. In fact, mediation or arbitration can be faster, less expensive, more satisfying alternatives than going to court. Workplace experts are hailing these less confrontational methods of solving workplace disputes as the hallmark of forward-thinking companies. And many employers are jumping on the bandwagon by adding clauses to their written employment agreements and employee manuals requiring that workplace disputes be resolved by arbitration or mediation.

Although mediation and arbitration are often lumped together under the general heading of alternative dispute resolution, there are significant differences between the two.

Mediation: Two or more people or groups get a third person—a mediator—to help them communicate. The mediator does not represent either side, or impose a decision, but helps the disagreeing parties formulate their own resolution of their dispute.

Arbitration: Both sides agree on the issue but cannot resolve it themselves. They agree to pick an arbitrator who will come up with a solution. Essentially, the arbitrator acts as an informal judge, but at far less cost and expense than most legal proceedings require.

Mediation or arbitration are sometimes used to help work out the terms of an agreement to end a work relationship, but they are most effective where those involved have a continuing relationship and want to find a mutually acceptable way to work together.

1. When Mediation Works Best

Mediation offers benefits to many employers and employees, since the resolution to a particular problem is reached quickly and creatively. And because all involved feel they have a stake in fashioning the agreement, they are more likely to abide by the solution.

Mediation is not the best solution for all types of disputes, since success depends on both sides being willing to meet in the middle and deal directly with one another. However, many workplace experts have found that mediation is particularly effective in resolving a number of common workplace conflicts.

- *Disputes between employees.* Many disputes fester because two people are not able to talk with one another. By setting up a nonjudgmental, nonconfrontational way for them to air their differences, mediation may offer a way for them to change their behavior so they can work together more effectively.
- *Deteriorating performance.* Good employees may stop performing well for any number of reasons. Again, encouraging judgment-free discussion, mediation can help remove the dynamics of browbeating and defensive-

ness that often result when a supervisor confronts an employee about a slipping work record.

- *Sexual harassment complaints.* Many such problems involve an initial misperception about what is and what is not considered acceptable workplace behavior—and are made worse by an inability to discuss the differences openly. Mediation can open communication and so help ease the hostility that may pollute a work environment.

- *Termination.* While a firing is usually unpleasant for both employers and employees, mediation can help an employee receive a fair hearing of differences when that deck is so often weighted in favor of the company. For the employer, it can offer hope for a peaceful parting, free from the threat of future litigation.

2. Where to Get More Information

Leading sources of professional arbitrators and mediators and of information on how to use these approaches to resolve disputes are:

American Arbitration Association

> 140 West 51st Street
> New York, NY 10020
> 212/484-4000

> American Bar Association
> Standing Committee on Dispute Resolution
> 1800 M Street, NW
> Washington, DC 20036
> 202/331-2258

> National Institute for Dispute Resolution
> 1726 Street, NW; Suite 500
> Washington, DC 20036
> 202/466-4764

THE TIMES THEY HAVE A-CHANGED

Courts used to look with disfavor on resolving workplace disputes through arbitration and mediation rather than in front of juries. Their reasoning was somewhat murky, but usually hinted that while arbitrators did fine at handling black-and-white problems such as contract disputes, they were universally less adept at enforcing legislation, which lies at the root of many workplace disputes.

But courts' gradual willingness to enforce arbitration clauses was boosted recently by a strong directive from the U.S. Supreme Court. In the 1991 case of *Gilmer v. Interstate Johnson Lane Corp.*, the Court upheld the clause in a stock exchange agreement requiring that disputes be arbitrated. A host of state courts followed suit—upholding arbitration clauses in age and physical handicap discrimination, sexual harassment and wrongful termination claims.

In light of this new judicial attitude, Congress is currently considering an amendment to the Civil Rights Act—the federal law that broadly prohibits discrimination. The proposed legislation "encourages alternative means of dispute resolution" in resolving discrimination claims.

The changed wind is not universally welcomed. Some plaintiffs' attorneys question the fairness of taking issues such as sexual harassment and racial discrimination out of the courtroom. They say that mandatory arbitration agreements can be coercive if employees feel that they have to agree to arbitration to get or keep a job.

B. Small Claims Court

Some disputes over workplace law, such as wages owed to you by a former employer, involve only relatively small amounts of money. In many of those cases, you can file your own lawsuit in small claims court to collect the money that is owed to you.

The hallmark of small claims court is that it is inexpensive and easy to file a case there, and court procedures have been simplified. You do not need to hire a lawyer to represent you, and in some states, lawyers are not even allowed. The small claims hearing will be held before a judge, magistrate, commissioner or volunteer attorney, who will usually decide the case on the spot or within a few days.

The amount you can sue for is limited—usually to between $2,000 and $5,000, depending on your state. But these limits increase regularly, so check first with the local court clerk if you decide to use small claims court.[1]

C. Class Action Lawsuits

The federal courts sometimes allow lawsuits to be filed jointly by groups of people who have all been injured by the same or similar conduct of an employer. These are called class actions. Because they spread the legal costs among many people who are injured, class actions can make it feasible to sue an employer or former employer where the expense would be too great for an individual. Of course, all those who join in the lawsuit will also share in any judgment.

The legal requirements for pursuing a class action are complex, and almost always require a lawyer's help. But keep this option in mind if a number of other workers suffered similar wrongs or injuries to yours.

Your local office of the American Civil Liberties Union (ACLU) should be able to direct you to lawyers who specialize in civil rights class action lawsuits. (See the Appendix for contact details of the national headquarters.)

---

[1]For details on using small claims courts, see *Everybody's Guide to Small Claims Court*, by Ralph Warner (Nolo Press).

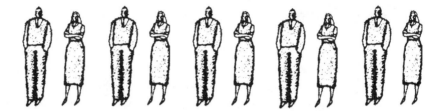

A CASE SHOWING THE STRENGTH OF NUMBERS

About 14,000 current and former female grocery store employees in northern California emerged a little richer and a lot more satisfied when they shared in a multi-million dollar class action settlement recently.

The lawsuit began in 1988 when five women sued Lucky Stores, Inc. in a San Francisco federal court, alleging the store discriminated against female employees by denying them advancement opportunities. The store at first defended that women were "not as interested in promotions as men."

But the plaintiffs in the case disagreed. Loudly. One of them, Reba Barber-Money claimed that she was hired as a checker in 1979 and made to stay in the position—bypassed for more than ten years by male employees who were given management training and then promoted. Diane Skillsky, another plaintiff, claimed she was also denied training necessary for a promotion—training that Lucky urged upon her teen-age son while he was employed at the same store.

After a ten-week trial, a California district court in 1992 found Lucky liable for sex discrimination against its female employees in job assignments, promotions and allocating work hours. Women who had worked at Lucky Stores for three months or more and who earned average salaries less than male employees were considered eligible to join in the class action.

After much legal wrangling and years of heated negotiations to determine appropriate damages, Lucky agreed in early 1994 to a $107 million settlement. It included $60 million to settle all damage claims and $20 million to pay for affirmative action programs aimed to bring more women into top management positions at Lucky.

D. Hiring a Lawyer

If your workplace problem involves a complex or ambiguous area of law—negotiating a complicated settlement, filing a claim of blacklisting or a violation of public policy—you will probably need to hire a lawyer for help. Depending on your circumstances and location, a number of places may provide referrals to lawyers with special expertise in workplace law.

- Legal aid clinics. In some cases, local legal clinics only make referrals to lawyers with appropriate knowledge and experience. And some may have lawyers on staff who will handle your case for a low cost or free of charge. Locate your community's legal aid clinics by looking in the telephone directory under Legal Aid Society or Legal Services—or check with the nearest law school.

- Organizations in your area that serve as advocates for the legal rights of minority groups, such as gay rights coalitions and local chapters of the National Association for the Advancement of Colored People (NAACP).

- National organizations that deal with specific types of workplace rights, such as the National Safe Workplace Institute, the National Association of Working Women or the National Coalition Against Sexual Assault.

- Groups of specialized employees may have access to legal help offered by special interest groups. Union workers, for example, can contact the Coalition for Labor Union Women for legal guidance and referrals to experienced attorneys.

See the Appendix for listings of organizations that provide legal referrals.

BEWARE OF LAWYER-RUN REFERRAL SERVICES

Bar associations and other lawyer groups often maintain and advertise lawyer referral services. Usually, there is little or no screening before a lawyer can get listed in these services. While it is always possible you will find a good lawyer through one of these services, your chances are hit and miss.

1. Comparison Shopping for a Lawyer

Take detailed notes on each lawyer mentioned during your research, and you should soon have your own small directory of lawyers with employment-related expertise from which to choose.

Be careful that people do not merely give you the names of lawyers they have heard of—or one who handled an entirely different kind of case, such as a divorce or a house closing. Any lawyer can become well-known just by buying a lot of advertising time on television or a large block in the yellow pages. Beware that in many states, lawyers can advertise any area of specialization they choose—even if they have never before handled a case in the area.

a. Questions to ask your referral source

Keep in mind that individual preferences for a particular lawyer are guided by intangibles such as personality. Here are a few questions you may want to ask a person who gives you a glowing review of a particular employment law lawyer.

- Did this lawyer respond to all your telephone calls and other communications promptly?
- Did the lawyer take the time to listen to your explanation and understand your situation fully?
- Were all the bills you received properly itemized and in line with the costs projections you got at the start of your case?
- Did this lawyer personally handle your case, or was it handed off to a younger, less experienced lawyer in the same firm?
- Did the lawyer deliver what he or she promised?

It may be slightly more difficult to evaluate a lawyer referral you get from an agency or special interest group. Reputable organizations will strike from their referral lists the names of lawyers about whom they have received negative reviews. You can help groups that make referrals keep their information accurate and useful to others if you let them know of both your good and bad experiences with a particular individual.

b. Deciding on a particular lawyer

Once you have a referral to a lawyer—or even better, several referrals—you should contact each and see whether he or she meets your needs.

Come forearmed with some inside knowledge.

Most lawyers are guided by the principle that Time Is Money. And time and money should also be your guiding concerns in deciding whether to hire a lawyer to help with your workplace claim.

Even the simplest problems can take a long time to be resolved through the legal system. And potential legal problems in the workplace do not often present themselves in straightforward issues. Unless a case is settled—most cases are—a court proceeding can take from five to eight years before a final judgment is reached.

A lawyer's help rarely comes cheap. Legal organizations estimate that workplace rights cases eat up an average of between $8,000 to $30,000 in lawyers' time and other legal costs such as court filings and witness interviews.

Lawyers often take on workplace cases for little or no money upfront. They depend on court-ordered fees and often a percentage of your recovery, or a contingency fee. (See Section 3.) This means that a lawyer will be assessing whether your case is likely to pay off so that he or she will be compensated.

Given these dire circumstances, you will want to be as certain as possible that any lawyer you hire will be doing the utmost to represent you fairly and efficiently—and that you are comfortable with his or her representation. Keep in mind that lawsuits can get dirty; the other side may try to probe deeply into your private life to gain the upper edge. A lawyer can represent you best if you are willing and able to speak candidly and comfortably to him or her about your case.

2. The Initial Interview

Start by calling for an appointment. Some lawyers will try to screen you over the phone by asking you to discuss the basics of your case. A little of this can be helpful to you both. You can begin to assess the lawyer's phoneside manner; he or she can begin to assess whether you truly need expert legal advice.

Many lawyers will agree not to charge you for an initial consultation to decide whether your situation requires legal action. But be prepared to pay a reasonable fee for legal advice. A charge of between $75 and $150 for a one-hour consultation is typical. Organize the facts in your case well before going to your consultation and be clear about what you are after—whether it's a financial settlement or being reinstated to your old job. An hour should be more than enough to explain your case and obtain at least a basic opinion on how it might be approached and what it is likely to cost. If you find the right lawyer and can afford the charge, it can be money well spent.

Keep in mind that very few employment law disputes actually end up in a courtroom. Most are settled or resolved in some other way. So you need not be swayed by a lawyer's likely effect on a jury alone. A good lawyer may also offer the valuable advice that you do not have a good case—or may suggest a good strategy for negotiating a settlement.

3. Paying a Lawyer

Some words to the wise about legal bills: Get It In Writing.

After you have interviewed a few lawyers and decided which one can best handle your case, don't just turn the case over to the lawyer of your choice. Most disagreements between lawyers and clients involve fees, so be sure to get all the details involving money in writing—including the per-hour billing rate or the contingency fee arrangement, the frequency of billing and whether you will be required to deposit money in advance to cover expenses.

Most workplace cases are handled under some form of contingent fee arrangement in which a lawyer agrees to handle a case for a fixed percentage of the amount finally recovered in a lawsuit. If you win the case, the lawyer's fee comes out of the money awarded to you. If you lose, neither you nor the lawyer will get any money.

A lawyer's willingness to take your case on a contingent fee is a hopeful sign of faith in the strength of your claim. A lawyer who is not firmly convinced that your case is a winner is unlikely to take you on as a contingency fee client. Be very wary of a lawyer who wants to take your case on an hourly payment basis. That usually signals that he or she does not think your case is very strong in terms of the money you might be able to recover. It could also mean financial disaster for you, as your legal bills are likely to mount up with no useful results. At the very least, insist that the lawyer write down some specific objectives to be accomplished in your case—and puts a limit on how high the fees can accumulate.

Although there is no set percentage for contingency fees in most types of cases, lawyers demand about 35% if the case is settled before a lawsuit is filed with the courts, and 40% if a case has to be tried. Keep in mind that the terms of a contingency fee agreement may be negotiable. You can try to get your lawyer to agree to a lower percentage—especially if the case is settled quickly—or to absorb some of the court costs.

Sometimes, a lawyer working for you under a contingency agreement will require that you pay all out-of-pocket expenses, such as filing fees charged by the courts and the cost of transcribing depositions—interviews of witnesses and others involved in a lawsuit who may provide additional information about the facts and circumstances. If this is so, the lawyer will want you to deposit a substantial amount of money—a thousand dollars or more—with the law firm to cover these expenses. From your standpoint, it is a much better arrangement for the lawyer to advance such costs and get repaid out of your recovery. A common sense arrangement might involve you advancing a small amount of money for some costs, with the attorney advancing the rest.

In some types of workplace lawsuits, such as Civil Rights Act violations, there is also the possibility of the court awarding you attorneys' fees as part of final judgment. However, this award may not be large enough to cover the entire amount owed to your attorney under the legal fee contract. Therefore, the contingency fee contract should spell out what happens to a court award of attorneys' fees. One approach is to have the fees paid to the attorney in their entirety—and subtract that amount from the contingency fee to which you have agreed.

4. Managing Your Lawyer

Many complaints against lawyers have to do with their failure to communicate with their clients. Your lawyer may be the one with the legal expertise, but the rights that are being pursued are yours—and you are the most important person involved in your case. You have the right to demand that your lawyer be reasonably available to answer your questions and to keep you posted on your case.

You may need to put some energy into managing your lawyer.

Carefully check every statement. Each statement or bill should list costs that the lawyer has paid or that you are expected to pay. If you question whether a particular bill complies with your written fee agreement, call your lawyer and politely demand that a new, more detailed version be sent before you pay it. Don't feel as though you are being too pushy: The laws in many states actually require thorough detail in lawyers' statements.

Learn as much as you can about the laws and decisions involved in your case. By doing so, you will be able to monitor your lawyer's work and may even be able to make a suggestion or provide information that will move your case along faster. Certainly if the other side offers a settlement, you will be in a better position to evaluate whether or not it makes sense to accept it.

Keep your own calendar of dates and deadlines. Note when papers and appearances are due in court. If you rely on your lawyer to keep your case on schedule, you may be unpleasantly surprised to find that an important deadline has been missed. Many a good case has been thrown out simply because of a lawyer's forgetfulness. Call or write to your lawyer at least a week before any important deadline in your case to inquire about plans to meet it.

Maintain your own file on your case. By having a well-organized file of your own, you will be able to discuss your case with your lawyer intelligently and efficiently—even over the telephone. Being well-informed will help keep your lawyer's effectiveness up and your costs down. Be aware that if your lawyer is working on a hourly basis, you'll probably be charged for telephone consultations. But they're likely to be less expensive than office visits.

DISAGREEING ON A SETTLEMENT OFFER

In many cases, your employer may offer a cash amount to settle the case. The problem is that you and your lawyer may have different interests at heart. If your lawyer is rushed or needs money, he or she may be ready to settle your case quickly for an inadequate amount. You, on the other hand, may want to hold out for what you consider to be more adequate. At this critical juncture, you may wish to get a second legal opinion as to whether the amount offered is realistic given the facts of your situation.

---

5. Firing a Lawyer

Change lawyers if you feel it is necessary. If your relationship does not seem to be working out, or if you feel that your case is not progressing as it should, consider asking another lawyer to take over. Be clear with the first lawyer that you are taking your business elsewhere, and immediately put your decision in writing. Otherwise, you could end up receiving bills from both lawyers—both of whom will claim they handled the lion's share of your case.

Before you pay anything, be sure that the total amount of the bills does not amount to more than you agreed to pay. If you have a contingency fee arrangement, it is up to your new lawyer and former lawyer to work out how to split the fee.

Take prompt action against any behavior by a lawyer that appears to be deceptive, unethical or otherwise illegal. A call to the local bar association, listed in the telephone directory under Attorneys, should provide you with guidance on what types of lawyer behavior are prohibited and how to file a complaint. In most states, attorney regulatory bodies are biased toward lawyers. Unless the lawyer's conduct is plainly dishonest or he or she has abandoned your case, you will probably not get much satisfaction. However, sometimes the threat of filing a complaint can move your lawyer into action. And if worst comes to worst, filing a formal complaint will create a document that you will need if you later file a lawsuit against a lawyer for malpractice.

E. Legal Research

This book gives you a general understanding of the legal principles involved in common workplace disputes. However, in negotiating with your employer, presenting your workplace problem to government investigators, preparing for mediation or arbitration, or working with a lawyer you hire, you may gain additional power and speed the resolution of your dispute by having detailed and specific legal knowledge.

In these situations, you may want to do some legal research of your own.[2]

---

[2]If you are new to legal research, you may find that you need more guidance than we provide here. Excellent resources on legal research for the novice include *Legal Research Made Easy*—a 2½ hour video that explains how to do technical legal research and how to set priorities to get results in a reasonable time. Also, *Legal Research: How to Find and Understand the Law*, by Steve Elias and Susan Levinkind, contains clear explanations and examples of all legal research techniques. Both are published by Nolo Press.

DON'T START FROM SCRATCH

For more general information about specific workplace issues, check the Appendix. Many legal and special interest groups publish helpful bibliographies and pamphlets on the legal aspects of workplace issues such as sexual harassment and age discrimination. Before you do extensive research on your own, check to see what others have done.

1. Libraries

The reference sections in most larger public libraries contain a set of local and state laws, as well as a set of the federal statutes. The reference librarian should be able to help you look up any laws that might affect your situation. However, if you want to look up a court case or a ruling by a government agency such as the Equal Employment Opportunity Commission, you will probably have to visit a law library.

In many states, county law libraries are free and open to the public. You can also try the library of the nearest law school, particularly if it's affiliated with a public university funded by tax dollars. Law school libraries offer one big advantage: They are usually open from early in the morning until late at night—even on weekends and some holidays. Whatever library you choose, you will find that most librarians are not only well-versed in legal research techniques, but also are open to helping you through the mazes of legal citations.

2. Where to Begin Your Research

There are several types of research materials concentrating on employment law that you may find useful: secondary sources such as books and law review articles, and also primary sources such as statutes and cases. These resources serve different purposes.

Secondary sources—general books and scholarly articles—are usually used to get an overview of a particular topic. If you find a good article or chapter on a topic you're interested in, it will give both an explanation of the law and citations to other materials—especially cases—that may prove helpful.

Primary sources—statutes (state and federal laws) and cases (published decisions of state and federal courts)—tell you the current status of the law. Very often, your goals in doing legal research are first to find the statutes that apply to you, and then to find the court cases that interpret the statutes in situations similar to yours. There may be cases with similar facts—for example, a supervisor who persistently asked a female employee to go out with him after she repeatedly said no. Or there may be a court case that raises a similar issue or legal question—for example, whether an employer is legally responsible for paying for an independent contractor's commuting costs. These court decisions may give you some indication of how a government agency or court is likely to decide your case.

The best place to begin your research depends on your situation. If you want some additional general information about a particular workplace issue, or an update on the law since this book was published, you will probably find a recent book or article more than adequate. However, if you want very specific legal information—for example, whether wrongful discharge is a valid legal theory in your state—you will probably need to look at both your state fair employment practice law and any judicial decisions dealing with the issue. The sections that follow describe how to find and use several types of resources to learn about the law that applies to your situation.

THE TWO RESEARCH TRACKS: FEDERAL AND STATE

Two separate sets of laws control the workplace—federal law and state law. Each has separate statutes, regulations and court cases, so you must decide which law you are relying on before you start to research.

The U.S. Civil Rights Act, for example, is a federal law, and the court decisions which interpret it—including those involving the EEOC—are federal cases. However, not all federal decisions carry equal weight. The cases which will be most persuasive in federal court are those from the highest court in that jurisdiction: the United States Supreme Court. On the second level in the hierarchy are the federal courts of appeal. You should look first for cases in the same judicial circuit or geographical region as yours, since these will be more authoritative. And finally, on the lowest level are the federal district courts—again, look first for cases in your geographical area.

If you are researching your state's laws, you will be looking at state court cases. Most state court systems are similar to the federal system, in that there are three hierarchical levels of courts. The most authoritative cases will be those from your state's highest court—usually called the supreme court—followed by decisions issued by your state appellate court, followed by decisions issued by your state trial court.

3. Statutes

When people refer to The Law, they are usually talking about statutes—the written laws created by state and federal legislatures.

Federal statutes are contained in the United States Code. For example, if you are looking for the Civil Rights Act, 42 U.S.C. 2000, locate Title 42 of the United States Code and turn to Section 2000.

Finding state statutes is a bit trickier, because states use slightly different systems to number and organize their statutes. Most states use one of the following methods:

• By topic. California uses this type of organization. To find Cal. Govt. Code §12900, locate the volumes that contain the state's government code and turn to Section 12900.

- By number. Florida, for example, lists statutes numerically, without flagging the topics the laws cover. To find Fla. Stat. §760.01, turn to Section 760.01.
- By title. Vermont, for example, divides its statutes into titles, similar to the federal citation system. To find 21 Vt. Stat. §495, locate Title 21 of the Vermont Statutes—and turn to Section 495.

Inside the back cover of the volume, you will find an unbound supplement called a pocket part. This material will update the information in the main volume, including any amendments or changes to the law that have happened since the main volume was published. It is organized just like the main volume, using the same numerical system. Be sure to check the pocket part every time you use a statute. If you forget this crucial step, you may be relying on law that is no longer valid.

4. Regulations

In some situations, you may also want to consult the regulations that pertain to a statute. Regulations are the rules created by administrative agencies for carrying out legislation. If, for example, a statute requires an agency to investigate complaints about workplace safety hazards, there will probably be regulations that give more detail about what form the investigation will take, who will conduct it and how it will be done.

Federal regulations can be found in the Code of Federal Regulations—usually abbreviated as CFR.

DON'T FORGET LOCAL LAWS

Many major cities and some counties also have their own laws on illegal workplace practices, such as discriminating against gay and lesbian workers, and regulations detailing how these laws should be carried out. Do not neglect these in your research. Sometimes a local law will contain the best protections against workplace problems or provide the best remedies. Ask your law librarian how to find and use your city or county code.

5. Cases

Sometimes, you will find all the information you need in the statutes and regulations. However, laws can be deceptively straightforward, impossibly complex—or somewhere in between. To be sure you get the point, it is wise to also look at court cases that involve the statute and see how the courts apply and interpret it. Courts have been known to take a law with an apparently obvious meaning and turn it on its head.

And sometimes, there will be no statute that applies to your situation. For example, when you are researching whether a legal theory such as the intentional infliction of emotional distress applies to your situation, you will absolutely need to look at some court decisions, since these issues are decided on a case-by-case basis.

Many court cases are cited throughout this book. Be sure to look at them as possible leads. If the discussion here makes a case seem similar in some way to your situation, you might want to look it up and read the court's ruling. For information on how to interpret case citations, see Subsection c, below.

a. Finding a case interpreting a statute

If you want to track down how a certain statute has been referred to by the courts in a case, your research task will be fairly simple: All you have to do is consult an annotated code. An annotated code is a version of the state or federal statutes that contains summaries of cases that have interpreted various provisions of a statute. There are two sets of federal annotated codes: the United States Code Service and the United States Code Annotated. Most states also have annotated codes. Ask the law librarian where you can find them.

To use an annotated code, look for the numbered section of the statute that is relevant to your situation. If there have been any court cases interpreting that statute, they will be listed after the specific section of the statute, along with a sentence or two describing the case. If the summary of the case leaves you wanting to know more about it, you can track down the case and read it by following the citation given there.

b. Finding a case using secondary sources

In some situations, you will want to find court decisions on a particular topic without referring to a statute. For example, if you want to find out whether some uncomfortable situation at work might form the basis of a tort action in your state, you should probably not begin your research with a statute. Common law tort actions were developed almost exclusively by case decisions. Sometimes these torts are also written into code—such as a state criminal statute defining and setting out the punishment for assault—but more likely, you will have to hunt down a few cases.

One good way to find relevant cases is through secondary sources (discussed in Section E2). Quite often, a law review article or book—including this one—will discuss key cases and give citations for them. If you find a source that analyzes an issue that is important in your case, you will likely get some good leads there.

c. Digests

Another good resource for finding cases is the digest system. These digests, published by the West Publishing Company, provide brief summaries of cases organized by topic. There are many sets of digests, divided by geographic region.

To use the digest system to find cases, first choose the relevant volumes—regional, state or federal. Next, look in the descriptive word index. You will find a number of categories listed under each heading. Look in the digest under topics that are relevant to your search—for example, Wrongful Discharge, Employer Negligence, Blacklisting. Under each topic, there will be short summaries of cases, arranged chronologically. If a case interests you, you can find the complete decision in the state or regional reporter by using the case citation.

The digests have a handy feature: the key number system. All of the digests use the same headings to categorize cases. Topics are divided into subtopics; each subtopic is given a number. If you find a topic in the state digest that seems relevant, and want to find federal cases on the same point, look in the federal practice digest under the same key number.

HOW TO READ A CASE CITATION

There are several places where a case may be reported. If it is a case decided by the U.S. Supreme Court, you can find it in either the United States Reports (U.S.) or the Supreme Court Reporter (S.Ct.). If it is a federal case decided by a court other than the U.S. Supreme Court, it will be in either the Federal Reporter, Second Series (F.2d) or the Federal Supplement (F. Supp.).

Most states publish their own official state reports. All published state courts decisions are also included in the West Reporter System. West has divided the country into seven regions—and publishes all the decisions of the supreme and appellate state courts in the region together. These reporters are:

A. and A.2d. Atlantic Reporter (First and Second Series), which includes decisions from Connecticut, Delaware, the District of Columbia, Maine, Maryland, New Hampshire, New Jersey, Pennsylvania, Rhode Island and Vermont.

N.E. and N.E.2d. Northeastern Reporter (First and Second Series), which includes decisions from New York*, Illinois, Indiana, Massachusetts and Ohio.

N.W. and N.W.2d. Northwestern Reporter (First and Second Series), which includes decisions from Iowa, Michigan, Minnesota, Nebraska, North Dakota, South Dakota and Wisconsin.

P. and P.2d. Pacific Reporter (First and Second Series), which includes decisions from Alaska, Arizona, California*, Colorado, Hawaii, Idaho, Kansas, Montana, Nevada, New Mexico, Oklahoma, Oregon, Utah, Washington and Wyoming.

S.E. and S.E.2d. Southeastern Reporter (First and Second Series), which includes decisions from Georgia, North Carolina, South Carolina, Virginia and West Virginia.

So. and So.2d. Southern Reporter (First and Second Series), which includes decisions from Alabama, Florida, Louisiana and Mississippi.

S.W. and S.W.2d. Southwestern Reporter (First and Second Series), which includes decisions from Arkansas, Kentucky, Missouri, Tennessee and Texas.

A case citation will give you the names of the people or companies on each side of a case, the volume of the reporter in which the case can be found, the page number on which it begins and the year in which the case was decided. For example:

Smith v. Jones Int'l, 123 N.Y.S.2d 456 (1994)

Smith and Jones are the names of the parties having the legal dispute. The case is reported in volume 123 of the New York Supplement, Second Series, beginning on page 456; the court issued the decision in 1994.

---

*All California appellate decisions are published in a separate volume, the California Reporter (Cal. Rptr.), and all decisions from New York appellate courts are published in a separate volume, New York Supplement (N.Y.S.).

d. Employment law reporters

Perhaps the best way to find cases is through one of two specialized legal publications that gather both state and federal cases on employment law issues:

- Fair Employment Practices Cases (Fair Empl. Prac. Cas.) published by the Bureau of National Affairs, and
- Employment Practices Decisions (Empl. Prac. Dec.) published by Commerce Clearing House.

To use these publications, look in the index volumes and glance through for specific topics that interest you. Then use the case citations listed to look for relevant court decisions in the reporter volumes.

e. Finding similar cases

Once you find a case that seems relevant to your situation, you can determine if there are more by using a publication called *Shepard's Citations*. *Shepard's* collects and lists every reference to a particular case. In other words, you can look up any case—state or federal—in the *Shepard's* volumes, and get a list of every case decided after it that has mentioned your case. This is very valuable for finding cases on the same subject, as well as for determining whether the original case you found has been influential or discredited.

6. Treatises

There are several books—sometimes called treatises—that cover workplace issues. The drawbacks of most treatises is that nearly all of them are written by and for lawyers—with little effort made to translate legalese into English. Also, these books oftentimes devote many pages to lawyerly concerns, such as how to plead and prove picayune points of law. Still, these volumes will often provide you with helpful background information—and will also often lead you to cases that pertain to your situation. When using a legal treatise, be sure to check the back inside cover; most publishers update the books periodically by issuing pocket parts, bound pamphlets noting changes and additions to the text.

8. Law Review Articles

Law reviews are periodicals containing articles written by lawyers, law professors and law students—usually covering a unique or evolving legal topic. Since workplace law is of great current interest, you'll find lots of articles about it. The inside joke about law review articles is that they are made up mostly of footnotes. While annoying to many readers, these footnotes—which contain references (citations) to other relevant cases, statutes and articles—can be goldmines for researchers. Look especially for articles that are published in law reviews from schools in your state, since these will be most likely to discuss your state's law and court decisions.

There are two tools in every law library that can help you find law review articles on topics that interest you: the Current Law Index and the Index to Legal Periodicals. These volumes are published annually, except for the most recent listings, which are published every month. Both list articles by subject, by author and by the cases and statutes referred to in the article. If you don't have a case name or a specific statute in mind to guide you, turn to the index and peruse the listings of articles there.

HOW TO READ LAW REVIEW CITATIONS

Both the Current Law Index and the Index to Legal Periodicals will give you the author, title and citations of law review articles. The citations will give the title of the publication and the volume and page numbers of the articles you want to look at. For example, if you look under Sexual Harassment—Analysis, you will see a listing for Susan Estrich's article "Sex at Work." The citation reads:

43 Stan. L. Rev. 813 (1991)

This article can be found in volume 43 of the Stanford Law Review, beginning on page 813; 1991 is the year of publication. If you have trouble deciphering the law review names, check the listing of abbreviations in the index—or ask a law librarian for help. ■

APPENDIX

The organizations listed here can give you additional information or assistance on specific workplace issues. Some groups offer a wide variety of services—including publications and written materials, telephone counseling and hotlines for advice, support groups or in-person counseling for workplace problems, attorney referrals and workplace training resources, including on-site training programs and written and video training materials.

Some organizations offer only limited services or restrict services to their members or to a limited geographic area. Be sure to ask whether you are eligible to use their services. Also, be sure to ask for an additional, more appropriate referral if the group you contact is not able to help.

AIDS/HIV

ACLU AIDS Project. (See American Civil Liberties Union under Civil Rights.)
AIDS Action Council
1875 Connecticut Avenue, NW; Suite 700
Washington, DC 20009
202/986-1300

National advocacy organization working for more effective AIDS policy, education and funding. No direct service for individuals.

American Foundation for AIDS Research (AmFAR)
733 Third Avenue
New York, NY 10017-3204
212/682-7440

Nonprofit public foundation funds programs for AIDS research, education for AIDS prevention and public policy development.

National Leadership Coalition on AIDS
1730 M Street, NW; Suite 905
Washington, DC 20036
202/429-0930

Business-related education, resource center and library.

Civil Rights

American Civil Liberties Union (ACLU)
132 West 43rd Street
New York, NY 10036
212/944-9800

Advocates individual rights through litigation and public education on a broad range of issues affecting individual freedom. Legal advice and counseling, as well as attorney referrals, provided by state offices. Check your phone book for the nearest location. The ACLU's National Task Force on Civil Liberties in the Workplace (in New York office, address above) answers questions on drug testing, discrimination, privacy, unjust dismissal, whistleblowing and has information on special projects on AIDS and on lesbian and gay rights.

Asian-American Legal Defense and Education Fund
99 Hudson Street, 12th Floor
New York, NY 10013
212/966-9800

Free legal advice, counseling and attorney referrals for Asians and Asian-Americans. Focus on issues of immigration, family, employment and anti-Asian violence.

Disabled Workers

ABLEDATA
8455 Colesville Road
Silver Spring, MD 20910
800/346-2742 or 800/227-0216

A consumer referral service that maintains a database of more than 17,000 adaptive devices from 2,000 companies.

Job Accommodation Network (JAN)
918 Chestnut Ridge Road; Suite 1
West Virginia University
P. O. Box 6080
Morgantown, WV 26506-6080
800/232-9675 or 800/526-7234
Computer bulletin board 800/342-5526

Provides free consulting services to people with disabilities seeking accommodation information under the Americans With Disabilities Act (ADA) and to employers seeking to accommodate employees with disabilities. Maintains a database of companies nationwide that have accommodated workers and organizations, support groups, government agencies and placement agencies that assist the disabled.

President's Committee on Employment of People With Disabilities
1331 F Street, NW
Washington, DC 20004-1107
202/376-6200
202/376-6205 (TDD)

Independent federal agency facilitates employment of people with disabilities and enforces Americans With Disabilities Act (ADA). Provides information, training and technical assistance.

Discrimination

Equal Employment Opportunity Commission
1801 L Street, NW
Washington, DC 20507
800/669-4000 To file charge or reach field office)
800/669-3362 Information and publication center)
800/800-3302 (TDD)
In Washington, DC, metropolitan area, call:
202/663-4900; 202/663-4494 (TDD)

Federal agency working to ensure equality of opportunity by enforcing federal laws prohibiting employment discrimination and sexual harassment through investigation, conciliation, litigation, coordination, education and technical assistance.

(See Chapter 8 for a list of regional EEOC offices and state Fair Employment Practices FEP/offices.)

Family Issues

See also organizations listed under Women's Issues.

Families and Work Institute
330 Seventh Avenue
New York, NY 10001
212/464-2044

Operates a national clearinghouse of information on work and family life, advises business, government, and community organizations and conducts management training on work and family issues.

Formerly Employed Mothers at the Leading Edge (FEMALE)
P.O. Box 31
Elmhurst, IL 60126
708/941-3553

Nationwide, membership-based support and advocacy group for women dealing with transition between paid employment and staying at home. Publishes monthly newsletter.

New Ways to Work
785 Market Street, Suite 950
San Francisco, CA 94103
415/552-1000

Educational and advocacy organization devoted to promoting flexible work arrangements. Serves as a clearinghouse for information, has an extensive publications list and offers seminars and training to companies.

Gay and Lesbian

ACLU National Lesbian and Gay Rights Project See American Civil Liberties Union under Civil Rights.

Gay and Lesbian Advocates and Defenders (GLAD)
P.O. Box 218
Boston, MA 02112
617/426-1350

Publishes information and provides general advice on sexual orientation and HIV status. Provides lawyer referrals.

Hollywood Supports
8455 Beverly Boulevard, Suite 305
Los Angeles, CA 90048
213/655-7705

Entertainment industry project founded to counter workplace fears and discrimination based on HIV status and sexual orientation. Provides model documents for domestic partnership benefit plans, lawyer referral and counseling in regards to AIDS and sexual orientation in the workplace.

Lambda Legal Defense and Education Fund
666 Broadway
12th Floor
New York, NY 10012
212/995-8585

Provides publications, advice and legal information on gay and lesbian job discrimination and HIV discrimination issues. Phone-in service for lawyer referrals.

National Center for Lesbian Rights
870 Market Street, Suite 570
San Francisco, CA 94102
415/392-6257

Offers publications, advice, counseling and lawyer referrals.

National Gay and Lesbian Task Force
1734 14th Street, NW
Washington, DC 20009-4309
202/332-6483; 202/332-6219 (TTY)

Political advocacy group. Publishes organizing manual for implementing domestic partnership benefit plans and non-discrimination policies. Provides referrals for counseling and lawyers.

Working It Out
The Newsletter for Gay and Lesbian Employment Issues
Ed Mickens
P.O. Box 2079
New York, NY 10108
212/769-2384

Quarterly publication for corporate human resource departments, management and others concerned with gay and lesbian issues in the workplace.

Health Insurance

Foundation of Employee Benefit Plans
18700 West Bluemound Road
P.O. Box 69
Brookfield, WI 53008-0069
414/786-6700

Publishes report *COBRA Continuation Coverage* on individual's rights to continue health insurance coverage.

Immigration

Immigration and Naturalization Service INS)
425 I Street, NW
Washington, DC 20507
202/663-4262

Federal agency responsible for overseeing and enforcing visa and lawful permanent resident applications and procedures.

Center for Immigrants Rights
48 Saint Marks Place
New York, NY 10003
212/505-6890

Provides advocacy and organizing advice for immigrant workers. Also gives advice and legal counseling on discrimination and compensation issues.

Labor Departments

U.S. Department of Labor
200 Constitution Avenue, NW
Washington, DC 20210
202/219-6666

Check government pages of the telephone book for nearest location.

State Labor Departments

Alabama	Labor Department 1789 Dickenson Drive, 2nd Floor Montgomery, AL 36130 205/242-3460
Alaska	Labor Department P.O. Box 21149 Juneau, AK 99802-1149 907/465-2700
Arizona	Labor Division 800 West Washington Street, Suite 102 Phoenix, AZ 85007 602/542-4515
Arkansas	Labor Department 10421 West Markham Street Little Rock, AR 72205 501/682-4500

California	Industrial Relations Department 455 Golden Gate Avenue P.O. Box 420603 San Francisco, CA 94142-0603 415/703-4281
Colorado	Labor Division 1120 Lincoln Street Denver, CO 80203 303/837-3800
Connecticut	Labor Department 200 Folly Brook Boulevard Wethersfield, CT 06109 203/566-4384
Delaware	Labor Department 820 North French Street; 6th Floor Wilmington, DE 19801 302/577-2710
District of Columbia	Wage and Hour Office 950 Upshur Street, NW; 2nd Floor Washington, DC 20011 202/576-6942
Florida	Labor Employment & Training Division Atkins Building, Suite 300 Tallahassee, FL 32399-0667 904/488-7228
Georgia	Labor Department 148 International Blvd, NE, Suite 600 Atlanta, GA 30303 404/656-3011
Hawaii	Labor & Industrial Relations Department 830 Punchbowl Street Honolulu, HI 96813 808/586-8842

Idaho	Labor & Industrial Services Department 277 North 6th Street State House Mail Boise, ID 83720 208/334-3950	Maryland	Labor & Industry Division 501 Saint Paul Place Baltimore, MD 21202 410/333-4179
Illinois	Labor Department 160 North LaSalle Street, 13th Floor Chicago, IL 60601 312/793-2800	Massachusetts	Labor & Industries Department 100 Cambridge Street, Room 1100 Boston, MA 02202 617/727-3454
Indiana	Labor Department 402 West Washington, Room W-195 Indianapolis, IN 46204 317/232-2655	Michigan	Labor Department Victor Office Building 201 North Washington Square P.O. Box 30015 Lansing, MI 48909 517/373-9600
Iowa	Labor Services Commission 1000 East Grand Avenue Des Moines, IA 50319 515/281-8067	Minnesota	Labor & Industry Department 443 Lafayete Road St. Paul, MN 55155 612/296-2342
Kansas	Public Employee Relations Board 512 West 6th Topeka, KS 66603 913/296-3094	Mississippi	Employment Security Commission 1520 West Capitol P.O. Box 1699 Jackson, MS 39215 601/354-8711
Kentucky	Labor Cabinet US Hwy. 127, South Building Frankfort, KY 40601 502/564-3070	Missouri	Labor & Industrial Relations Department 3315 West Truman Boulevard Jefferson City, MO 65109 314/751-4091
Louisiana	Labor Department P.O. Box 94094 Baton Rouge, LA 70804-9094 504/342-3011	Montana	Labor & Industry Department 1327 Lockey Avenue P.O. Box 1728 Helena, MT 59624 406/444-3555
Maine	Labor Department 20 Union Street P.O. Box 309 Augusta, ME 04332-0309 207/287-3788		

Nebraska	Labor Department P.O. Box 94600 Lincoln, NE 68509 402/471-9000	Oklahoma	Labor Department 4001 Lincoln Boulevard Oklahoma City, OK 73105 405/528-1500
Nevada	Labor Commission 1445 Hot Springs Road, Suite 108 Carson City, NV 89710 702/687-4850	Oregon	Labor & Industries Bureau 800 NE Oregon Portland, OR 97232 503/731-4200
New Hampshire	Labor Department 95 Pleasant Street Concord, NH 03301 603/271-3171	Pennsylvania	Labor & Industry Department Labor & Industry Building Harrisburg, PA 17120 717/787-3756
New Jersey	Labor Department John Fitch Plaza, CN 110 Trenton, NJ 08625 609/292-2323	Rhode Island	Labor Department 610 Manton Avenue Providence, RI 02909 401/457-1800
New Mexico	Labor & Industrial Division 1596 Pacheco Street Santa Fe, NM 87501 505/827-6808	South Carolina	Labor Department P.O. Box 11329 Columbia, SC 29211-1329 803/734-9594
New York	Labor Department State Campus, Bldg. 12 Albany, NY 12240 518/457-2741	South Dakota	Labor Department 700 Governors Drive Pierre, SD 57501 605/773-3101
North Carolina	Labor Department 4 W. Edenton Street Raleigh, NC 27601 919/733-7166	Tennessee	Labor Department 710 James Robertson Parkway, 2nd Floor Nashville, TN 37243-0655 615/741-2582
North Dakota	Labor Department 600 East Boulevard Bismarck, ND 58505 701/224-2660	Texas	Licensing & Regulation Department P.O. Box 12157, Capitol Station Austin, TX 78711 512/463-5522
Ohio	Industrial Relations Department 2323 West 5th Avenue P.O. Box 825 Columbus, OH 43216 614/644-2223	Utah	Labor Division 160 E. 300 South, 3rd Floor P.O Box 146630 Salt Lake City, UT 84114-6630 801/530-6921

Vermont	Labor & Industry Department National Life Building, Drawer 20 Montpelier, VT 05620-3401 802/828-2286
Virginia	Labor & Industry Department 13 South 13th Street Richmond, VA 23219 804/786-2377
Washington	Labor & Industries Department P.O. Box 44001 Olympia, WA 98504-4001 206/956-4213
West Virginia	Labor Division 1800 Washington Street E Charleston, WV 25305 304/558-7890
Wisconsin	Industry, Labor & Human Relations Department P.O. Box 7946 Madison, WI 53707 608/266-7552
Wyoming	Labor & Statistics Department U.S. West Building 6101 Yellowstone Road, Room 259C Cheyenne, WY 82002 307/777-7261

Legal Referrals

National Employment Lawyers Association
535 Pacific Avenue
San Francisco, CA 94133

National directory of employment law attorneys, including brief descriptions of their practices. Send a stamped, self-addressed envelope for more information.

National Resource Center for Consumers of Legal Services
P.O. Box 340
Gloucester, VA 23061
804/693-9330

Nationwide legal referrals to attorneys experienced in employment law. Publishes materials on how to choose a lawyer and articles about job rights. Send a stamped, self-addressed envelope for more information.

Mediation and Arbitration

American Arbitration Association
140 West 51st Street
New York, NY 10020
212/484-4000

National nonprofit organization offering mediation and arbitration services through local offices across the country. Also conducts neutral investigations of workplace disputes. Provides education and training in alternative dispute resolution. General information about out-of-court settlement, negotiation opportunities, rules and procedures of mediation.

National Institute for Dispute Resolution
1726 M Street, NW, Suite 500
Washington, DC 20036
202/466-4764

Provides publications, advice and referrals on alternative dispute resolution.

Miscellaneous Workplace Issues

Bureau of National Affairs BNA/Communications
9439 Key West Avenue
Rockville, MD 20850
800/233-6067

Special reports, audio-video materials and manuals in many areas of employment, including disabilities, discrimination, diversity and management training.

Business and Legal Reports, Inc.
39 Academy Street
Madison, CT 06443
203/245-7448

Publishes booklets on numerous workplace issues including safety, workers' compensation, sexual harassment, family leave, drug testing and stress management.

Center for Working Life
3814 SE Martins
Portland, OR 97202
503/774-6088

National nonprofit organization providing training and consultation for development of programs to assist in relocating displaced workers and work-place education.

Older Americans

American Association of Retired Persons
601 E Street, NW
Washington, DC 20049
800/424-3410

Nonprofit membership organization of older Americans open to anyone age 50 or older. Wide range of publications on retirement planning, age discrimination and employment-related topics. Networking and direct services available through local chapters.

Older Women's League
730 Eleventh Street, NW, Suite 300
Washington, DC 20001
202/783-6686

Provides advice on claiming COBRA benefits, discrimination and other issues facing the elderly.

Retirement Plans and Pensions

American Association of Retired Persons. (See listing under Older Americans.)

Pension Benefit Guaranty Corporation
Coverage & Inquiries Branch
1200 G Street, NW
Washington, DC 20006
202/326-4000; 202/778-8859 (TDD)

Government agency established to protect pension benefits. Collects premiums from participating companies. Investigation with Labor Department.

Pension Rights Center
918 16th Street, NW; Suite 704
Washington, DC 20006
202/296-3778

Nonprofit organization and service network providing pension advice or lawyer referral. Publications list available.

Safety and Health Issues

American Psychological Association
750 First Street, NE
Washington, DC 20002-4242
202/336-5500

Information on career training, stress and well-being at work, counseling and psychotherapy for work dysfunctions.

Americans for Nonsmokers' Rights
2530 San Pablo Avenue, Suite J
Berkeley, CA 94702
510/841-3032

Nonprofit advocacy group that campaigns for legislation to assure that nonsmokers can avoid involuntary exposure to secondhand smoke in the workplace, restaurants, public places and public transportation. Offers educational programs for children on smoking prevention and the right to smokefree air.

Asbestos Victims of America
P.O. Box 559
Capitola, CA 95010
408/476-3646

Printed information on asbestos, including status of legal issues for people who have been exposed to asbestos at work.

National Institute for Occupational Safety and Health (NIOSH)
200 Independence Avenue, SW
HHH Building, Room 714-B
Washington, DC 20201
202/690-7134
Information hotline: 800/356-4674

Research institute offering publications on various workplace health and safety issues. Maintains database indoor air quality, carpal tunnel, workplace homicide and other current topics. Conducts evaluations of individual worksite. Also makes available training programs, materials and videos.

National Safe Workplace Institute
Courthouse Place
54 West Hubbard, Suite 403
Chicago, IL 60610
312/661-0690

Nonprofit organization addressing issues of occupational safety and health, reproductive issues, violence in the workplace, child labor and adolescents' rights. Reports available for fee. Threat assessment services, legal referral and expert witness service available.

Occupational Safety and Health Administration
200 Constitution Avenue, NW
Washington, DC 20210
202/219-8148

Federal agency responsible for establishing and overseeing workplace health and safety standards.

Smokefree Air for Everyone (SAFE)
P.O. Box 246
Newbury Park, CA 91319
803/499-8921

S.A.F.E. was formed by a group of individuals who have been injured or disabled by secondhand smoke. Maintains a resource list of doctors and attorneys to help with secondhand smoke problems. Works closely with health and tobacco control organizations to promote legislation restricting smoking in public places.

White Lung Association
P.O. Box 1483
Baltimore, MD 21203-1483
410/243-5864

National nonprofit organization of asbestos victims. Teaches consequences and effect, removal and disposal of asbestos. Provides literature.

Unions

American Federation of Labor and Congress of Industrial Organizations (AFL-CIO)
815-16th Street, NW
Washington, DC 20006
202/637-5000

Voluntary federation of 86 unions with over 14 million members. Printed materials on all aspects of union employment. Information and assistance for union-related issues at local levels.

AFL-CIO: Union Privilege
1444 I Street, NW, 8th Floor
Washington, DC 20005
202/336-5460; 800/452-9425 for lawyer referral in local area.

Nationwide legal services plan free to most members of AFL-CIO. Free initial consultation and document review; other fees discounted. Many locals have their own legal services plan.

Association for Union Democracy
500 State Street
Brooklyn, NY 11217
718/855-6650

Nationwide attorney referrals, legal advice, counseling and organizational assistance for union members.

Coalition of Labor Union Women (CLUW)
1126 16th Street, NW
Washington, DC 20036
202/296-1200

National organization with 75 local chapters. Provides education, organizes conferences and workshops, lobbies for legislation, supports strikes and boycotts. Newsletter and written materials. Provides referrals to attorneys and legal rights groups for union workers.

National Right to Work Committee
8001 Braddock Road
Springfield, VA 22160
703/321-9820

Citizens' lobbying organization to pass more right to work legislation and combat compulsory unionism.

National Right to Work Legal Defense Foundation
8001 Braddock Road
Springfield, VA 22160
703/321-8510; 800/336-3600

Nonprofit charitable organization which offers free legal aid to employees whose rights are violated by compulsory unionism abuses.

Women's Issues

Catalyst
250 Park Avenue South
New York, NY 10003
212/777-8900

Promotes the advancement of women in business by working with corporate management to analyze existing barriers to women's advancement and recommend ways to eliminate those barriers. Publishes a national directory of career resource centers that counsel individuals.

Equal Rights Advocates
1663 Mission Street, Suite 550
San Francisco, CA 94103
415/621-0672 (General information)
415/621-0505 (Advice and counseling hotline)

Nonprofit public interest law firm providing legal advice and counseling in both English and Spanish.

Federation of Organizations for Professional Women
2001 S Street, NW; Suite 540
Washington, DC 20009
202/328-1415

Telephone advice and counseling on sexual harassment and discrimination. Publishes written materials. Support groups in Washington, DC area.

Fund for the Feminist Majority
1600 Wilson Boulevard
Arlington, VA 22209
703/522-2214 (General information)
703/522-2501 (Sexual harassment hotline)

The Fund is political and does lobbying. The Foundation with which it is associated is nonprofit research organization which provides public information about battered women, sexual harassment and international women's issues.

9to5, National Association of Working Women
614 Superior Avenue, NW
Cleveland, OH 44113
216/566-9308 (General information)
800/522-0925 (Hotline)

National nonprofit membership organization for working women. Counseling, information and referrals for problems on the job, including family leave, pregnancy disability, termination, compensation and sexual harassment. Newsletter and publications. Local chapters throughout the country.

NOW Legal Defense and Education Fund
99 Hudson Street, 12th Floor
New York, NY 10013
212/925-6635

Legal referrals available through the mail.
National Women's Law Center
1616 P Street, NW; Suite 100
Washington, DC 20036
202/328-5160

National nonprofit civil rights organization focusing on key issues affecting women, including employment discrimination and sexual harassment

U.S. Department of Labor, Women's Bureau
200 Constitution Avenue, NW
Washington, DC 20210
800/827-5355

National clearinghouse of information on pregnancy discrimination, sexual harassment, family and medical leave, child care programs and other topics of interest to working women.

Wider Opportunities for Women (WOW)
1325 G Street, NW
Washington, DC 20005
202/638-3143

National nonprofit organization, primarily focusing on economic opportunities for women and girls. Publishes reports and other materials.

Women's Legal Defense Fund
1875 Connecticut Avenue, NW; Suite 710
Washington, DC 20009
202/986-2600

National nonprofit membership organization. Promotes policies that help women achieve economic opportunities, quality health care and financial security. Provides public education, written information, and targeted litigation on sexual harassment. Some lawyer referrals. ■

INDEX

E

CATALOG

... more books from Nolo Press

ESTATE PLANNING & PROBATE

Make Your Own Living Trust, Clifford	1st Ed	$19.95	LITR
Plan Your Estate With a Living Trust, Clifford	2nd Ed	$19.95	NEST
Nolo's Simple Will Book, Clifford	2nd Ed	$17.95	SWIL
Who Will Handle Your Finances If You Can't?, Clifford & Randolph	1st Ed	$19.95	FINA
The Conservatorship Book (California), Goldoftas & Farren	2nd Ed	$29.95	CNSV
How to Probate an Estate (California), Nissley	7th Ed	$34.95	PAE
Nolo's Law Form Kit: Wills, Clifford & Goldoftas	1st Ed	$14.95	KWL
Write Your Will (audio cassette), Warner & Greene	1st Ed	$14.95	TWYW
5 Ways to Avoid Probate (audio cassette), Warner & Greene	1st Ed	$14.95	TPRO

GOING TO COURT

Represent Yourself in Court, Bergman & Berman-Barrett	1st Ed	$29.95	RYC
Everybody's Guide to Municipal Court (California), Duncan	1st Ed	$29.95	MUNI
Everybody's Guide to Small Claims Court (California), Warner	11th Ed	$18.95	CSCC
Everybody's Guide to Small Claims Court (National), Warner	5th Ed	$18.95	NSCC
Fight Your Ticket (California), Brown	5th Ed	$18.95	FYT
Collect Your Court Judgment (California), Scott, Elias & Goldoftas	2nd Ed	$19.95	JUDG
How to Change Your Name (California), Loeb & Brown	6th Ed	$24.95	NAME
The Criminal Records Book (California), Siegel	3rd Ed	$19.95	CRIM
Winning in Small Claims Court, Warner & Greene (audio cassette)	1st Ed	$14.95	TWIN

LEGAL REFORM

Fed Up with the Legal System: What's Wrong and How to Fix It, Nolo Press	2nd Ed	$9.95	LEG

BUSINESS & WORKPLACE

💾 Software Development: A Legal Guide, Fishman	1st Ed	$44.95	SFT
The Legal Guide for Starting & Running a Small Business, Steingold	1st Ed	$22.95	RUNS
Sexual Harassment on the Job, Petrocelli & Repa	1st Ed	$14.95	HARS
Your Rights in the Workplace, Repa	2nd Ed	$15.95	YRW
How to Write a Business Plan, McKeever	4th Ed	$19.95	SBS

💾 = BOOKS WITH DISK

Marketing Without Advertising, Phillips & Rasberry	1st Ed	$14.00	MWAD
The Partnership Book, Clifford & Warner	4th Ed	$24.95	PART`
The California Nonprofit Corporation Handbook, Mancuso	6th Ed	$29.95	NON
💾 The California Nonprofit Corporation Handbook, Mancuso	DOS	$39.95	NPI
	MAC	$39.95	NPM
💾 How to Form a Nonprofit Corporation (National), Mancuso	DOS	$39.95	NNP
How to Form Your Own California Corporation, Mancuso	7th Ed	$29.95	CCOR
How to Form Your Own California Corporation with Corporate Records Binder and Disk, Mancuso	1st Ed	$39.95	CACI
The California Professional Corporation Handbook, Mancuso	5th Ed	$34.95	PROF
💾 How to Form Your Own Florida Corporation, Mancuso	DOS	$39.95	FLCO
How to Form Your Own New York Corporation, Mancuso	2nd Ed	$29.95	NYCO
💾 How to Form Your Own New York Corporation, Mancuso	DOS	$39.95	NYCI
How to Form Your Own Texas Corporation, Mancuso	4th Ed	$29.95	TCOR
💾 How to Form Your Own Texas Corporation, Mancuso	DOS	$39.95	TCI
The Independent Paralegal's Handbook, Warner	2nd Ed	$24.95	PARA
Getting Started as an Independent Paralegal, Warner (audio cassette)	2nd Ed	$44.95	GSIP
How To Start Your Own Business: Small Business Law, Warner & Greene (audio cassette)	1st Ed	$14.95	TBUS

THE NEIGHBORHOOD

Neighbor Law: Fences, Trees, Boundaries & Noise, Jordan	1st Ed	$14.95	NEI
Safe Home, Safe Neighborhoods: Stopping Crime Where You Live, Mann & Blakeman	1st Ed	$14.95	SAFE
Dog Law, Randolph	2nd Ed	$12.95	DOG

MONEY MATTERS

Stand Up to the IRS, Daily	2nd Ed	$21.95	SIRS
Money Troubles: Legal Strategies to Cope With Your Debts, Leonard	2nd Ed	$16.95	MT
How to File for Bankruptcy, Elias, Renauer & Leonard	4th Ed	$25.95	HFB
Simple Contracts for Personal Use, Elias & Stewart	2nd Ed	$16.95	CONT
Nolo's Law Form Kit: Power of Attorney, Clifford, Randolph & Goldoftas	1st Ed	$14.95	KPA
Nolo's Law Form Kit: Personal Bankruptcy, Elias, Renauer, Leonard & Goldoftas	1st Ed	$14.95	KBNK
Nolo's Law Form Kit: Rebuild Your Credit, Leonard & Goldoftas	1st Ed	$14.95	KCRD
Nolo's Law Form Kit: Loan Agreements, Stewart & Goldoftas	1st Ed	$14.95	KLOAN
Nolo's Law Form Kit: Buy & Sell Contracts, Elias, Stewart & Goldoftas	1st Ed	$9.95	KCONT

FAMILY MATTERS

How to Raise or Lower Child Support In California, Duncan & Siegal	2nd Ed	$17.95	CHLD
Divorce & Money, Woodhouse & Felton-Collins with Blakeman	2nd Ed	$21.95	DIMO

💾 = **BOOKS WITH DISK**

The Living Together Kit, Ihara & Warner	6th Ed	$17.95	LTK
The Guardianship Book (California), Goldoftas & Brown	1st Ed	$19.95	GB
A Legal Guide for Lesbian and Gay Couples, Curry & Clifford	8th Ed	$26.95	LG
How to Do Your Own Divorce in California, Sherman	19th Ed	$21.95	CDIV
Practical Divorce Solutions, Sherman	1st Ed	$14.95	PDS
California Marriage & Divorce Law, Warner, Ihara & Elias	11th Ed	$19.95	MARR
How to Adopt Your Stepchild in California, Zagone & Randolph	4th Ed	$22.95	ADOP
Nolo's Pocket Guide to Family Law, Leonard & Elias	3rd Ed	$14.95	FLD
Divorce: A New Yorker's Guide to Doing it Yourself, *Alexandra*	1st Ed	$24.95	NYDIV

JUST FOR FUN

29 Reasons Not to Go to Law School, Warner & Ihara	3rd Ed	$9.95	29R
Devil's Advocates, Roth & Roth	1st Ed	$12.95	DA
Poetic Justice, Roth & Roth	1st Ed	$9.95	PJ

PATENT, COPYRIGHT & TRADEMARK

Trademark: How To Name Your Business & Product, McGrath & Elias, with Shena	1st Ed	$29.95	TRD
Patent It Yourself, Pressman	3rd Ed	$39.95	PAT
The Inventor's Notebook, Grissom & Pressman	1st Ed	$19.95	INOT
The Copyright Handbook, Fishman	2nd Ed	$24.95	COHA

LANDLORDS & TENANTS

The Landlord's Law Book, Vol. 1: Rights & Responsibilities (California), Brown & Warner	4th Ed	$32.95	LBRT
The Landlord's Law Book, Vol. 2: Evictions (California), Brown	4th Ed	$32.95	LBEV
Tenants' Rights (California), Moskovitz & Warner	11th Ed	$15.95	CTEN
Nolo's Law Form Kit: Leases & Rental Agreements (California), Warner & Stewart	1st Ed	$14.95	KLEAS

HOMEOWNERS

How to Buy a House in California, Warner, Serkes & Devine	3rd Ed	$24.95	BHCA
For Sale By Owner, Devine	2nd Ed	$24.95	FSBO
Homestead Your House, Warner, Sherman & Ihara	8th Ed	$9.95	HOME
The Deeds Book, Randolph	2nd Ed	$15.95	DEED

OLDER AMERICANS

Beat the Nursing Home Trap: A Consumer's Guide to Choosing & Financing Long Term Care, Matthews	2nd Ed	$18.95	ELD
Social Security, Medicare & Pensions, Matthews with Berman	5th Ed	$18.95	SOA

RESEARCH/REFERENCE

Legal Research, Elias & Levinkind	3rd Ed	$19.95	LRES
Legal Research Made Easy: A Roadmap Through the Law Library			
Maze (2 1/2 hr videotape & manual), Nolo & Legal Star	1st Ed	$89.95	LRME

CONSUMER

How To Get A Green Card:			
Legal Ways To Stay In The U.S.A., Nicolas Lewis	1st Ed	$22.95	GRN
How to Win Your Personal Injury Claim, Matthews	1st Ed	$24.95	PICL
Nolo's Pocket Guide to California Law, Guerin & Nolo Press Editors	2nd Ed	$10.95	CLAW
Nolo's Pocket Guide to California Law on Disk,	Windows	$24.95	CLWIN
Guerin & Nolo Press Editors	MAC	$24.95	CLM
Nolo's Law Form Kit: Hiring Child Care & Household Help,			
Repa & Goldoftas	1st Ed	$14.95	KCHLD
Nolo's Pocket Guide to Consumer Rights, Kaufman	2nd Ed	$12.95	CAG

IMMIGRATION

How to Get a Green Card: Legal Ways to Stay in the U.S.A.,			
Lewis with Madlanscay	1st Ed	$22.95	GRN

SOFTWARE

WillMaker 5.0, Nolo Press	Windows	$69.95	WI5
	DOS	$69.95	WI5
	MAC	$69.95	WM5
Nolo's Personal RecordKeeper 3.0, Pladsen & Warner	DOS	$49.95	FRI3
	MAC	$49.95	FRM3
Nolo's Living Trust 1.0, Randolph	MAC	$79.95	LTM1
Nolo's Partnership Maker 1.0, Mancuso & Radtke	DOS	$129.95	PAGI1
California Incorporator 1.0, Mancuso	DOS	$129.00	INCI
Patent It Yourself 1.0, Pressman	Windows	$229.95	PYW1

RECYCLE YOUR OUT-OF-DATE BOOKS AND GET 25% OFF YOUR NEXT PURCHASE

It's important to have the most current legal information. Because laws and legal procedures change often, we update our books regularly. To help keep you up-to-date we are extending this special offer. Cut out and mail the title portion of the cover of any old Nolo book with your next order and we'll give you a 25% discount off the retail price of ANY new Nolo book you purchase directly from us. For current prices and editions call us at 1 (800) 992-6656. This offer is to individuals only. Prices subject to change.

VISIT OUR STORE

If you live in the Bay Area, be sure to visit the Nolo Press Bookstore on the corner of 9th & Parker Streets in west Berkeley. You'll find our complete line of books and software—all at a discount. CALL 1-510-704-2248 for hours.

TO ORDER CALL 800-992-6656

ORDER FORM

Code	Quantity	Title	Unit price	Total

	Subtotal	
	California residents add Sales Tax	
	Shipping & Handling ($4 for 1st item; $1 each additional)	
	2nd day UPS (additional $5; $8 in Alaska and Hawaii)	
	TOTAL	

Name

Address

(UPS to street address, Priority Mail to P.O. boxes)

FOR FASTER SERVICE, USE YOUR CREDIT CARD AND OUR TOLL-FREE NUMBERS

Monday-Friday, 7 a.m. to 6 p.m. Pacific Time

Order Line	1 (800) 992-6656 (in the 510 area code, call 549-1976)
General Information	1 (510) 549-1976
Fax your order	1 (800) 645-0895 (in the 510 area code, call 548-5902)

METHOD OF PAYMENT

☐ Check enclosed

☐ VISA   ☐ Mastercard   ☐ Discover Card   ☐ American Express

Account #   Expiration Date

Authorizing Signature

Daytime Phone

Allow 2-3 weeks for delivery. Prices subject to change.

NOLO PRESS, 950 PARKER ST., BERKELEY, CA 94710